W9-DGU-883

Date: 6/9/17

GRA 741.5 DEA
Posehn, Brian,
Deadpool. Dracula's gauntlet /

DEADPOOL
Dracula's Gauntlet

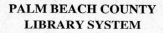
**PALM BEACH COUNTY
LIBRARY SYSTEM**
3650 Summit Boulevard
West Palm Beach, FL 33406-4198

COLLECTION EDITOR **ALEX STARBUCK**
ASSOCIATE EDITOR **SARAH BRUNSTAD**
EDITORS, SPECIAL PROJECTS **JENNIFER GRÜNWALD & MARK D. BEAZLEY**
VP, PRODUCTION & SPECIAL PROJECTS **JEFF YOUNGQUIST**
SVP PRINT, SALES & MARKETING **DAVID GABRIEL**
BOOK DESIGNER **NELSON RIBEIRO**

EDITOR IN CHIEF **AXEL ALONSO**
CHIEF CREATIVE OFFICER **JOE QUESADA**
PUBLISHER **DAN BUCKLEY**
EXECUTIVE PRODUCER **ALAN FINE**

DEADPOOL CREATED BY **ROB LIEFELD** & **FABIAN NICIEZA**

DEADPOOL: DRACULA'S GAUNTLET. Contains material originally published in magazine form as DEADPOOL: DRACULA'S GAUNTLET #1-7. First printing 2016. ISBN# 978-1-302-90121-9. Published by MARVEL WORLDWIDE, INC., a subsidiary of MARVEL ENTERTAINMENT, LLC. OFFICE OF PUBLICATION: 135 West 50th Street, New York, NY 10020. Copyright © 2016 MARVEL No similarity between any of the names, characters, persons, and/or institutions in this magazine with those of any living or dead person or institution is intended, and any such similarity which may exist is purely coincidental. **Printed in the U.S.A.** ALAN FINE, President, Marvel Entertainment; DAN BUCKLEY, President, TV, Publishing & Brand Management; JOE QUESADA, Chief Creative Officer; TOM BREVOORT, SVP of Publishing; DAVID BOGART, SVP of Business Affairs & Operations, Publishing & Partnership; C.B. CEBULSKI, VP of Brand Management & Development, Asia; DAVID GABRIEL, SVP of Sales & Marketing, Publishing; JEFF YOUNGQUIST, VP of Production & Special Projects; DAN CARR, Executive Director of Publishing Technology; ALEX MORALES, Director of Publishing Operations; SUSAN CRESPI, Production Manager; STAN LEE, Chairman Emeritus. For information regarding advertising in Marvel Comics or on Marvel.com, please contact Vit DeBellis, Integrated Sales Manager, at vdebellis@marvel. com. For Marvel subscription inquiries, please call 888-511-5480. **Manufactured between 4/29/2016 and 6/6/2016 by R.R. DONNELLEY, INC., OWENSVILLE, MO, USA.**

10 9 8 7 6 5 4 3 2 1

DEADPOOL
Dracula's Gauntlet

STORY **BRIAN POSEHN**
& GERRY DUGGAN

WRITER **GERRY DUGGAN**

STORYBOARDS **REILLY BROWN**
PENCILERS **REILLY BROWN** (Chapters 1-8, 10-14)
WITH **KHARY RANDOLPH** (9) & **SCOTT KOBLISH** (11-13)
INKERS **REILLY BROWN** (1-4),
NELSON DECASTRO (5-7, 10, 12-14),
TERRY PALLOT (7-8, 11-13), **KHARY RANDOLPH** (9)
& **SCOTT KOBLISH** (11-13)

COLORISTS **JIM CHARALAMPIDIS** (1-5, 7, 9, 12-13) &
JIM CAMPBELL (6, 8, 10-11, 14)
LETTERERS **VC'S JOE SABINO**
WITH **CHRIS ELIOPOULOS** (11)
COVER ARTISTS **REILLY BROWN** &
JIM CHARALAMPIDIS

ASSISTANT EDITORS **FRANKIE JOHNSON** & **XANDER JAROWEY**
EDITOR **JORDAN D. WHITE**

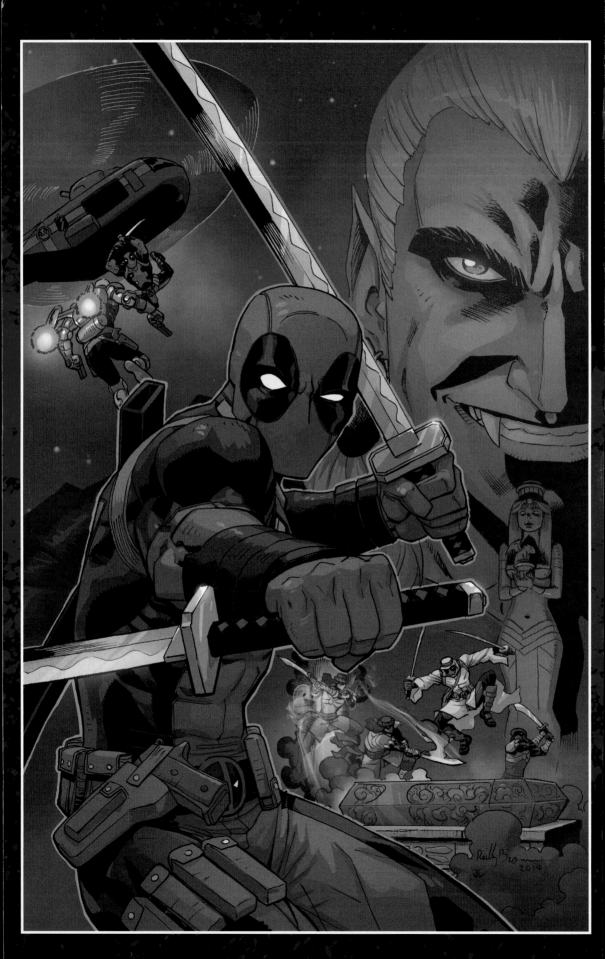

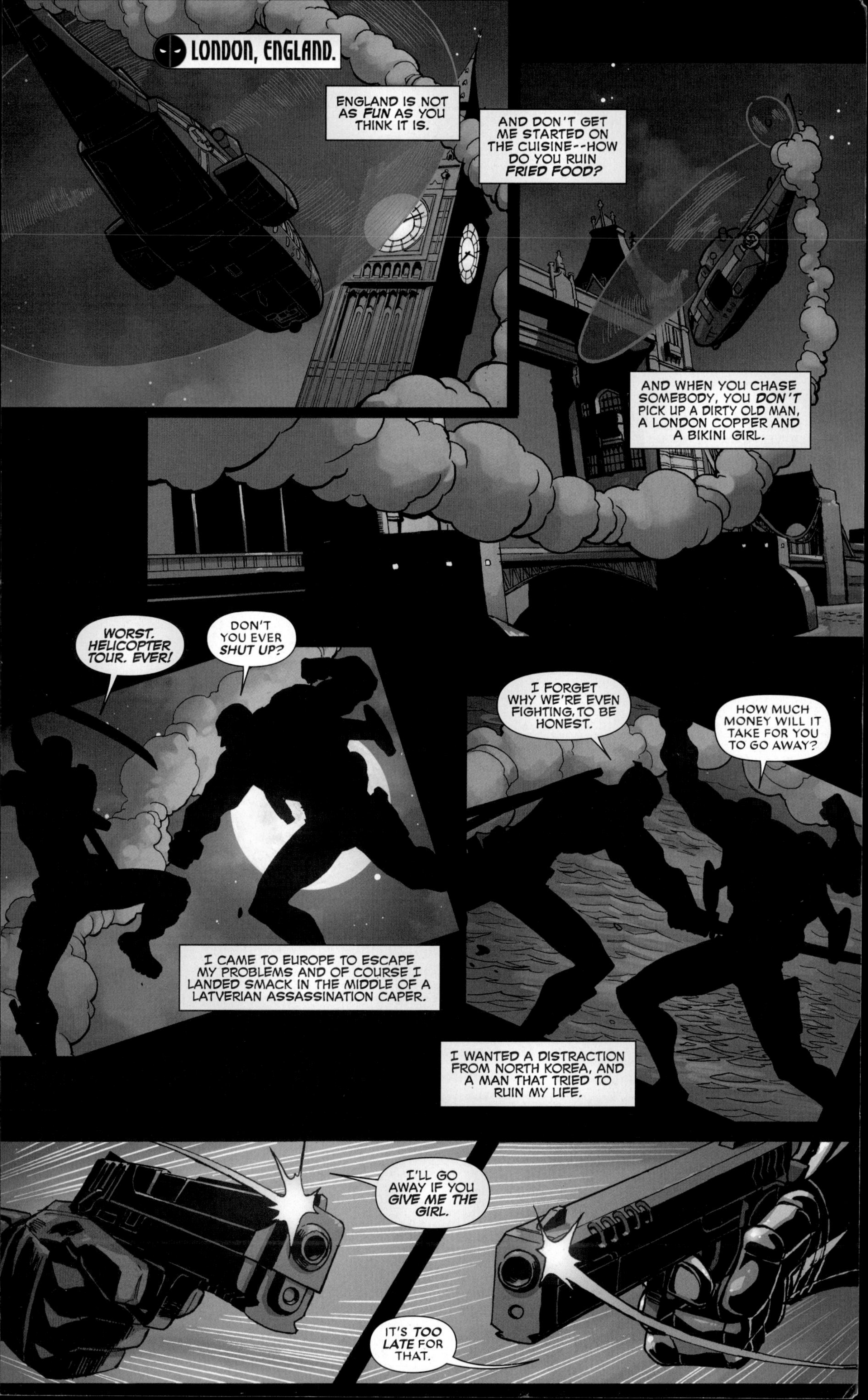
LONDON, ENGLAND.
ENGLAND IS NOT AS FUN AS YOU THINK IT IS.
AND DON'T GET ME STARTED ON THE CUISINE--HOW DO YOU RUIN FRIED FOOD?
AND WHEN YOU CHASE SOMEBODY, YOU DON'T PICK UP A DIRTY OLD MAN, A LONDON COPPER AND A BIKINI GIRL.
WORST. HELICOPTER TOUR. EVER!
DON'T YOU EVER SHUT UP?
I CAME TO EUROPE TO ESCAPE MY PROBLEMS AND OF COURSE I LANDED SMACK IN THE MIDDLE OF A LATVERIAN ASSASSINATION CAPER.
I FORGET WHY WE'RE EVEN FIGHTING, TO BE HONEST.
HOW MUCH MONEY WILL IT TAKE FOR YOU TO GO AWAY?
I WANTED A DISTRACTION FROM NORTH KOREA, AND A MAN THAT TRIED TO RUIN MY LIFE.
I'LL GO AWAY IF YOU GIVE ME THE GIRL.
IT'S TOO LATE FOR THAT.

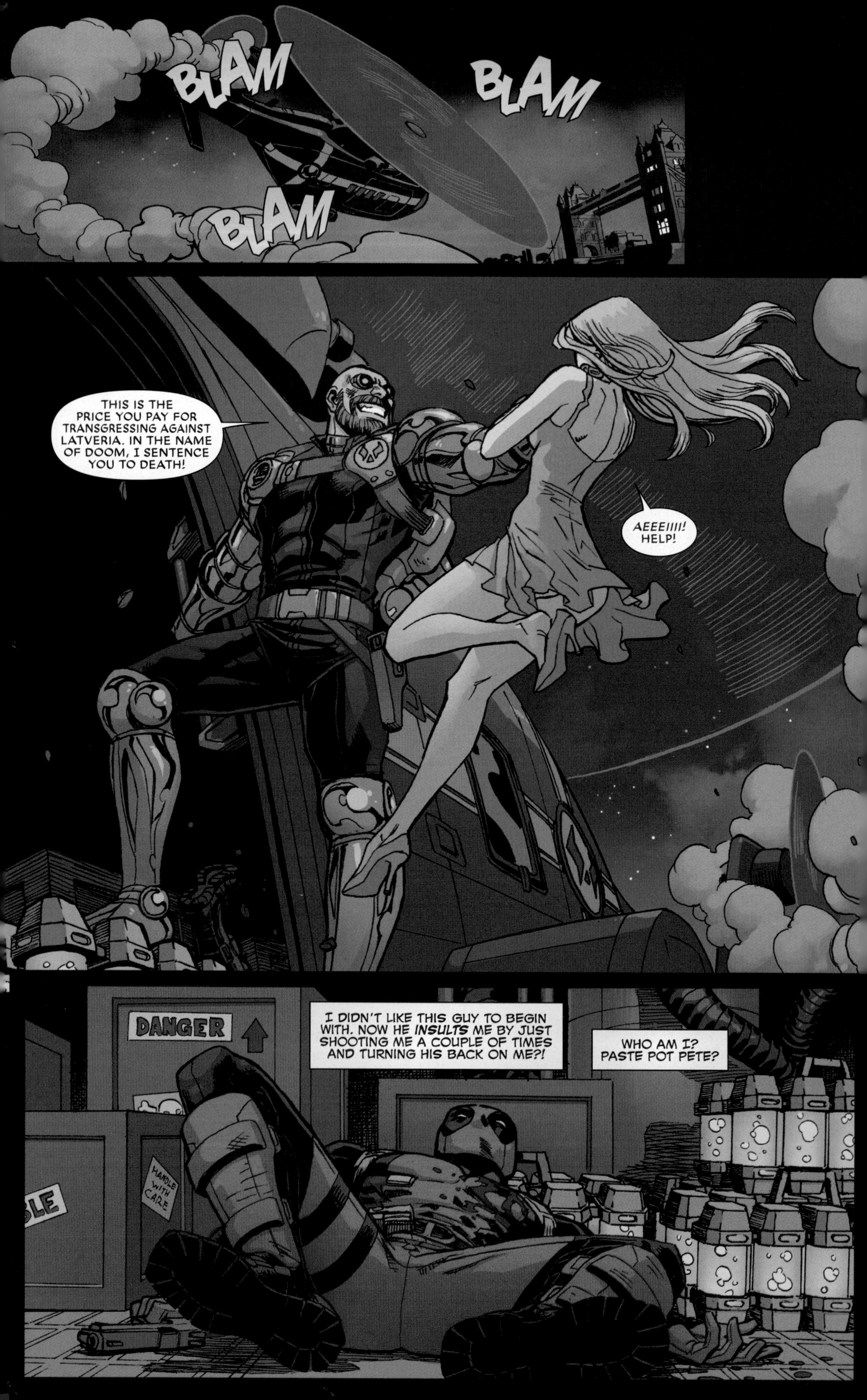

BLAM
BLAM
BLAM
THIS IS THE PRICE YOU PAY FOR TRANSGRESSING AGAINST LATVERIA. IN THE NAME OF DOOM, I SENTENCE YOU TO DEATH!
AEEEIIII! HELP!
DANGER
HANDLE WITH CARE
I DIDN'T LIKE THIS GUY TO BEGIN WITH. NOW HE INSULTS ME BY JUST SHOOTING ME A COUPLE OF TIMES AND TURNING HIS BACK ON ME?!
WHO AM I? PASTE POT PETE?

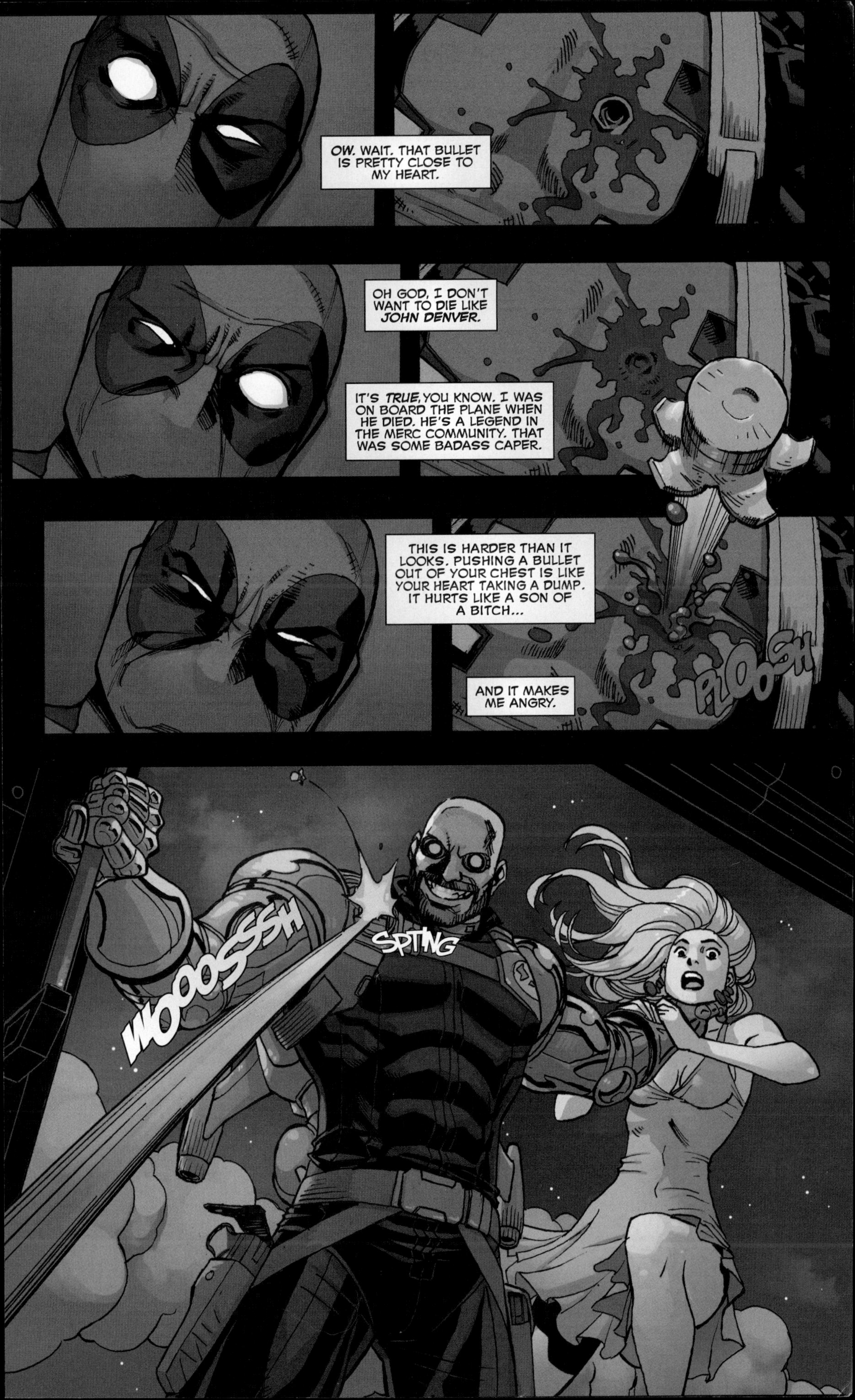
OW. WAIT. THAT BULLET IS PRETTY CLOSE TO MY HEART.
OH GOD, I DON'T WANT TO DIE LIKE JOHN DENVER.
IT'S TRUE, YOU KNOW. I WAS ON BOARD THE PLANE WHEN HE DIED. HE'S A LEGEND IN THE MERC COMMUNITY. THAT WAS SOME BADASS CAPER.
THIS IS HARDER THAN IT LOOKS. PUSHING A BULLET OUT OF YOUR CHEST IS LIKE YOUR HEART TAKING A DUMP. IT HURTS LIKE A SON OF A BITCH...
PLOOSH
AND IT MAKES ME ANGRY.
WOOOSSSH
SPTING

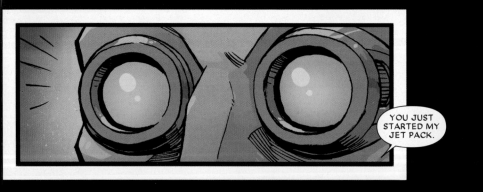

YOU JUST STARTED MY JET PACK.

YES, I KNOW.

SORRY YOU'VE BEEN... BUMPED FROM THIS FLIGHT.

OFF! TURN OFF, DAMN YOU!

OH NO! ON! ON!

ZZZSHWICK

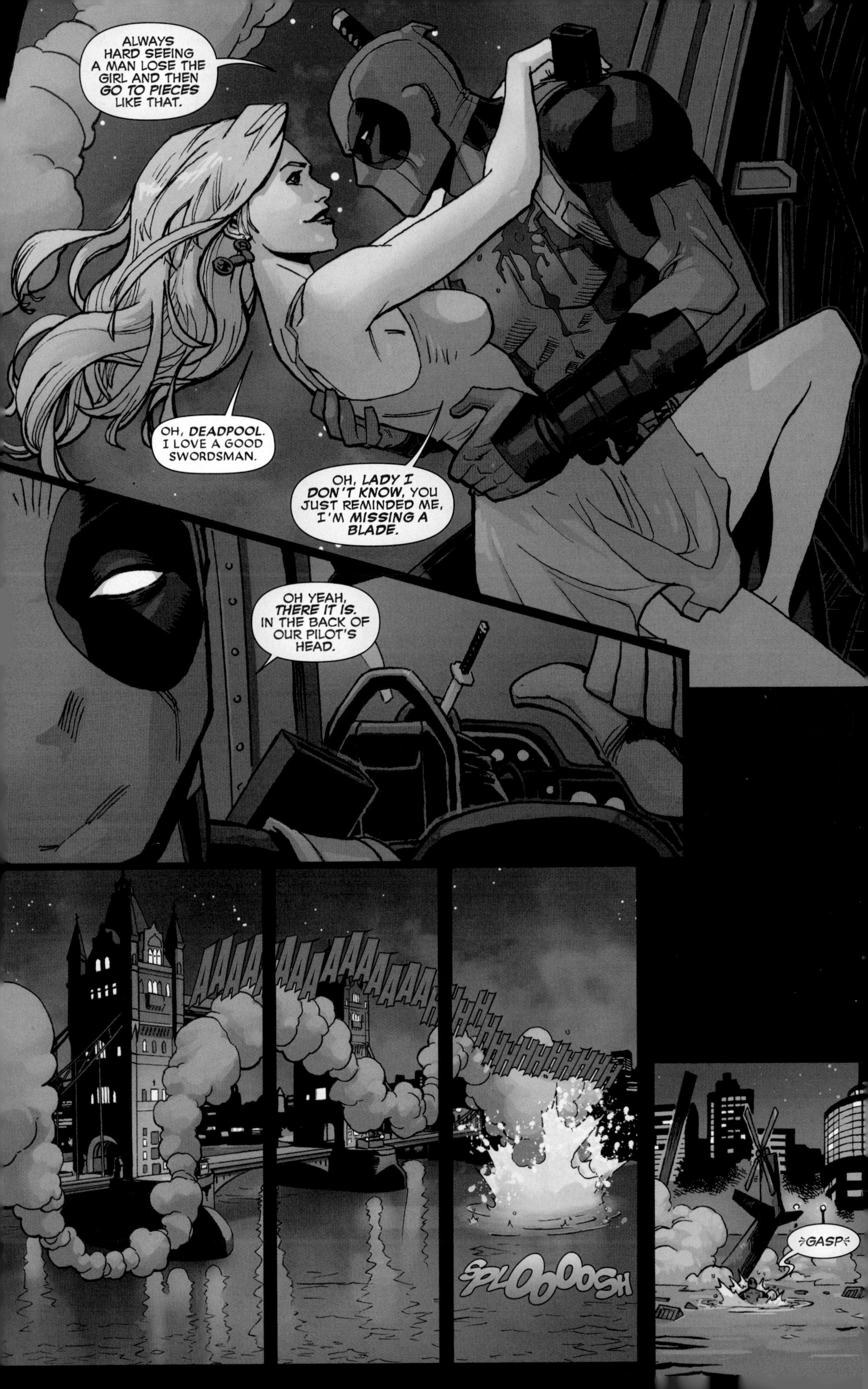
ALWAYS HARD SEEING A MAN LOSE THE GIRL AND THEN GO TO PIECES LIKE THAT.
OH, DEADPOOL. I LOVE A GOOD SWORDSMAN.
OH, LADY I DON'T KNOW, YOU JUST REMINDED ME, I'M MISSING A BLADE.
OH YEAH, THERE IT IS. IN THE BACK OF OUR PILOT'S HEAD.
AAAAAAAAAAAAAAAHHHHHHHHHHHHHH
SPLOOOOOSH
GASP

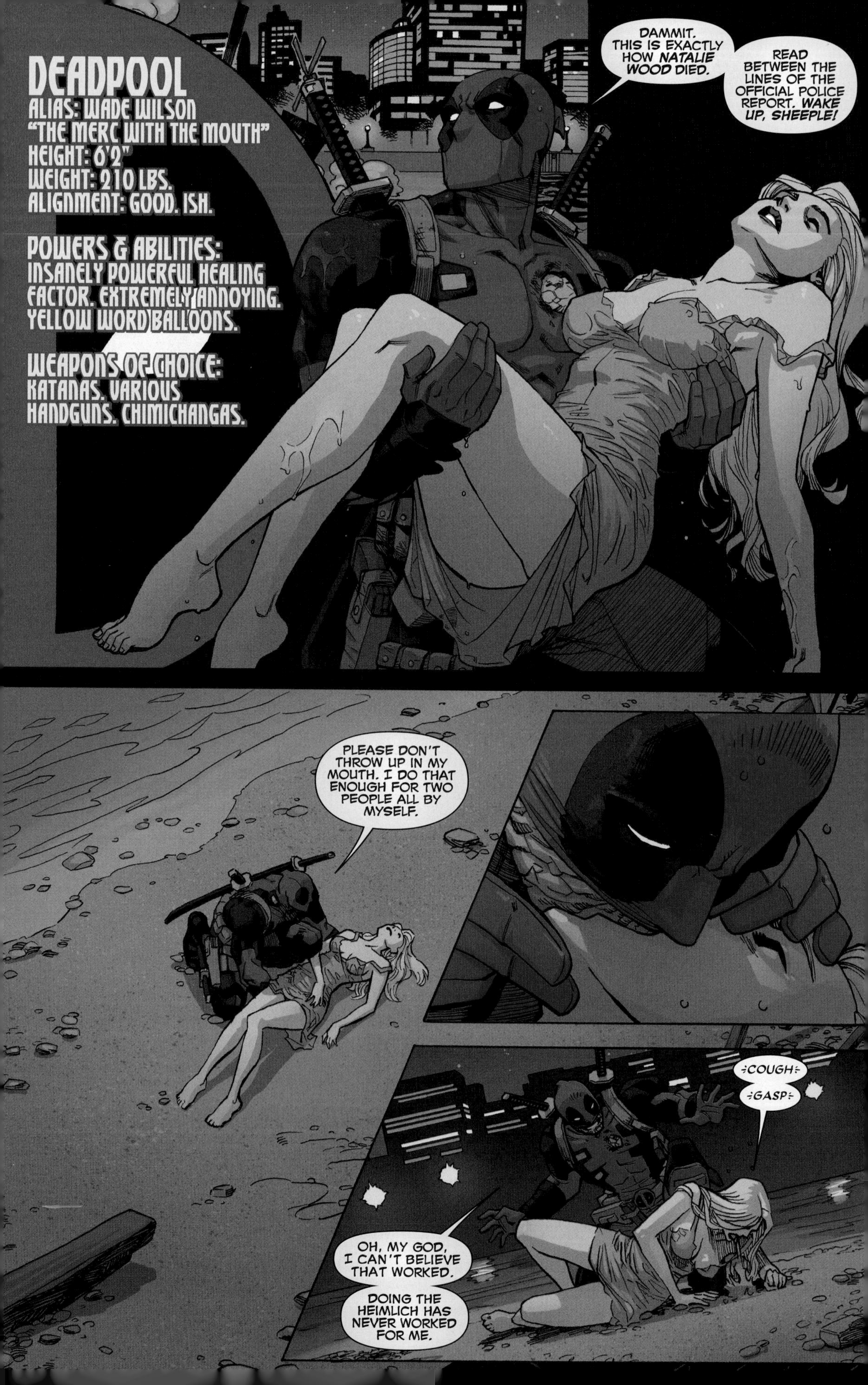
DEADPOOL
ALIAS: WADE WILSON
"THE MERC WITH THE MOUTH"
HEIGHT: 6'2"
WEIGHT: 210 LBS.
ALIGNMENT: GOOD. ISH.
POWERS & ABILITIES:
INSANELY POWERFUL HEALING FACTOR. EXTREMELY ANNOYING. YELLOW WORD BALLOONS.
WEAPONS OF CHOICE:
KATANAS. VARIOUS HANDGUNS. CHIMICHANGAS.
DAMMIT. THIS IS EXACTLY HOW NATALIE WOOD DIED.
READ BETWEEN THE LINES OF THE OFFICIAL POLICE REPORT. WAKE UP, SHEEPLE!
PLEASE DON'T THROW UP IN MY MOUTH. I DO THAT ENOUGH FOR TWO PEOPLE ALL BY MYSELF.
COUGH
GASP
OH, MY GOD, I CAN'T BELIEVE THAT WORKED.
DOING THE HEIMLICH HAS NEVER WORKED FOR ME.

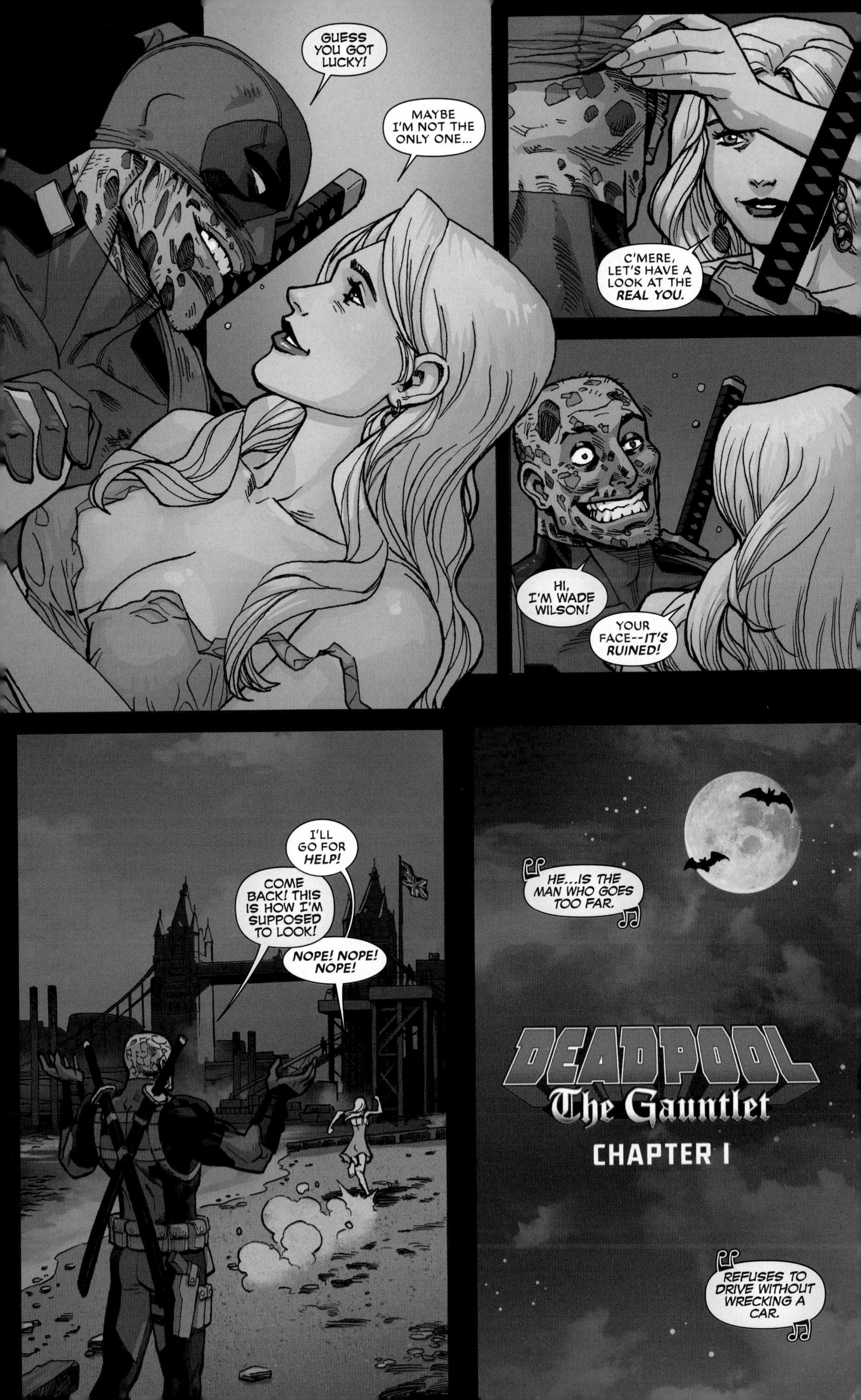
GUESS YOU GOT LUCKY!
MAYBE I'M NOT THE ONLY ONE...
C'MERE, LET'S HAVE A LOOK AT THE REAL YOU.
HI, I'M WADE WILSON!
YOUR FACE--IT'S RUINED!
I'LL GO FOR HELP!
COME BACK! THIS IS HOW I'M SUPPOSED TO LOOK!
NOPE! NOPE! NOPE!
HE...IS THE MAN WHO GOES TOO FAR.
DEADPOOL
The Gauntlet
CHAPTER 1
REFUSES TO DRIVE WITHOUT WRECKING A CAR.

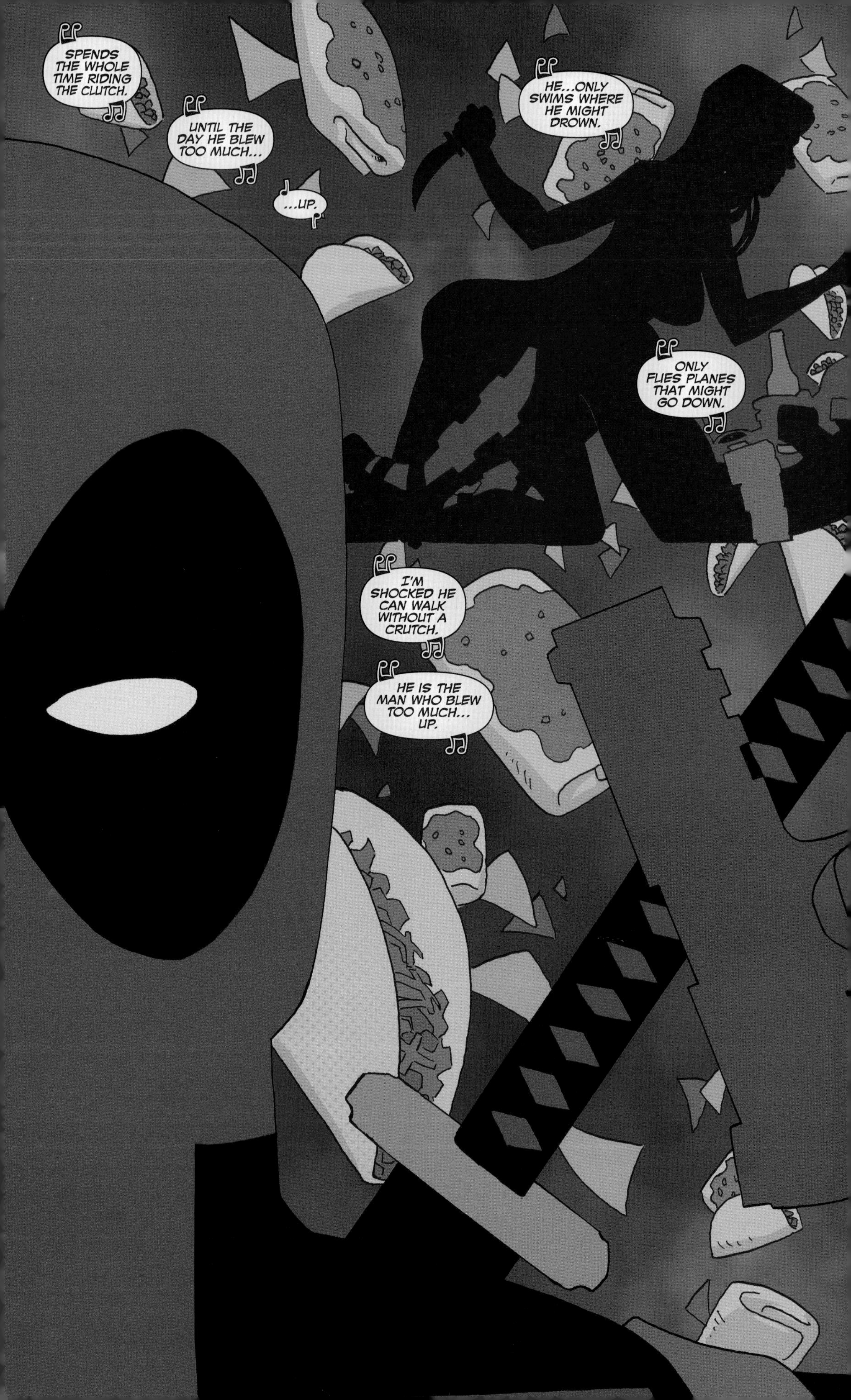
SPENDS THE WHOLE TIME RIDING THE CLUTCH.
UNTIL THE DAY HE BLEW TOO MUCH...
...UP.
HE...ONLY SWIMS WHERE HE MIGHT DROWN.
ONLY FLIES PLANES THAT MIGHT GO DOWN.
I'M SHOCKED HE CAN WALK WITHOUT A CRUTCH.
HE IS THE MAN WHO BLEW TOO MUCH... UP.

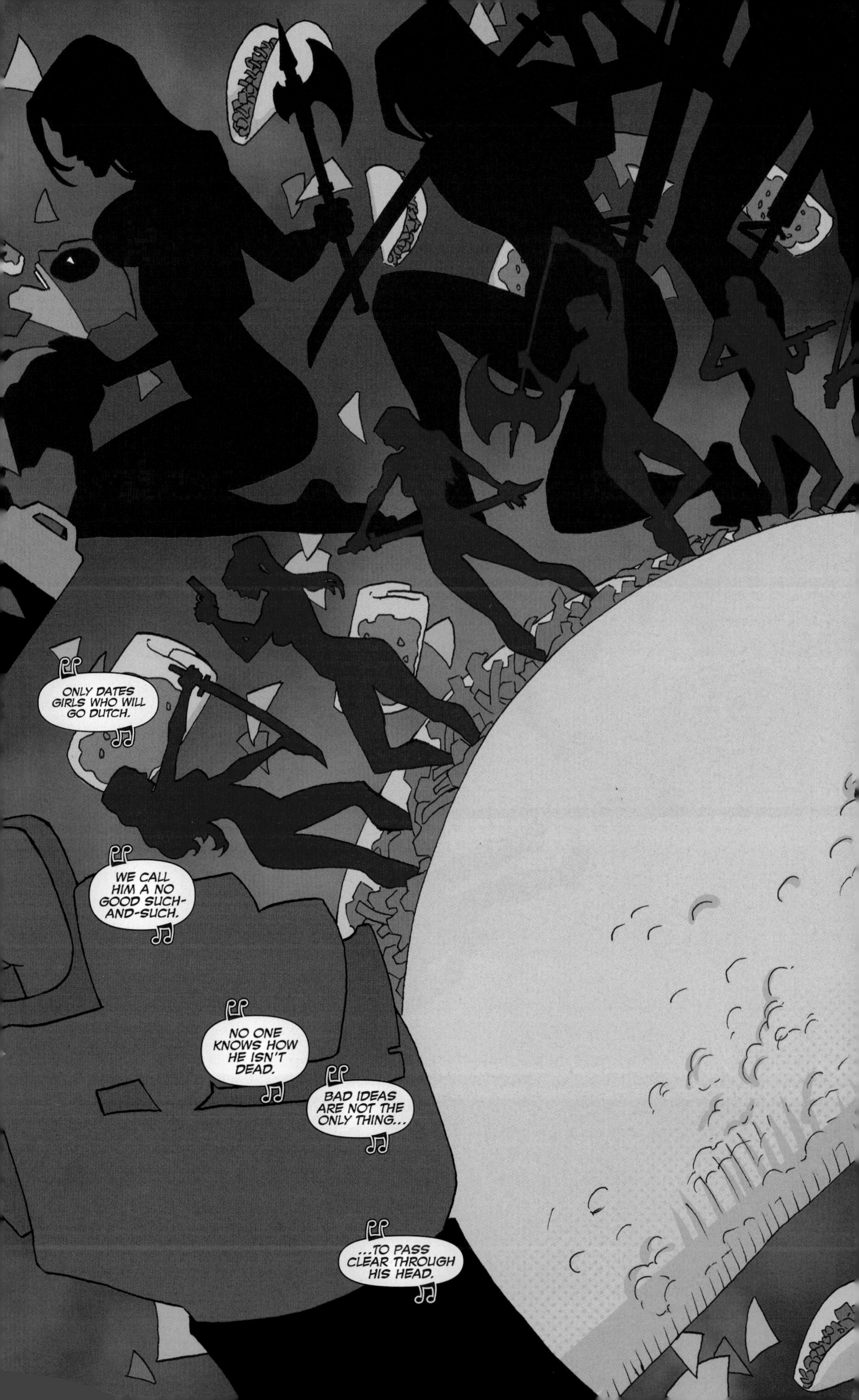
ONLY DATES GIRLS WHO WILL GO DUTCH.
WE CALL HIM A NO GOOD SUCH-AND-SUCH.
NO ONE KNOWS HOW HE ISN'T DEAD.
BAD IDEAS ARE NOT THE ONLY THING...
...TO PASS CLEAR THROUGH HIS HEAD.

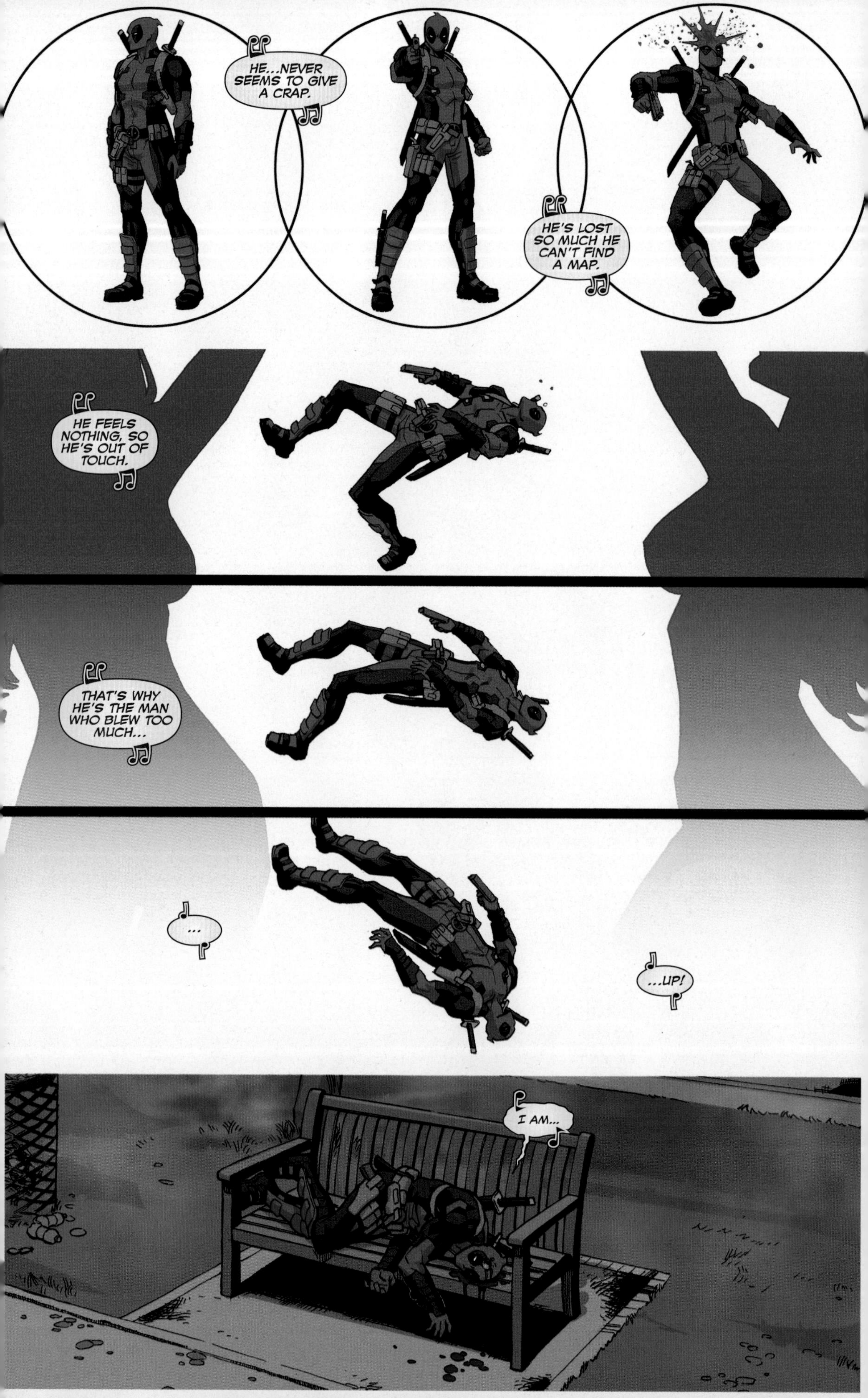
HE...NEVER SEEMS TO GIVE A CRAP.
HE'S LOST SO MUCH HE CAN'T FIND A MAP.
HE FEELS NOTHING, SO HE'S OUT OF TOUCH.
THAT'S WHY HE'S THE MAN WHO BLEW TOO MUCH...
...
...UP!
I AM...

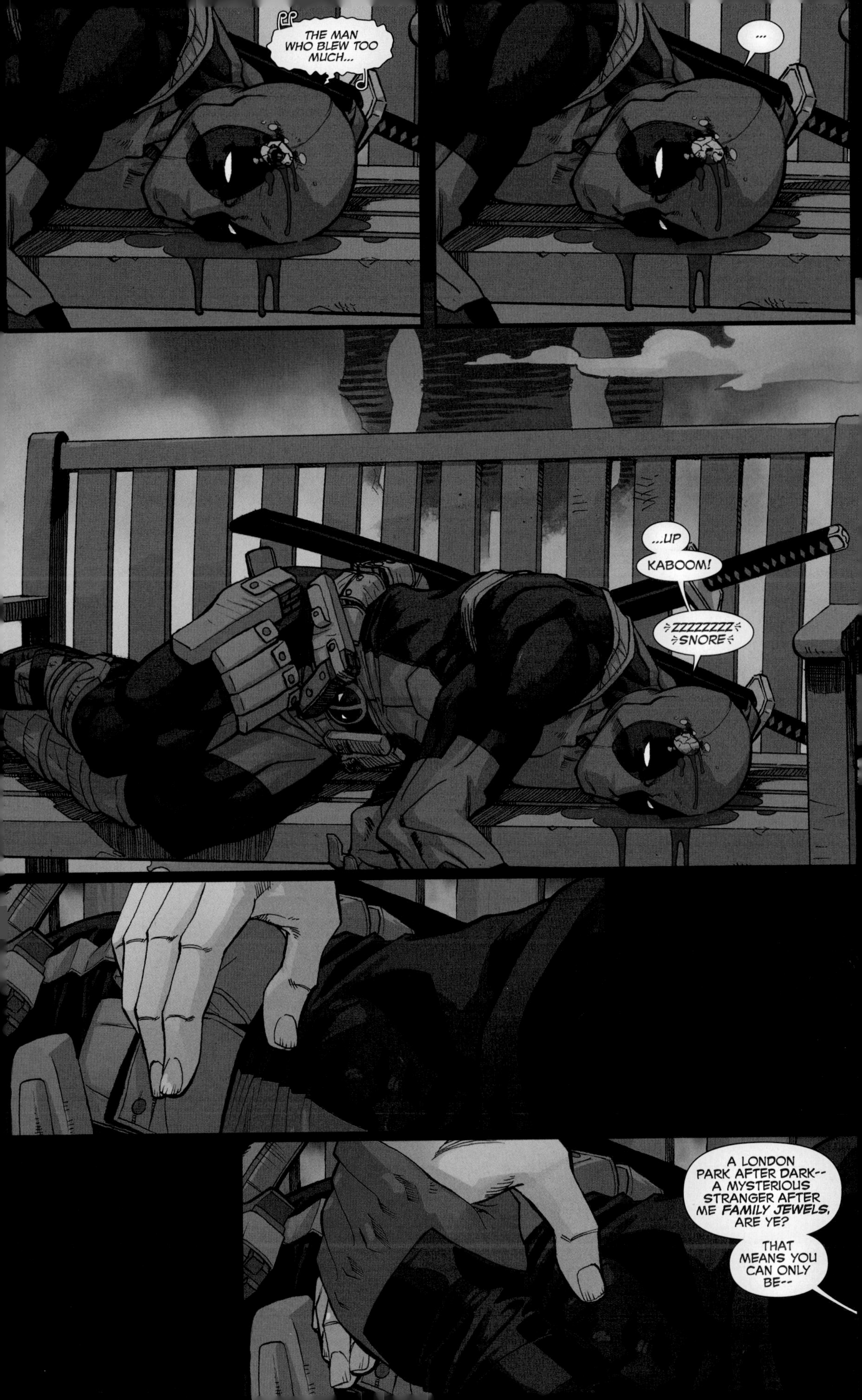
THE MAN WHO BLEW TOO MUCH...
...
...UP
KABOOM!
ZZZZZZZZ SNORE
A LONDON PARK AFTER DARK-- A MYSTERIOUS STRANGER AFTER ME *FAMILY JEWELS*, ARE YE?
THAT MEANS YOU CAN ONLY BE--

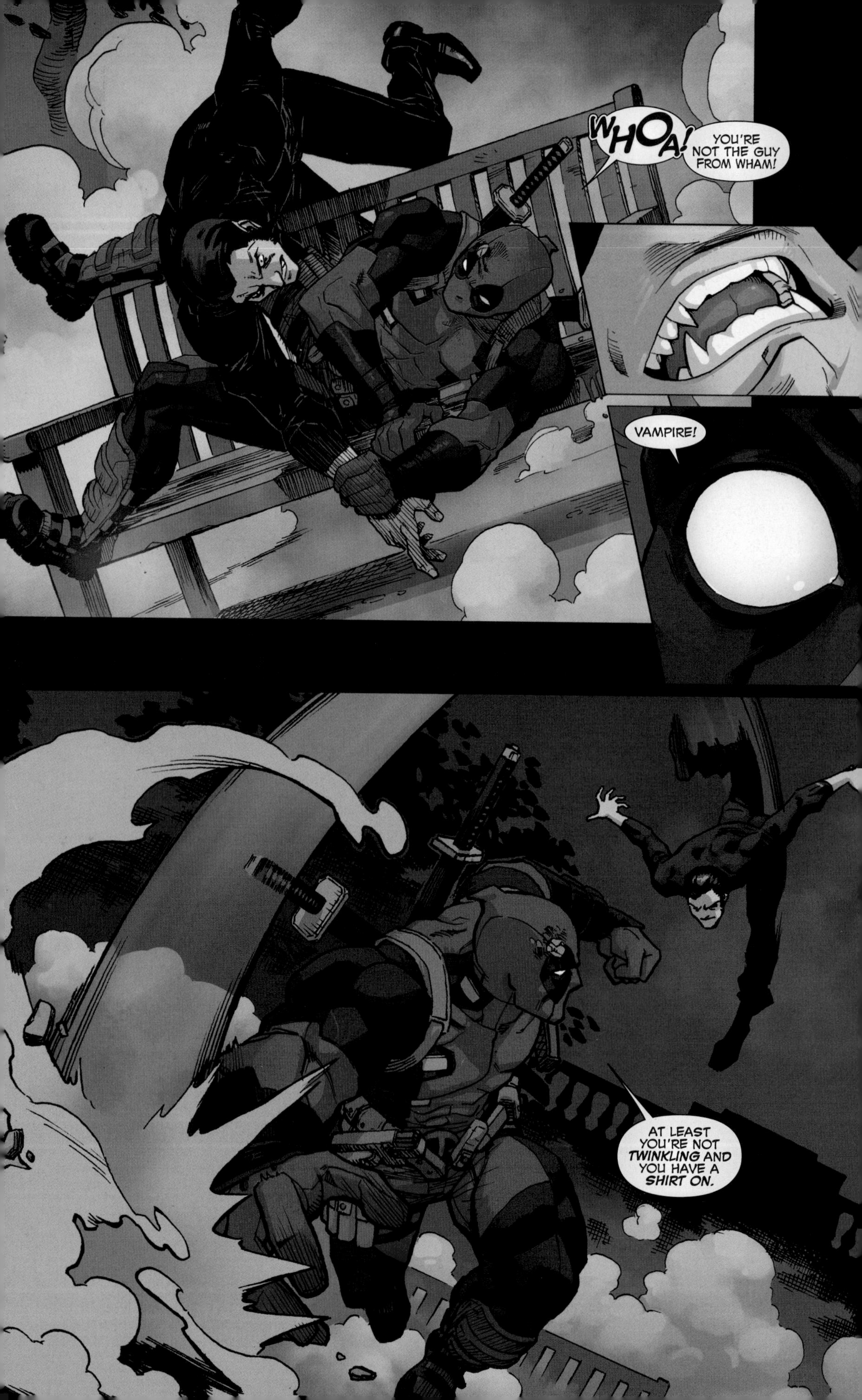
WHOA!
YOU'RE NOT THE GUY FROM WHAM!
VAMPIRE!
AT LEAST YOU'RE NOT *TWINKLING* AND YOU HAVE A *SHIRT ON*.

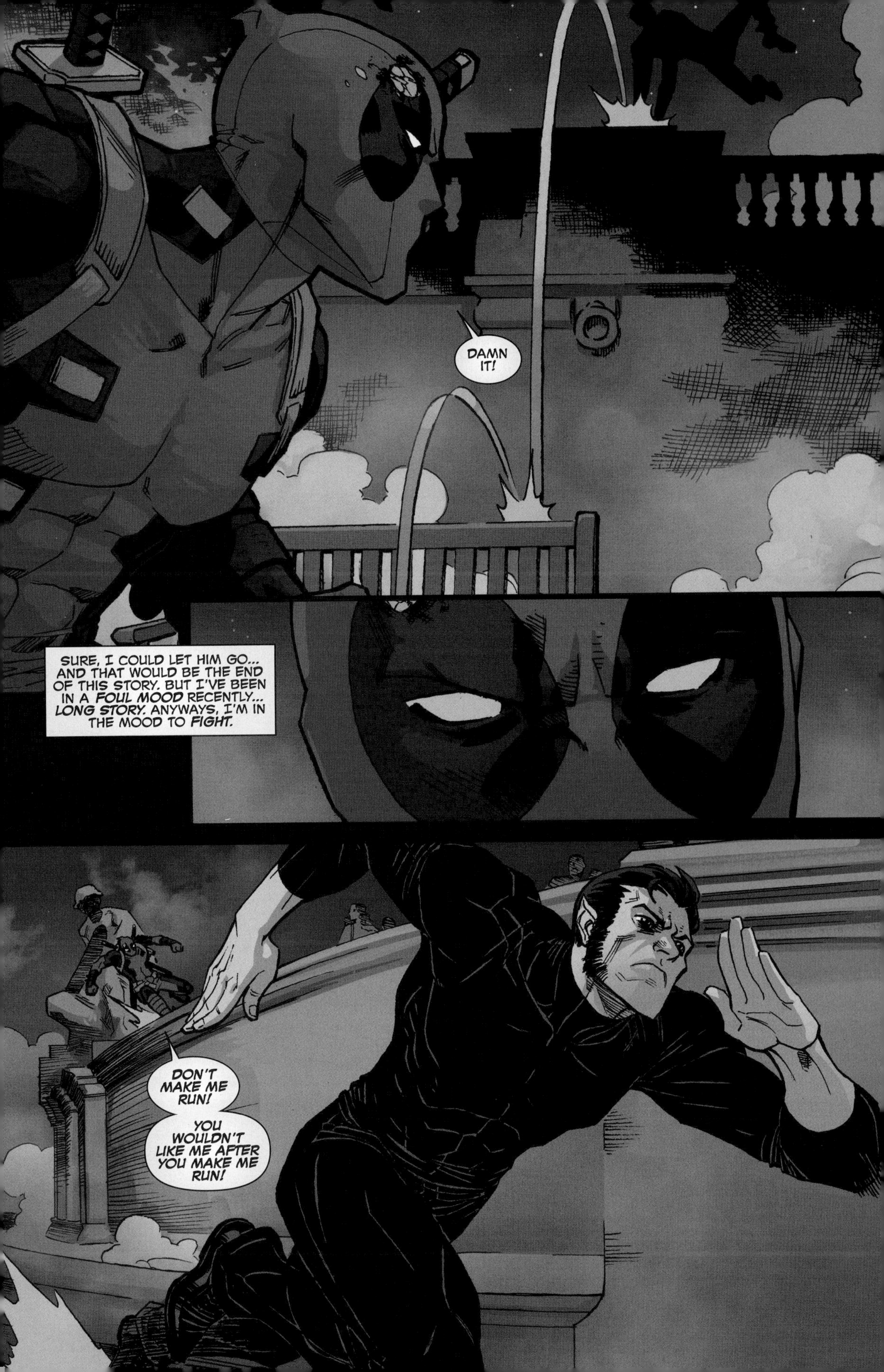
DAMN IT!
SURE, I COULD LET HIM GO... AND THAT WOULD BE THE END OF THIS STORY. BUT I'VE BEEN IN A FOUL MOOD RECENTLY... LONG STORY. ANYWAYS, I'M IN THE MOOD TO FIGHT.
DON'T MAKE ME RUN!
YOU WOULDN'T LIKE ME AFTER YOU MAKE ME RUN!

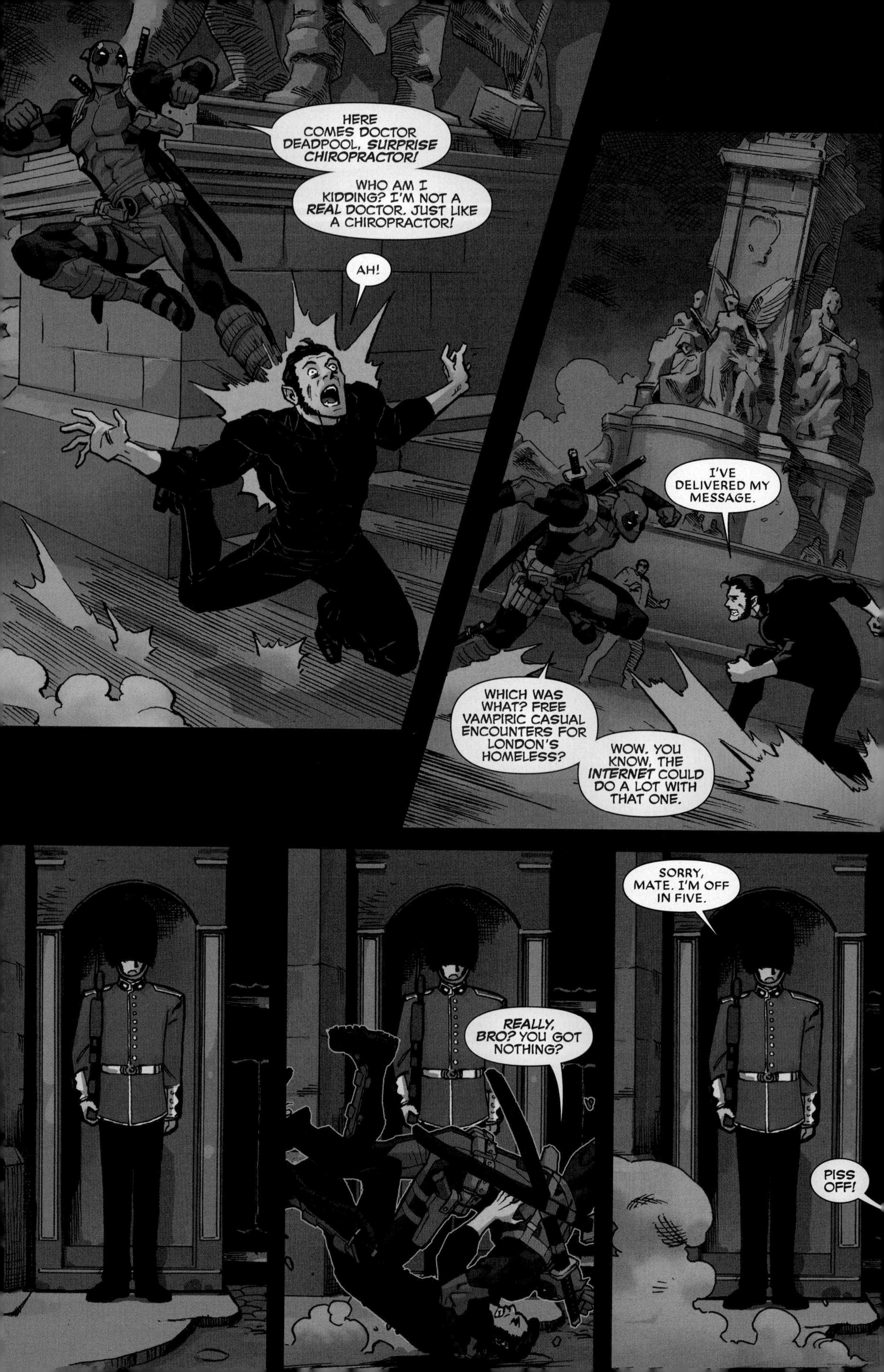
HERE COMES DOCTOR DEADPOOL, SURPRISE CHIROPRACTOR!
WHO AM I KIDDING? I'M NOT A REAL DOCTOR. JUST LIKE A CHIROPRACTOR!
AH!
I'VE DELIVERED MY MESSAGE.
WHICH WAS WHAT? FREE VAMPIRIC CASUAL ENCOUNTERS FOR LONDON'S HOMELESS?
WOW. YOU KNOW, THE INTERNET COULD DO A LOT WITH THAT ONE.
REALLY, BRO? YOU GOT NOTHING?
SORRY, MATE. I'M OFF IN FIVE.
PISS OFF!

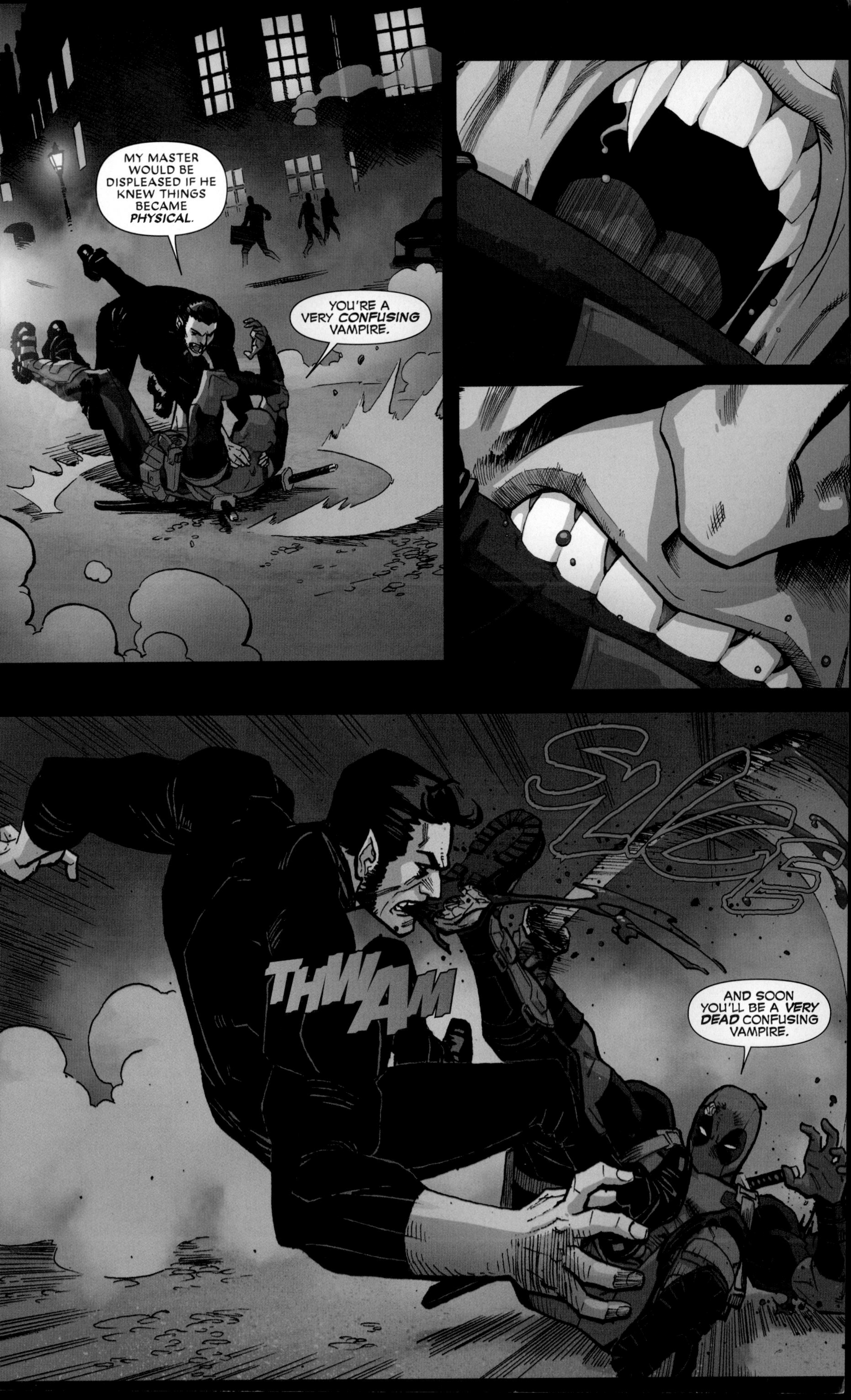
MY MASTER WOULD BE DISPLEASED IF HE KNEW THINGS BECAME PHYSICAL.
YOU'RE A VERY CONFUSING VAMPIRE.
SHLCK
THWAM
AND SOON YOU'LL BE A VERY DEAD CONFUSING VAMPIRE.

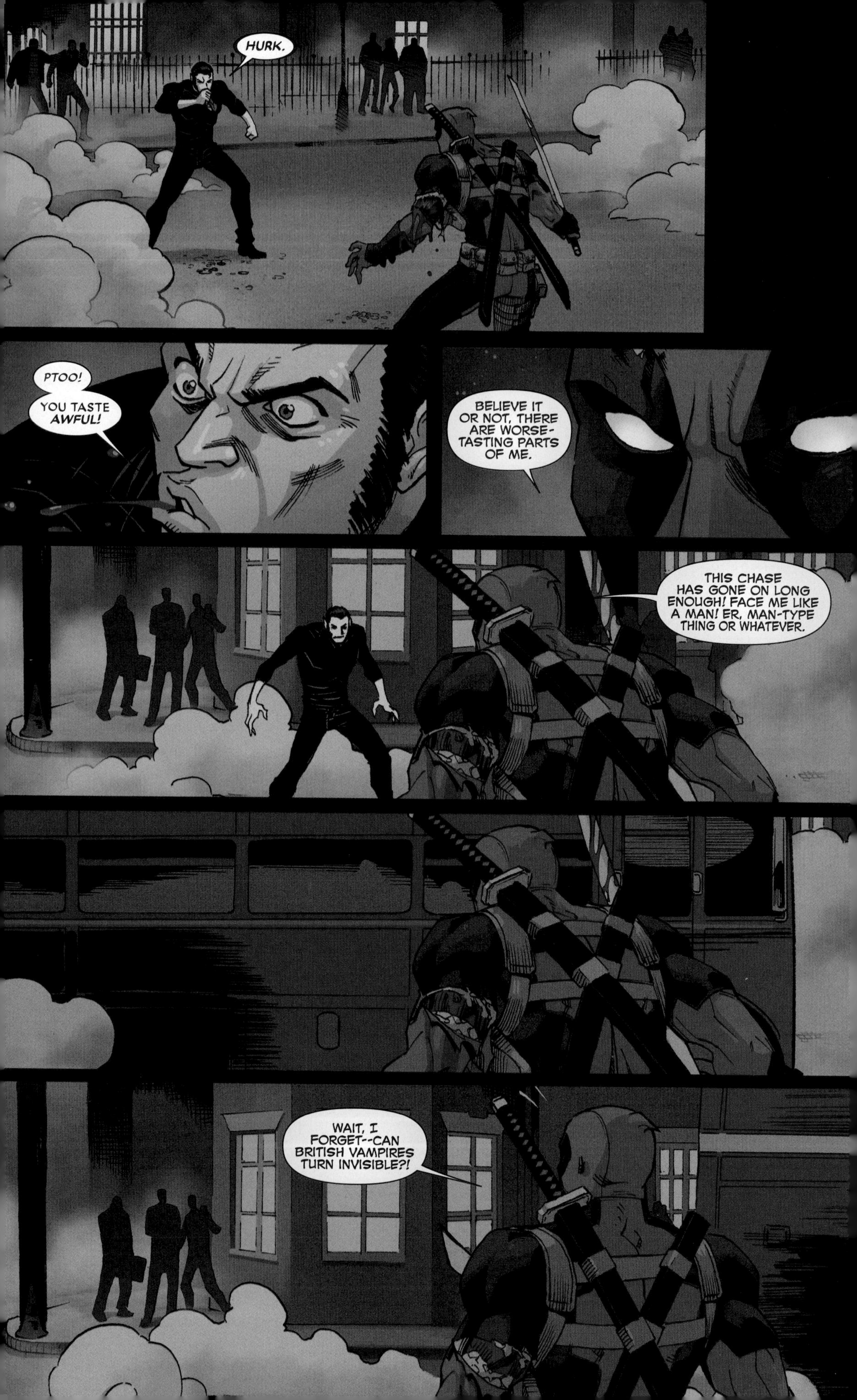
HURK.
PTOO!
YOU TASTE AWFUL!
BELIEVE IT OR NOT, THERE ARE WORSE-TASTING PARTS OF ME.
THIS CHASE HAS GONE ON LONG ENOUGH! FACE ME LIKE A MAN! ER, MAN-TYPE THING OR WHATEVER.
WAIT, I FORGET--CAN BRITISH VAMPIRES TURN INVISIBLE?!

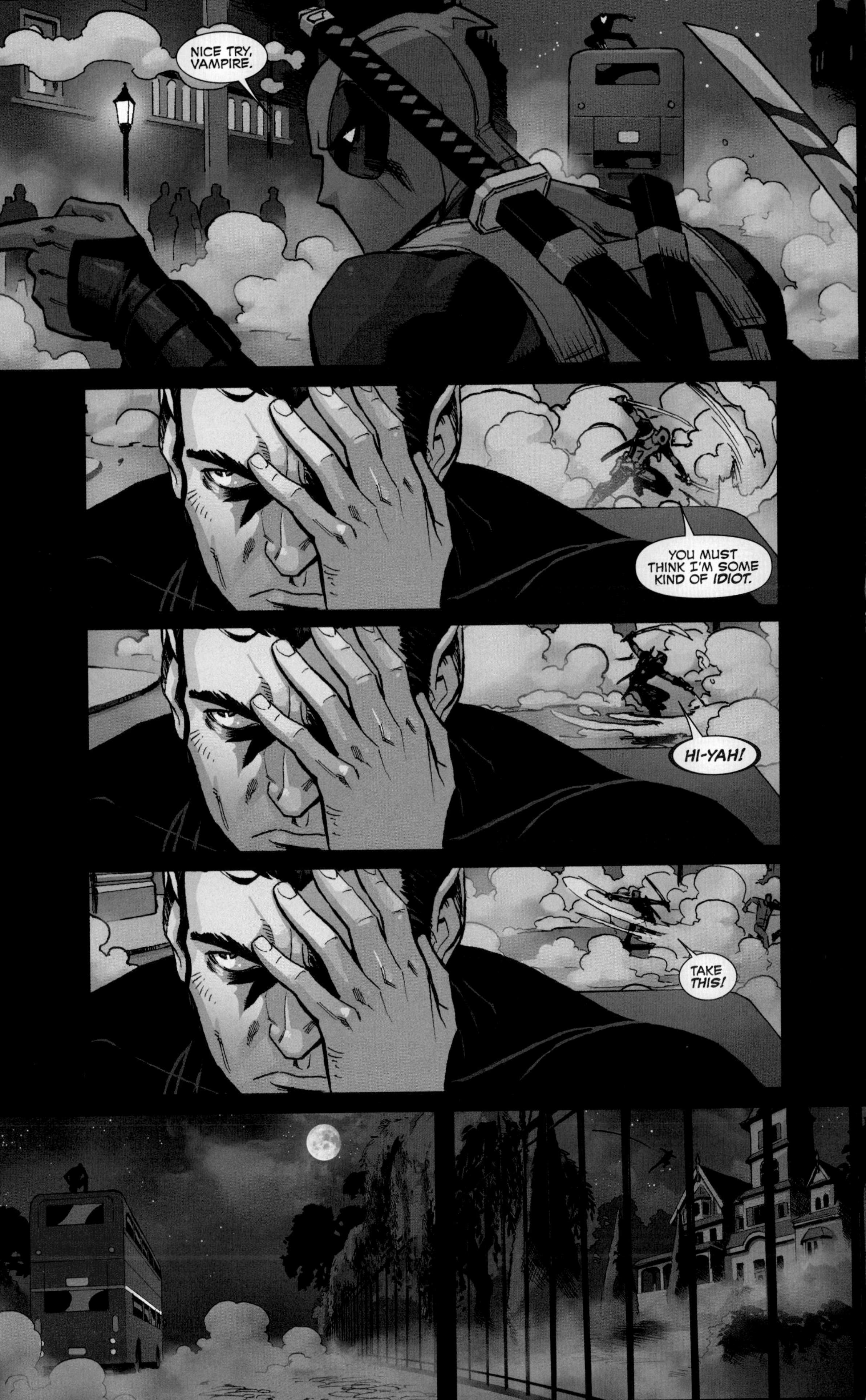
NICE TRY, VAMPIRE.
YOU MUST THINK I'M SOME KIND OF *IDIOT*.
HI-YAH!
TAKE *THIS!*

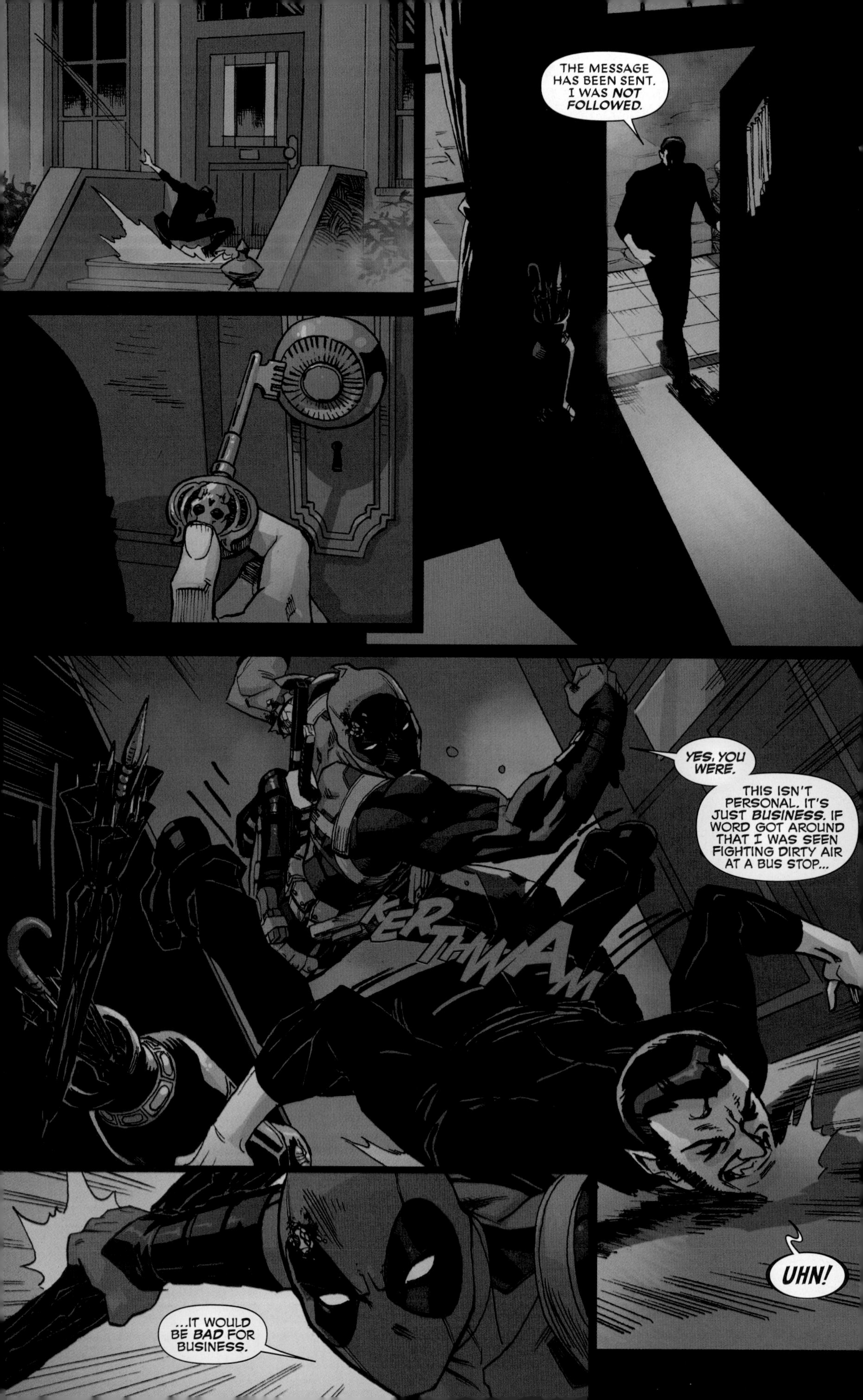

THE MESSAGE HAS BEEN SENT. I WAS NOT FOLLOWED.
YES, YOU WERE.
THIS ISN'T PERSONAL. IT'S JUST BUSINESS. IF WORD GOT AROUND THAT I WAS SEEN FIGHTING DIRTY AIR AT A BUS STOP...
KERTHWAM
...IT WOULD BE BAD FOR BUSINESS.
UHN!

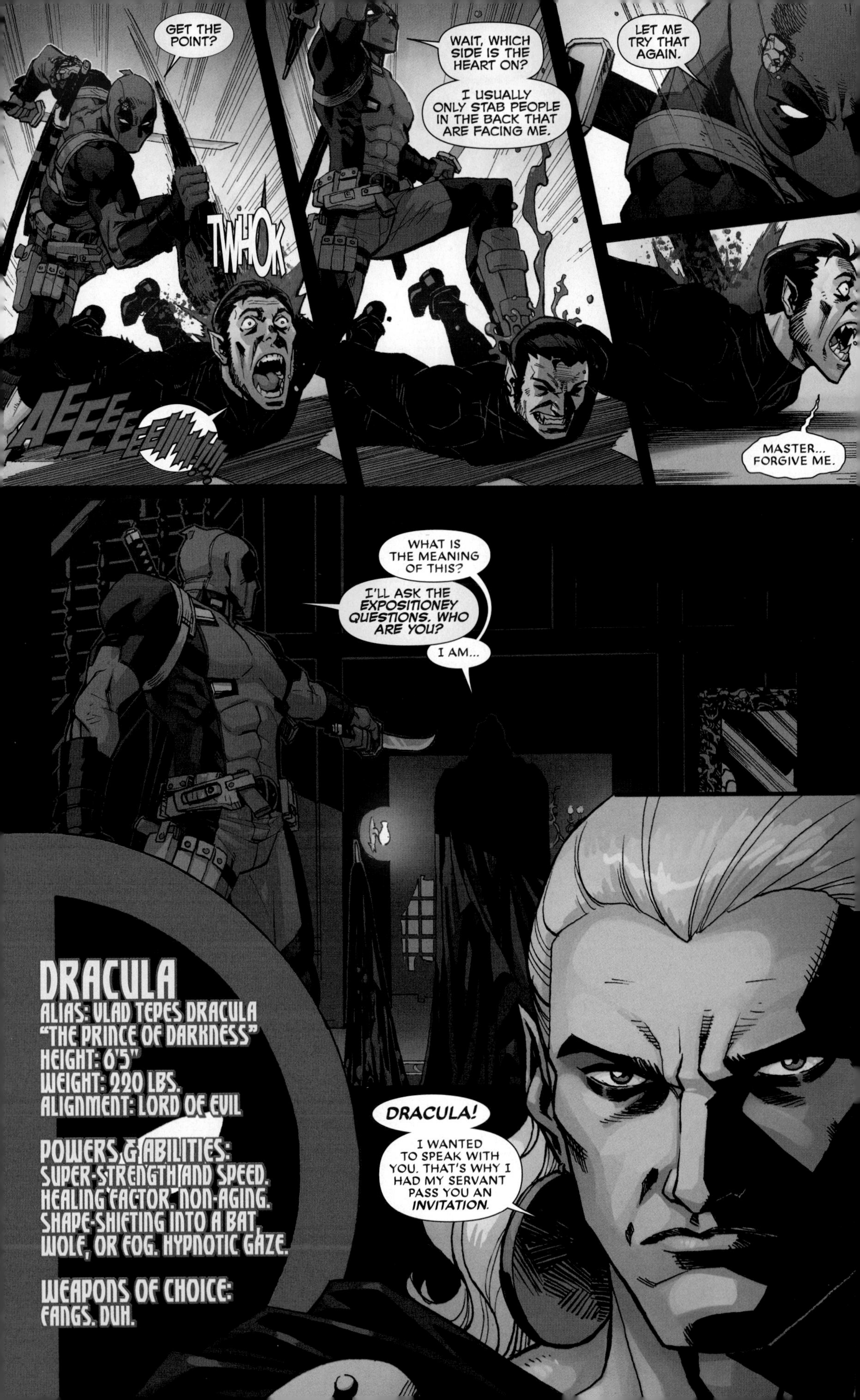
GET THE POINT?
TWHOK
AEEEEEEIIIIII!!!
WAIT, WHICH SIDE IS THE HEART ON?
I USUALLY ONLY STAB PEOPLE IN THE BACK THAT ARE FACING ME.
LET ME TRY THAT AGAIN.
MASTER... FORGIVE ME.
WHAT IS THE MEANING OF THIS?
I'LL ASK THE EXPOSITIONEY QUESTIONS. WHO ARE YOU?
I AM...
DRACULA
ALIAS: VLAD TEPES DRACULA
"THE PRINCE OF DARKNESS"
HEIGHT: 6'5"
WEIGHT: 220 LBS.
ALIGNMENT: LORD OF EVIL
POWERS & ABILITIES:
SUPER-STRENGTH AND SPEED. HEALING FACTOR. NON-AGING. SHAPE-SHIFTING INTO A BAT, WOLF, OR FOG. HYPNOTIC GAZE.
WEAPONS OF CHOICE:
FANGS. DUH.
DRACULA!
I WANTED TO SPEAK WITH YOU. THAT'S WHY I HAD MY SERVANT PASS YOU AN INVITATION.

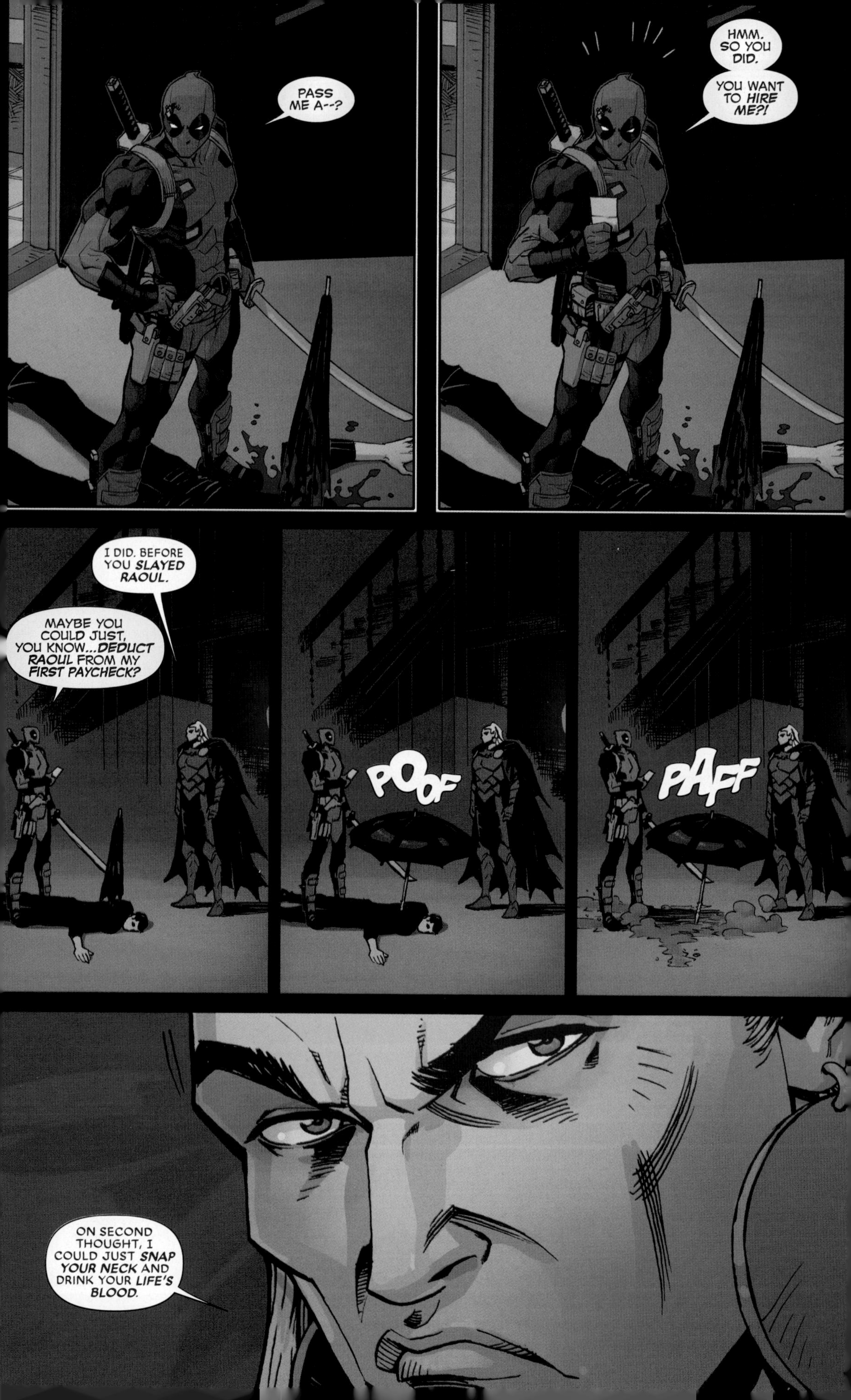
PASS ME A--?
HMM. SO YOU DID.
YOU WANT TO HIRE ME?!
I DID. BEFORE YOU SLAYED RAOUL.
MAYBE YOU COULD JUST, YOU KNOW...DEDUCT RAOUL FROM MY FIRST PAYCHECK?
POOF
PAFF
ON SECOND THOUGHT, I COULD JUST SNAP YOUR NECK AND DRINK YOUR LIFE'S BLOOD.

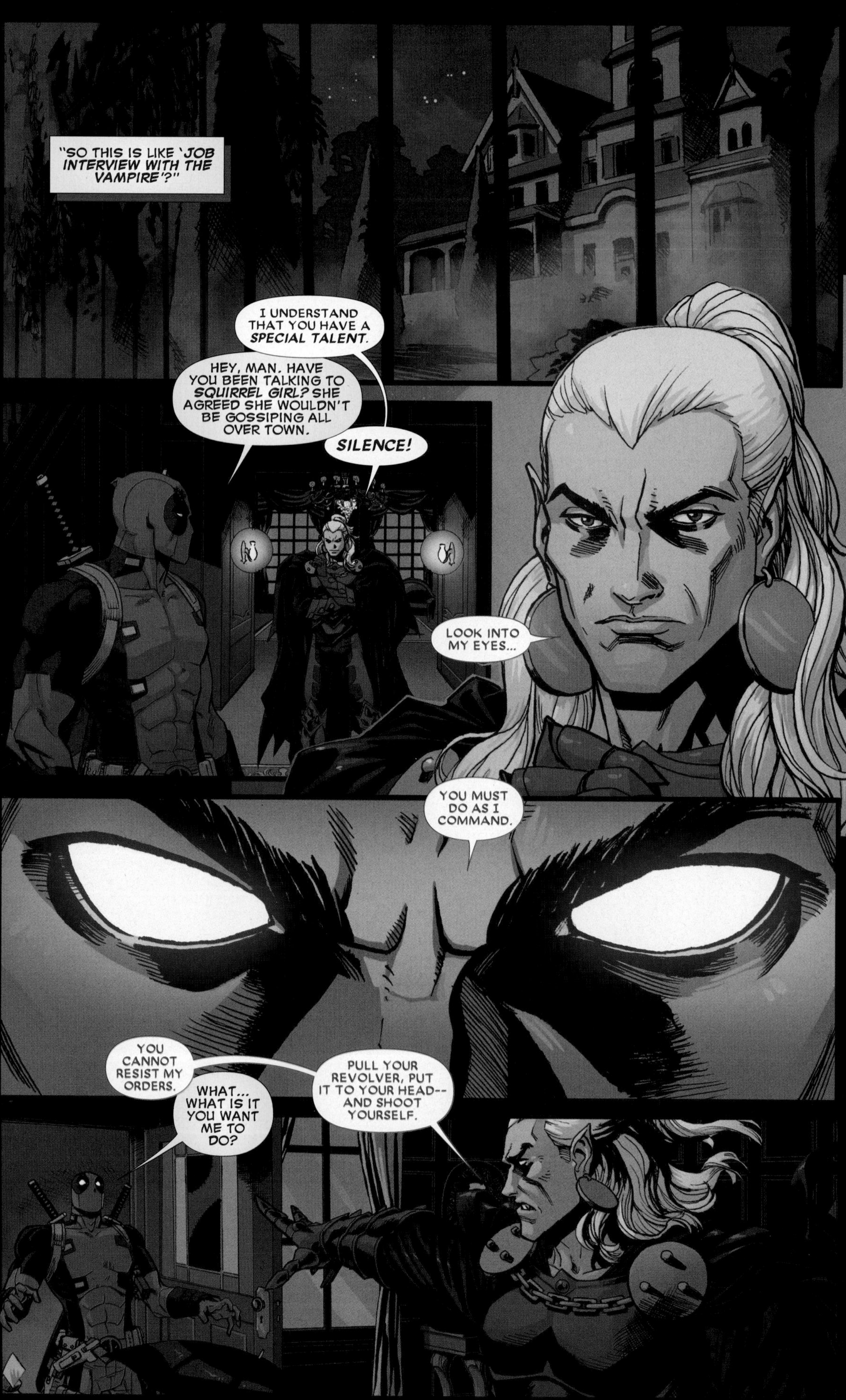
"SO THIS IS LIKE 'JOB INTERVIEW WITH THE VAMPIRE'?"
I UNDERSTAND THAT YOU HAVE A SPECIAL TALENT.
HEY, MAN. HAVE YOU BEEN TALKING TO SQUIRREL GIRL? SHE AGREED SHE WOULDN'T BE GOSSIPING ALL OVER TOWN.
SILENCE!
LOOK INTO MY EYES...
YOU MUST DO AS I COMMAND.
YOU CANNOT RESIST MY ORDERS.
WHAT... WHAT IS IT YOU WANT ME TO DO?
PULL YOUR REVOLVER, PUT IT TO YOUR HEAD-- AND SHOOT YOURSELF.

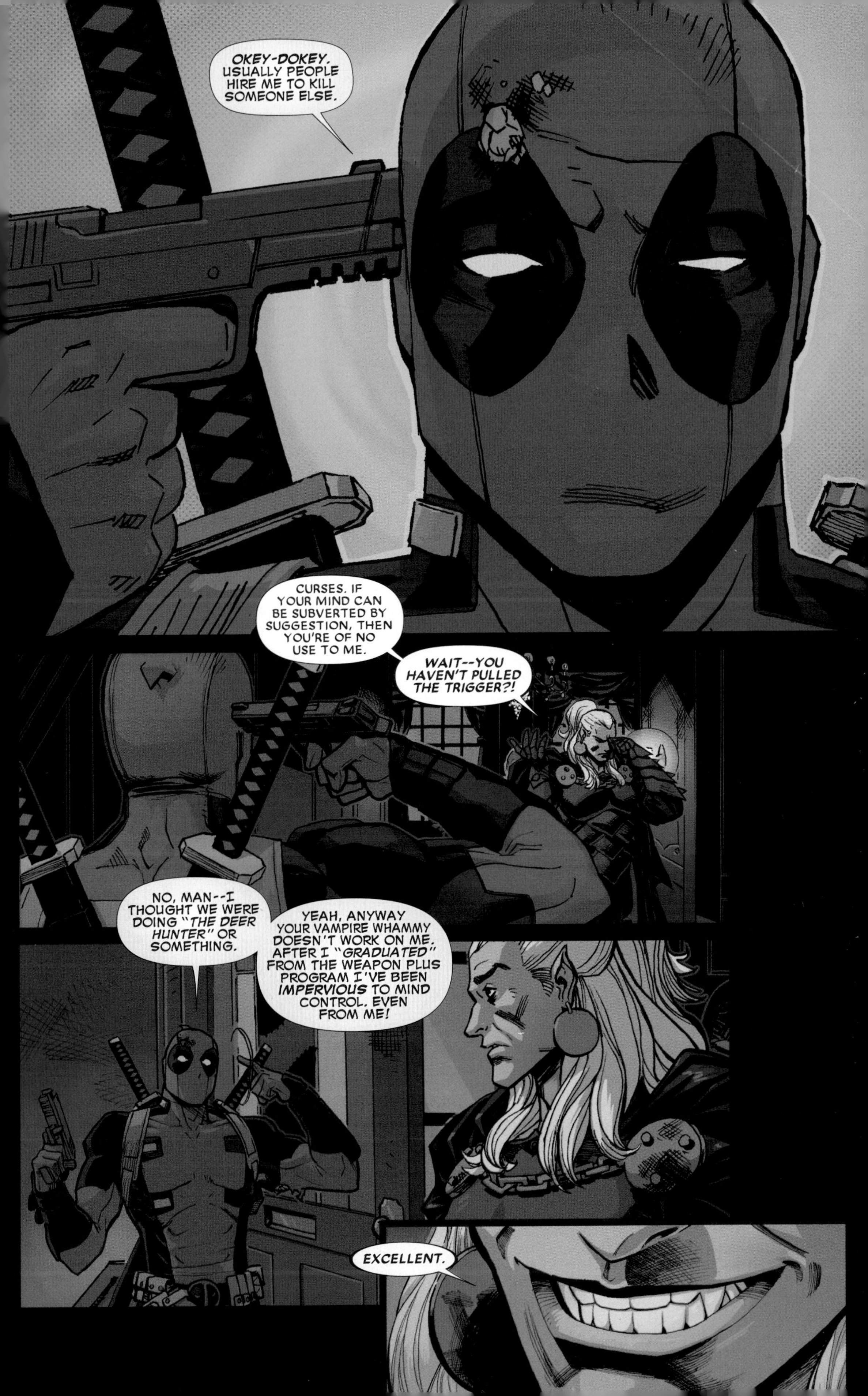
OKEY-DOKEY. USUALLY PEOPLE HIRE ME TO KILL SOMEONE ELSE.
CURSES. IF YOUR MIND CAN BE SUBVERTED BY SUGGESTION, THEN YOU'RE OF NO USE TO ME.
WAIT--YOU HAVEN'T PULLED THE TRIGGER?!
NO, MAN--I THOUGHT WE WERE DOING "THE DEER HUNTER" OR SOMETHING.
YEAH, ANYWAY YOUR VAMPIRE WHAMMY DOESN'T WORK ON ME. AFTER I "GRADUATED" FROM THE WEAPON PLUS PROGRAM I'VE BEEN IMPERVIOUS TO MIND CONTROL. EVEN FROM ME!
EXCELLENT.

CHAPTER 2:
DEADPOOL & THE TEMPLE OF BOOM!

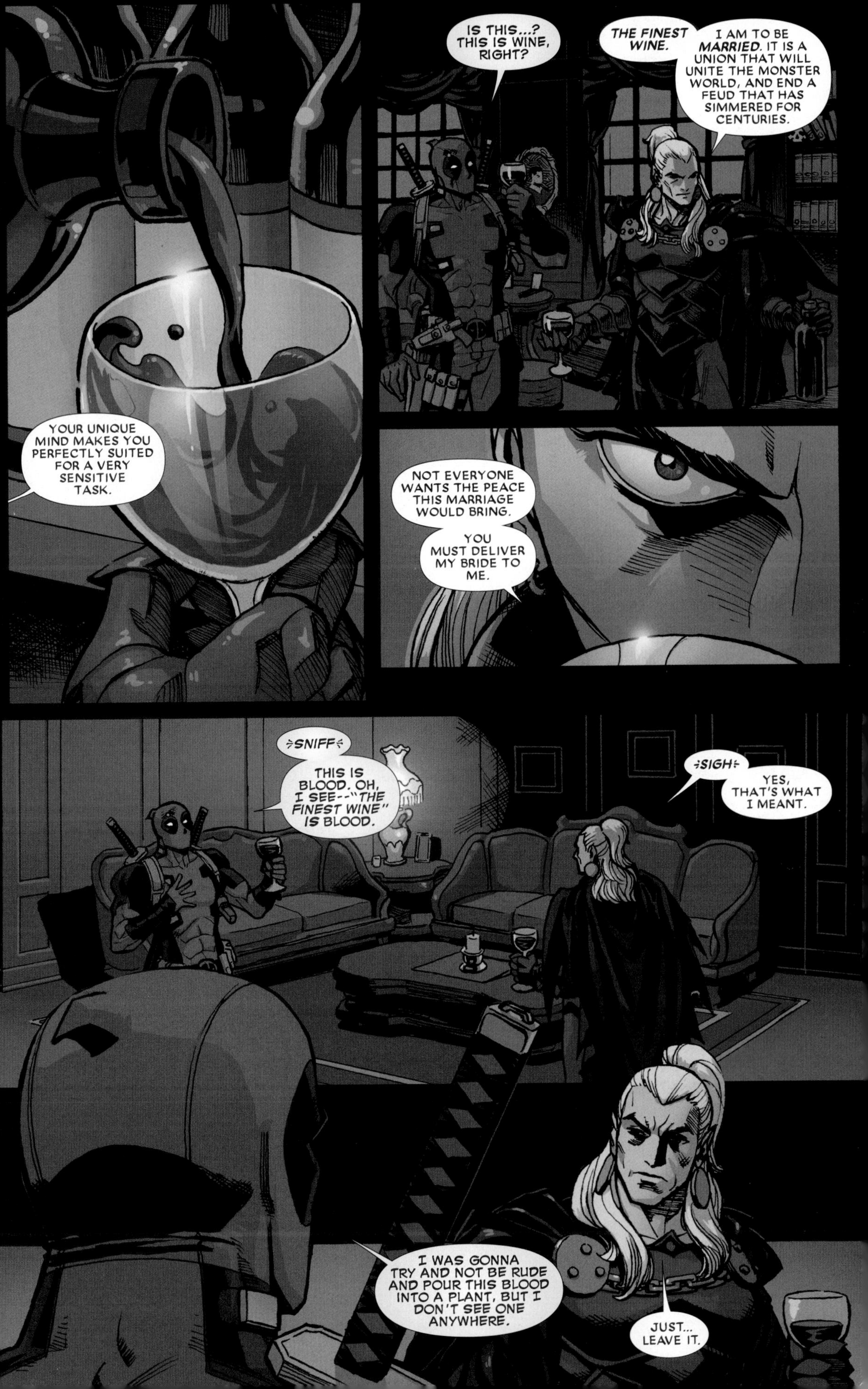
IS THIS...? THIS IS WINE, RIGHT?
THE FINEST WINE.
I AM TO BE MARRIED. IT IS A UNION THAT WILL UNITE THE MONSTER WORLD, AND END A FEUD THAT HAS SIMMERED FOR CENTURIES.
YOUR UNIQUE MIND MAKES YOU PERFECTLY SUITED FOR A VERY SENSITIVE TASK.
NOT EVERYONE WANTS THE PEACE THIS MARRIAGE WOULD BRING.
YOU MUST DELIVER MY BRIDE TO ME.
SNIFF
THIS IS BLOOD. OH, I SEE--"THE FINEST WINE" IS BLOOD.
SIGH
YES, THAT'S WHAT I MEANT.
I WAS GONNA TRY AND NOT BE RUDE AND POUR THIS BLOOD INTO A PLANT, BUT I DON'T SEE ONE ANYWHERE.
JUST... LEAVE IT.

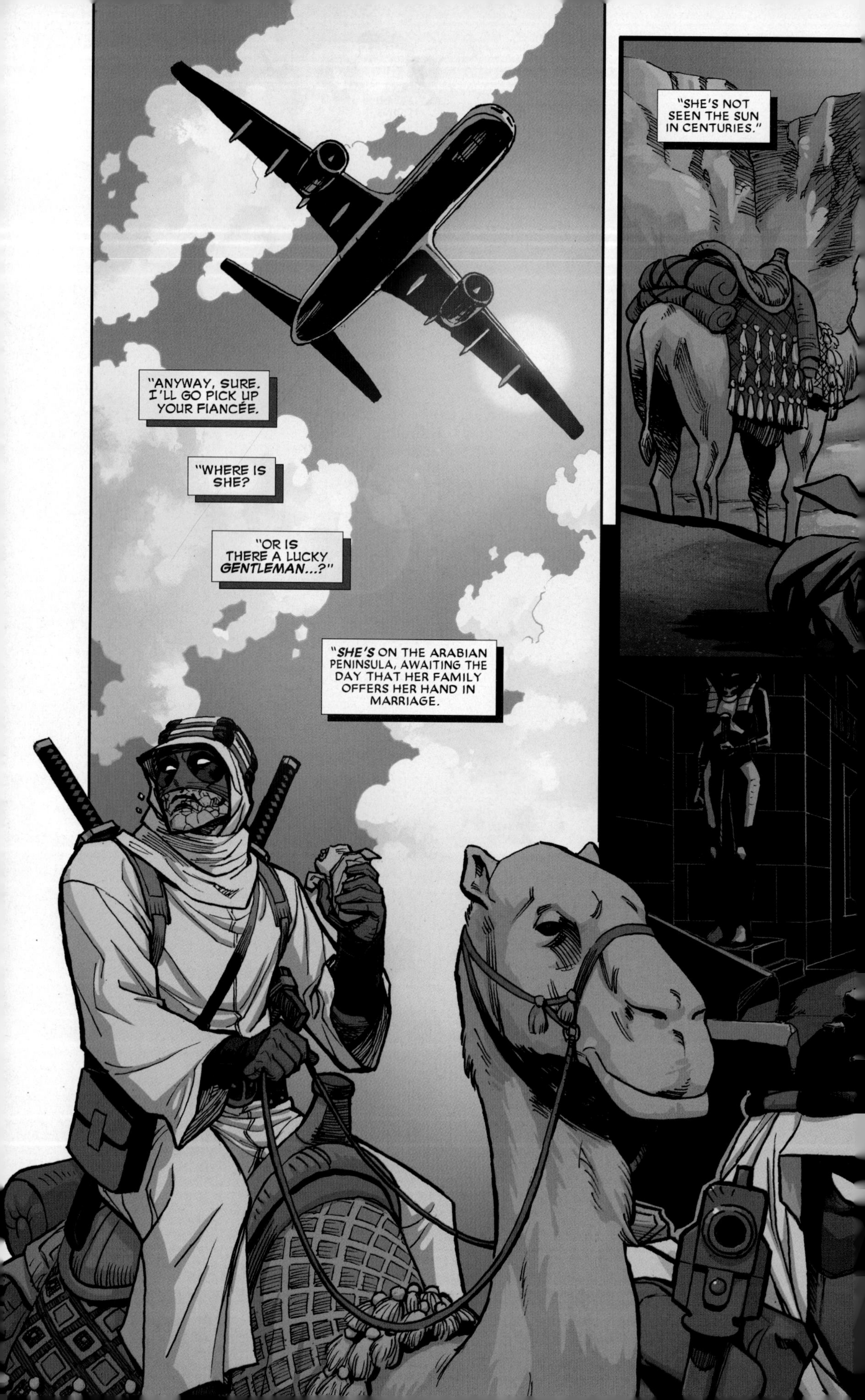
"ANYWAY, SURE. I'LL GO PICK UP YOUR FIANCÉE.
"WHERE IS SHE?
"OR IS THERE A LUCKY GENTLEMAN...?"
"SHE'S ON THE ARABIAN PENINSULA, AWAITING THE DAY THAT HER FAMILY OFFERS HER HAND IN MARRIAGE.
"SHE'S NOT SEEN THE SUN IN CENTURIES."

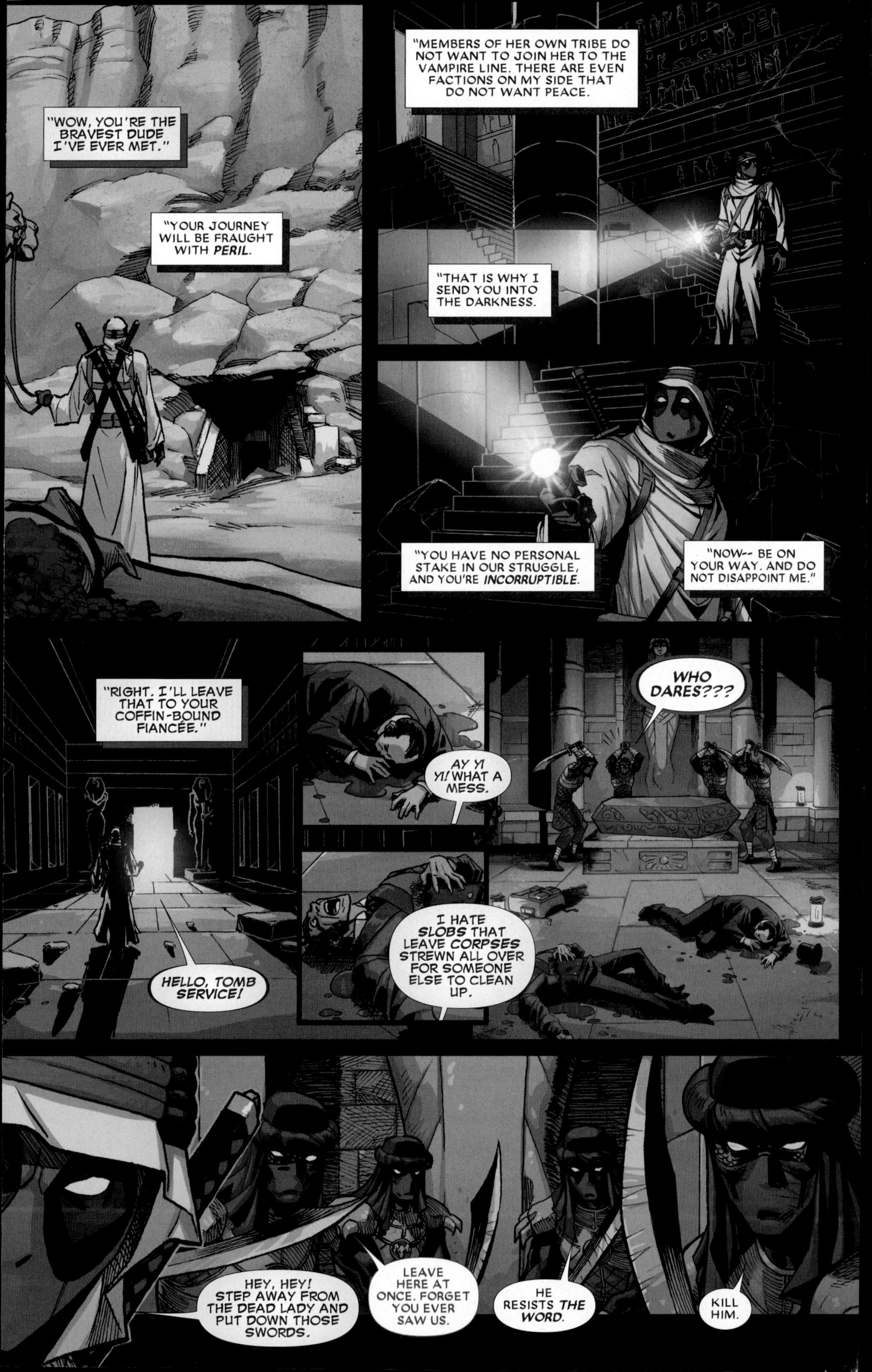
"WOW, YOU'RE THE BRAVEST DUDE I'VE EVER MET."
"YOUR JOURNEY WILL BE FRAUGHT WITH PERIL.
"MEMBERS OF HER OWN TRIBE DO NOT WANT TO JOIN HER TO THE VAMPIRE LINE. THERE ARE EVEN FACTIONS ON MY SIDE THAT DO NOT WANT PEACE.
"THAT IS WHY I SEND YOU INTO THE DARKNESS.
"YOU HAVE NO PERSONAL STAKE IN OUR STRUGGLE, AND YOU'RE INCORRUPTIBLE.
"NOW-- BE ON YOUR WAY. AND DO NOT DISAPPOINT ME."
"RIGHT. I'LL LEAVE THAT TO YOUR COFFIN-BOUND FIANCÉE."
HELLO, TOMB SERVICE!
AY YI YI! WHAT A MESS.
I HATE SLOBS THAT LEAVE CORPSES STREWN ALL OVER FOR SOMEONE ELSE TO CLEAN UP.
WHO DARES???
HEY, HEY! STEP AWAY FROM THE DEAD LADY AND PUT DOWN THOSE SWORDS.
LEAVE HERE AT ONCE. FORGET YOU EVER SAW US.
HE RESISTS THE WORD.
KILL HIM.

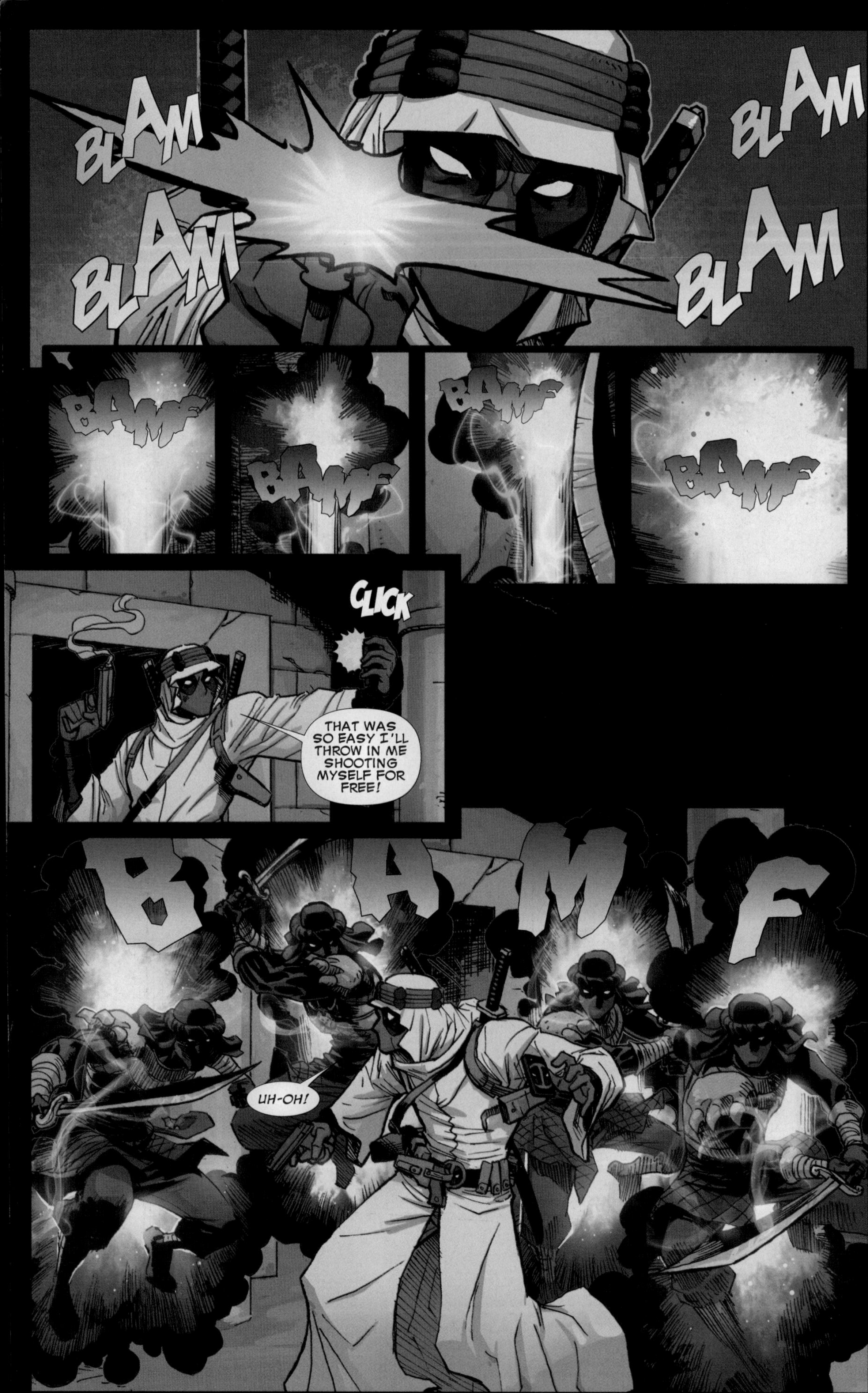

BLAM
BLAM
BLAM
BLAM
BAMF
BAMF
BAMF
BAMF
CLICK
THAT WAS SO EASY I'LL THROW IN ME SHOOTING MYSELF FOR FREE!
BAMF
UH-OH!

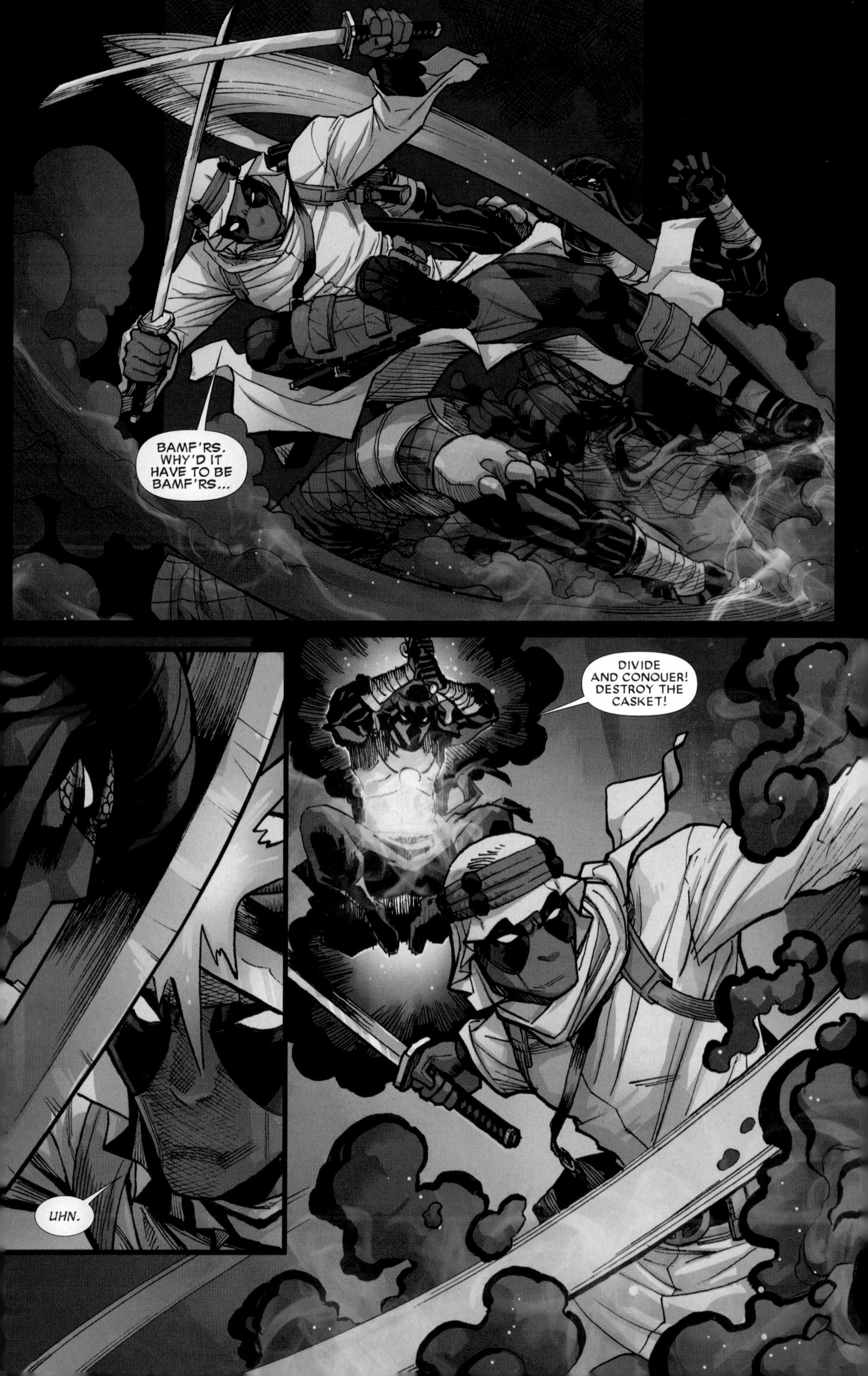
BAMF'RS. WHY'D IT HAVE TO BE BAMF'RS...
UHN.
DIVIDE AND CONQUER! DESTROY THE CASKET!

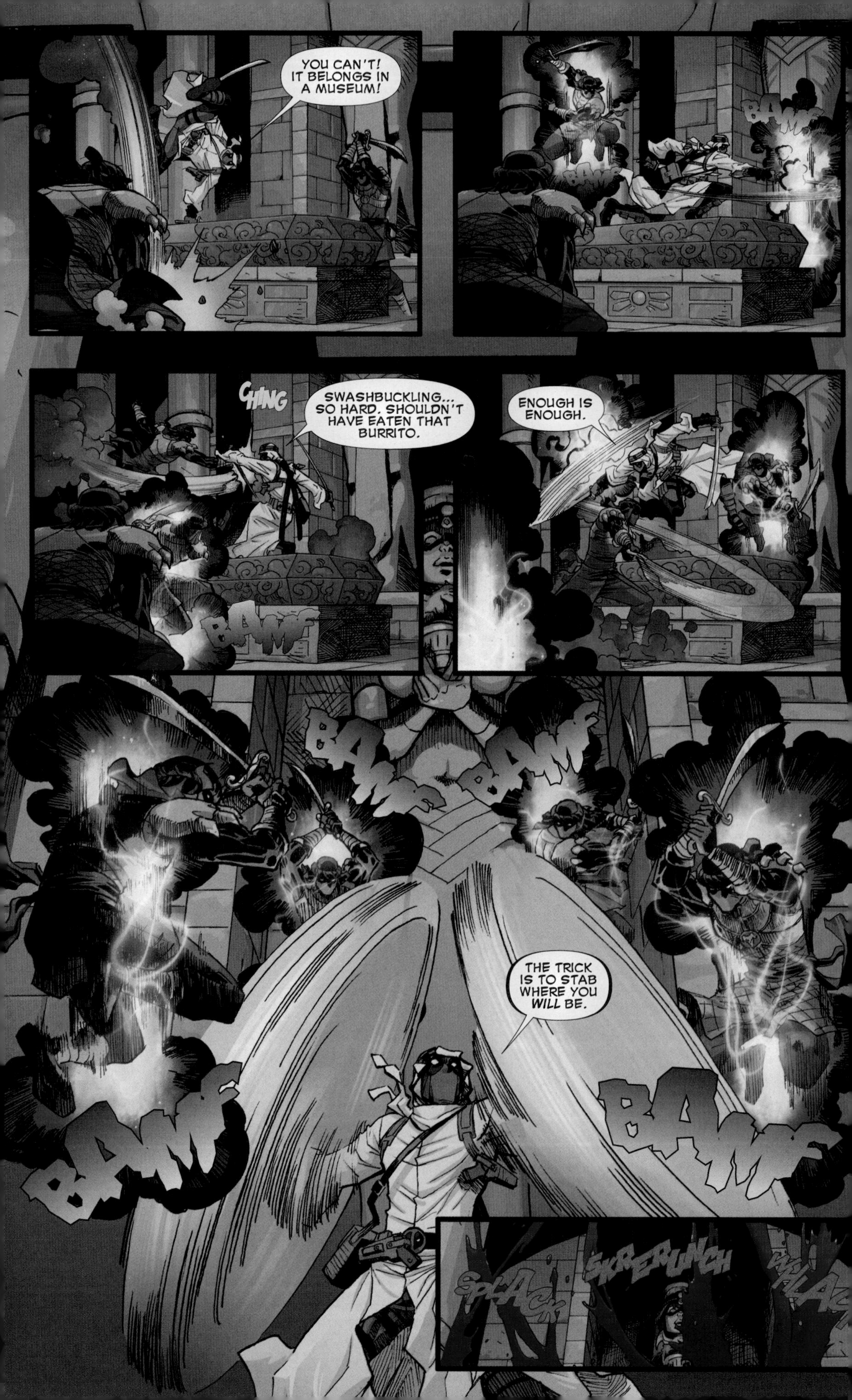
YOU CAN'T! IT BELONGS IN A MUSEUM!
BAMF
CHING
SWASHBUCKLING... SO HARD. SHOULDN'T HAVE EATEN THAT BURRITO.
BAMF
ENOUGH IS ENOUGH.
BAMF
BAMF
THE TRICK IS TO STAB WHERE YOU *WILL* BE.
BAMF
BAMF
SPLACK
SKRERUNCH

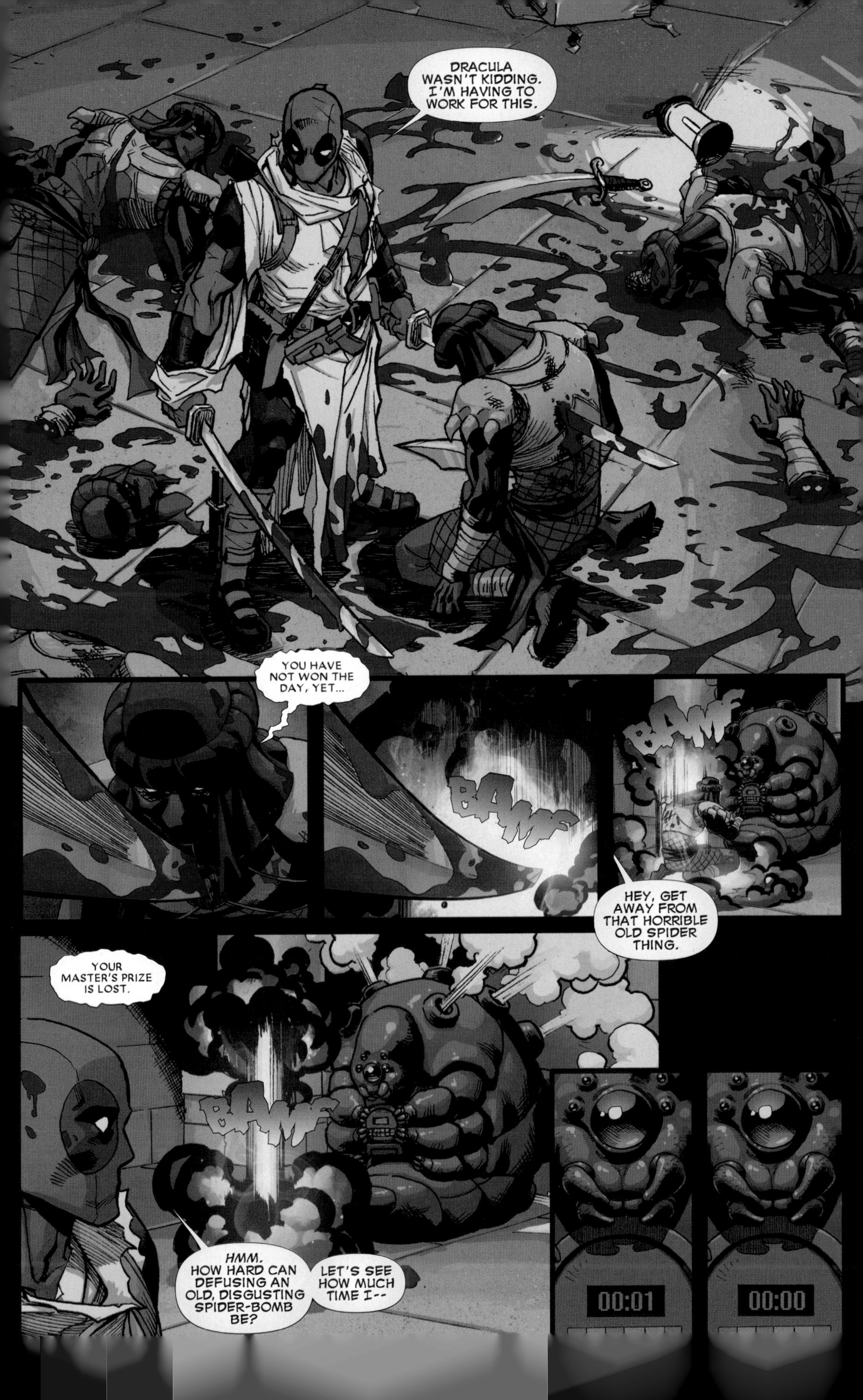
DRACULA WASN'T KIDDING. I'M HAVING TO WORK FOR THIS.
YOU HAVE NOT WON THE DAY, YET...
BAMF
BAMF
HEY, GET AWAY FROM THAT HORRIBLE OLD SPIDER THING.
YOUR MASTER'S PRIZE IS LOST.
BAMF
HMM. HOW HARD CAN DEFUSING AN OLD, DISGUSTING SPIDER-BOMB BE?
LET'S SEE HOW MUCH TIME I--
00:01
00:00

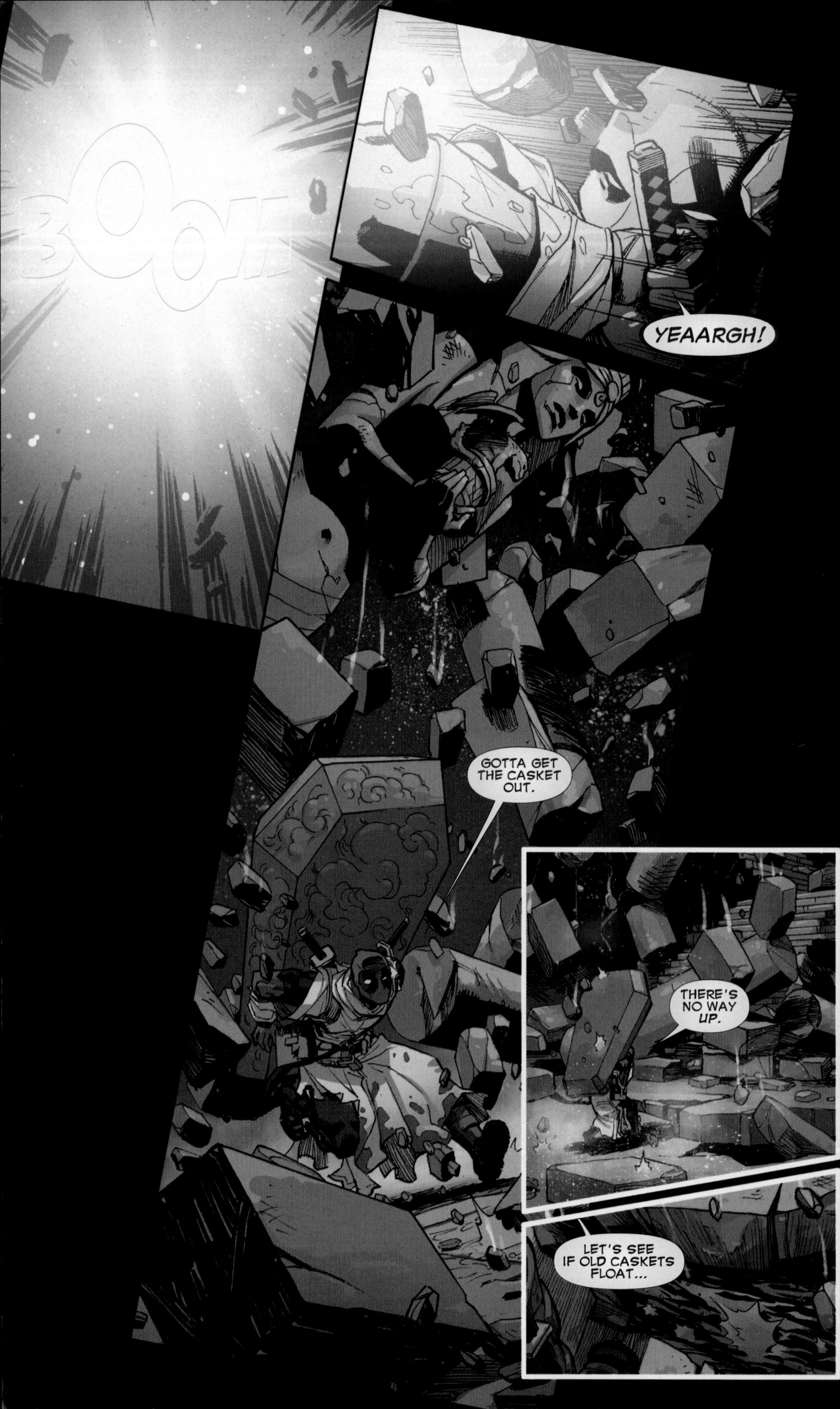
BOOM
YEAARGH!
GOTTA GET THE CASKET OUT.
THERE'S NO WAY UP.
LET'S SEE IF OLD CASKETS FLOAT...

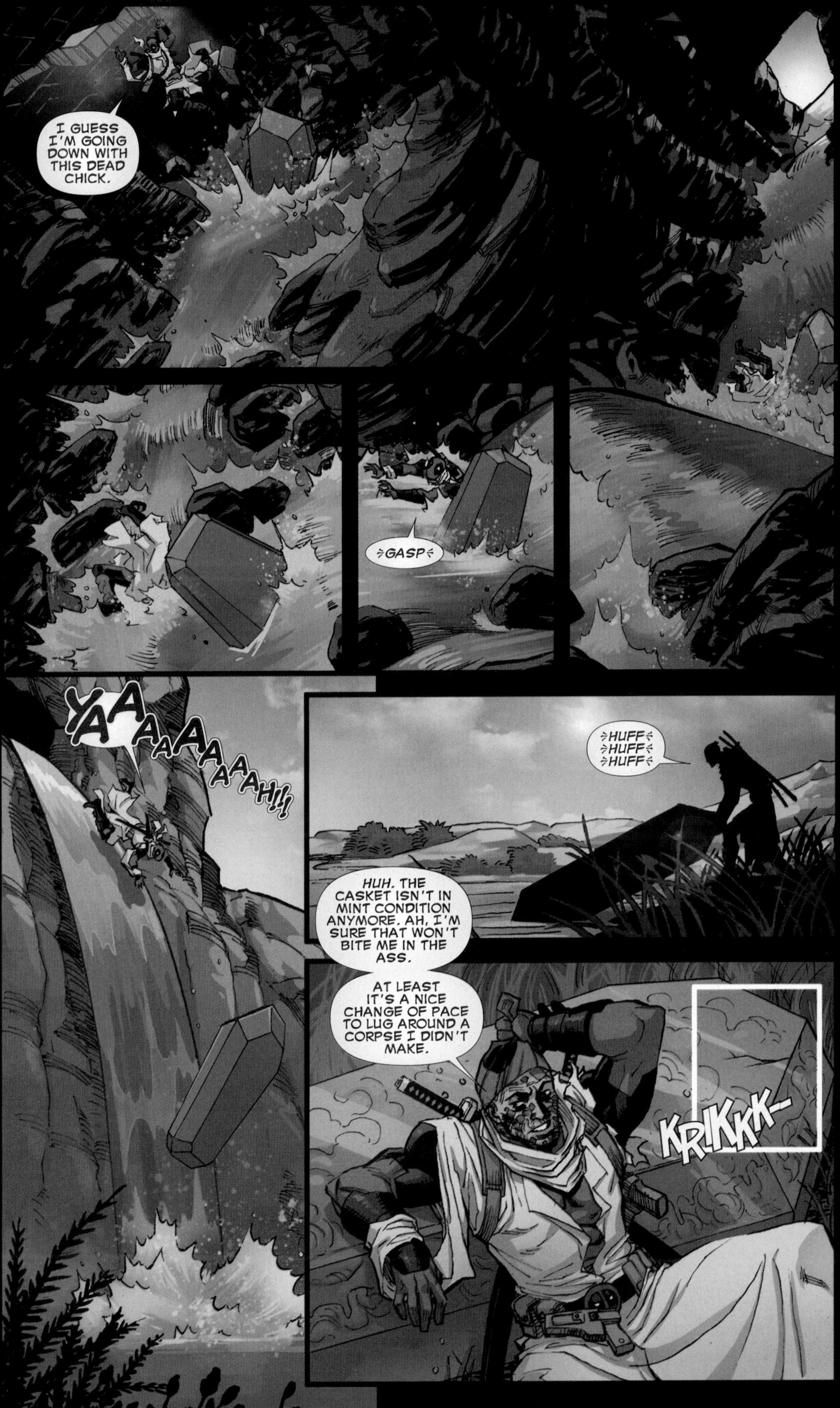

I GUESS I'M GOING DOWN WITH THIS DEAD CHICK.
GASP
YAAAAAAAAAAAH!!!
HUFF HUFF HUFF
HUH. THE CASKET ISN'T IN MINT CONDITION ANYMORE. AH, I'M SURE THAT WON'T BITE ME IN THE ASS.
AT LEAST IT'S A NICE CHANGE OF PACE TO LUG AROUND A CORPSE I DIDN'T MAKE.
KRIKKK-

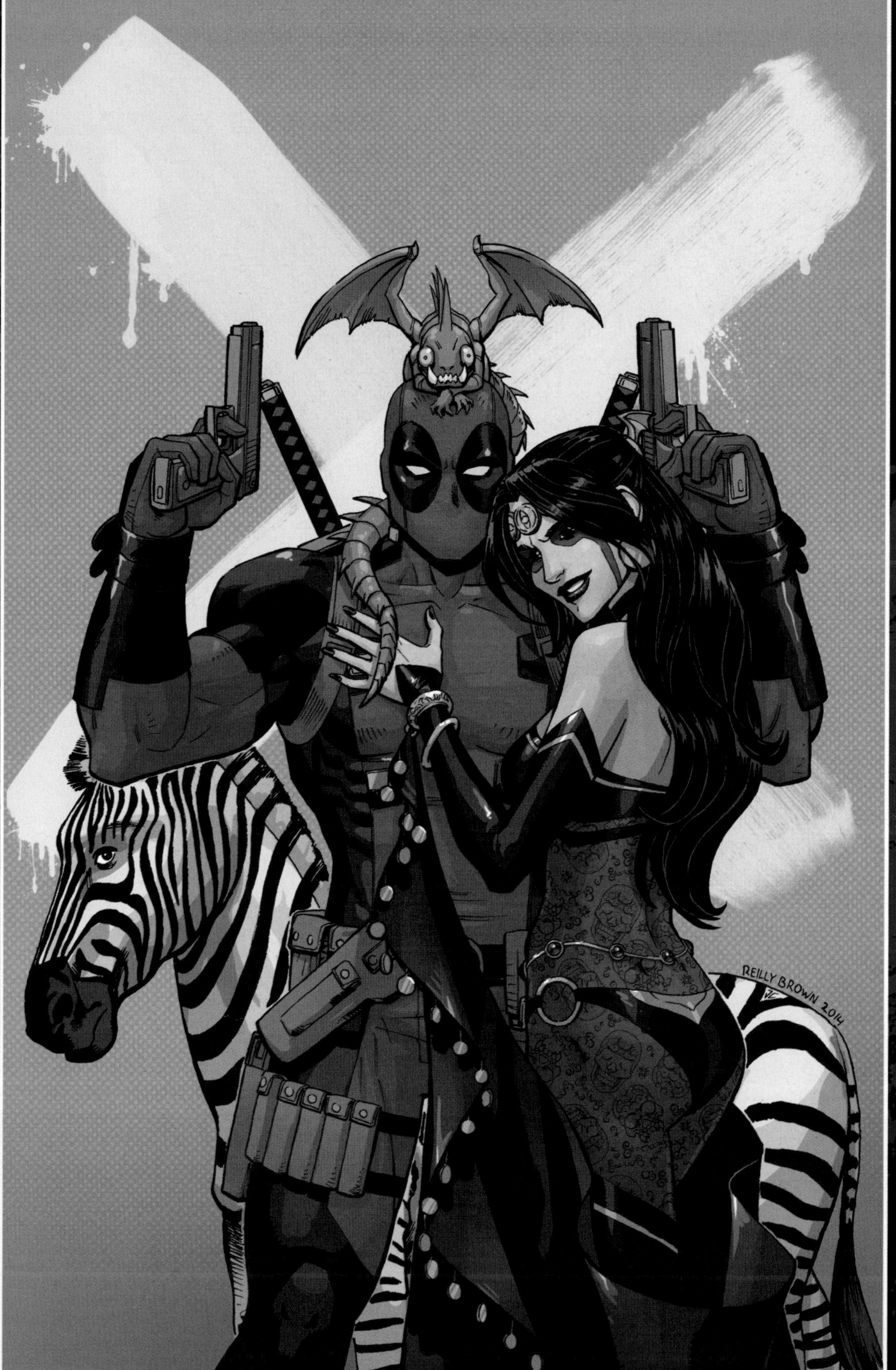
REILLY BROWN 2014

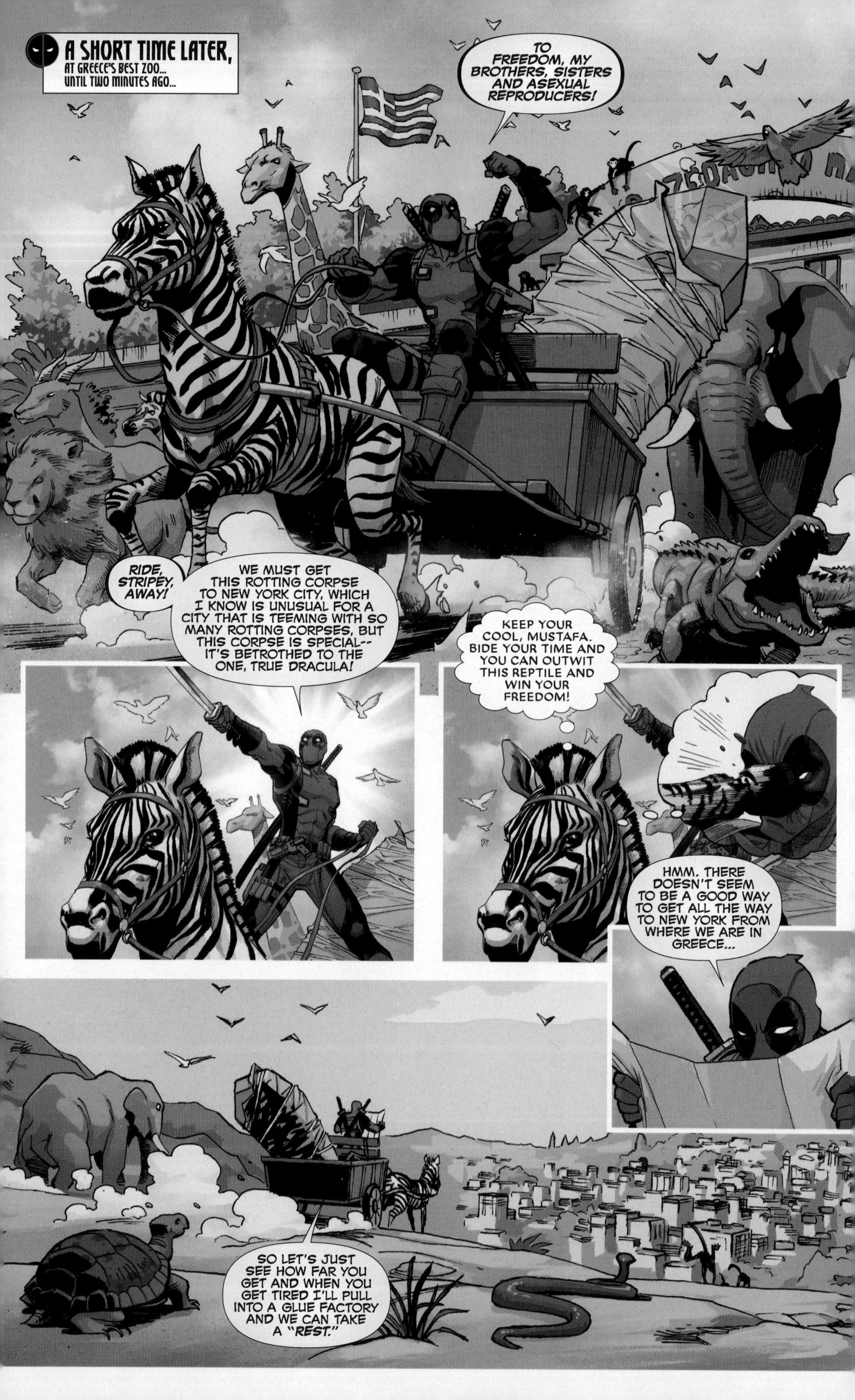
A SHORT TIME LATER,
AT GREECE'S BEST ZOO... UNTIL TWO MINUTES AGO...
TO FREEDOM, MY BROTHERS, SISTERS AND ASEXUAL REPRODUCERS!
RIDE, STRIPEY, AWAY!
WE MUST GET THIS ROTTING CORPSE TO NEW YORK CITY, WHICH I KNOW IS UNUSUAL FOR A CITY THAT IS TEEMING WITH SO MANY ROTTING CORPSES, BUT THIS CORPSE IS SPECIAL-- IT'S BETROTHED TO THE ONE, TRUE DRACULA!
KEEP YOUR COOL, MUSTAFA. BIDE YOUR TIME AND YOU CAN OUTWIT THIS REPTILE AND WIN YOUR FREEDOM!
HMM. THERE DOESN'T SEEM TO BE A GOOD WAY TO GET ALL THE WAY TO NEW YORK FROM WHERE WE ARE IN GREECE...
SO LET'S JUST SEE HOW FAR YOU GET AND WHEN YOU GET TIRED I'LL PULL INTO A GLUE FACTORY AND WE CAN TAKE A "REST."

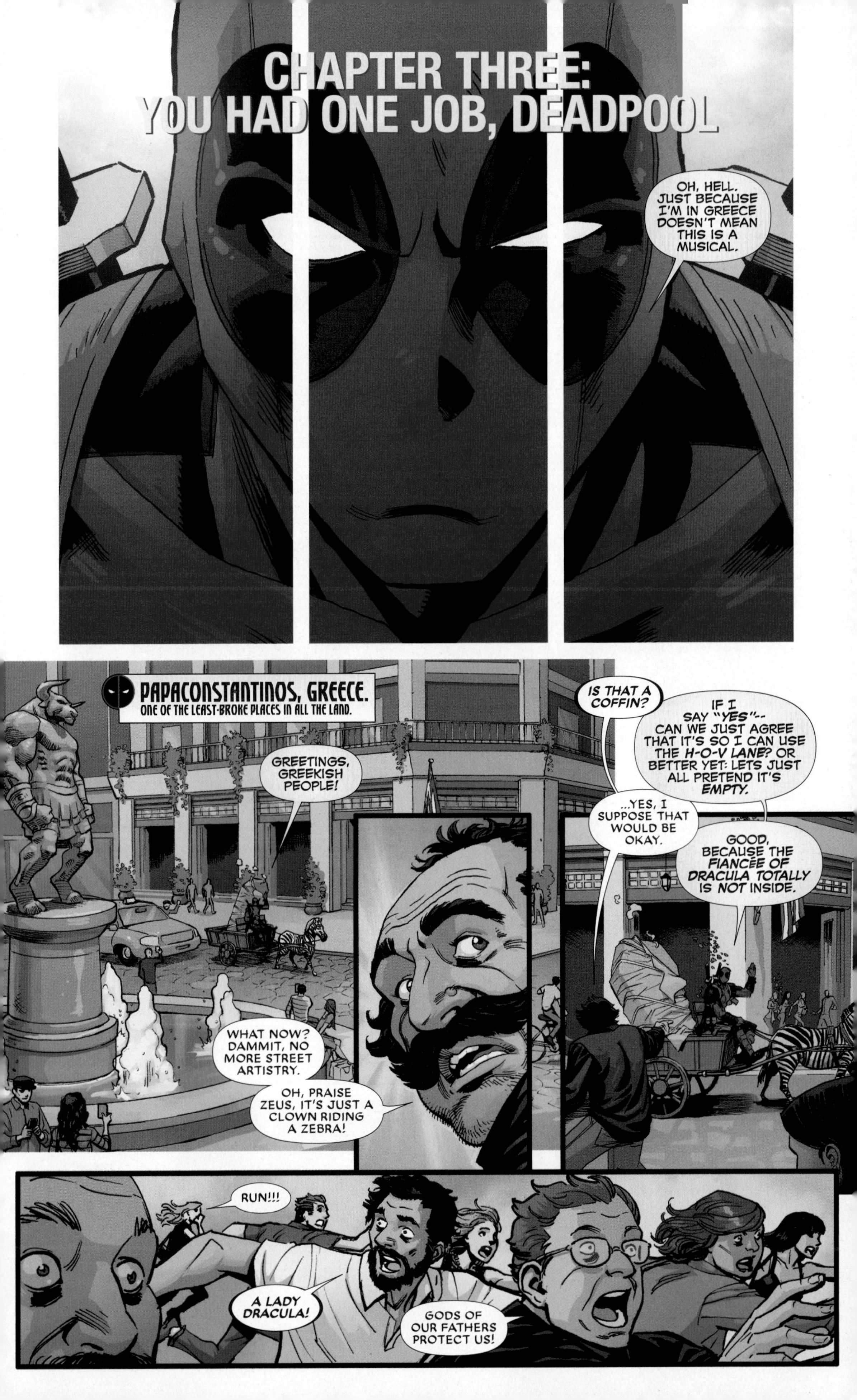
CHAPTER THREE:
YOU HAD ONE JOB, DEADPOOL
OH, HELL. JUST BECAUSE I'M IN GREECE DOESN'T MEAN THIS IS A MUSICAL.
PAPACONSTANTINOS, GREECE.
ONE OF THE LEAST-BROKE PLACES IN ALL THE LAND.
GREETINGS, GREEKISH PEOPLE!
WHAT NOW? DAMMIT, NO MORE STREET ARTISTRY.
OH, PRAISE ZEUS, IT'S JUST A CLOWN RIDING A ZEBRA!
IS THAT A COFFIN?
IF I SAY "YES"-- CAN WE JUST AGREE THAT IT'S SO I CAN USE THE H-O-V LANE? OR BETTER YET: LETS JUST ALL PRETEND IT'S EMPTY.
...YES, I SUPPOSE THAT WOULD BE OKAY.
GOOD, BECAUSE THE FIANCÉE OF DRACULA TOTALLY IS NOT INSIDE.
RUN!!!
A LADY DRACULA!
GODS OF OUR FATHERS PROTECT US!

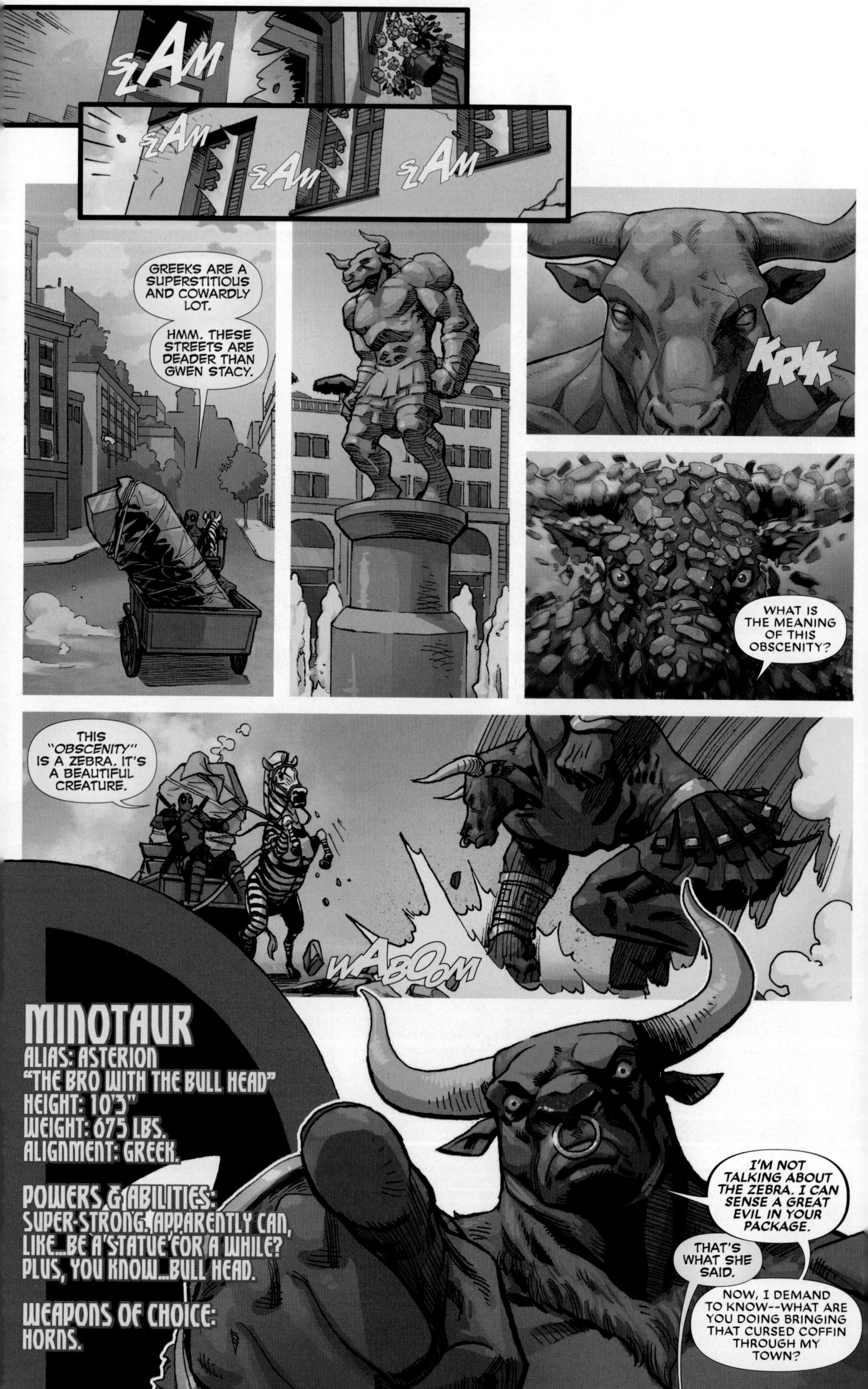
SLAM
SLAM
SLAM
SLAM
GREEKS ARE A SUPERSTITIOUS AND COWARDLY LOT.
HMM. THESE STREETS ARE DEADER THAN GWEN STACY.
KRAK
WHAT IS THE MEANING OF THIS OBSCENITY?
THIS "OBSCENITY" IS A ZEBRA. IT'S A BEAUTIFUL CREATURE.
WABOOM
MINOTAUR
ALIAS: ASTERION
"THE BRO WITH THE BULL HEAD"
HEIGHT: 10'3"
WEIGHT: 675 LBS.
ALIGNMENT: GREEK.
POWERS & ABILITIES:
SUPER-STRONG, APPARENTLY CAN, LIKE...BE A STATUE FOR A WHILE? PLUS, YOU KNOW...BULL HEAD.
WEAPONS OF CHOICE:
HORNS.
I'M NOT TALKING ABOUT THE ZEBRA. I CAN SENSE A GREAT EVIL IN YOUR PACKAGE.
THAT'S WHAT SHE SAID.
NOW, I DEMAND TO KNOW--WHAT ARE YOU DOING BRINGING THAT CURSED COFFIN THROUGH MY TOWN?

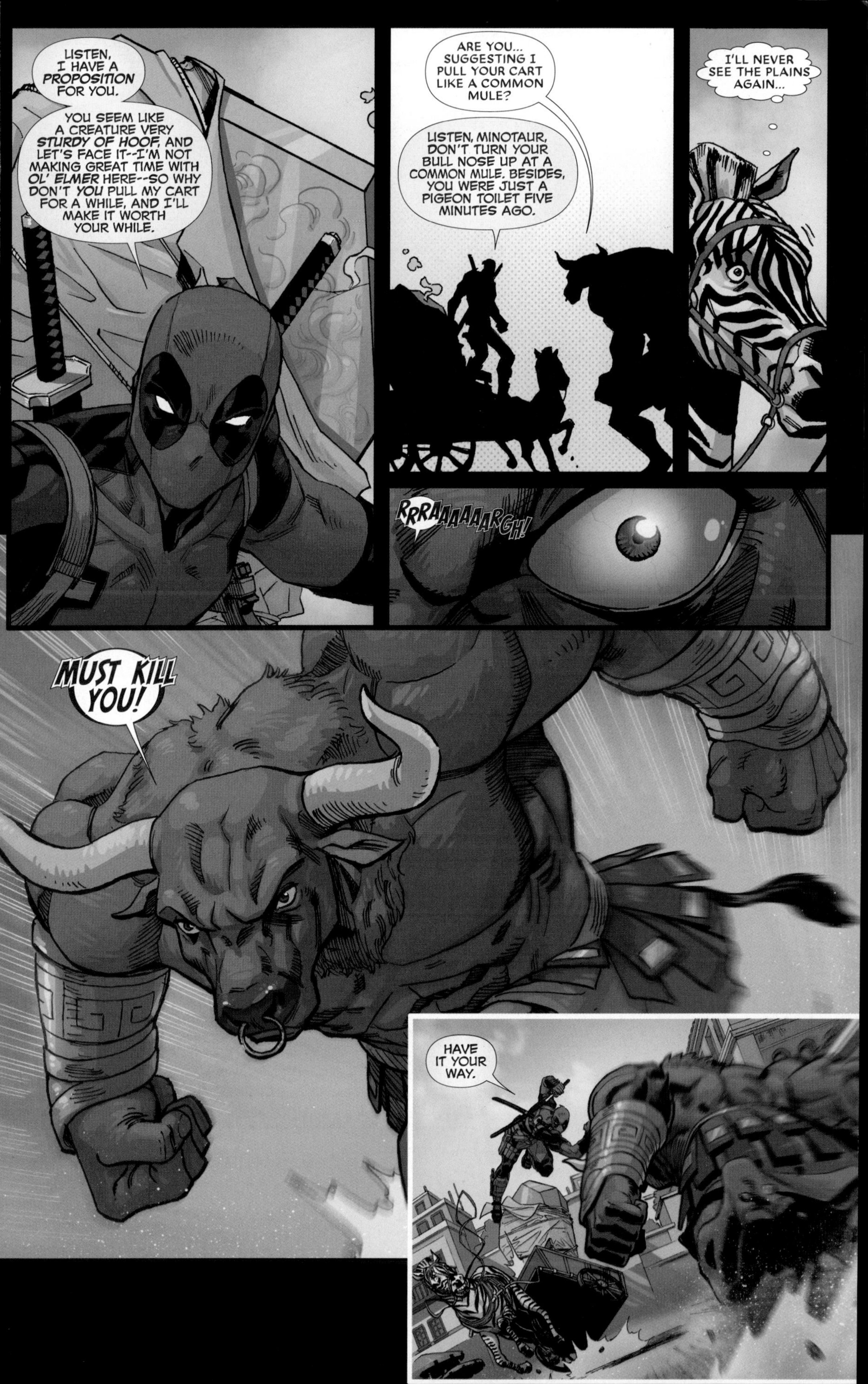
LISTEN, I HAVE A PROPOSITION FOR YOU.
YOU SEEM LIKE A CREATURE VERY STURDY OF HOOF, AND LET'S FACE IT--I'M NOT MAKING GREAT TIME WITH OL' ELMER HERE--SO WHY DON'T YOU PULL MY CART FOR A WHILE, AND I'LL MAKE IT WORTH YOUR WHILE.
ARE YOU... SUGGESTING I PULL YOUR CART LIKE A COMMON MULE?
LISTEN, MINOTAUR, DON'T TURN YOUR BULL NOSE UP AT A COMMON MULE. BESIDES, YOU WERE JUST A PIGEON TOILET FIVE MINUTES AGO.
I'LL NEVER SEE THE PLAINS AGAIN...
RRRAAAAAARGH!
MUST KILL YOU!
HAVE IT YOUR WAY.

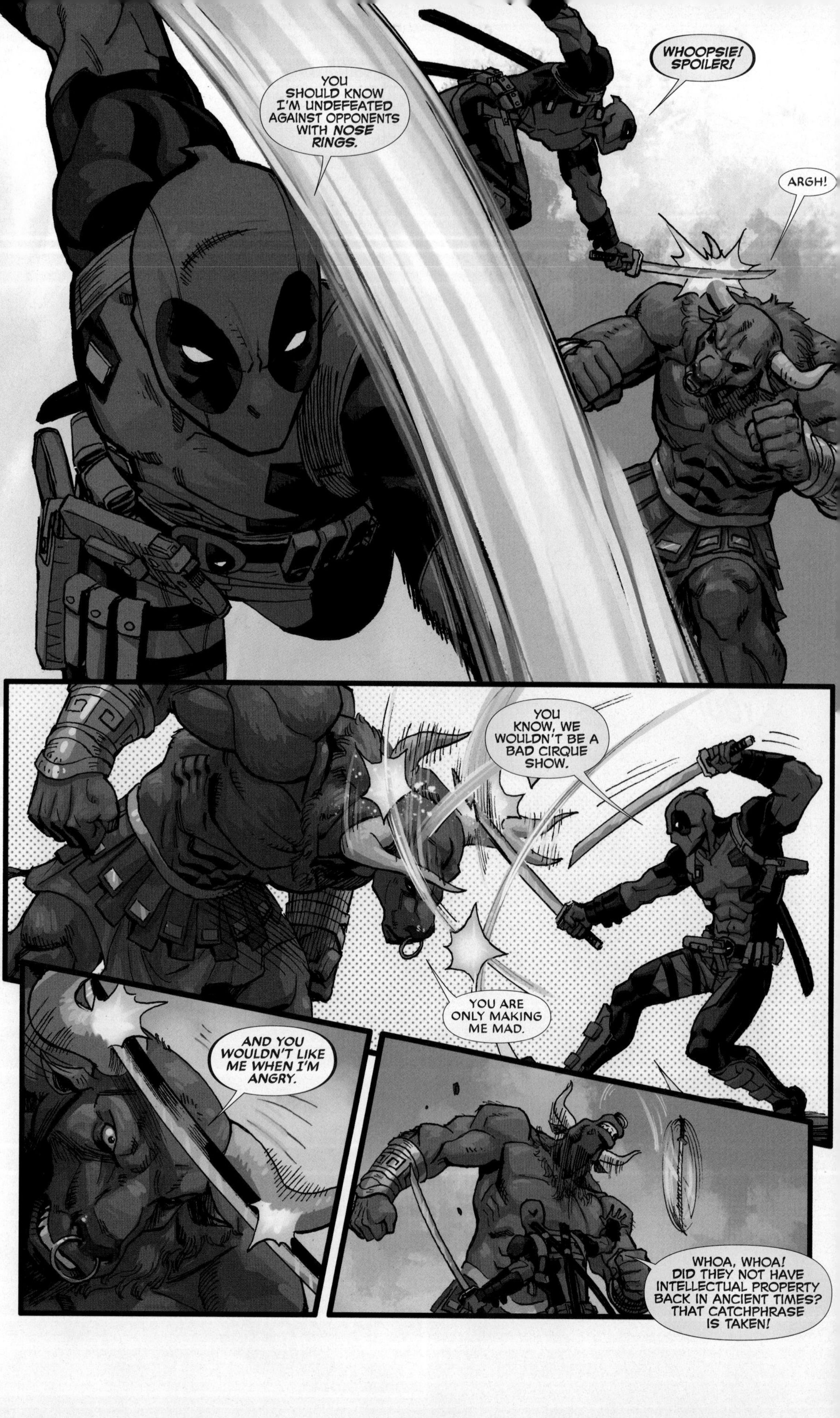
YOU SHOULD KNOW I'M UNDEFEATED AGAINST OPPONENTS WITH NOSE RINGS.
WHOOPSIE! SPOILER!
ARGH!
YOU KNOW, WE WOULDN'T BE A BAD CIRQUE SHOW.
YOU ARE ONLY MAKING ME MAD.
AND YOU WOULDN'T LIKE ME WHEN I'M ANGRY.
WHOA, WHOA! DID THEY NOT HAVE INTELLECTUAL PROPERTY BACK IN ANCIENT TIMES? THAT CATCHPHRASE IS TAKEN!

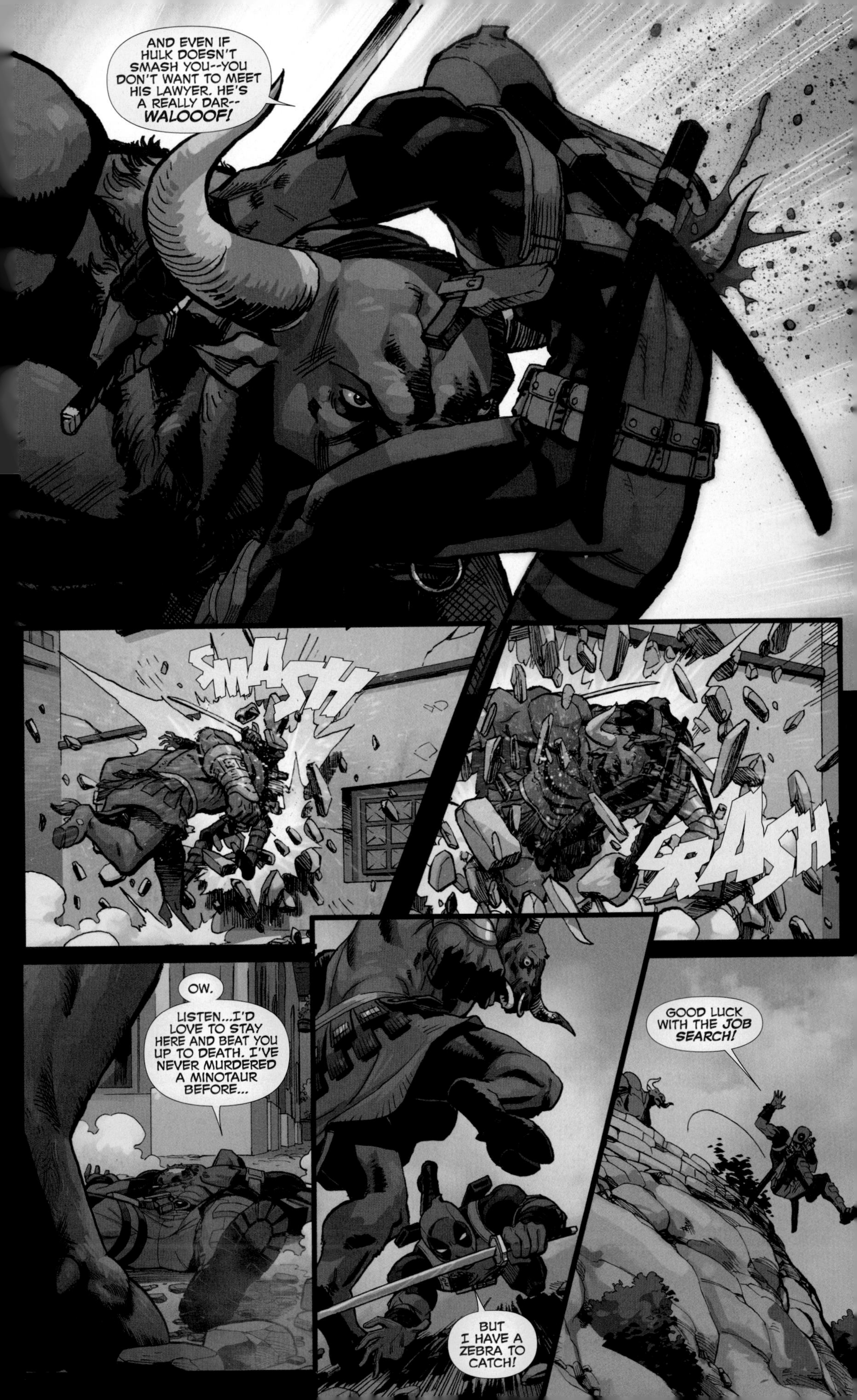
AND EVEN IF HULK DOESN'T SMASH YOU--YOU DON'T WANT TO MEET HIS LAWYER. HE'S A REALLY DAR-- WALOOOF!
SMASH
CRASH
OW.
LISTEN...I'D LOVE TO STAY HERE AND BEAT YOU UP TO DEATH. I'VE NEVER MURDERED A MINOTAUR BEFORE...
BUT I HAVE A ZEBRA TO CATCH!
GOOD LUCK WITH THE JOB SEARCH!

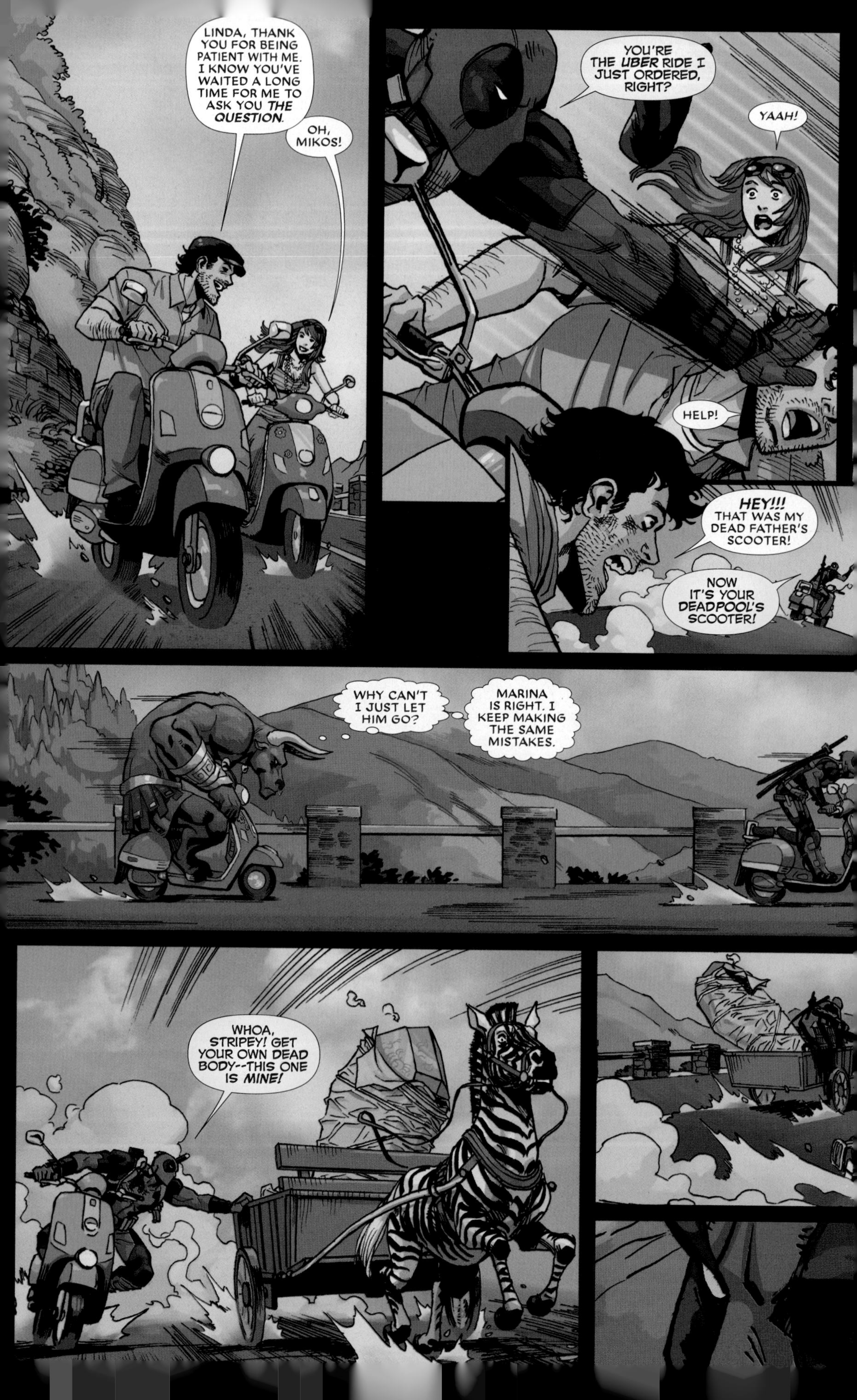
LINDA, THANK YOU FOR BEING PATIENT WITH ME. I KNOW YOU'VE WAITED A LONG TIME FOR ME TO ASK YOU THE QUESTION.
OH, MIKOS!
YOU'RE THE UBER RIDE I JUST ORDERED, RIGHT?
YAAH!
HELP!
HEY!!! THAT WAS MY DEAD FATHER'S SCOOTER!
NOW IT'S YOUR DEADPOOL'S SCOOTER!
WHY CAN'T I JUST LET HIM GO?
MARINA IS RIGHT. I KEEP MAKING THE SAME MISTAKES.
WHOA, STRIPEY! GET YOUR OWN DEAD BODY--THIS ONE IS MINE!

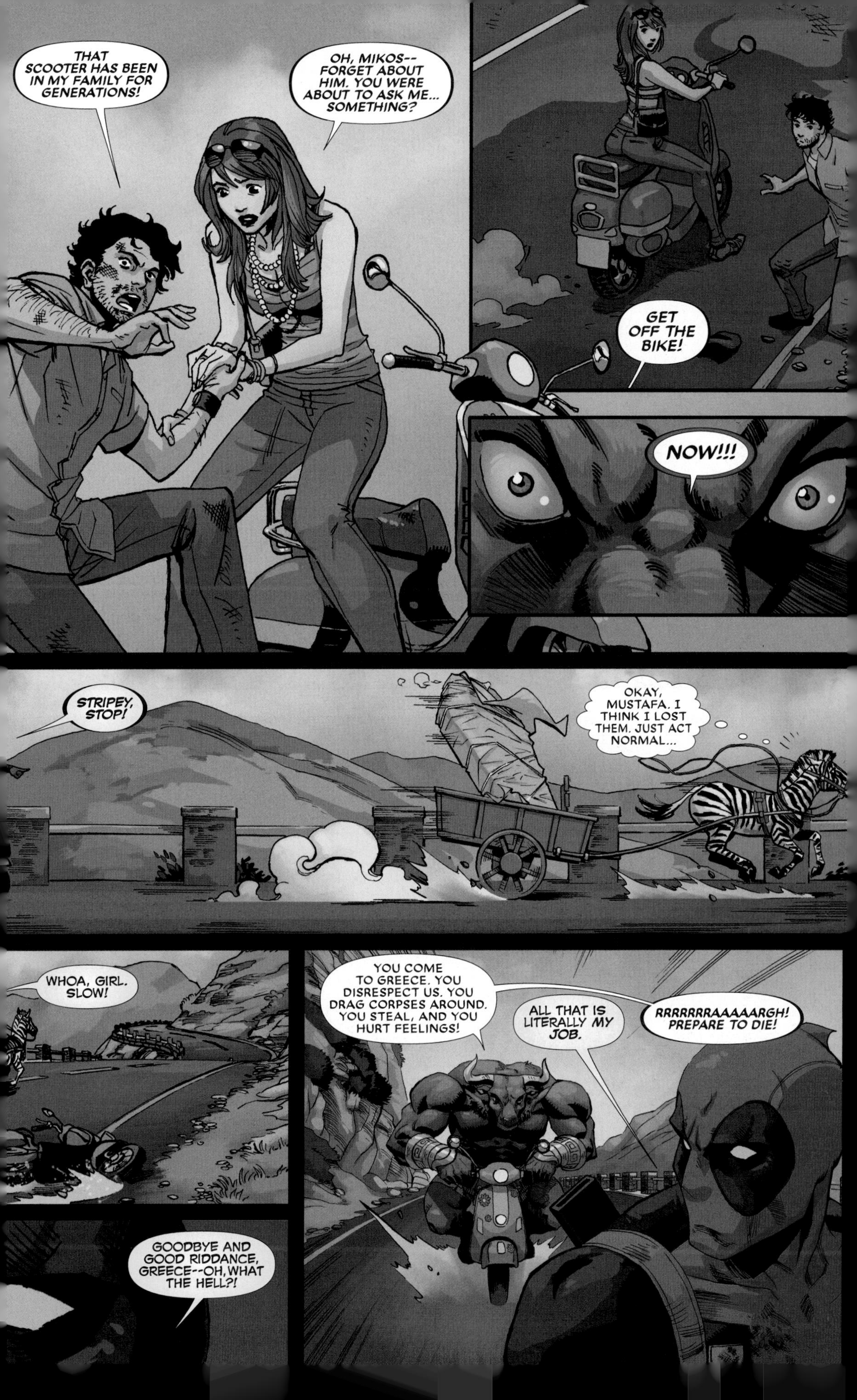
THAT SCOOTER HAS BEEN IN MY FAMILY FOR GENERATIONS!
OH, MIKOS-- FORGET ABOUT HIM. YOU WERE ABOUT TO ASK ME... SOMETHING?
GET OFF THE BIKE!
NOW!!!
STRIPEY, STOP!
OKAY, MUSTAFA. I THINK I LOST THEM. JUST ACT NORMAL...
WHOA, GIRL. SLOW!
GOODBYE AND GOOD RIDDANCE, GREECE--OH, WHAT THE HELL?!
YOU COME TO GREECE. YOU DISRESPECT US. YOU DRAG CORPSES AROUND. YOU STEAL, AND YOU HURT FEELINGS!
ALL THAT IS LITERALLY MY JOB.
RRRRRRRAAAAARGH! PREPARE TO DIE!

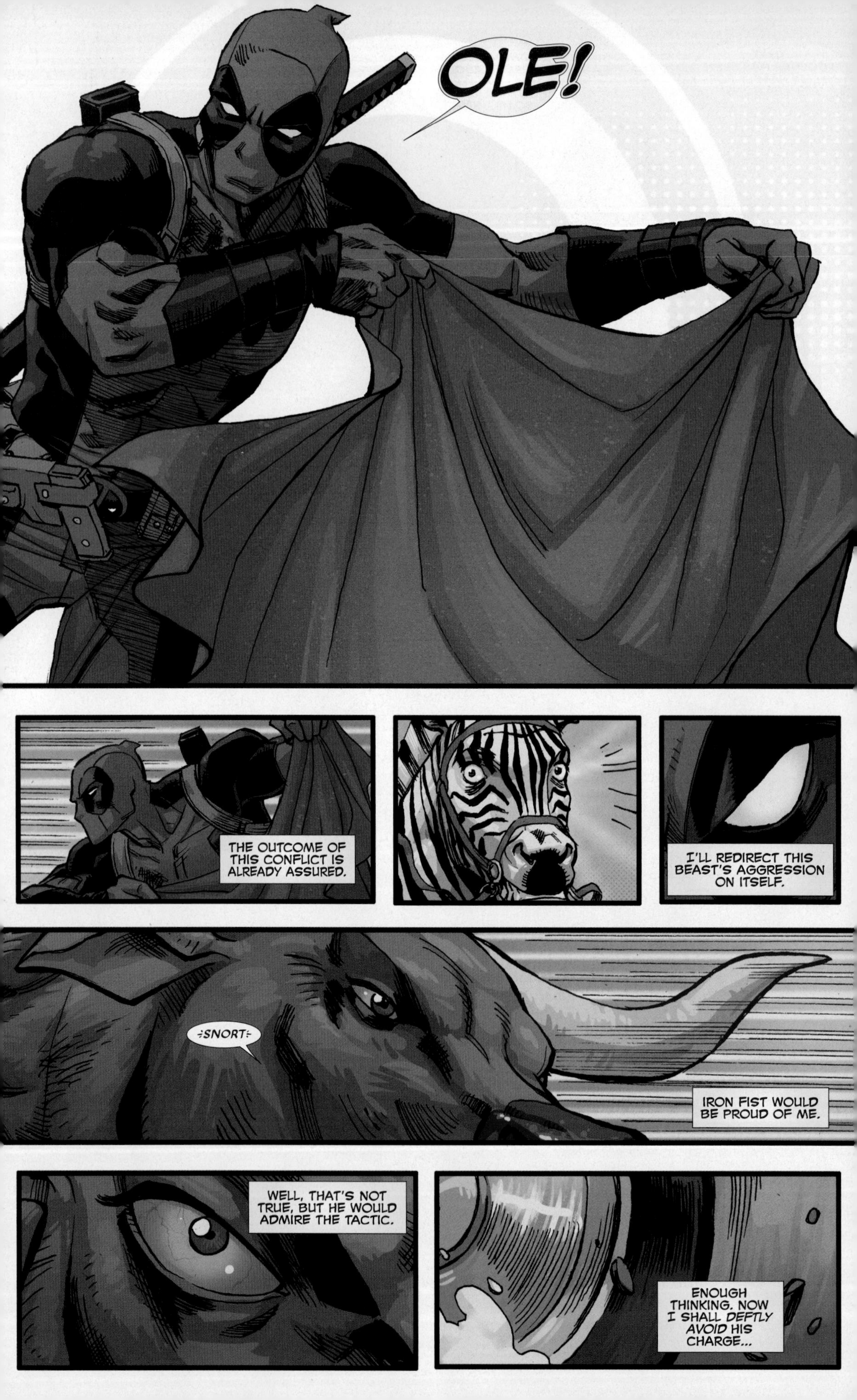

OLE!
THE OUTCOME OF THIS CONFLICT IS ALREADY ASSURED.
I'LL REDIRECT THIS BEAST'S AGGRESSION ON ITSELF.
SNORT
IRON FIST WOULD BE PROUD OF ME.
WELL, THAT'S NOT TRUE, BUT HE WOULD ADMIRE THE TACTIC.
ENOUGH THINKING. NOW I SHALL *DEFTLY AVOID* HIS CHARGE...

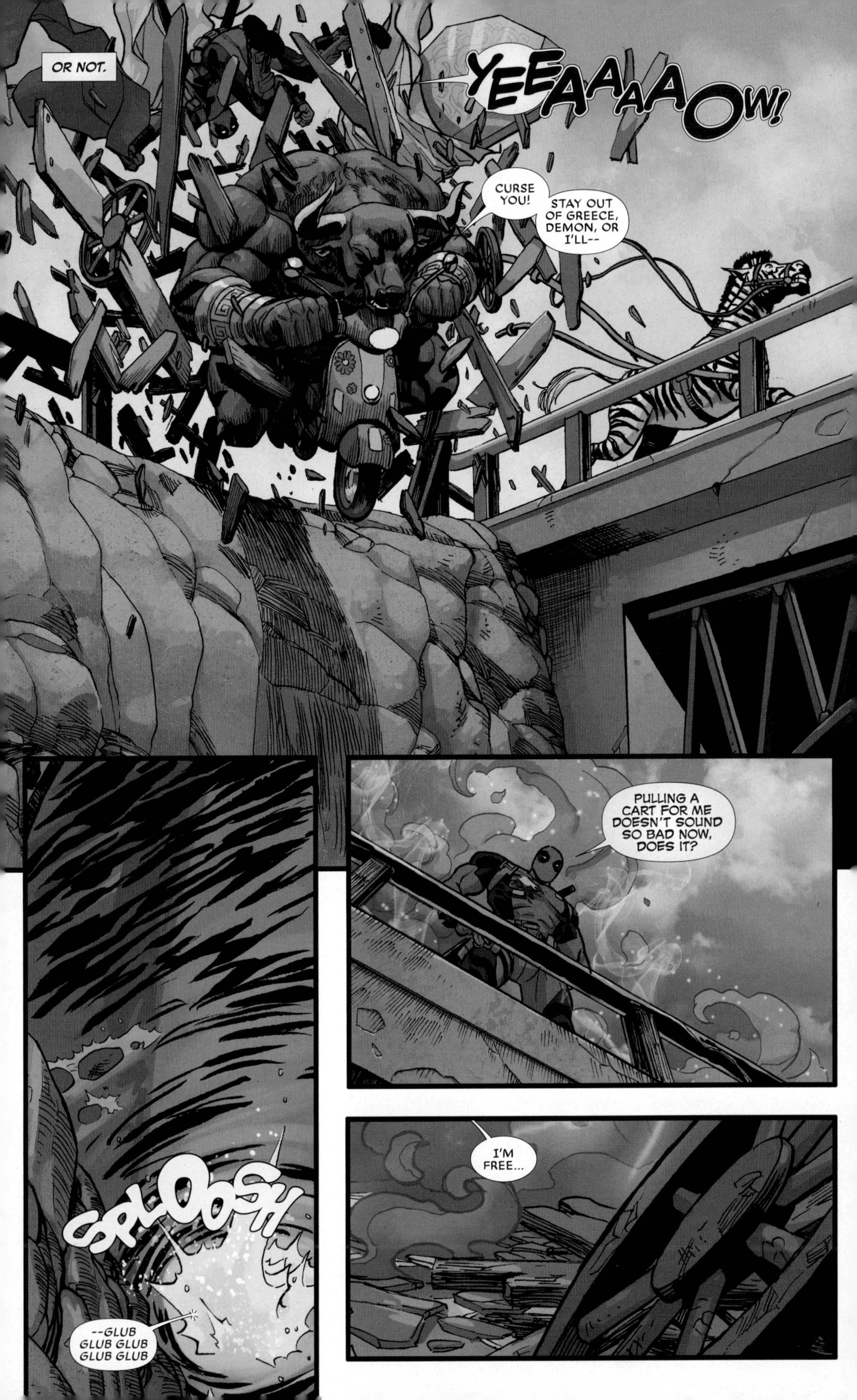
OR NOT.
YEEAAAAAOW!
CURSE YOU!
STAY OUT OF GREECE, DEMON, OR I'LL--
PULLING A CART FOR ME DOESN'T SOUND SO BAD NOW, DOES IT?
SPLOOSH
--GLUB GLUB GLUB GLUB GLUB
I'M FREE...

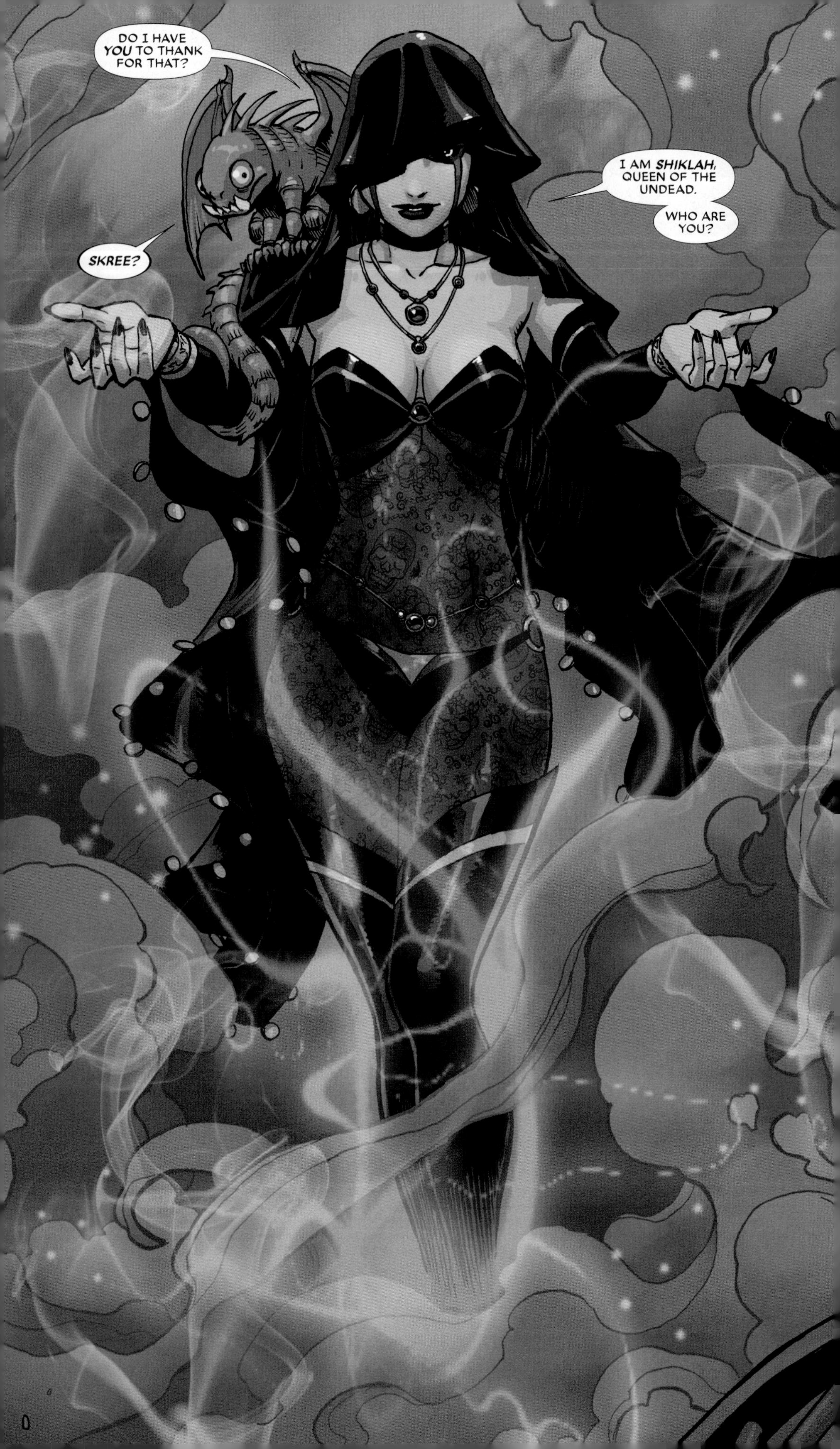
DO I HAVE YOU TO THANK FOR THAT?
SKREE?
I AM SHIKLAH, QUEEN OF THE UNDEAD.
WHO ARE YOU?

MEANWHILE, BACK IN THE DESERT...

A BURRITO.

THERE'S ONLY ONE THING THAT COULD MEAN.

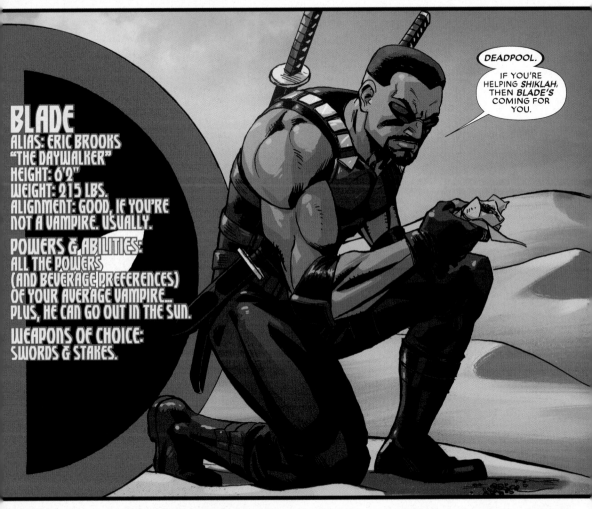

BLADE
ALIAS: ERIC BROOKS "THE DAYWALKER"
HEIGHT: 6'2"
WEIGHT: 215 LBS.
ALIGNMENT: GOOD, IF YOU'RE NOT A VAMPIRE. USUALLY.

POWERS & ABILITIES: ALL THE POWERS (AND BEVERAGE PREFERENCES) OF YOUR AVERAGE VAMPIRE... PLUS, HE CAN GO OUT IN THE SUN.

WEAPONS OF CHOICE: SWORDS & STAKES.

DEADPOOL. IF YOU'RE HELPING *SHIKLAH*, THEN *BLADE'S* COMING FOR YOU.

COUNT ON IT.

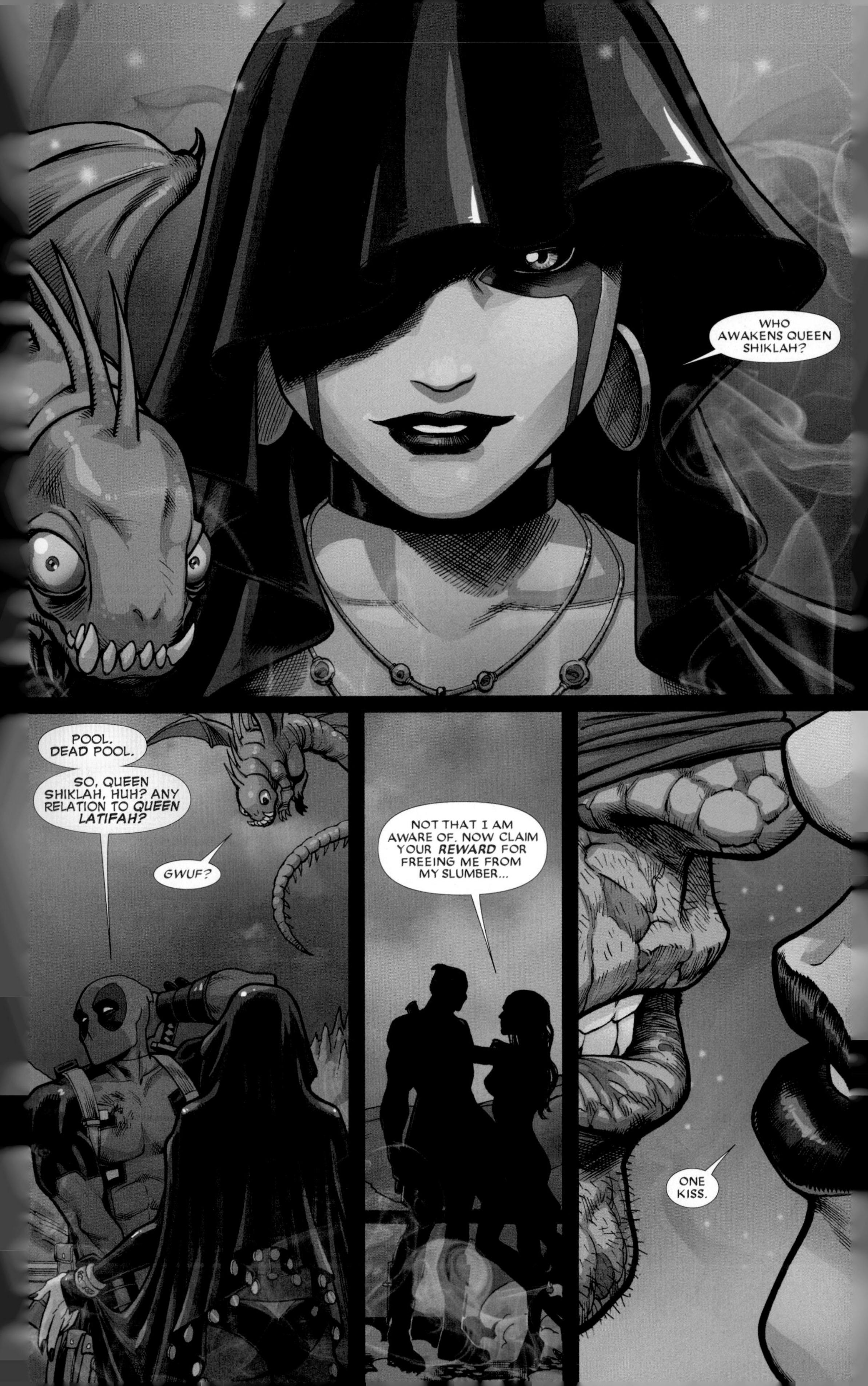
WHO AWAKENS QUEEN SHIKLAH?
POOL. DEAD POOL.
SO, QUEEN SHIKLAH, HUH? ANY RELATION TO QUEEN LATIFAH?
GWUF?
NOT THAT I AM AWARE OF. NOW CLAIM YOUR REWARD FOR FREEING ME FROM MY SLUMBER...
ONE KISS.

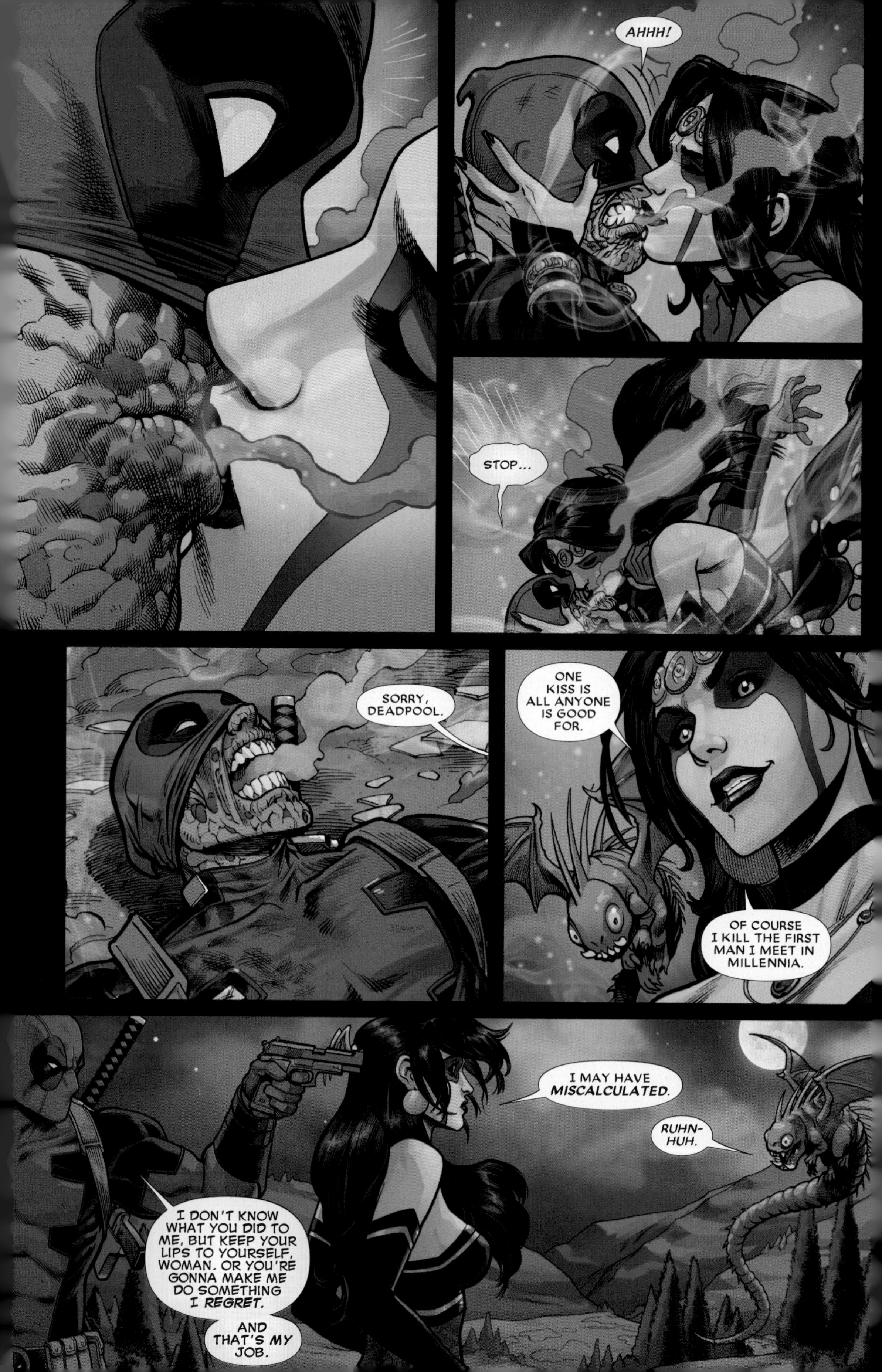
AHHH!
STOP...
SORRY, DEADPOOL.
ONE KISS IS ALL ANYONE IS GOOD FOR.
OF COURSE I KILL THE FIRST MAN I MEET IN MILLENNIA.
I MAY HAVE MISCALCULATED.
RUHN-HUH.
I DON'T KNOW WHAT YOU DID TO ME, BUT KEEP YOUR LIPS TO YOURSELF, WOMAN. OR YOU'RE GONNA MAKE ME DO SOMETHING I REGRET.
AND THAT'S MY JOB.

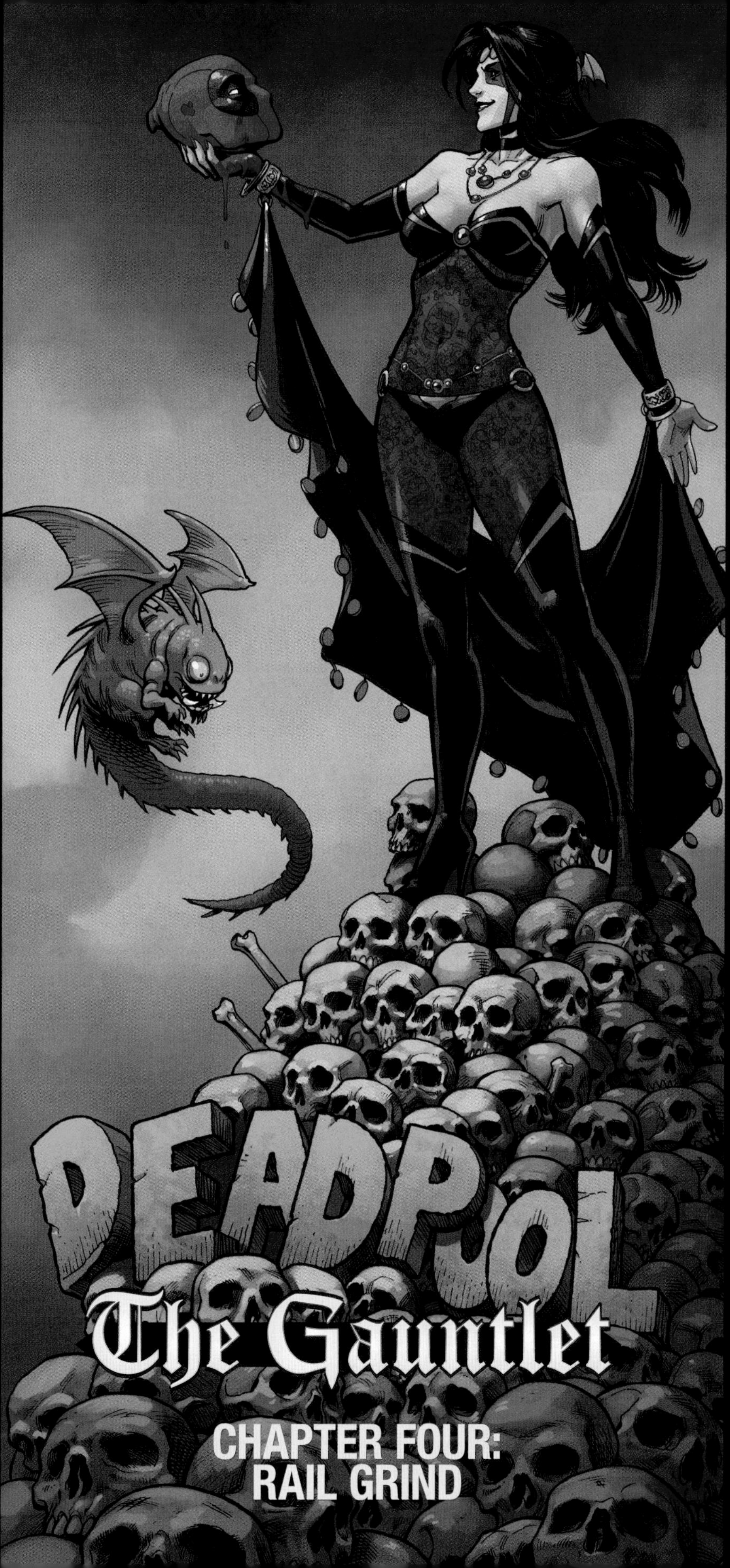
DEADPOOL
The Gauntlet
CHAPTER FOUR:
RAIL GRIND

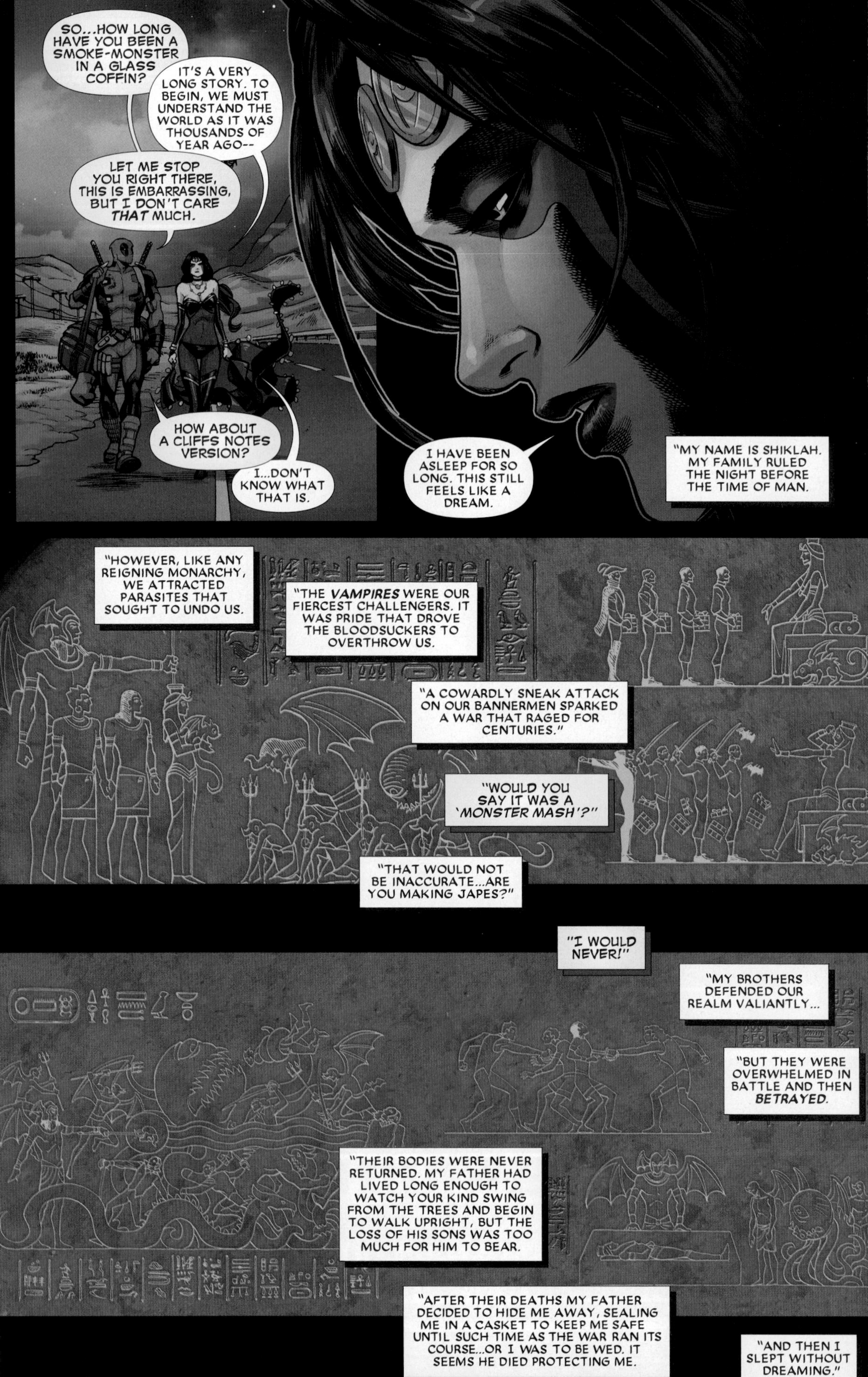

SO...HOW LONG HAVE YOU BEEN A SMOKE-MONSTER IN A GLASS COFFIN?
IT'S A VERY LONG STORY. TO BEGIN, WE MUST UNDERSTAND THE WORLD AS IT WAS THOUSANDS OF YEAR AGO--
LET ME STOP YOU RIGHT THERE, THIS IS EMBARRASSING, BUT I DON'T CARE THAT MUCH.
HOW ABOUT A CLIFFS NOTES VERSION?
I...DON'T KNOW WHAT THAT IS.
I HAVE BEEN ASLEEP FOR SO LONG. THIS STILL FEELS LIKE A DREAM.
"MY NAME IS SHIKLAH. MY FAMILY RULED THE NIGHT BEFORE THE TIME OF MAN.
"HOWEVER, LIKE ANY REIGNING MONARCHY, WE ATTRACTED PARASITES THAT SOUGHT TO UNDO US.
"THE VAMPIRES WERE OUR FIERCEST CHALLENGERS. IT WAS PRIDE THAT DROVE THE BLOODSUCKERS TO OVERTHROW US.
"A COWARDLY SNEAK ATTACK ON OUR BANNERMEN SPARKED A WAR THAT RAGED FOR CENTURIES."
"WOULD YOU SAY IT WAS A 'MONSTER MASH'?"
"THAT WOULD NOT BE INACCURATE...ARE YOU MAKING JAPES?"
"I WOULD NEVER!"
"MY BROTHERS DEFENDED OUR REALM VALIANTLY...
"BUT THEY WERE OVERWHELMED IN BATTLE AND THEN BETRAYED.
"THEIR BODIES WERE NEVER RETURNED. MY FATHER HAD LIVED LONG ENOUGH TO WATCH YOUR KIND SWING FROM THE TREES AND BEGIN TO WALK UPRIGHT, BUT THE LOSS OF HIS SONS WAS TOO MUCH FOR HIM TO BEAR.
"AFTER THEIR DEATHS MY FATHER DECIDED TO HIDE ME AWAY, SEALING ME IN A CASKET TO KEEP ME SAFE UNTIL SUCH TIME AS THE WAR RAN ITS COURSE...OR I WAS TO BE WED. IT SEEMS HE DIED PROTECTING ME.
"AND THEN I SLEPT WITHOUT DREAMING."

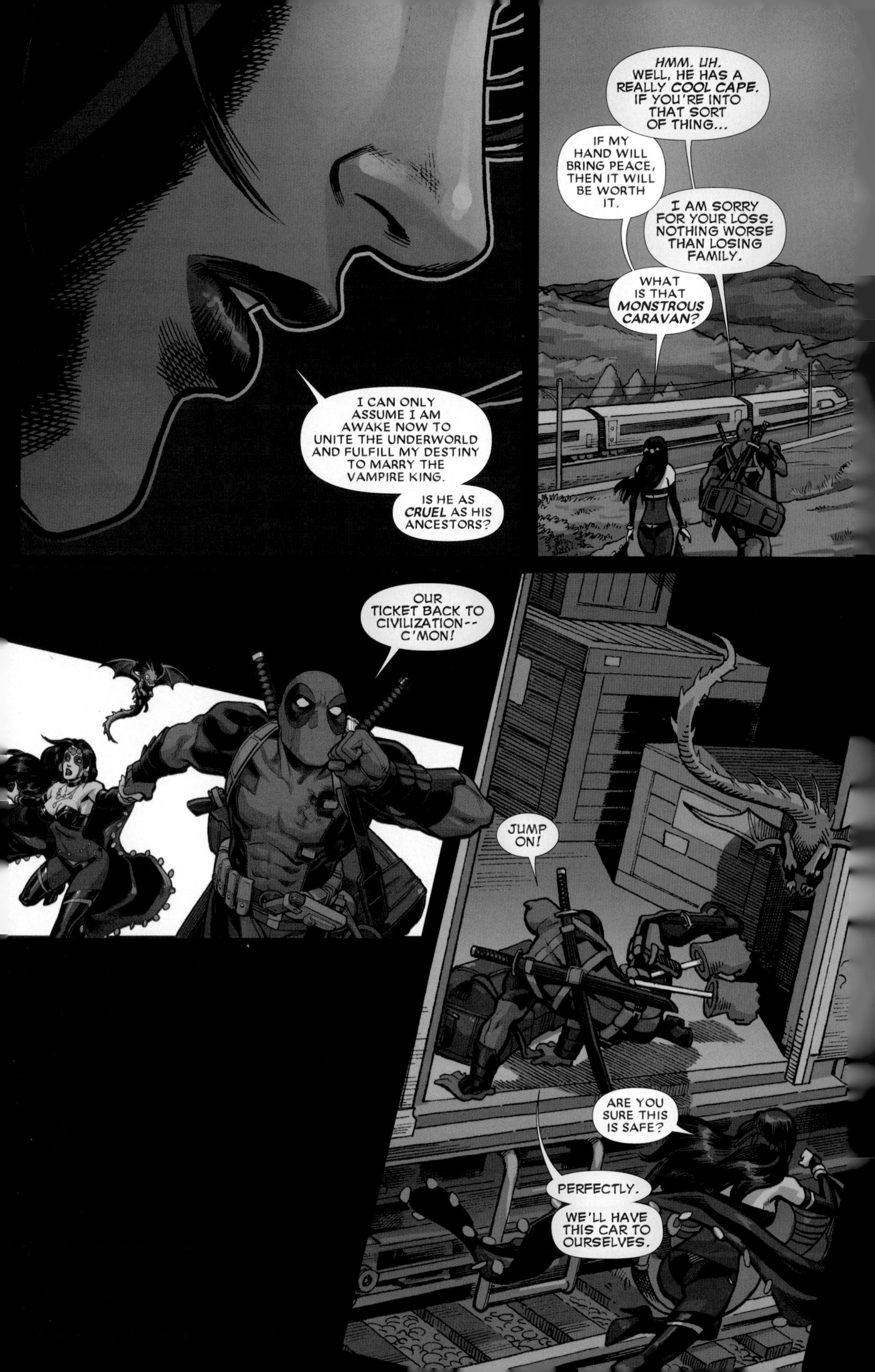
I CAN ONLY ASSUME I AM AWAKE NOW TO UNITE THE UNDERWORLD AND FULFILL MY DESTINY TO MARRY THE VAMPIRE KING.
IS HE AS CRUEL AS HIS ANCESTORS?
HMM. UH. WELL, HE HAS A REALLY COOL CAPE. IF YOU'RE INTO THAT SORT OF THING...
IF MY HAND WILL BRING PEACE, THEN IT WILL BE WORTH IT.
I AM SORRY FOR YOUR LOSS. NOTHING WORSE THAN LOSING FAMILY.
WHAT IS THAT MONSTROUS CARAVAN?
OUR TICKET BACK TO CIVILIZATION-- C'MON!
JUMP ON!
ARE YOU SURE THIS IS SAFE?
PERFECTLY.
WE'LL HAVE THIS CAR TO OURSELVES.

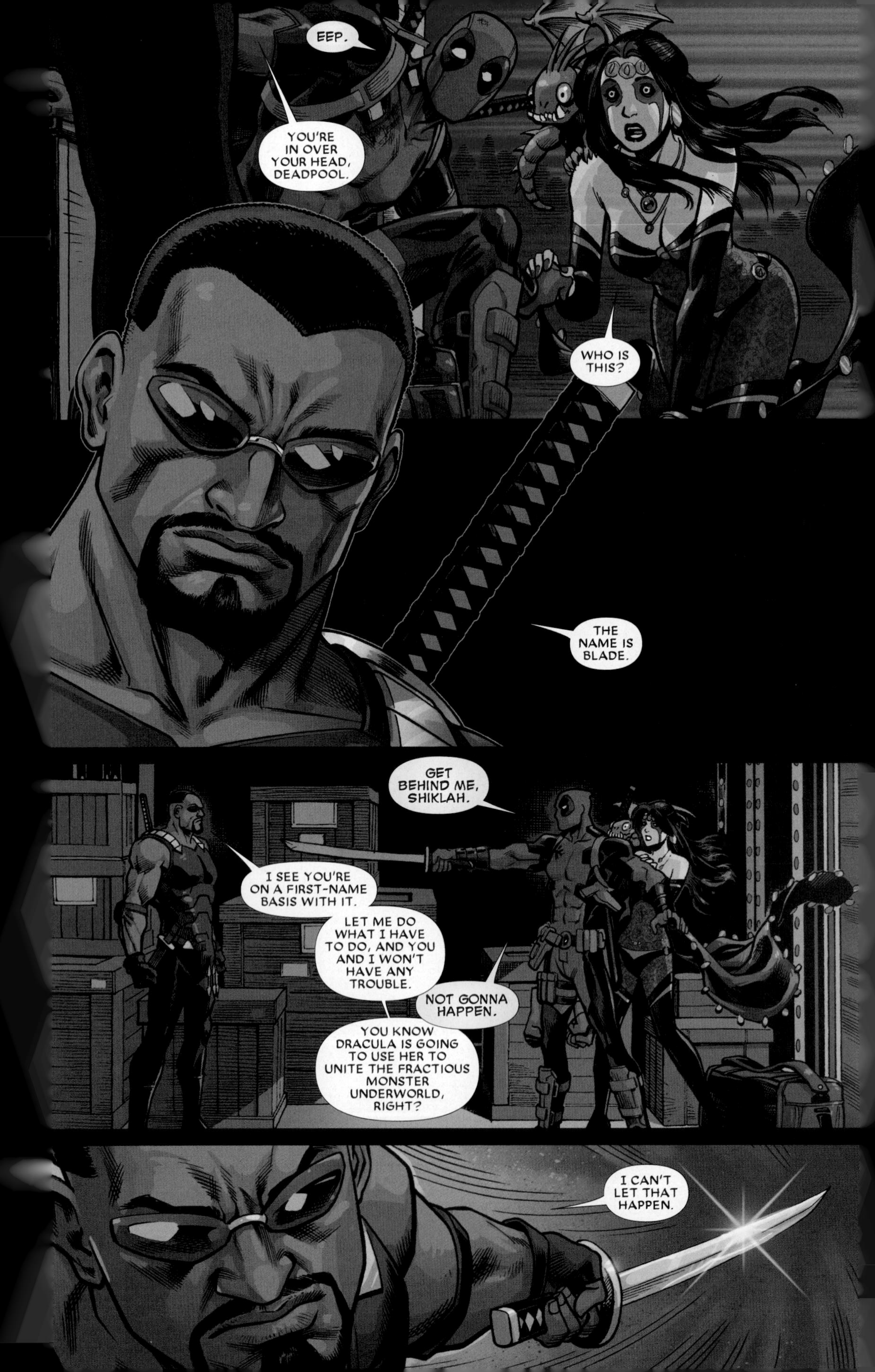
EEP.
YOU'RE IN OVER YOUR HEAD, DEADPOOL.
WHO IS THIS?
THE NAME IS BLADE.
GET BEHIND ME, SHIKLAH.
I SEE YOU'RE ON A FIRST-NAME BASIS WITH IT.
LET ME DO WHAT I HAVE TO DO, AND YOU AND I WON'T HAVE ANY TROUBLE.
NOT GONNA HAPPEN.
YOU KNOW DRACULA IS GOING TO USE HER TO UNITE THE FRACTIOUS MONSTER UNDERWORLD, RIGHT?
I CAN'T LET THAT HAPPEN.

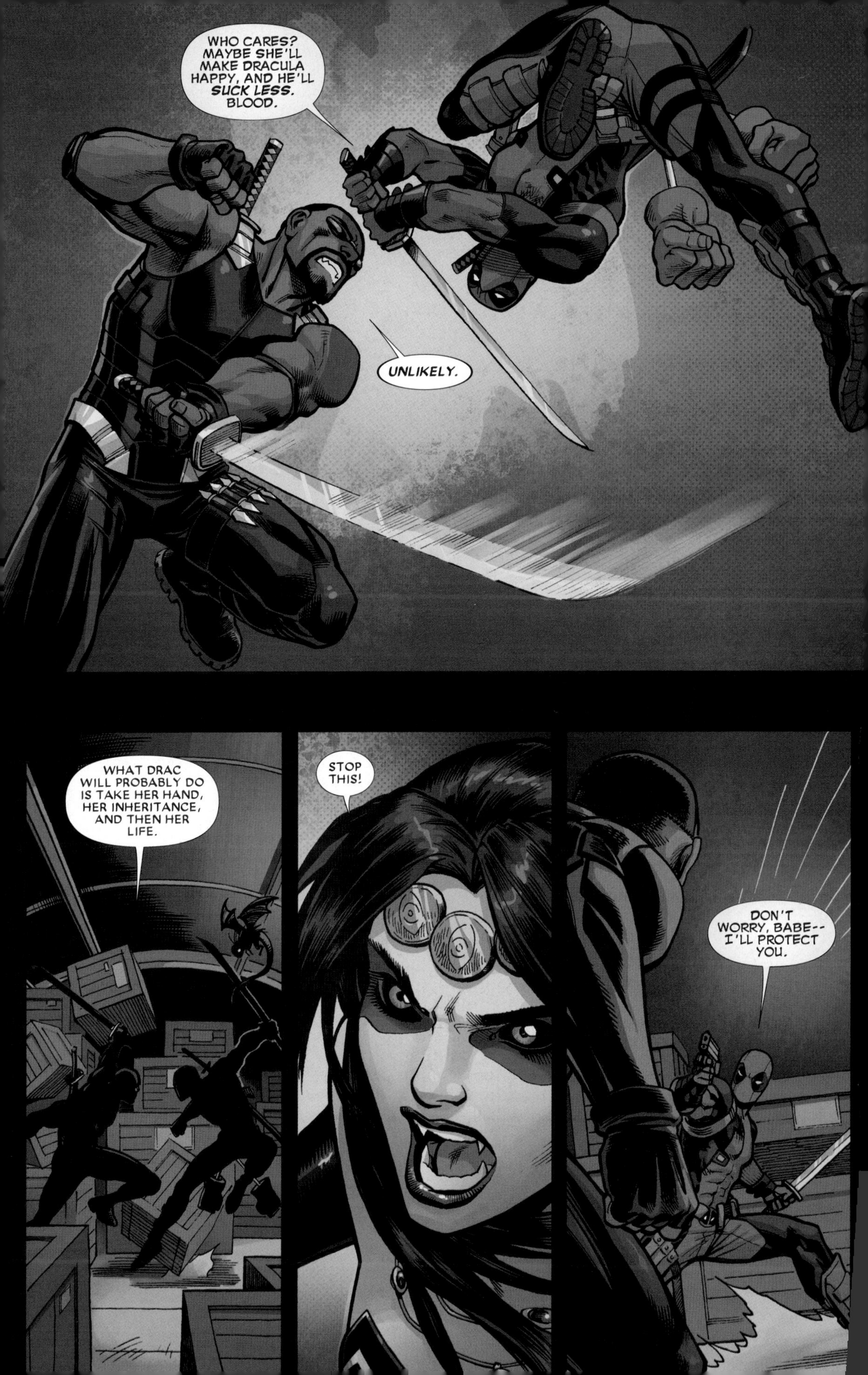

WHO CARES? MAYBE SHE'LL MAKE DRACULA HAPPY, AND HE'LL SUCK LESS. BLOOD.
UNLIKELY.
WHAT DRAC WILL PROBABLY DO IS TAKE HER HAND, HER INHERITANCE, AND THEN HER LIFE.
STOP THIS!
DON'T WORRY, BABE-- I'LL PROTECT YOU.

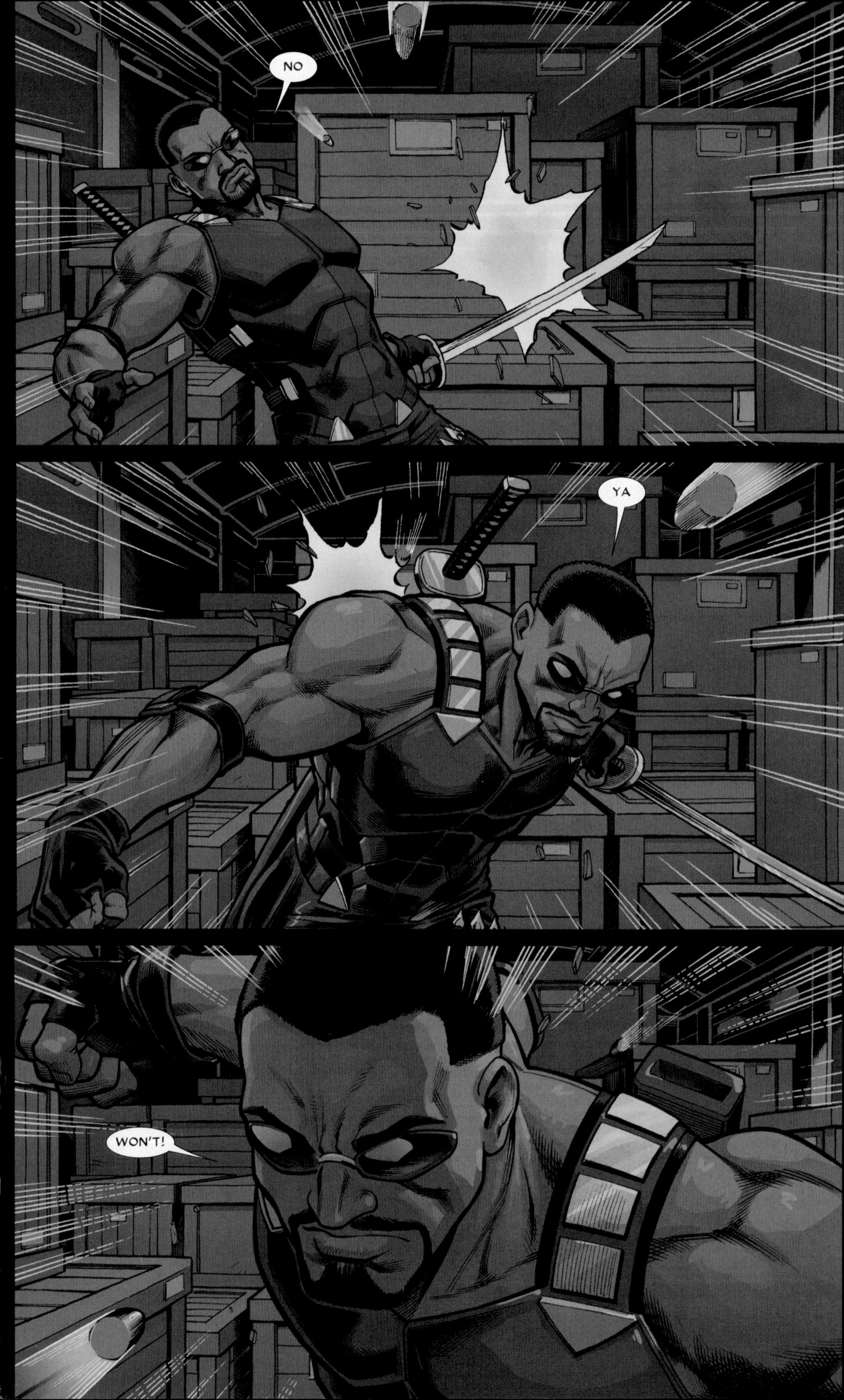
NO
YA
WON'T!

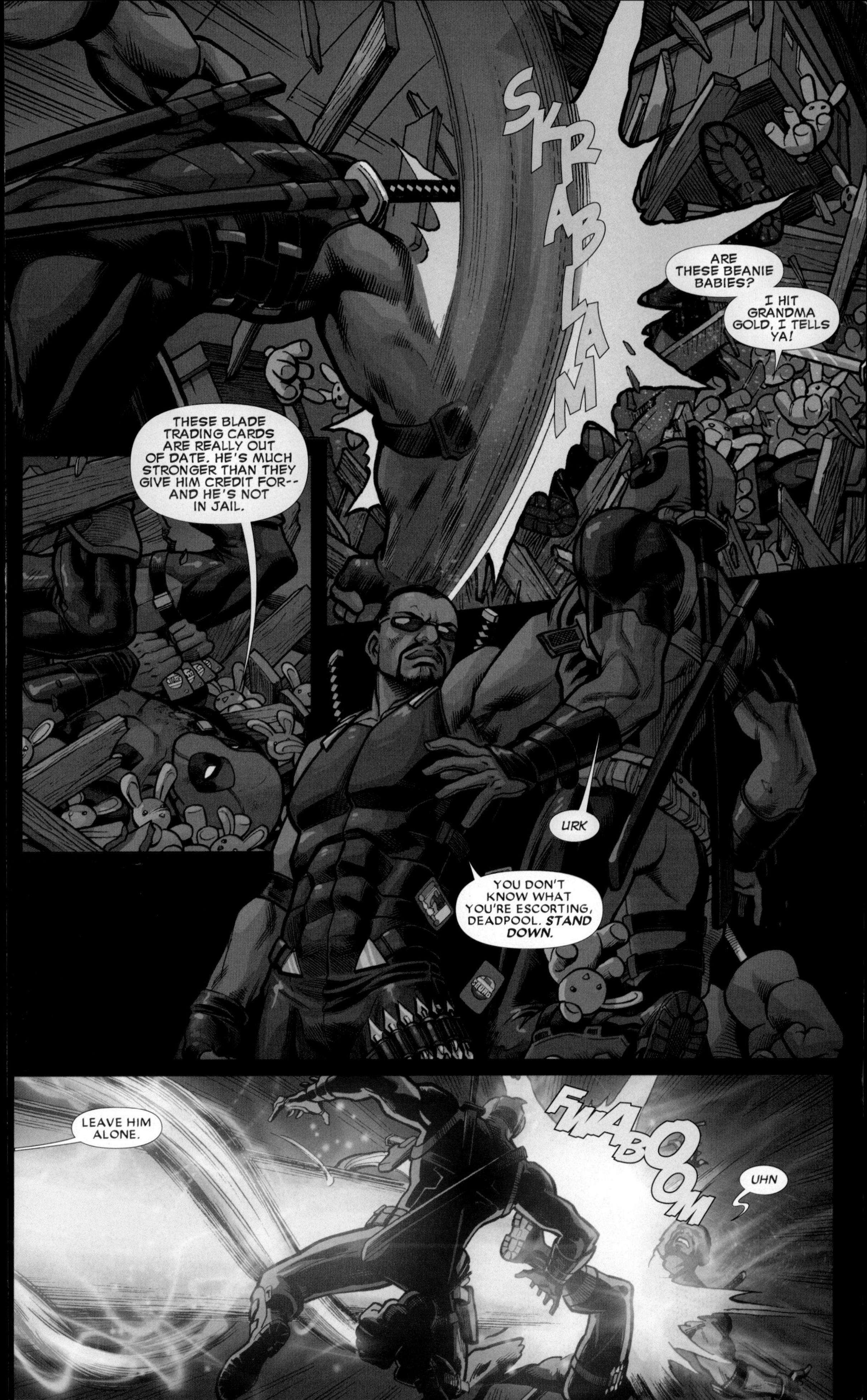
SKRABLAM
ARE THESE BEANIE BABIES?
I HIT GRANDMA GOLD, I TELLS YA!
THESE BLADE TRADING CARDS ARE REALLY OUT OF DATE. HE'S MUCH STRONGER THAN THEY GIVE HIM CREDIT FOR--AND HE'S NOT IN JAIL.
URK
YOU DON'T KNOW WHAT YOU'RE ESCORTING, DEADPOOL. STAND DOWN.
LEAVE HIM ALONE.
FWABOOM
UHN

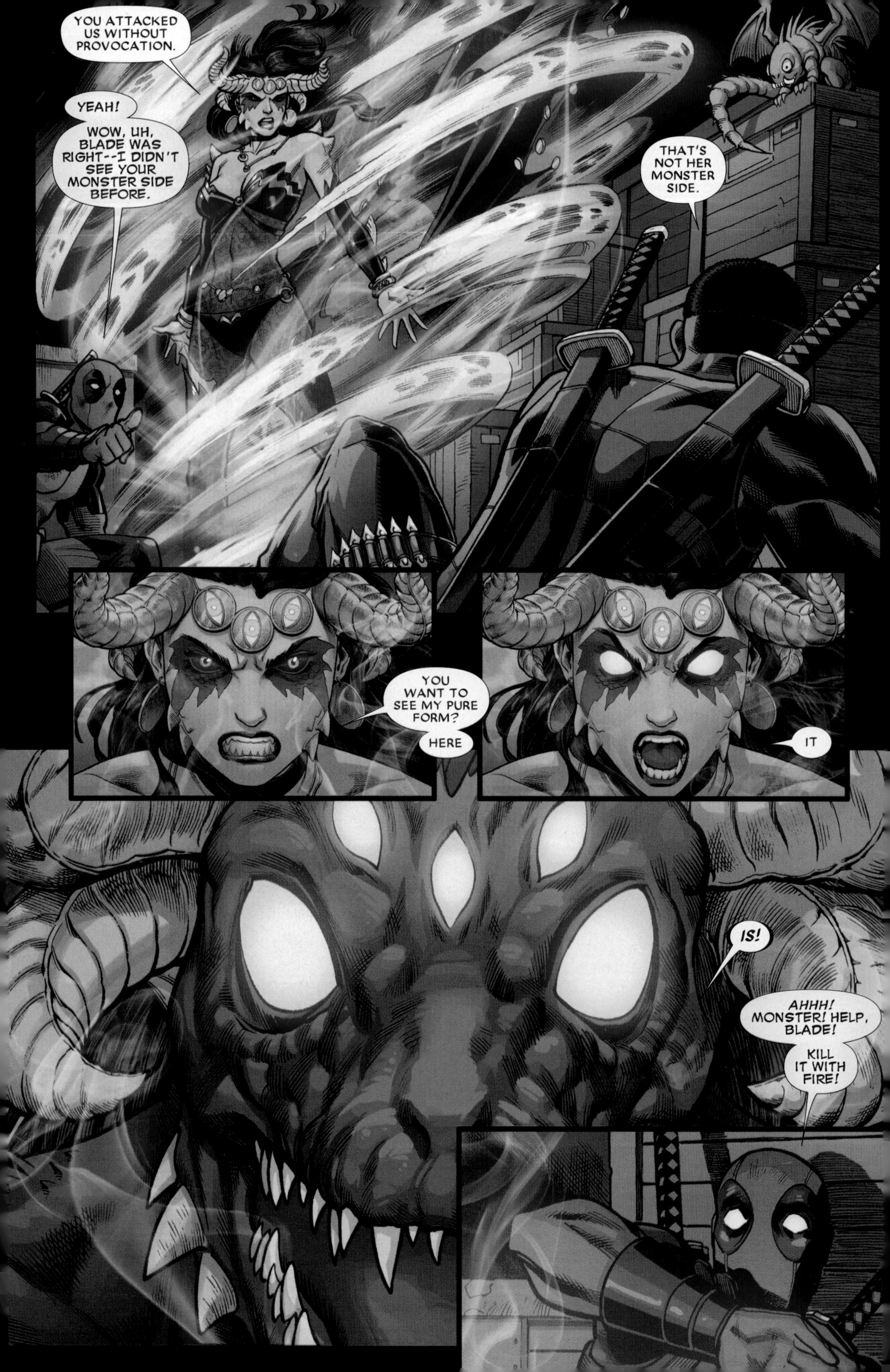
YOU ATTACKED US WITHOUT PROVOCATION.
YEAH!
WOW, UH, BLADE WAS RIGHT--I DIDN'T SEE YOUR MONSTER SIDE BEFORE.
THAT'S NOT HER MONSTER SIDE.
YOU WANT TO SEE MY PURE FORM?
HERE
IT
IS!
AHHH! MONSTER! HELP, BLADE!
KILL IT WITH FIRE!

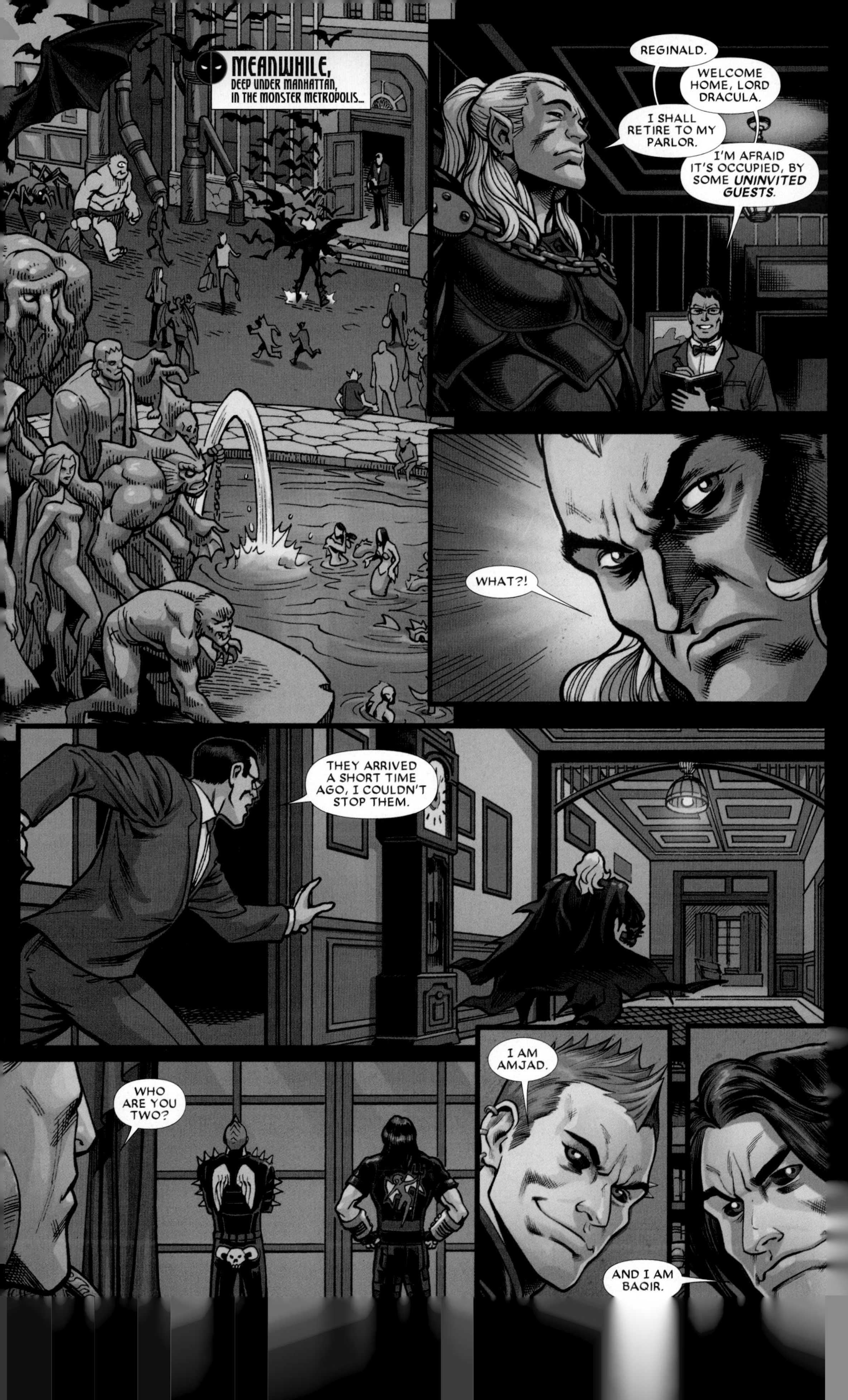
MEANWHILE, DEEP UNDER MANHATTAN, IN THE MONSTER METROPOLIS...
REGINALD.
WELCOME HOME, LORD DRACULA.
I SHALL RETIRE TO MY PARLOR.
I'M AFRAID IT'S OCCUPIED, BY SOME UNINVITED GUESTS.
WHAT?!
THEY ARRIVED A SHORT TIME AGO, I COULDN'T STOP THEM.
WHO ARE YOU TWO?
I AM AMJAD.
AND I AM BAQIR.

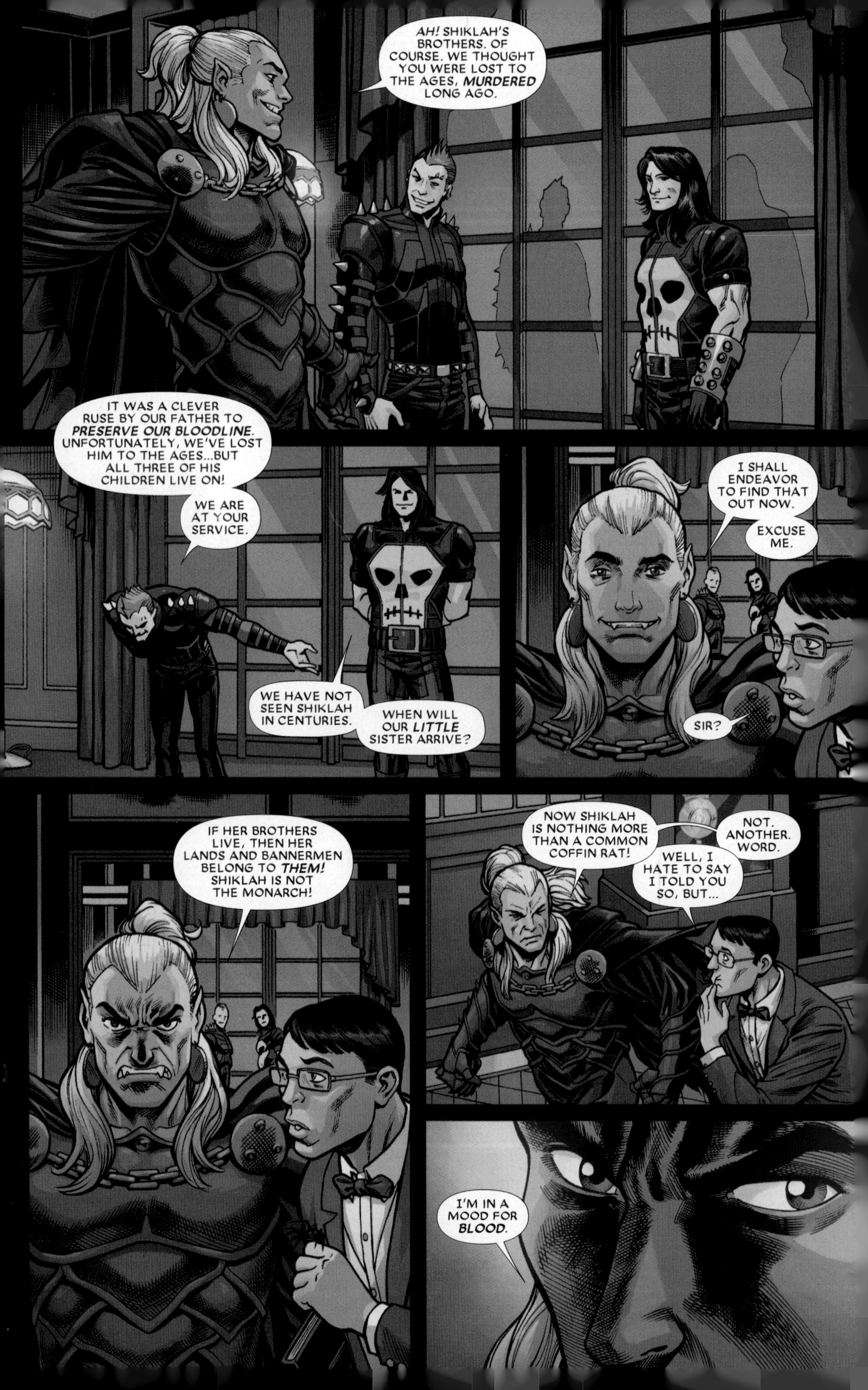

AH! SHIKLAH'S BROTHERS. OF COURSE. WE THOUGHT YOU WERE LOST TO THE AGES, MURDERED LONG AGO.
IT WAS A CLEVER RUSE BY OUR FATHER TO PRESERVE OUR BLOODLINE. UNFORTUNATELY, WE'VE LOST HIM TO THE AGES...BUT ALL THREE OF HIS CHILDREN LIVE ON!
WE ARE AT YOUR SERVICE.
WE HAVE NOT SEEN SHIKLAH IN CENTURIES.
WHEN WILL OUR LITTLE SISTER ARRIVE?
I SHALL ENDEAVOR TO FIND THAT OUT NOW.
EXCUSE ME.
SIR?
IF HER BROTHERS LIVE, THEN HER LANDS AND BANNERMEN BELONG TO THEM! SHIKLAH IS NOT THE MONARCH!
NOW SHIKLAH IS NOTHING MORE THAN A COMMON COFFIN RAT!
WELL, I HATE TO SAY I TOLD YOU SO, BUT...
NOT. ANOTHER. WORD.
I'M IN A MOOD FOR BLOOD.

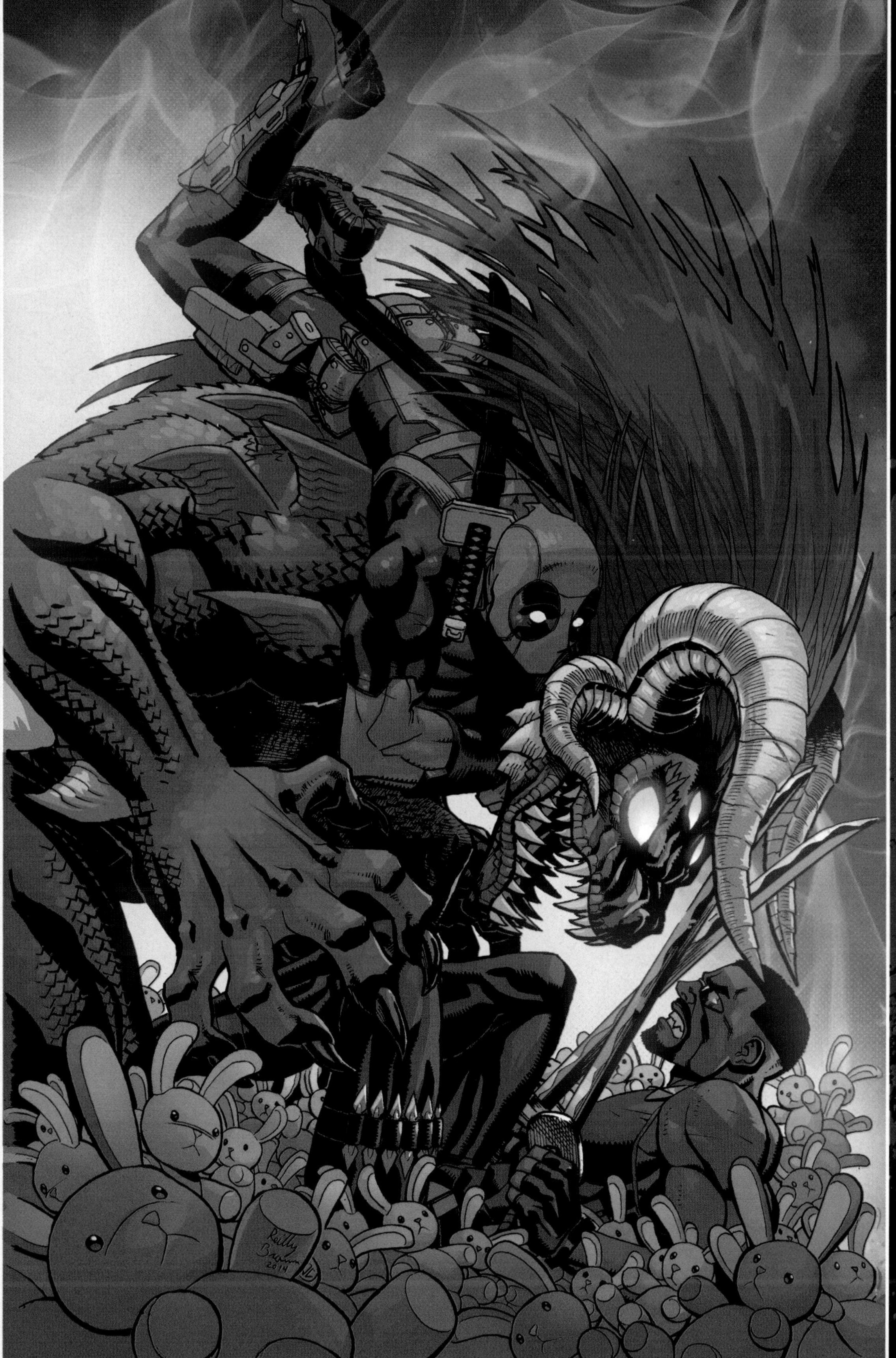
Reilly Brown 2014

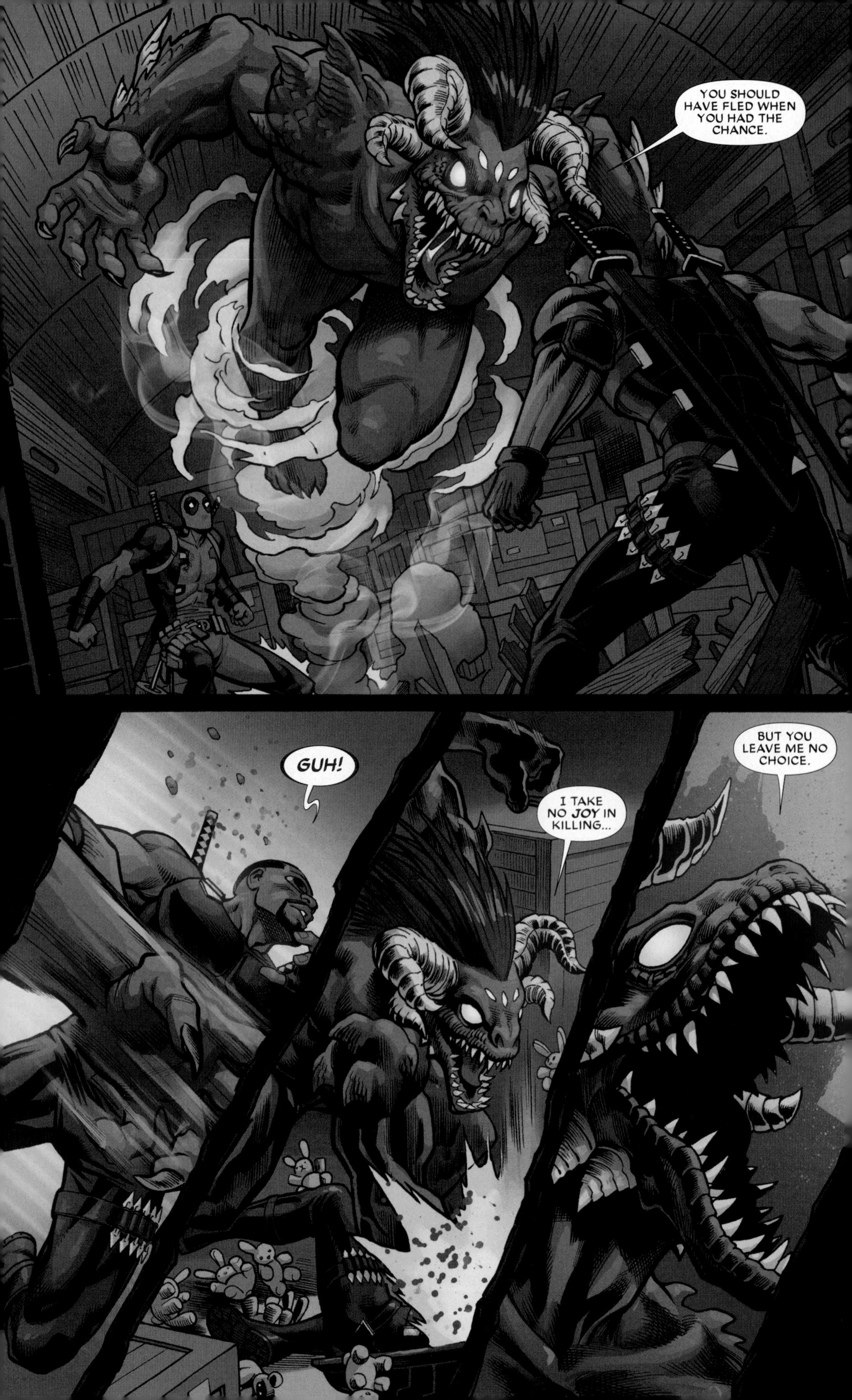
YOU SHOULD HAVE FLED WHEN YOU HAD THE CHANCE.
GUH!
I TAKE NO JOY IN KILLING...
BUT YOU LEAVE ME NO CHOICE.

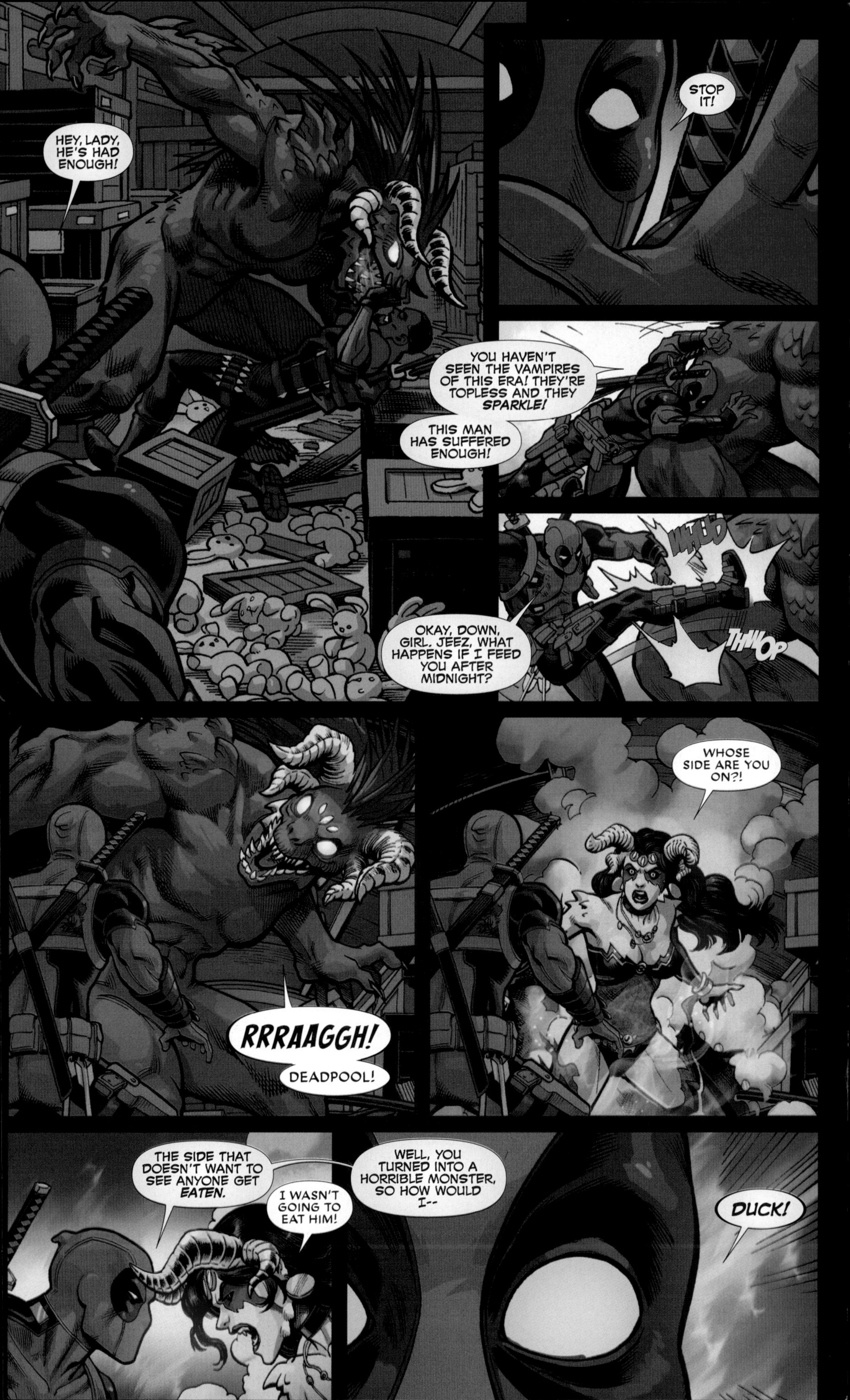
HEY, LADY, HE'S HAD ENOUGH!
STOP IT!
YOU HAVEN'T SEEN THE VAMPIRES OF THIS ERA! THEY'RE TOPLESS AND THEY SPARKLE!
THIS MAN HAS SUFFERED ENOUGH!
WHUD
THWOP
OKAY, DOWN, GIRL. JEEZ, WHAT HAPPENS IF I FEED YOU AFTER MIDNIGHT?
RRRAAGGH!
DEADPOOL!
WHOSE SIDE ARE YOU ON?!
THE SIDE THAT DOESN'T WANT TO SEE ANYONE GET EATEN.
I WASN'T GOING TO EAT HIM!
WELL, YOU TURNED INTO A HORRIBLE MONSTER, SO HOW WOULD I--
DUCK!

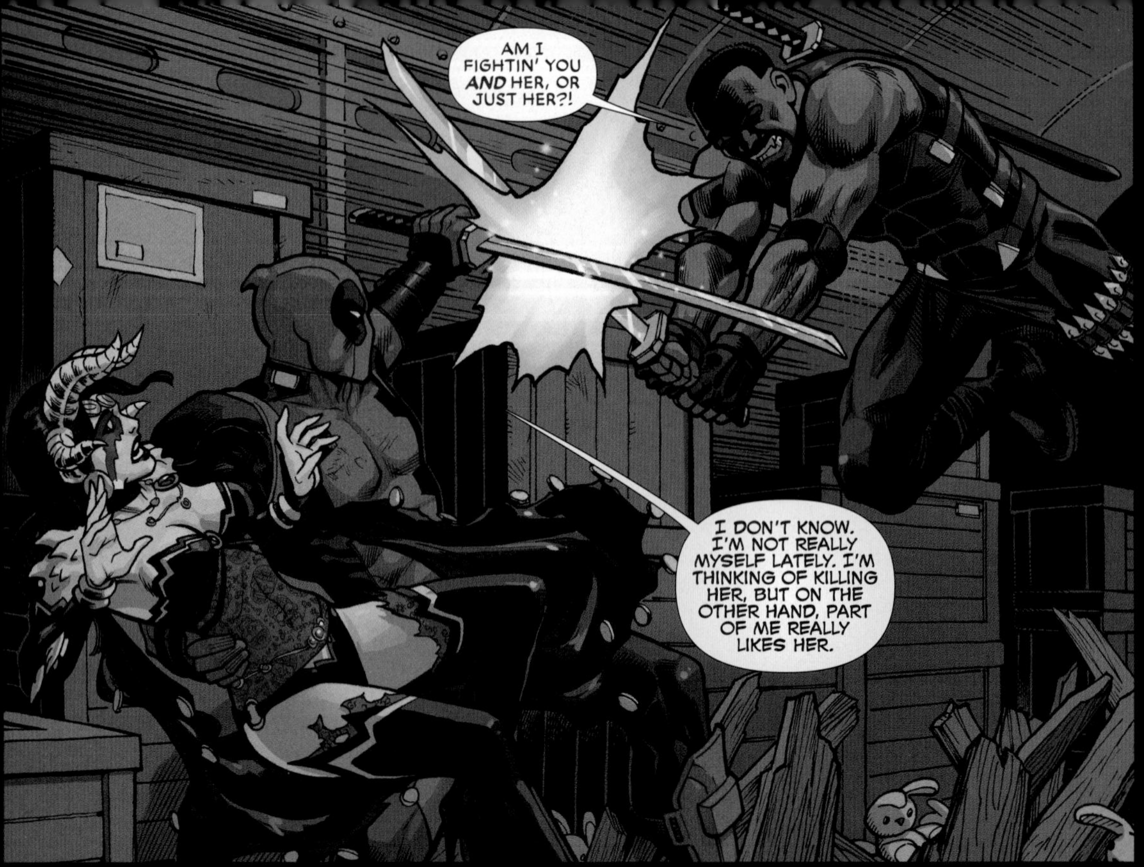
AM I FIGHTIN' YOU AND HER, OR JUST HER?!
I DON'T KNOW. I'M NOT REALLY MYSELF LATELY. I'M THINKING OF KILLING HER, BUT ON THE OTHER HAND, PART OF ME REALLY LIKES HER.

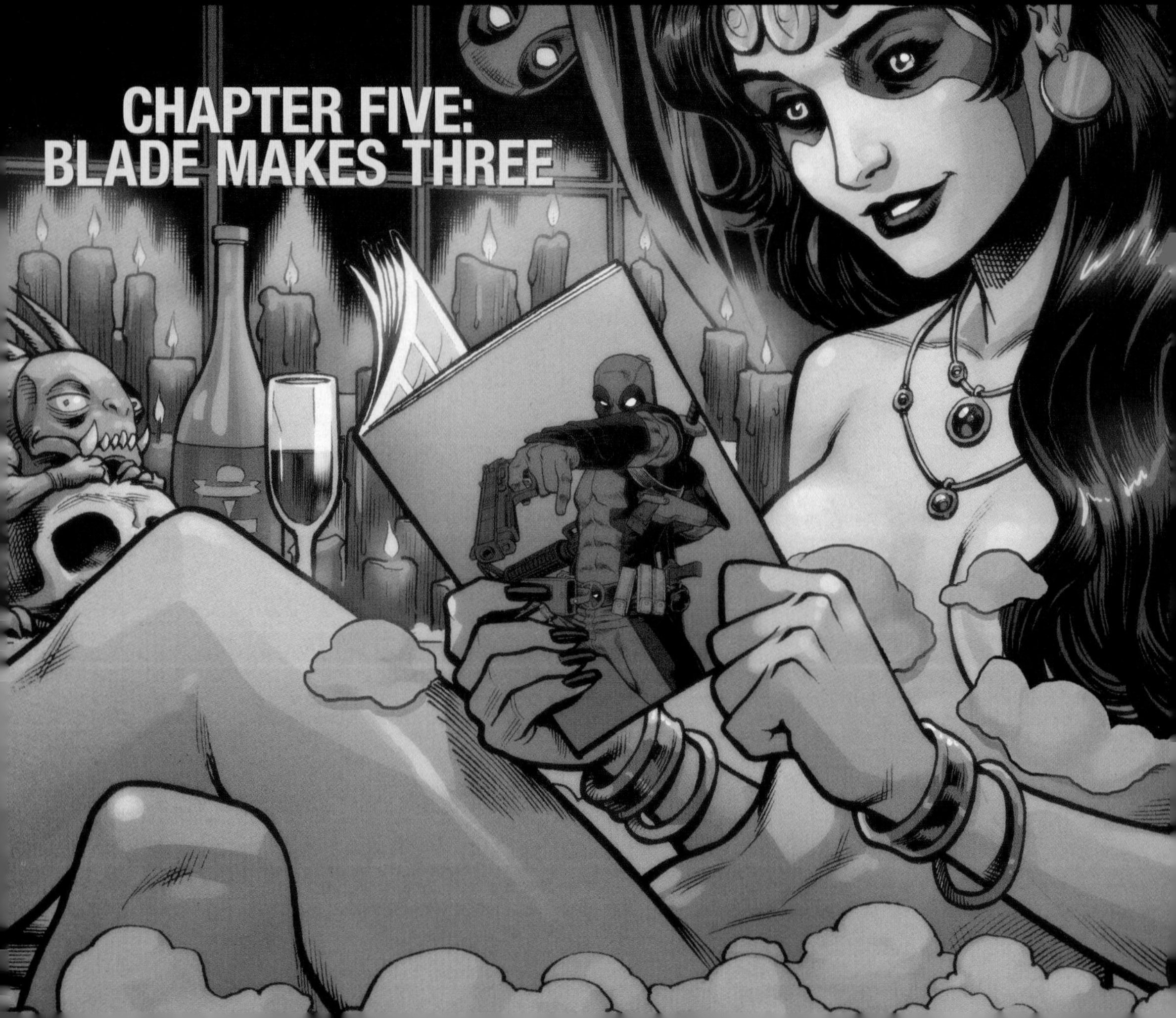
CHAPTER FIVE:
BLADE MAKES THREE

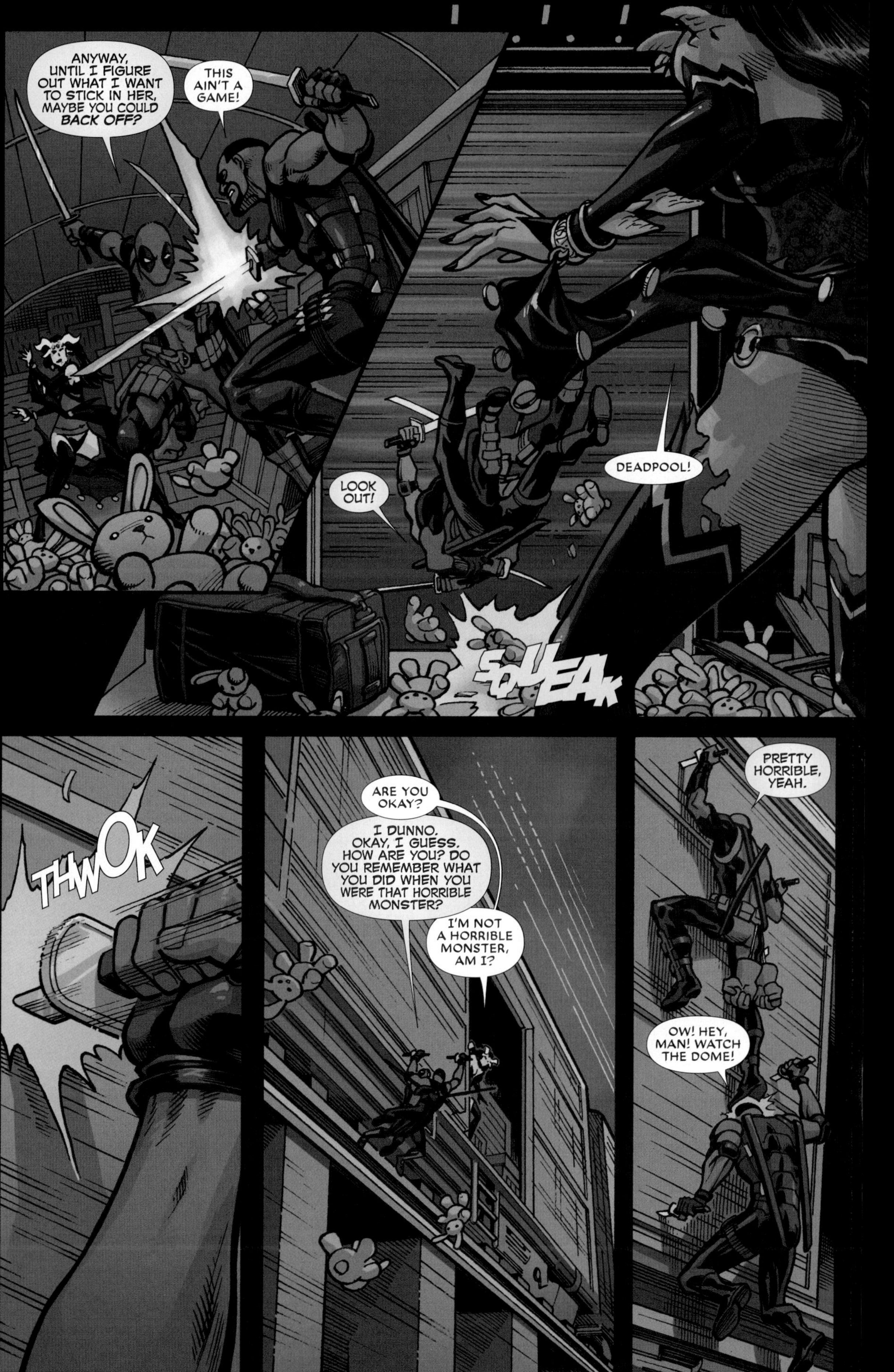
ANYWAY, UNTIL I FIGURE OUT WHAT I WANT TO STICK IN HER, MAYBE YOU COULD BACK OFF?
THIS AIN'T A GAME!
DEADPOOL!
LOOK OUT!
SQUEAK
THWOK
ARE YOU OKAY?
I DUNNO. OKAY, I GUESS. HOW ARE YOU? DO YOU REMEMBER WHAT YOU DID WHEN YOU WERE THAT HORRIBLE MONSTER?
I'M NOT A HORRIBLE MONSTER, AM I?
PRETTY HORRIBLE, YEAH.
OW! HEY, MAN! WATCH THE DOME!

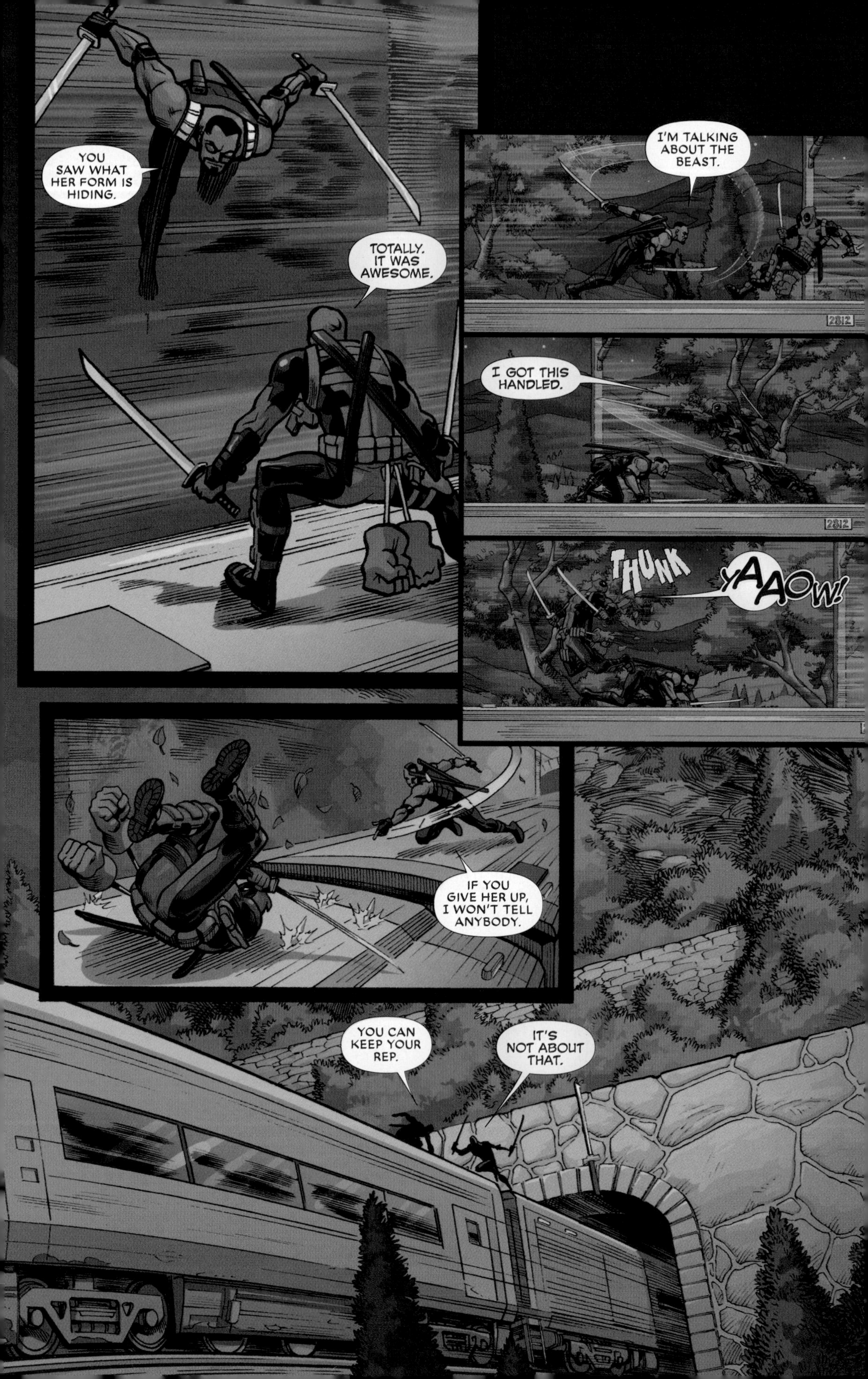
YOU SAW WHAT HER FORM IS HIDING.
TOTALLY. IT WAS AWESOME.
I'M TALKING ABOUT THE BEAST.
I GOT THIS HANDLED.
THUNK
YAAOW!
IF YOU GIVE HER UP, I WON'T TELL ANYBODY.
YOU CAN KEEP YOUR REP.
IT'S NOT ABOUT THAT.

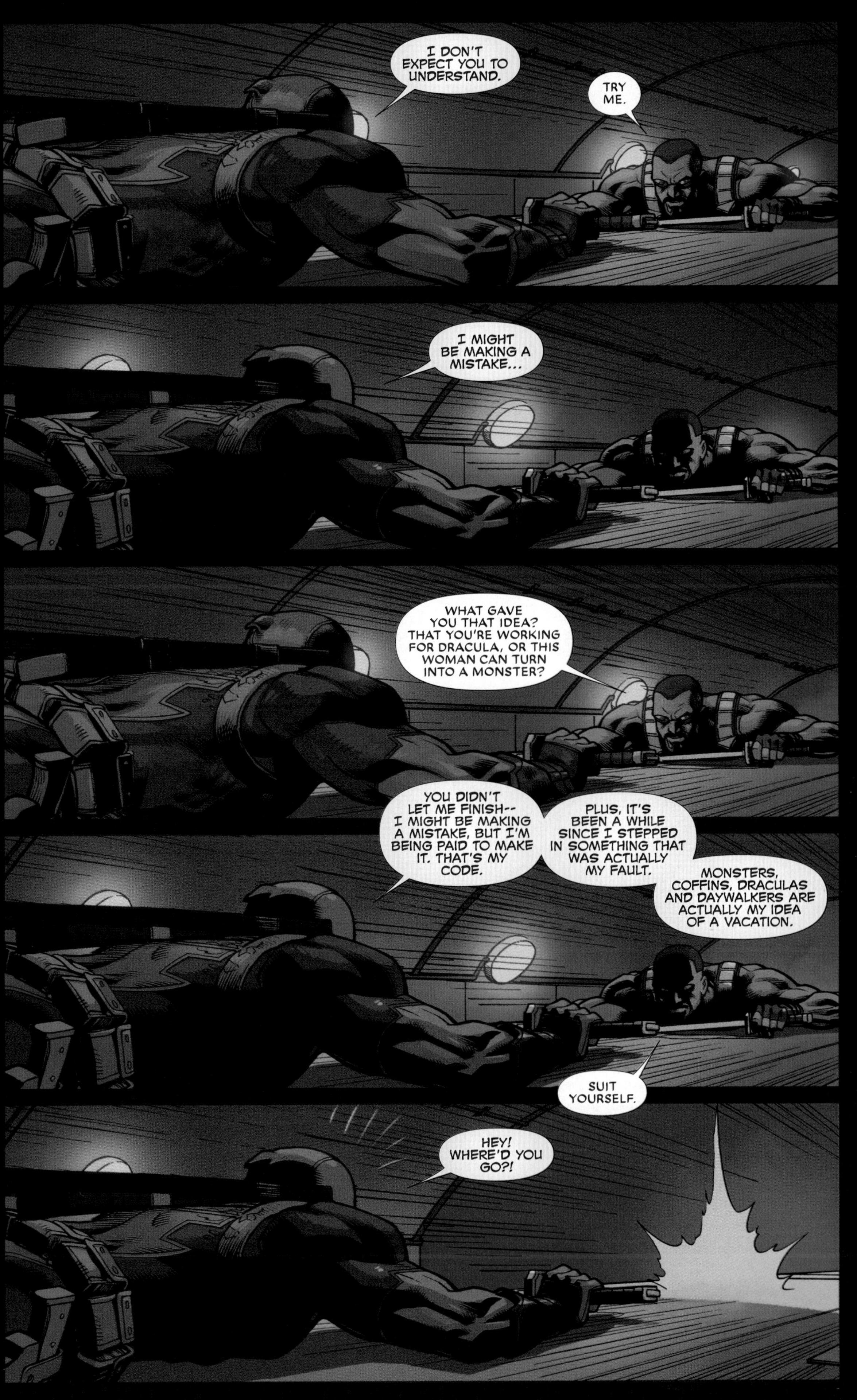
I DON'T EXPECT YOU TO UNDERSTAND.
TRY ME.
I MIGHT BE MAKING A MISTAKE...
WHAT GAVE YOU THAT IDEA? THAT YOU'RE WORKING FOR DRACULA, OR THIS WOMAN CAN TURN INTO A MONSTER?
YOU DIDN'T LET ME FINISH-- I MIGHT BE MAKING A MISTAKE, BUT I'M BEING PAID TO MAKE IT. THAT'S MY CODE.
PLUS, IT'S BEEN A WHILE SINCE I STEPPED IN SOMETHING THAT WAS ACTUALLY MY FAULT.
MONSTERS, COFFINS, DRACULAS AND DAYWALKERS ARE ACTUALLY MY IDEA OF A VACATION.
SUIT YOURSELF.
HEY! WHERE'D YOU GO?!

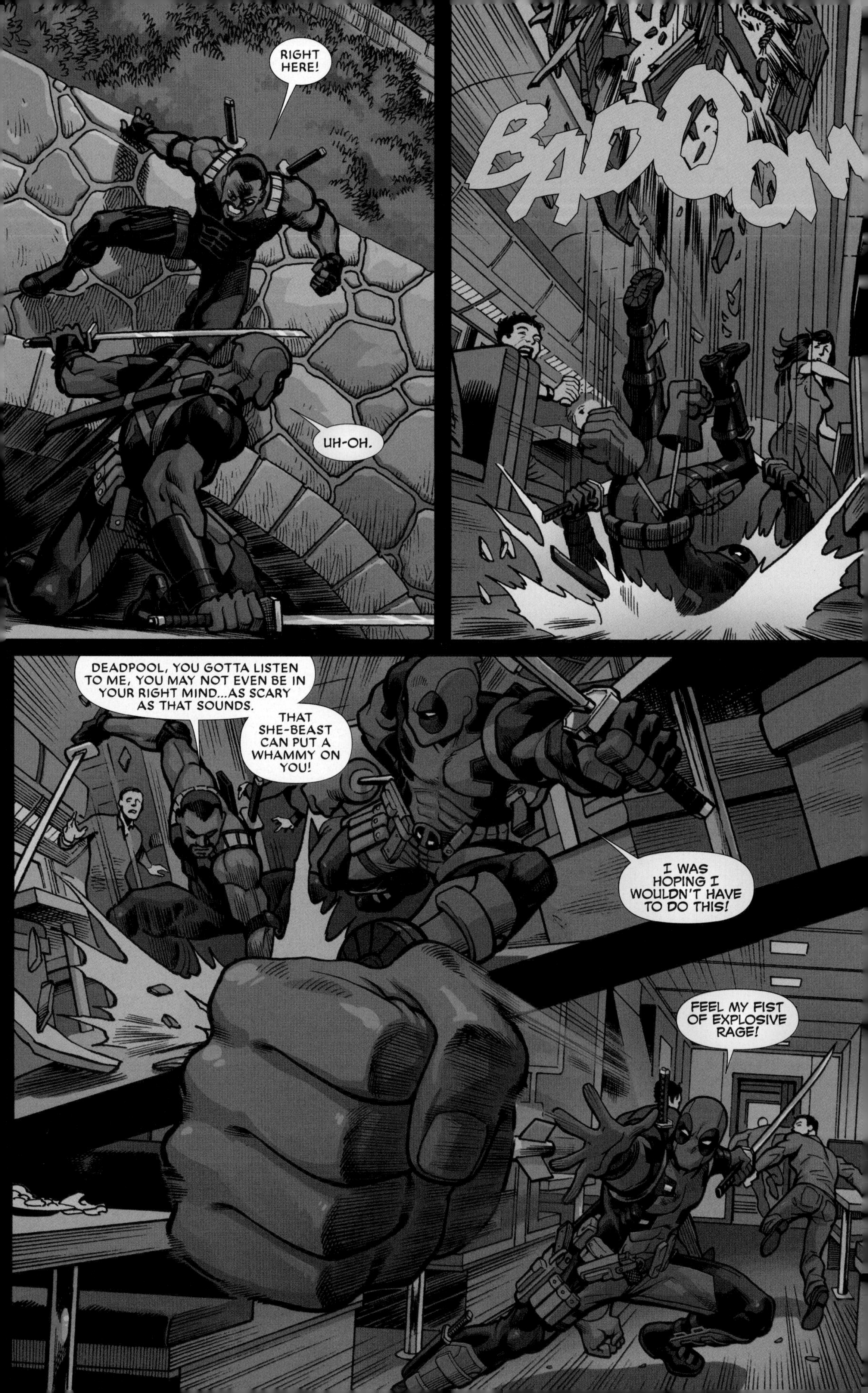
RIGHT HERE!
UH-OH.
BADOOM
DEADPOOL, YOU GOTTA LISTEN TO ME, YOU MAY NOT EVEN BE IN YOUR RIGHT MIND...AS SCARY AS THAT SOUNDS.
THAT SHE-BEAST CAN PUT A WHAMMY ON YOU!
I WAS HOPING I WOULDN'T HAVE TO DO THIS!
FEEL MY FIST OF EXPLOSIVE RAGE!

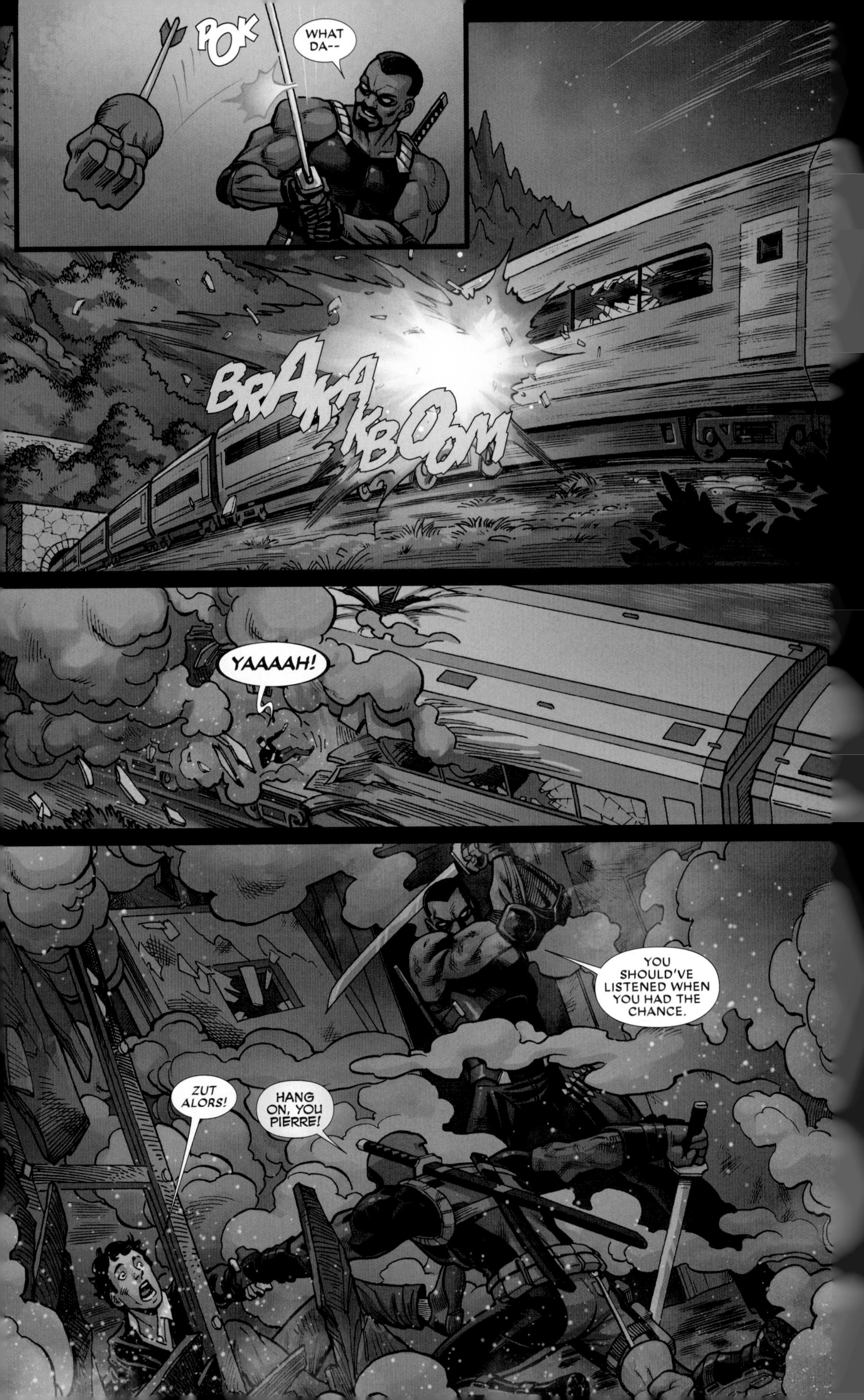
POK
WHAT DA--
BRAKA KBOOM
YAAAAH!
YOU SHOULD'VE LISTENED WHEN YOU HAD THE CHANCE.
ZUT ALORS!
HANG ON, YOU PIERRE!

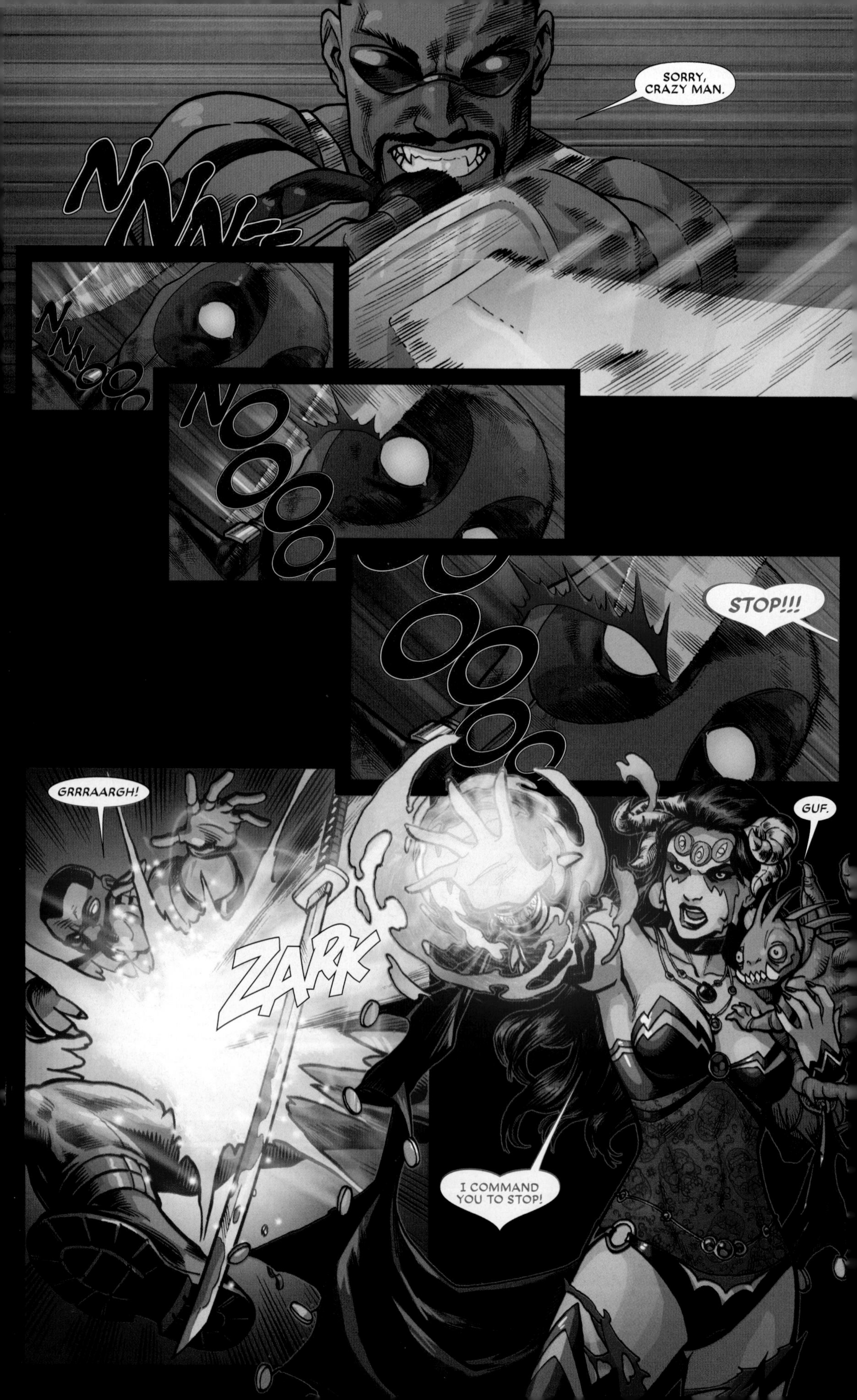
SORRY, CRAZY MAN.
NNNNNN
NNNOOOO
NOOOOO
OOOOOO
STOP!!!
GRRRAARGH!
GUF.
ZARK
I COMMAND YOU TO STOP!

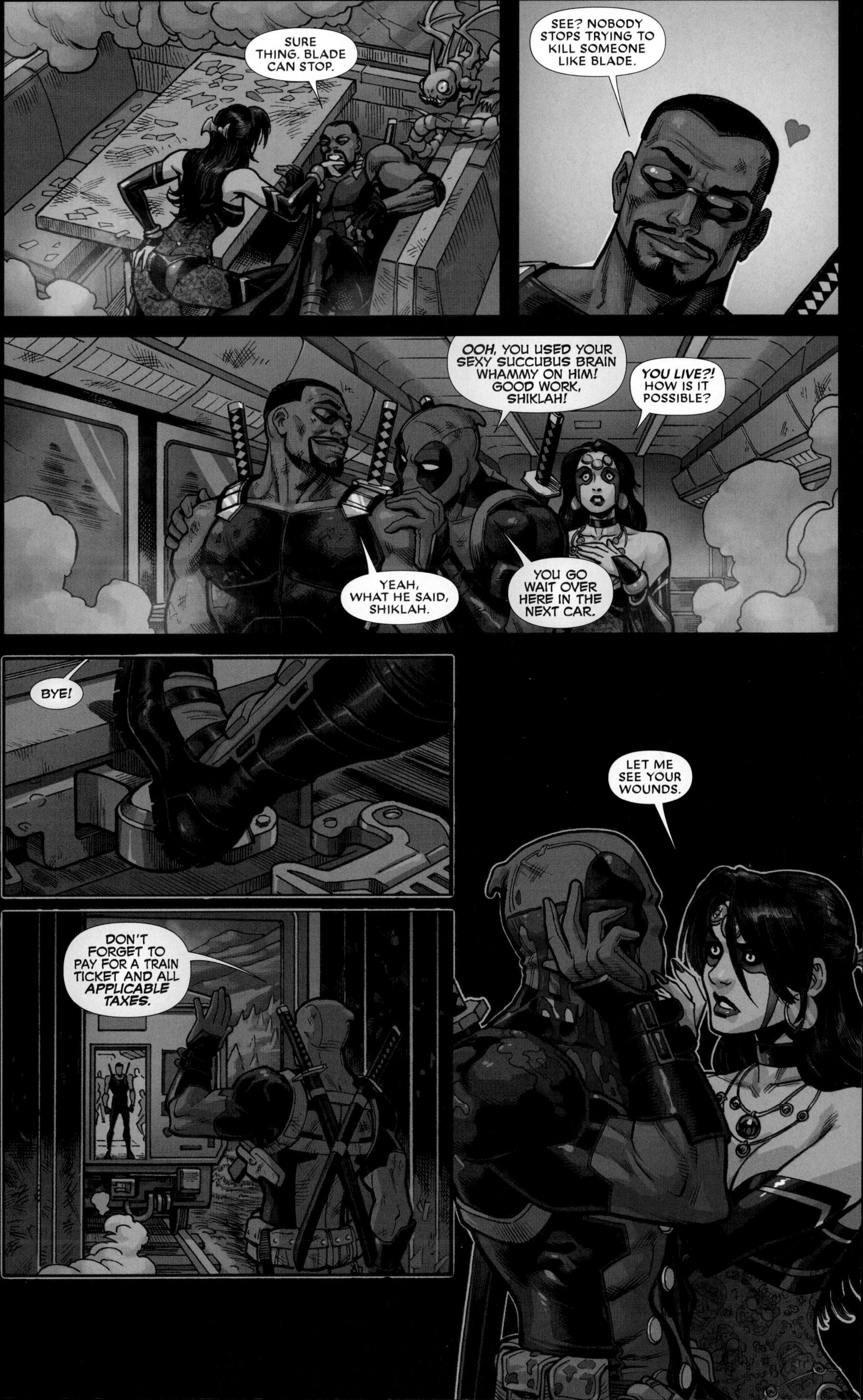
SURE THING. BLADE CAN STOP.
SEE? NOBODY STOPS TRYING TO KILL SOMEONE LIKE BLADE.
OOH, YOU USED YOUR SEXY SUCCUBUS BRAIN WHAMMY ON HIM! GOOD WORK, SHIKLAH!
YOU LIVE?! HOW IS IT POSSIBLE?
YEAH, WHAT HE SAID, SHIKLAH.
YOU GO WAIT OVER HERE IN THE NEXT CAR.
BYE!
DON'T FORGET TO PAY FOR A TRAIN TICKET AND ALL APPLICABLE TAXES.
LET ME SEE YOUR WOUNDS.

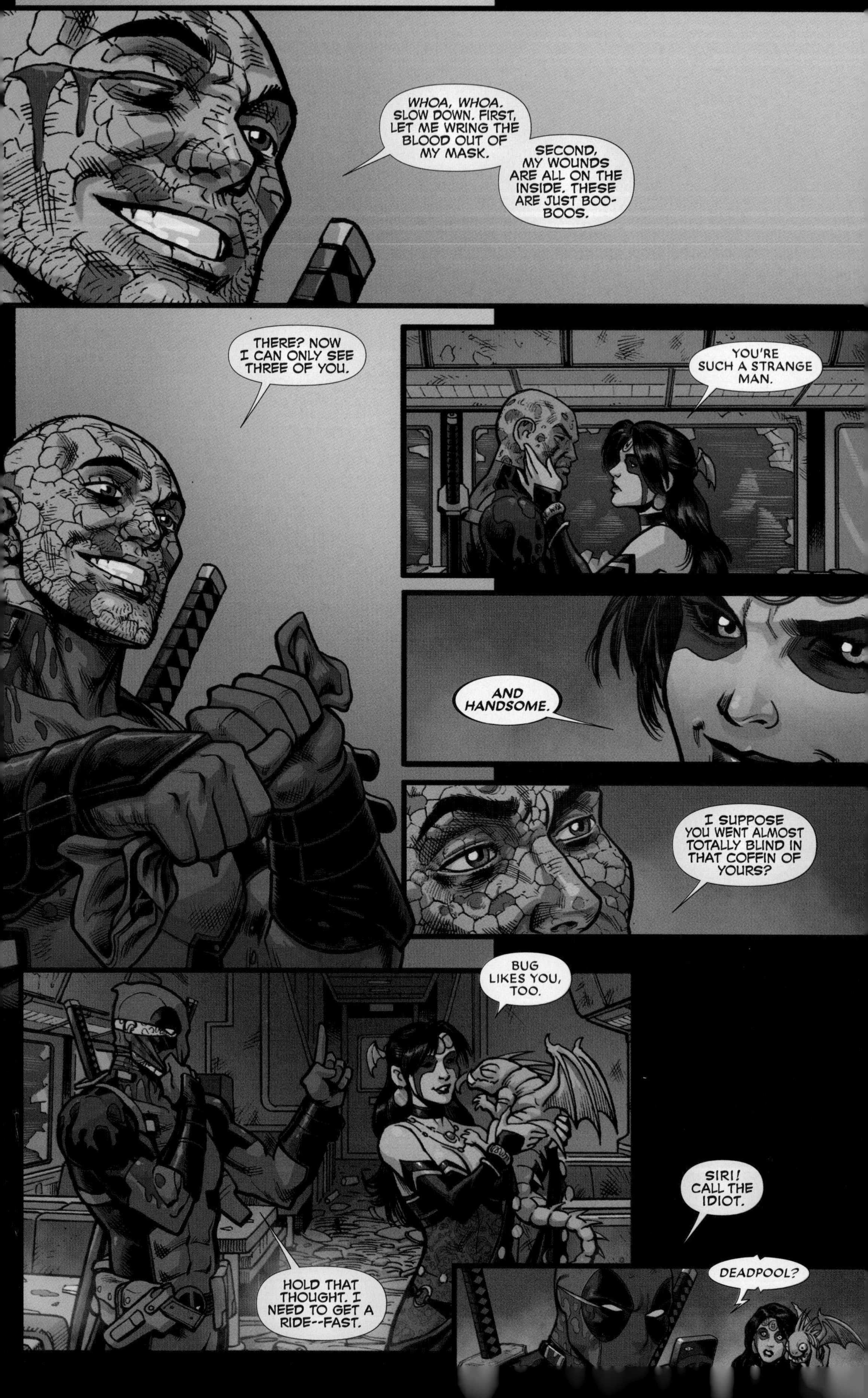
WHOA, WHOA. SLOW DOWN. FIRST, LET ME WRING THE BLOOD OUT OF MY MASK.
SECOND, MY WOUNDS ARE ALL ON THE INSIDE. THESE ARE JUST BOO-BOOS.
THERE? NOW I CAN ONLY SEE THREE OF YOU.
YOU'RE SUCH A STRANGE MAN.
AND HANDSOME.
I SUPPOSE YOU WENT ALMOST TOTALLY BLIND IN THAT COFFIN OF YOURS?
BUG LIKES YOU, TOO.
HOLD THAT THOUGHT. I NEED TO GET A RIDE--FAST.
SIRI! CALL THE IDIOT.
DEADPOOL?

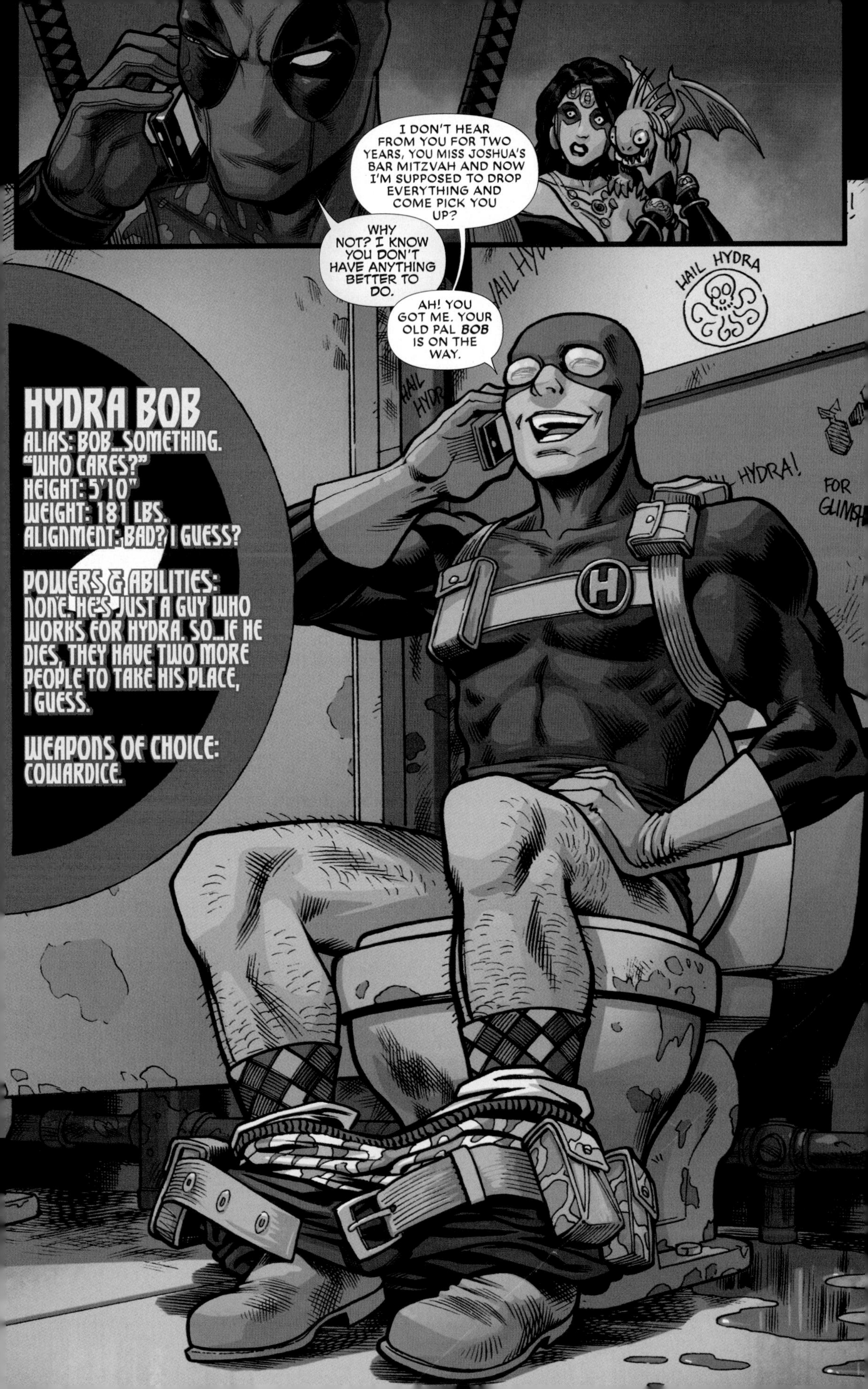
I DON'T HEAR FROM YOU FOR TWO YEARS, YOU MISS JOSHUA'S BAR MITZVAH AND NOW I'M SUPPOSED TO DROP EVERYTHING AND COME PICK YOU UP?
WHY NOT? I KNOW YOU DON'T HAVE ANYTHING BETTER TO DO.
AH! YOU GOT ME. YOUR OLD PAL BOB IS ON THE WAY.
HAIL HYDRA
HYDRA BOB
ALIAS: BOB...SOMETHING. "WHO CARES?"
HEIGHT: 5'10"
WEIGHT: 181 LBS.
ALIGNMENT: BAD? I GUESS?
POWERS & ABILITIES: NONE. HE'S JUST A GUY WHO WORKS FOR HYDRA. SO...IF HE DIES, THEY HAVE TWO MORE PEOPLE TO TAKE HIS PLACE, I GUESS.
WEAPONS OF CHOICE: COWARDICE.
HYDRA!
FOR GLINSH

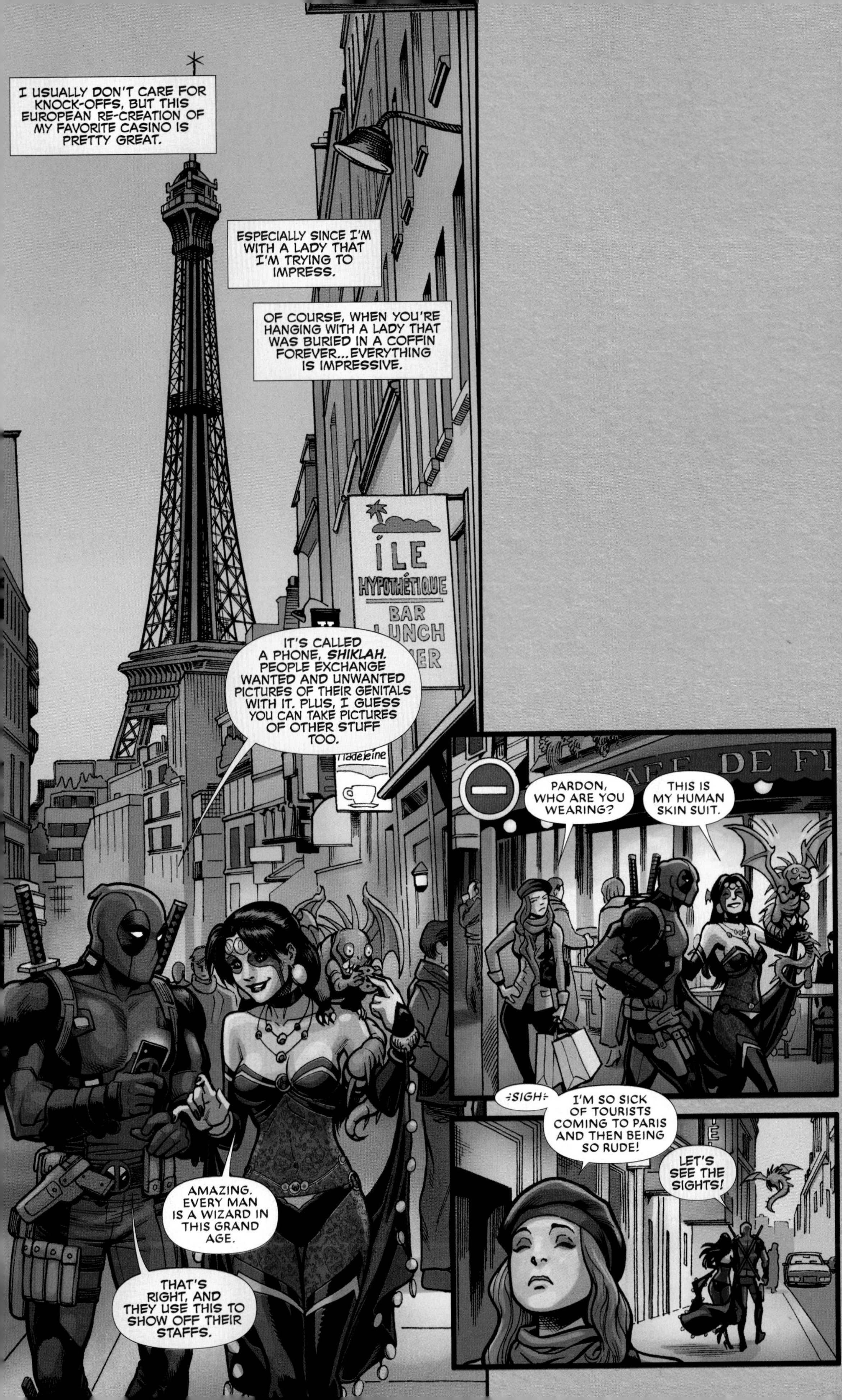
I USUALLY DON'T CARE FOR KNOCK-OFFS, BUT THIS EUROPEAN RE-CREATION OF MY FAVORITE CASINO IS PRETTY GREAT.
ESPECIALLY SINCE I'M WITH A LADY THAT I'M TRYING TO IMPRESS.
OF COURSE, WHEN YOU'RE HANGING WITH A LADY THAT WAS BURIED IN A COFFIN FOREVER... EVERYTHING IS IMPRESSIVE.
ÎLE
HYPOTHÉTIQUE
BAR
IT'S CALLED A PHONE, *SHIKLAH.* PEOPLE EXCHANGE WANTED AND UNWANTED PICTURES OF THEIR GENITALS WITH IT. PLUS, I GUESS YOU CAN TAKE PICTURES OF OTHER STUFF TOO.
AMAZING. EVERY MAN IS A WIZARD IN THIS GRAND AGE.
THAT'S RIGHT, AND THEY USE THIS TO SHOW OFF THEIR STAFFS.
PARDON, WHO ARE YOU WEARING?
THIS IS MY HUMAN SKIN SUIT.
SIGH
I'M SO SICK OF TOURISTS COMING TO PARIS AND THEN BEING SO RUDE!
LET'S SEE THE SIGHTS!

DEADPOOL

THE GAUNTLET

SOMEWHERE OLD AND PLEASANT-LOOKING.

THOSE GUYS ARE PROBABLY ALL DEAD BY NOW.

CHAPTER SIX

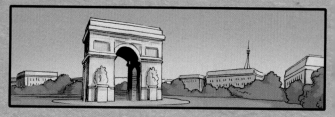

AN AMERICAN

MERCENARY

IF YOU WANT TO STAY IN THIS MUSEUM, YOU'RE GONNA WANT TO NOT LET THAT BUG OF YOURS GET SEXY ON ANYTHING IN HERE.

I'M SPEAKING FROM EXPERIENCE HERE.

MEANWHILE, AT THE DA VINCI CODE HALL OF JUSTICE...

ANCIENS SABRES JAPONAIS

ANCIENT JAPANESE SWORDS

THESE KATANAS AREN'T GOING TO SWING *THEMSELVES* INTO BODIES...BUT THAT WOULD BE PRETTY AWESOME IF THEY COULD.

IN PARIS

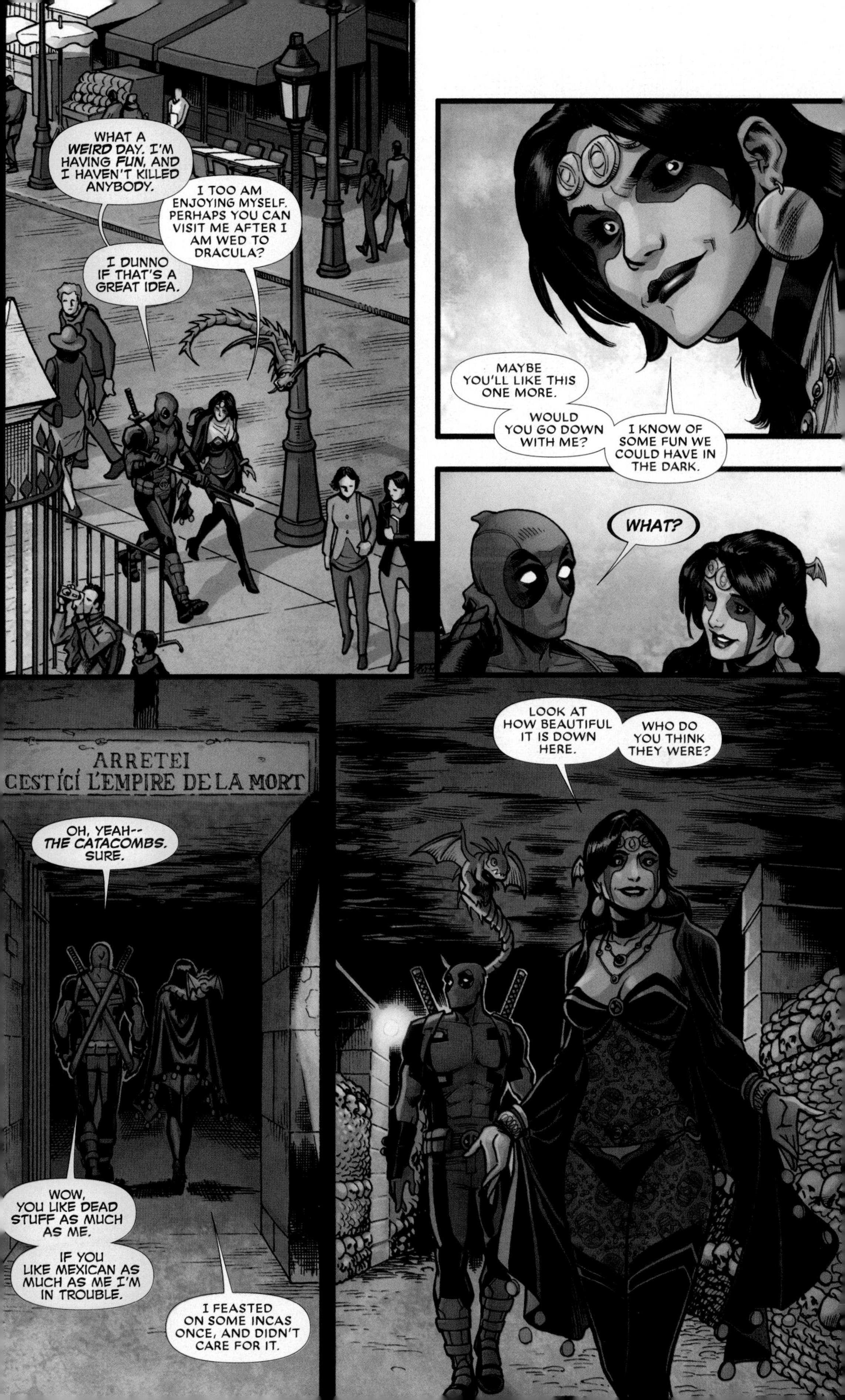
WHAT A WEIRD DAY. I'M HAVING FUN, AND I HAVEN'T KILLED ANYBODY.
I TOO AM ENJOYING MYSELF. PERHAPS YOU CAN VISIT ME AFTER I AM WED TO DRACULA?
I DUNNO IF THAT'S A GREAT IDEA.
MAYBE YOU'LL LIKE THIS ONE MORE.
WOULD YOU GO DOWN WITH ME?
I KNOW OF SOME FUN WE COULD HAVE IN THE DARK.
WHAT?
ARRETEI
CESTÍCÍ L'EMPIRE DE LA MORT
OH, YEAH-- THE CATACOMBS. SURE.
WOW, YOU LIKE DEAD STUFF AS MUCH AS ME.
IF YOU LIKE MEXICAN AS MUCH AS ME I'M IN TROUBLE.
I FEASTED ON SOME INCAS ONCE, AND DIDN'T CARE FOR IT.
LOOK AT HOW BEAUTIFUL IT IS DOWN HERE.
WHO DO YOU THINK THEY WERE?

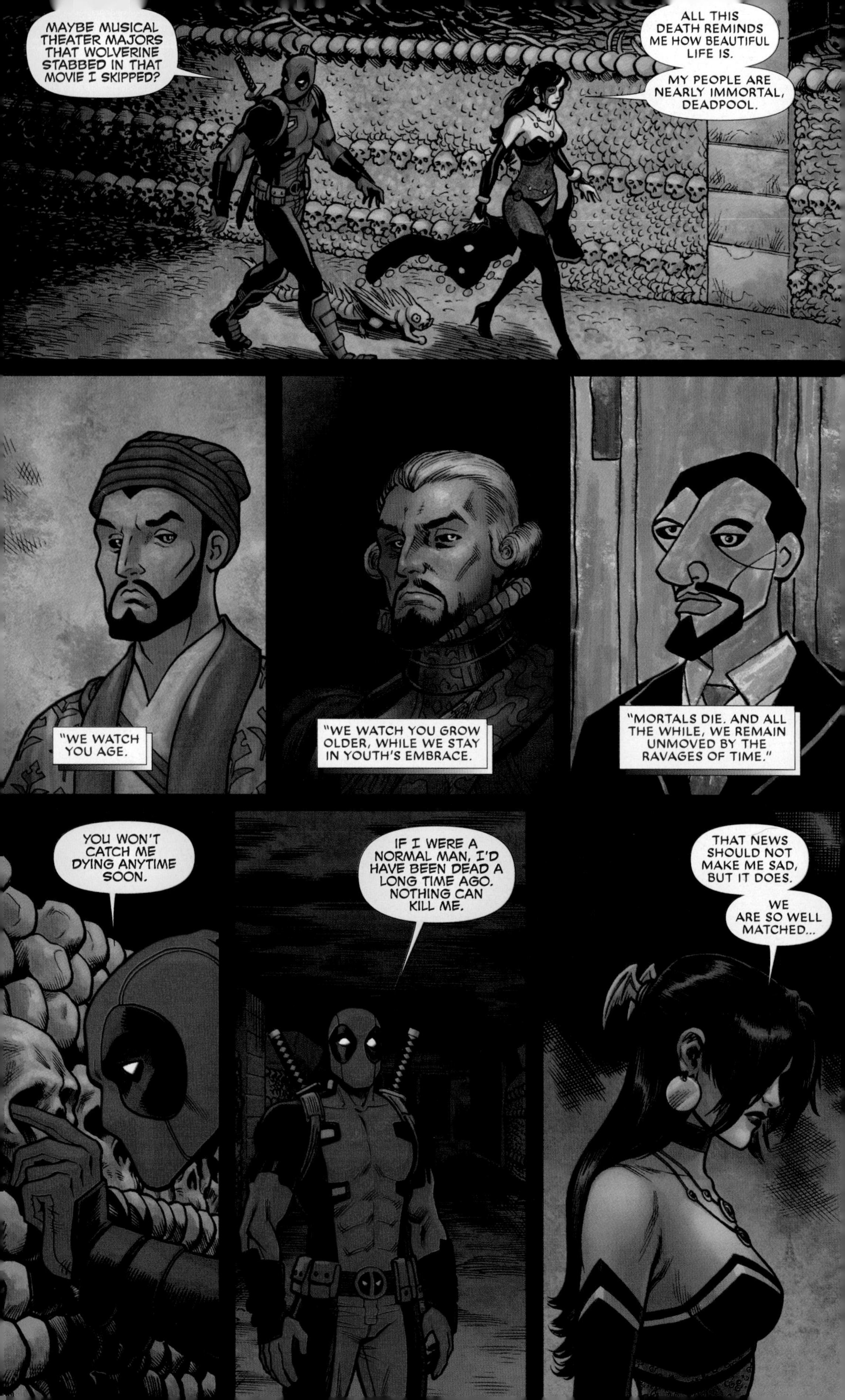
MAYBE MUSICAL THEATER MAJORS THAT WOLVERINE STABBED IN THAT MOVIE I SKIPPED?
ALL THIS DEATH REMINDS ME HOW BEAUTIFUL LIFE IS.
MY PEOPLE ARE NEARLY IMMORTAL, DEADPOOL.
"WE WATCH YOU AGE.
"WE WATCH YOU GROW OLDER, WHILE WE STAY IN YOUTH'S EMBRACE.
"MORTALS DIE. AND ALL THE WHILE, WE REMAIN UNMOVED BY THE RAVAGES OF TIME."
YOU WON'T CATCH ME DYING ANYTIME SOON.
IF I WERE A NORMAL MAN, I'D HAVE BEEN DEAD A LONG TIME AGO. NOTHING CAN KILL ME.
THAT NEWS SHOULD NOT MAKE ME SAD, BUT IT DOES.
WE ARE SO WELL MATCHED...

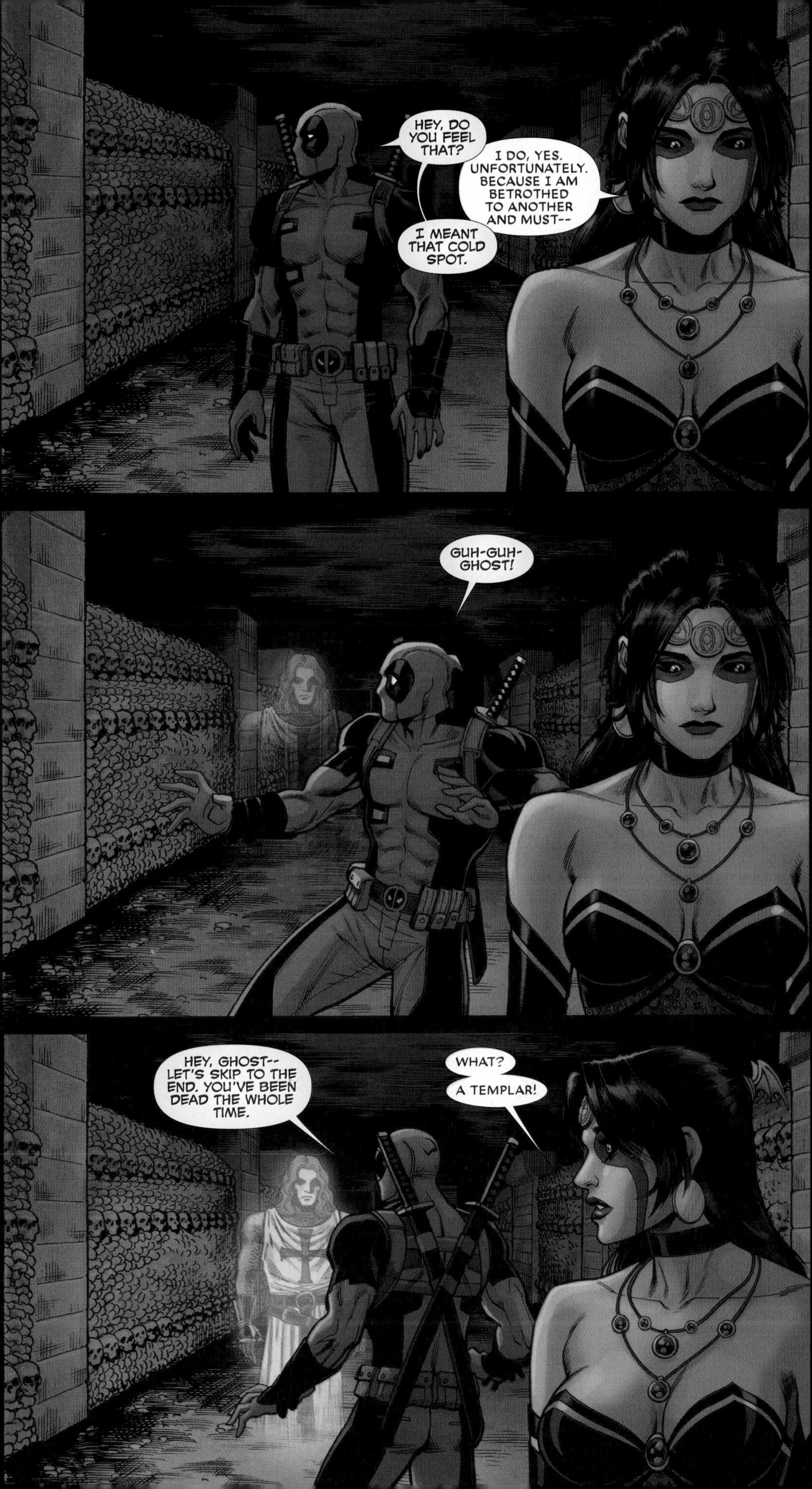
HEY, DO YOU FEEL THAT?
I DO, YES. UNFORTUNATELY. BECAUSE I AM BETROTHED TO ANOTHER AND MUST--
I MEANT THAT COLD SPOT.
GUH-GUH-GHOST!
HEY, GHOST-- LET'S SKIP TO THE END. YOU'VE BEEN DEAD THE WHOLE TIME.
WHAT?
A TEMPLAR!

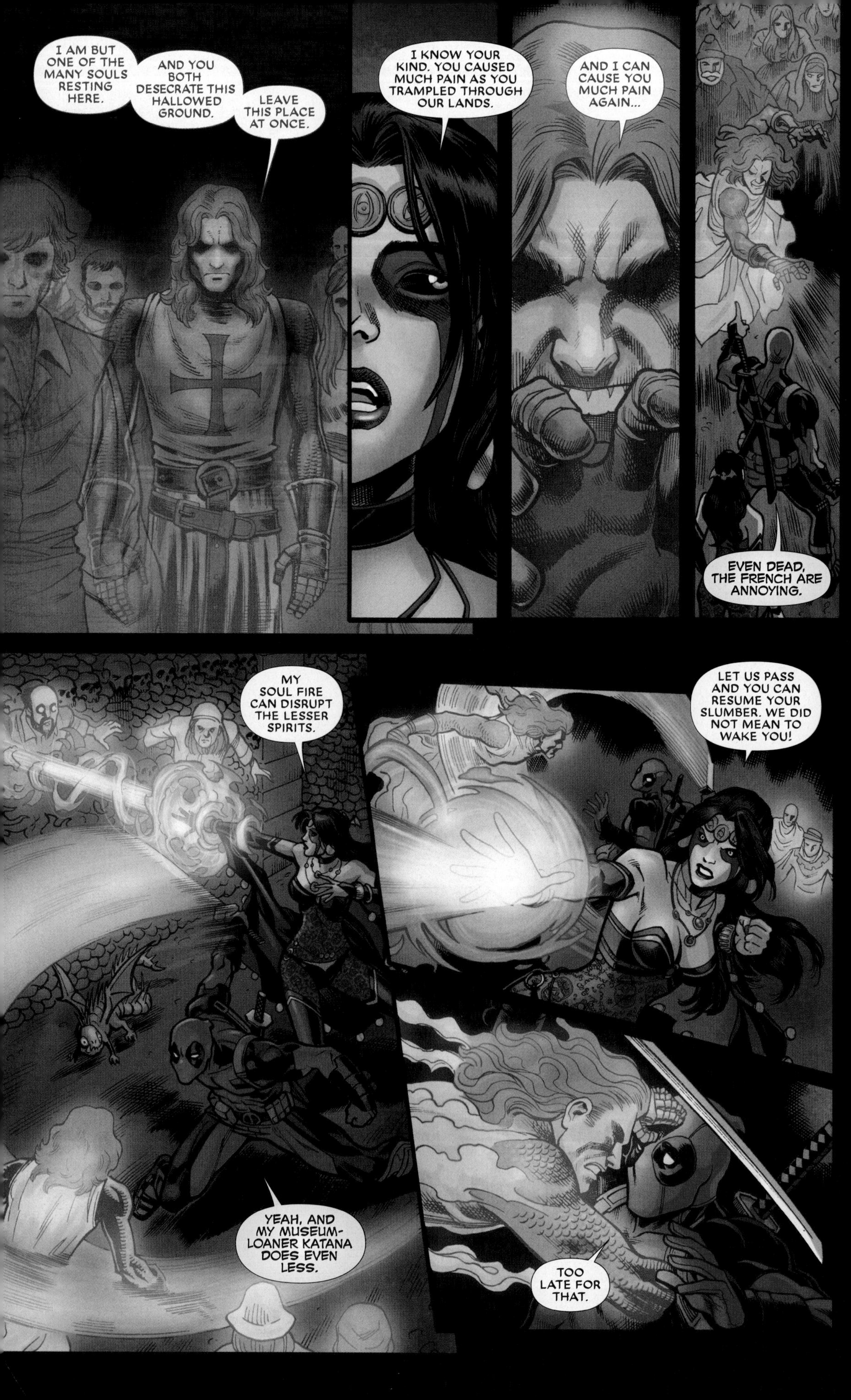
I AM BUT ONE OF THE MANY SOULS RESTING HERE.
AND YOU BOTH DESECRATE THIS HALLOWED GROUND.
LEAVE THIS PLACE AT ONCE.
I KNOW YOUR KIND. YOU CAUSED MUCH PAIN AS YOU TRAMPLED THROUGH OUR LANDS.
AND I CAN CAUSE YOU MUCH PAIN AGAIN...
EVEN DEAD, THE FRENCH ARE ANNOYING.
MY SOUL FIRE CAN DISRUPT THE LESSER SPIRITS.
YEAH, AND MY MUSEUM-LOANER KATANA DOES EVEN LESS.
LET US PASS AND YOU CAN RESUME YOUR SLUMBER. WE DID NOT MEAN TO WAKE YOU!
TOO LATE FOR THAT.

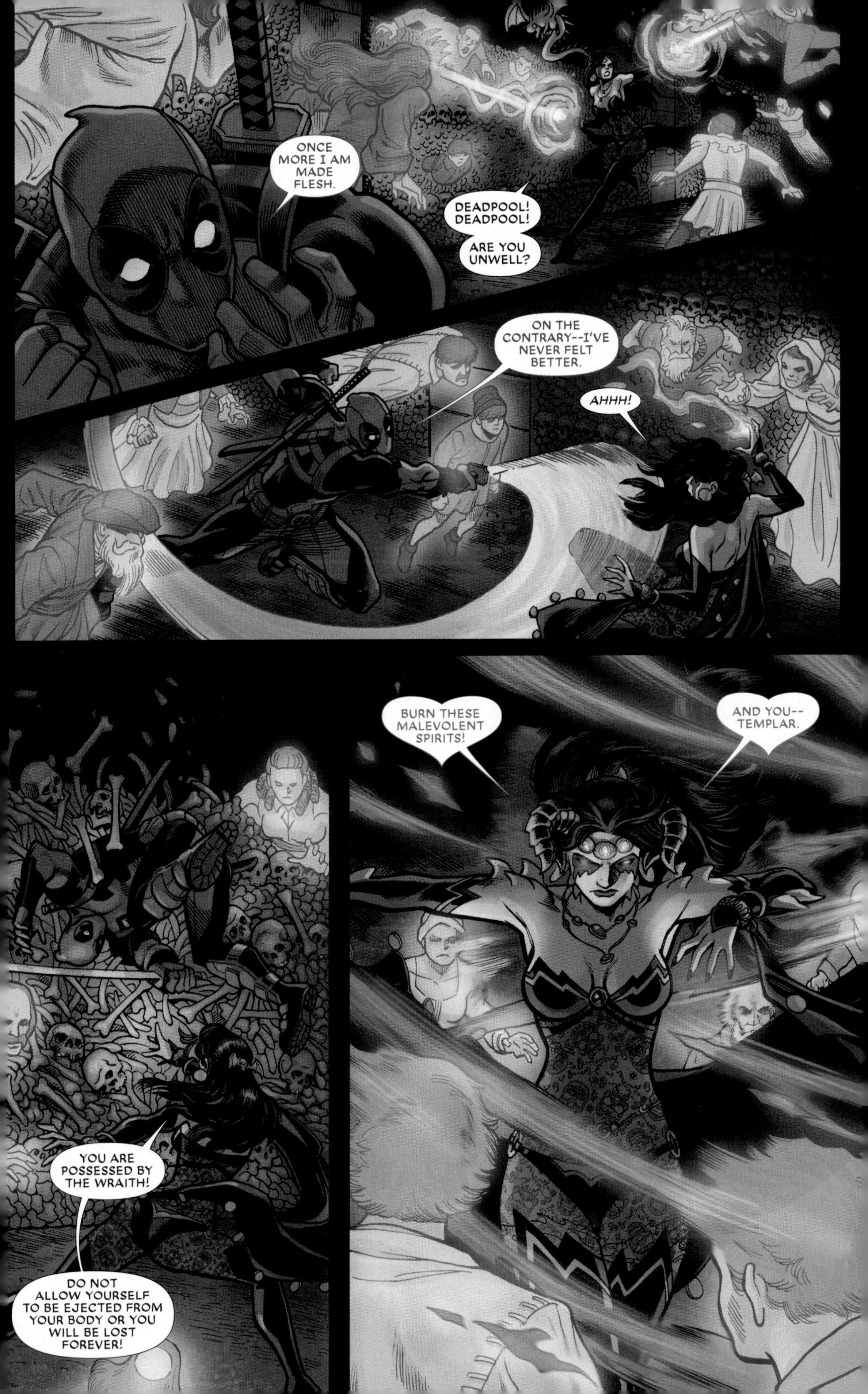
ONCE MORE I AM MADE FLESH.
DEADPOOL! DEADPOOL!
ARE YOU UNWELL?
ON THE CONTRARY--I'VE NEVER FELT BETTER.
AHHH!
YOU ARE POSSESSED BY THE WRAITH!
DO NOT ALLOW YOURSELF TO BE EJECTED FROM YOUR BODY OR YOU WILL BE LOST FOREVER!
BURN THESE MALEVOLENT SPIRITS!
AND YOU-- TEMPLAR.

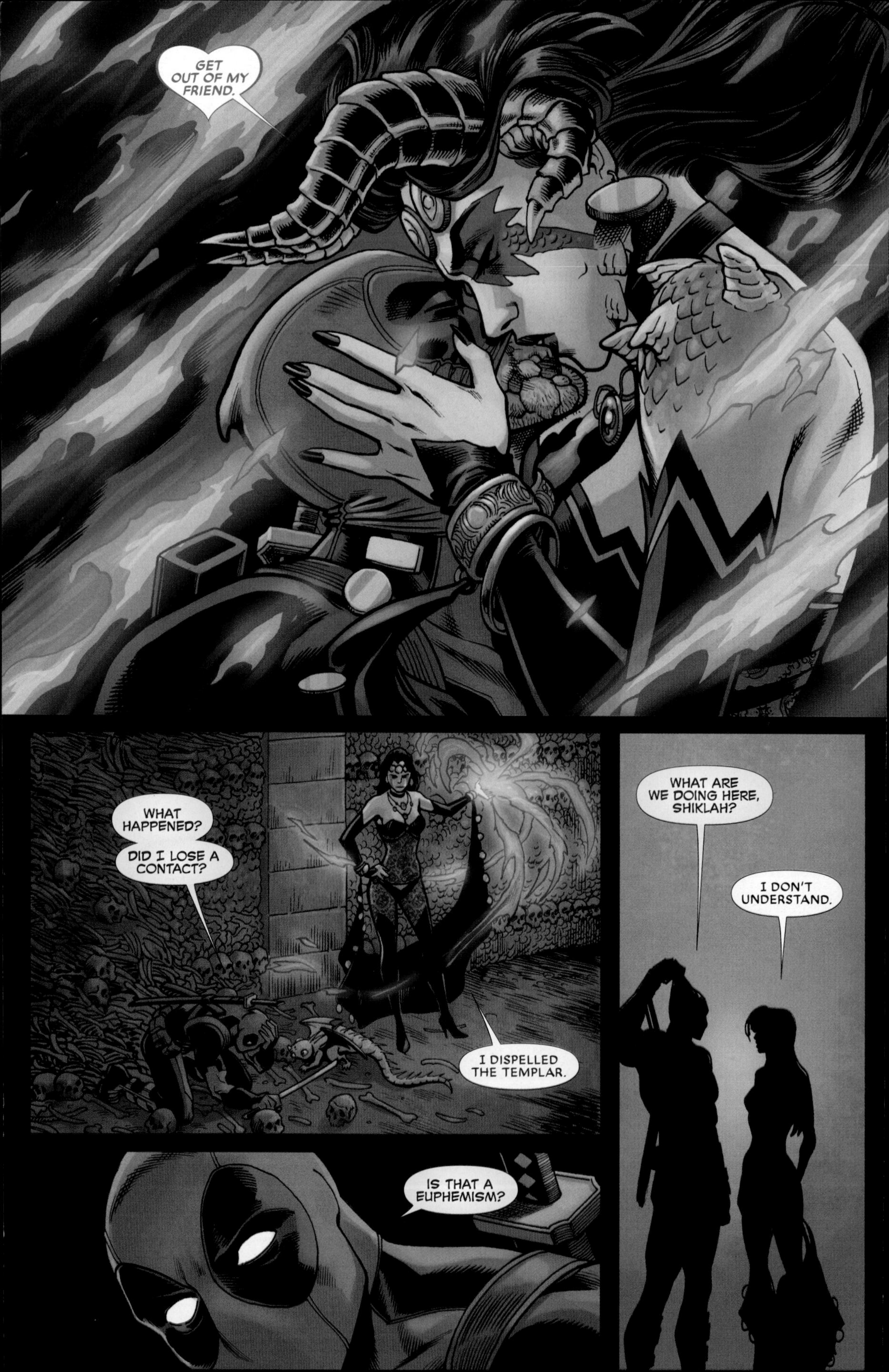
GET OUT OF MY FRIEND.
WHAT HAPPENED?
DID I LOSE A CONTACT?
I DISPELLED THE TEMPLAR.
IS THAT A EUPHEMISM?
WHAT ARE WE DOING HERE, SHIKLAH?
I DON'T UNDERSTAND.

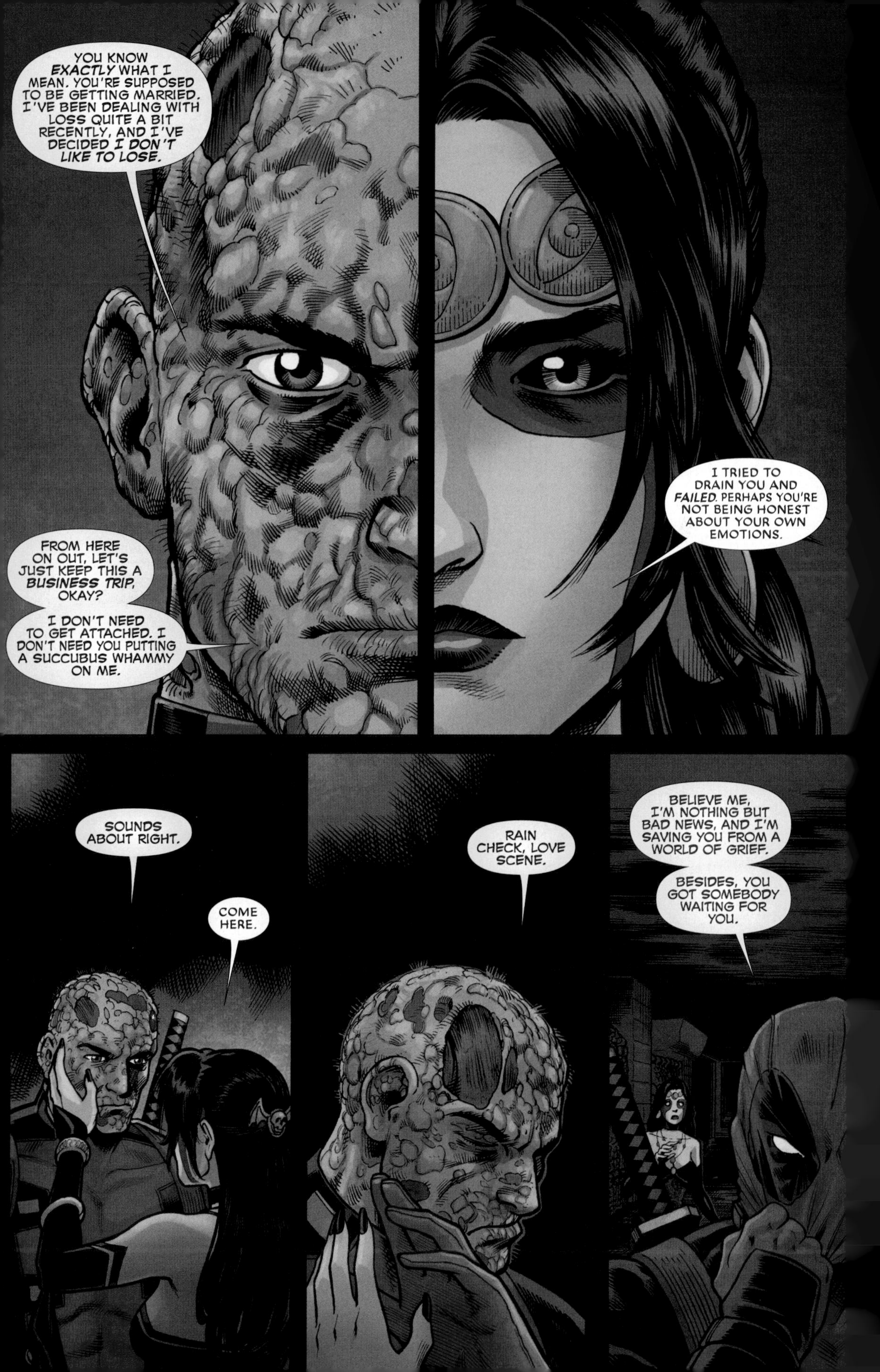

YOU KNOW EXACTLY WHAT I MEAN. YOU'RE SUPPOSED TO BE GETTING MARRIED. I'VE BEEN DEALING WITH LOSS QUITE A BIT RECENTLY, AND I'VE DECIDED I DON'T LIKE TO LOSE.
I TRIED TO DRAIN YOU AND FAILED. PERHAPS YOU'RE NOT BEING HONEST ABOUT YOUR OWN EMOTIONS.
FROM HERE ON OUT, LET'S JUST KEEP THIS A BUSINESS TRIP, OKAY?
I DON'T NEED TO GET ATTACHED. I DON'T NEED YOU PUTTING A SUCCUBUS WHAMMY ON ME.
SOUNDS ABOUT RIGHT.
COME HERE.
RAIN CHECK, LOVE SCENE.
BELIEVE ME, I'M NOTHING BUT BAD NEWS, AND I'M SAVING YOU FROM A WORLD OF GRIEF.
BESIDES, YOU GOT SOMEBODY WAITING FOR YOU.

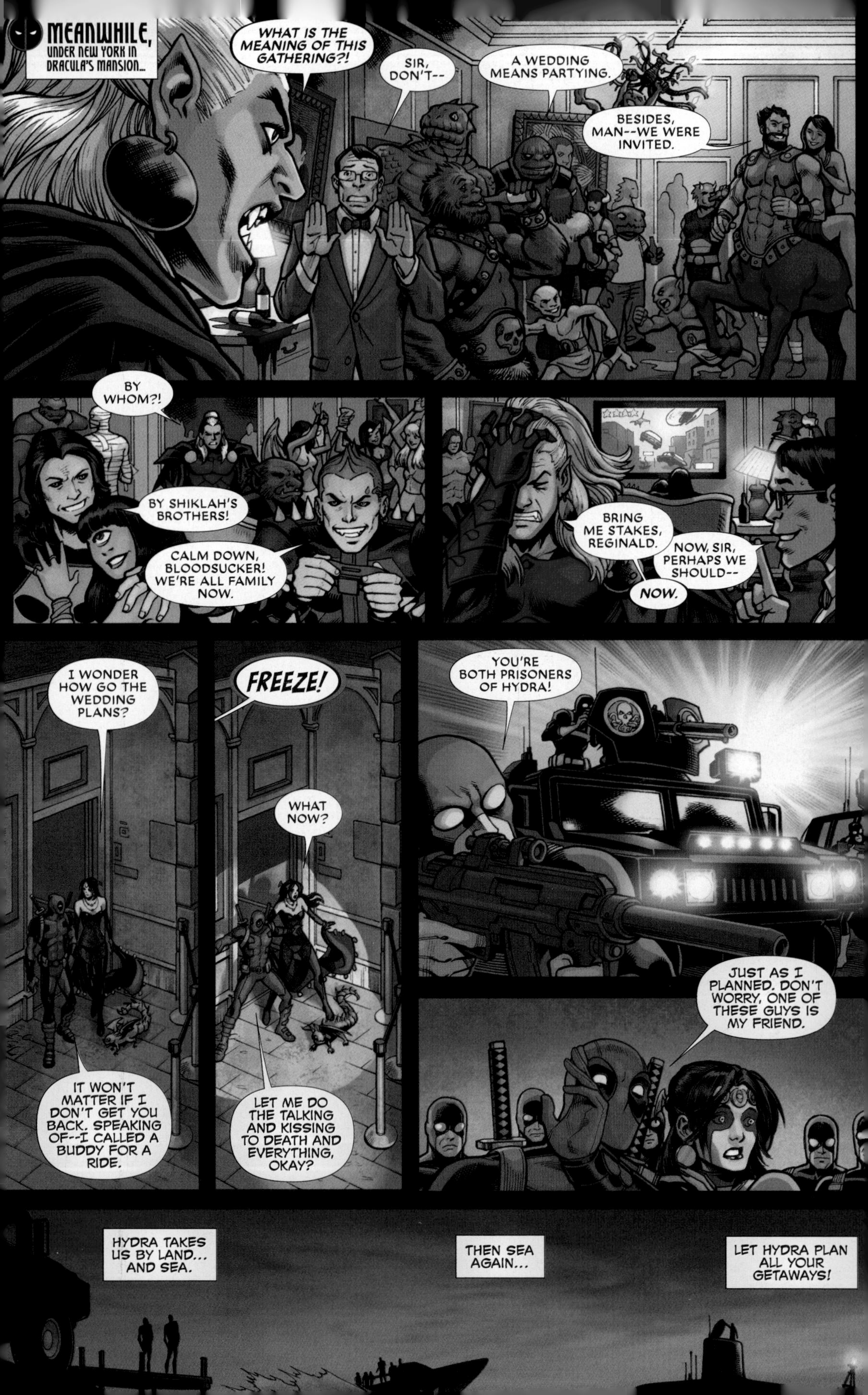
MEANWHILE, UNDER NEW YORK IN DRACULA'S MANSION...
WHAT IS THE MEANING OF THIS GATHERING?!
SIR, DON'T--
A WEDDING MEANS PARTYING.
BESIDES, MAN--WE WERE INVITED.
BY WHOM?!
BY SHIKLAH'S BROTHERS!
CALM DOWN, BLOODSUCKER! WE'RE ALL FAMILY NOW.
BRING ME STAKES, REGINALD.
NOW, SIR, PERHAPS WE SHOULD--
NOW.
I WONDER HOW GO THE WEDDING PLANS?
IT WON'T MATTER IF I DON'T GET YOU BACK. SPEAKING OF--I CALLED A BUDDY FOR A RIDE.
FREEZE!
WHAT NOW?
LET ME DO THE TALKING AND KISSING TO DEATH AND EVERYTHING, OKAY?
YOU'RE BOTH PRISONERS OF HYDRA!
JUST AS I PLANNED. DON'T WORRY, ONE OF THESE GUYS IS MY FRIEND.
HYDRA TAKES US BY LAND... AND SEA.
THEN SEA AGAIN...
LET HYDRA PLAN ALL YOUR GETAWAYS!

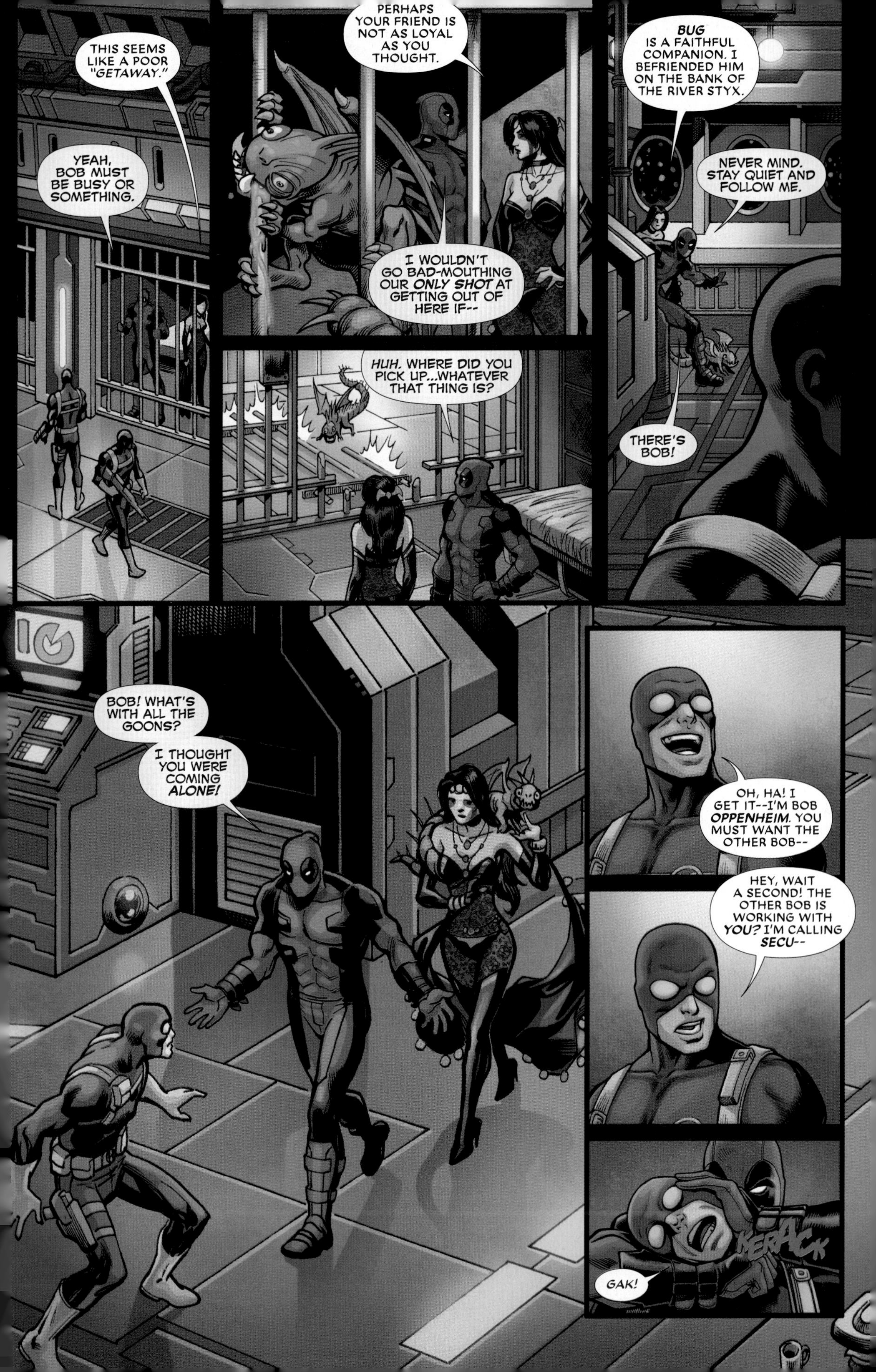

THIS SEEMS LIKE A POOR "GETAWAY."
YEAH, BOB MUST BE BUSY OR SOMETHING.
PERHAPS YOUR FRIEND IS NOT AS LOYAL AS YOU THOUGHT.
I WOULDN'T GO BAD-MOUTHING OUR ONLY SHOT AT GETTING OUT OF HERE IF--
BUG IS A FAITHFUL COMPANION. I BEFRIENDED HIM ON THE BANK OF THE RIVER STYX.
NEVER MIND. STAY QUIET AND FOLLOW ME.
HUH. WHERE DID YOU PICK UP...WHATEVER THAT THING IS?
THERE'S BOB!
BOB! WHAT'S WITH ALL THE GOONS?
I THOUGHT YOU WERE COMING ALONE!
OH, HA! I GET IT--I'M BOB OPPENHEIM. YOU MUST WANT THE OTHER BOB--
HEY, WAIT A SECOND! THE OTHER BOB IS WORKING WITH YOU? I'M CALLING SECU--
KERACK
GAK!

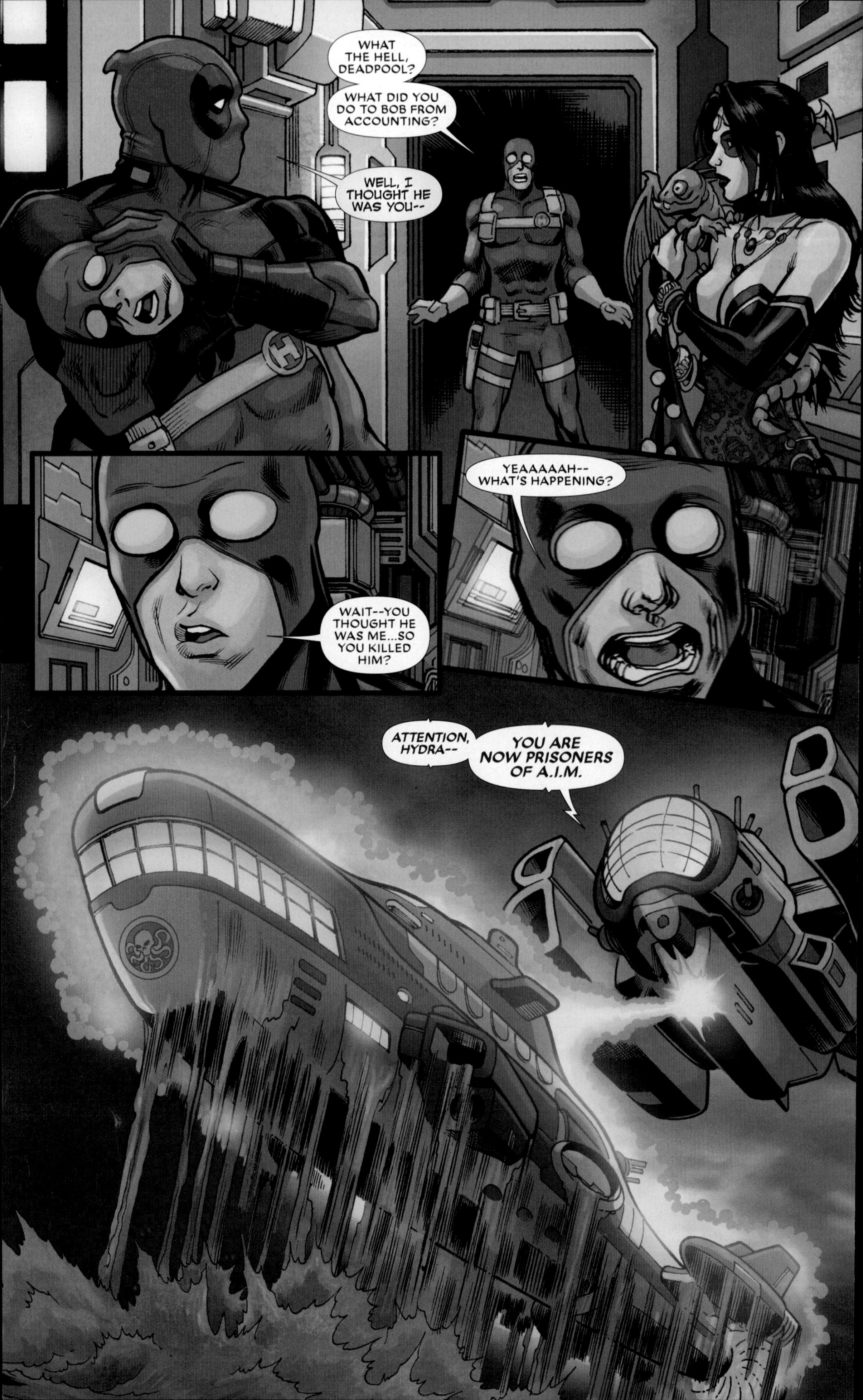
WHAT THE HELL, DEADPOOL?
WHAT DID YOU DO TO BOB FROM ACCOUNTING?
WELL, I THOUGHT HE WAS YOU--
WAIT--YOU THOUGHT HE WAS ME...SO YOU KILLED HIM?
YEAAAAAH-- WHAT'S HAPPENING?
ATTENTION, HYDRA--
YOU ARE NOW PRISONERS OF A.I.M.

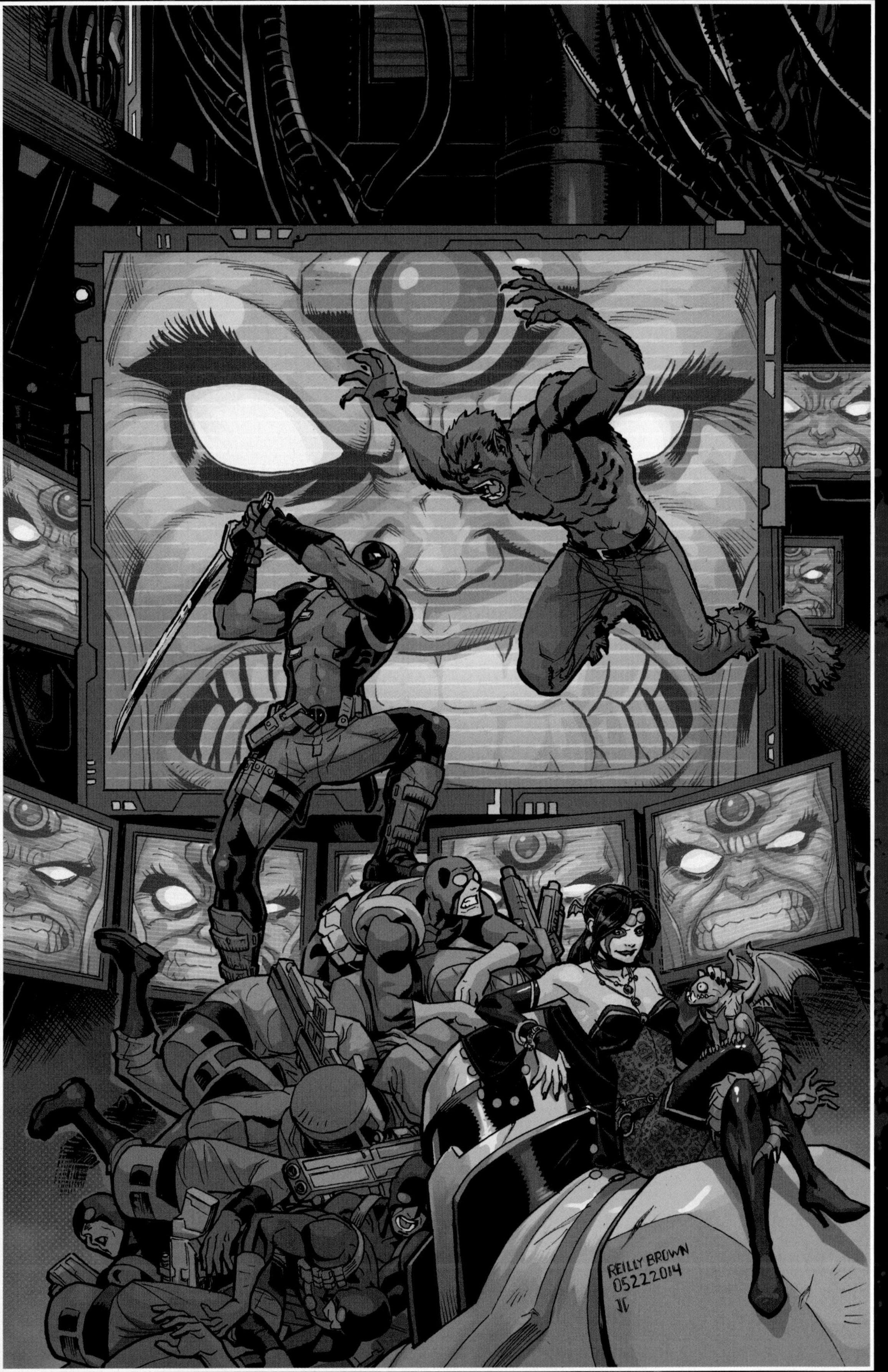
REILLY BROWN
05222014

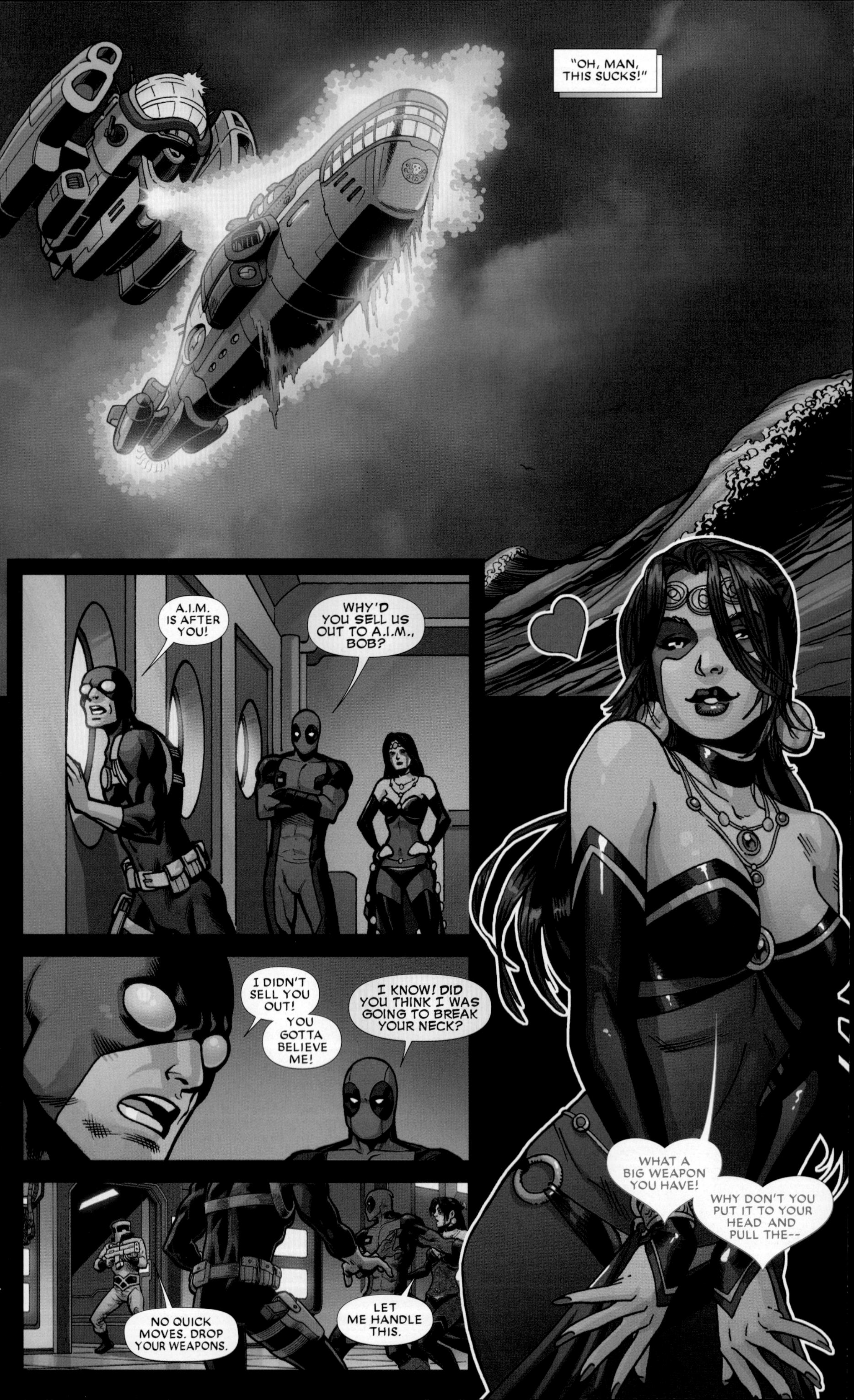
"OH, MAN, THIS SUCKS!"
A.I.M. IS AFTER YOU!
WHY'D YOU SELL US OUT TO A.I.M., BOB?
I DIDN'T SELL YOU OUT!
YOU GOTTA BELIEVE ME!
I KNOW! DID YOU THINK I WAS GOING TO BREAK YOUR NECK?
NO QUICK MOVES. DROP YOUR WEAPONS.
LET ME HANDLE THIS.
WHAT A BIG WEAPON YOU HAVE!
WHY DON'T YOU PUT IT TO YOUR HEAD AND PULL THE--

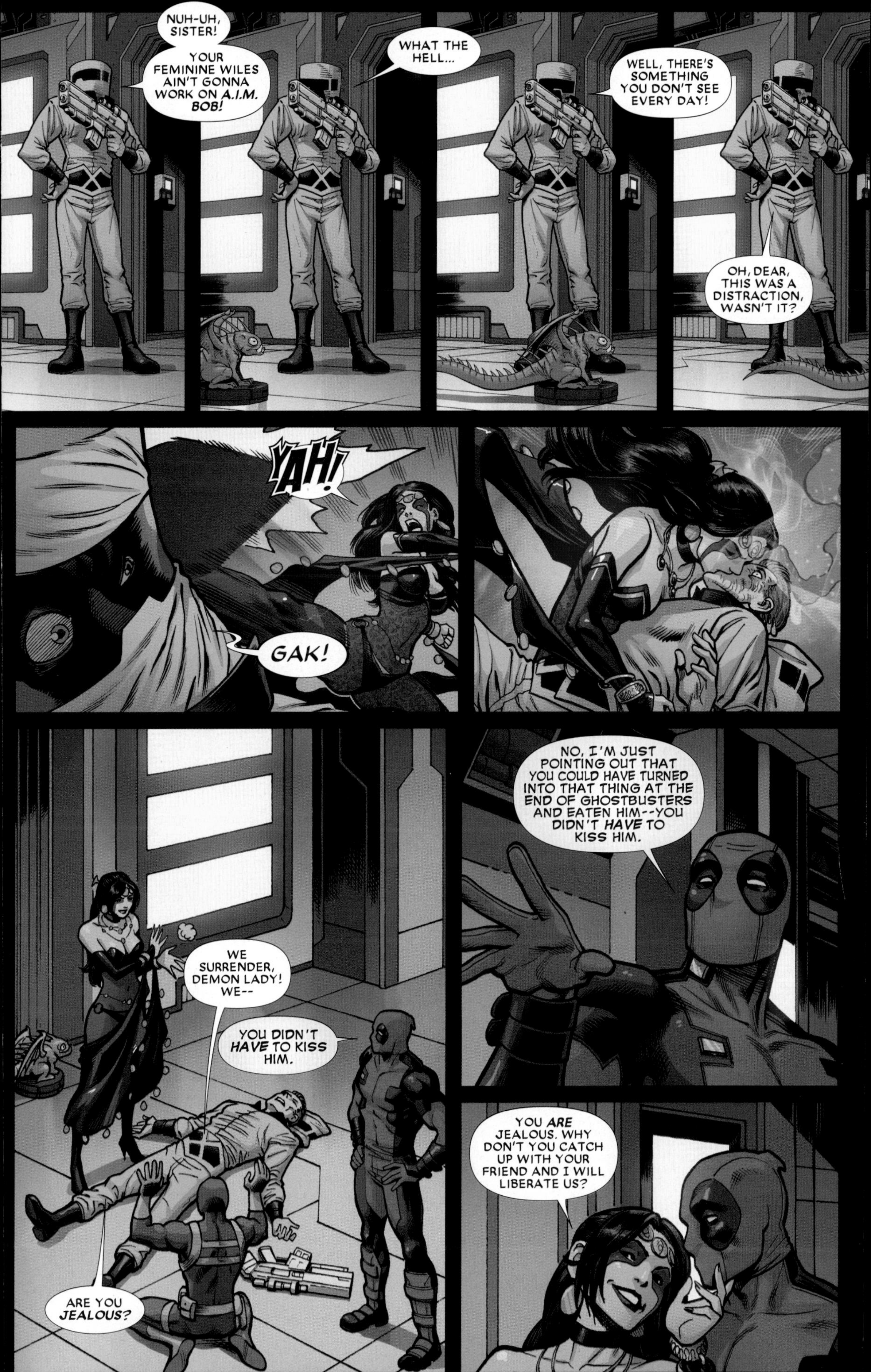
NUH-UH, SISTER!
YOUR FEMININE WILES AIN'T GONNA WORK ON A.I.M. BOB!
WHAT THE HELL...
WELL, THERE'S SOMETHING YOU DON'T SEE EVERY DAY!
OH, DEAR, THIS WAS A DISTRACTION, WASN'T IT?
YAH!
GAK!
WE SURRENDER, DEMON LADY! WE--
YOU DIDN'T HAVE TO KISS HIM.
ARE YOU JEALOUS?
NO, I'M JUST POINTING OUT THAT YOU COULD HAVE TURNED INTO THAT THING AT THE END OF GHOSTBUSTERS AND EATEN HIM--YOU DIDN'T HAVE TO KISS HIM.
YOU ARE JEALOUS. WHY DON'T YOU CATCH UP WITH YOUR FRIEND AND I WILL LIBERATE US?

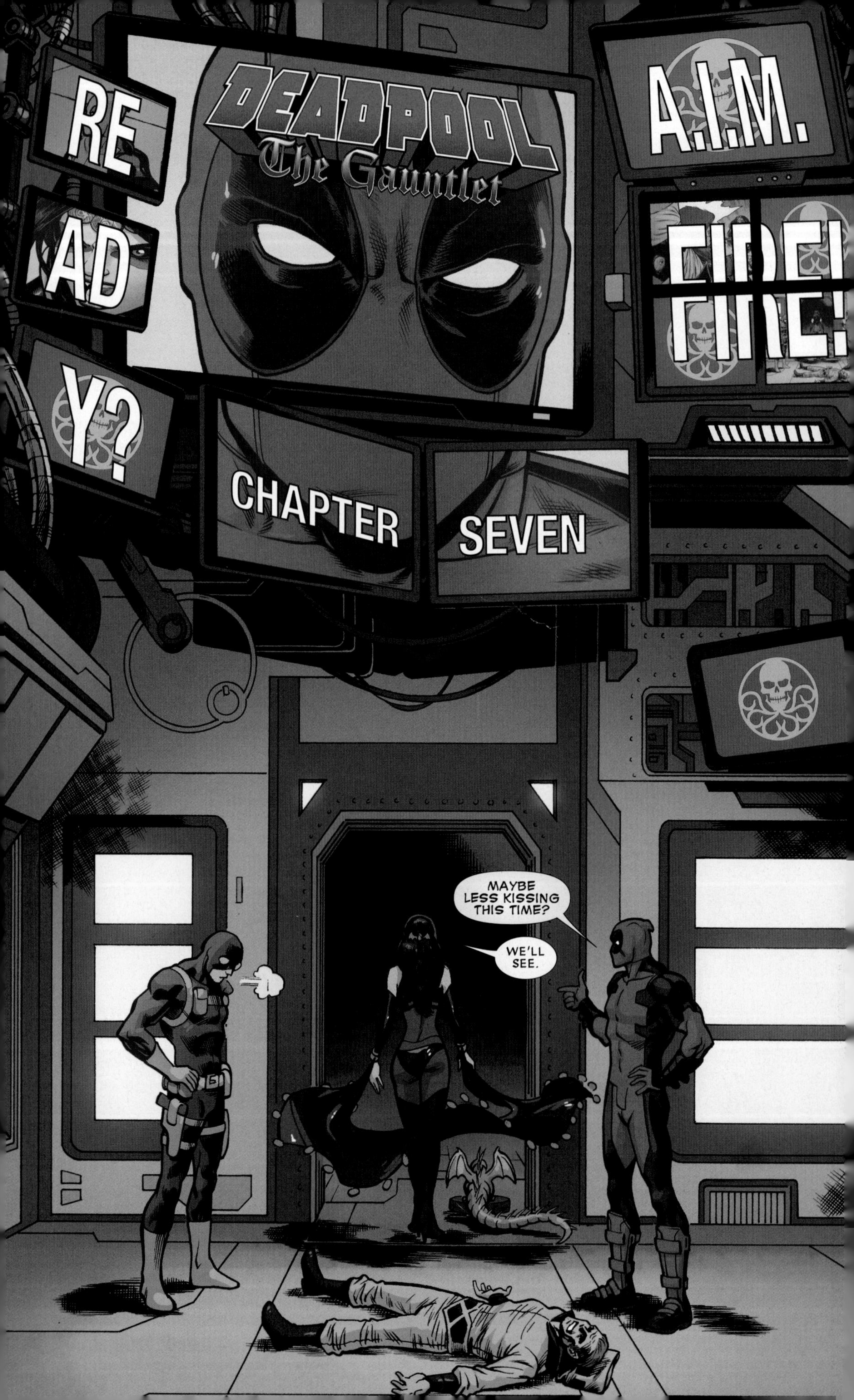
DEADPOOL
The Gauntlet
RE
AD
Y?
A.I.M.
FIRE!
CHAPTER
SEVEN
MAYBE LESS KISSING THIS TIME?
WE'LL SEE.

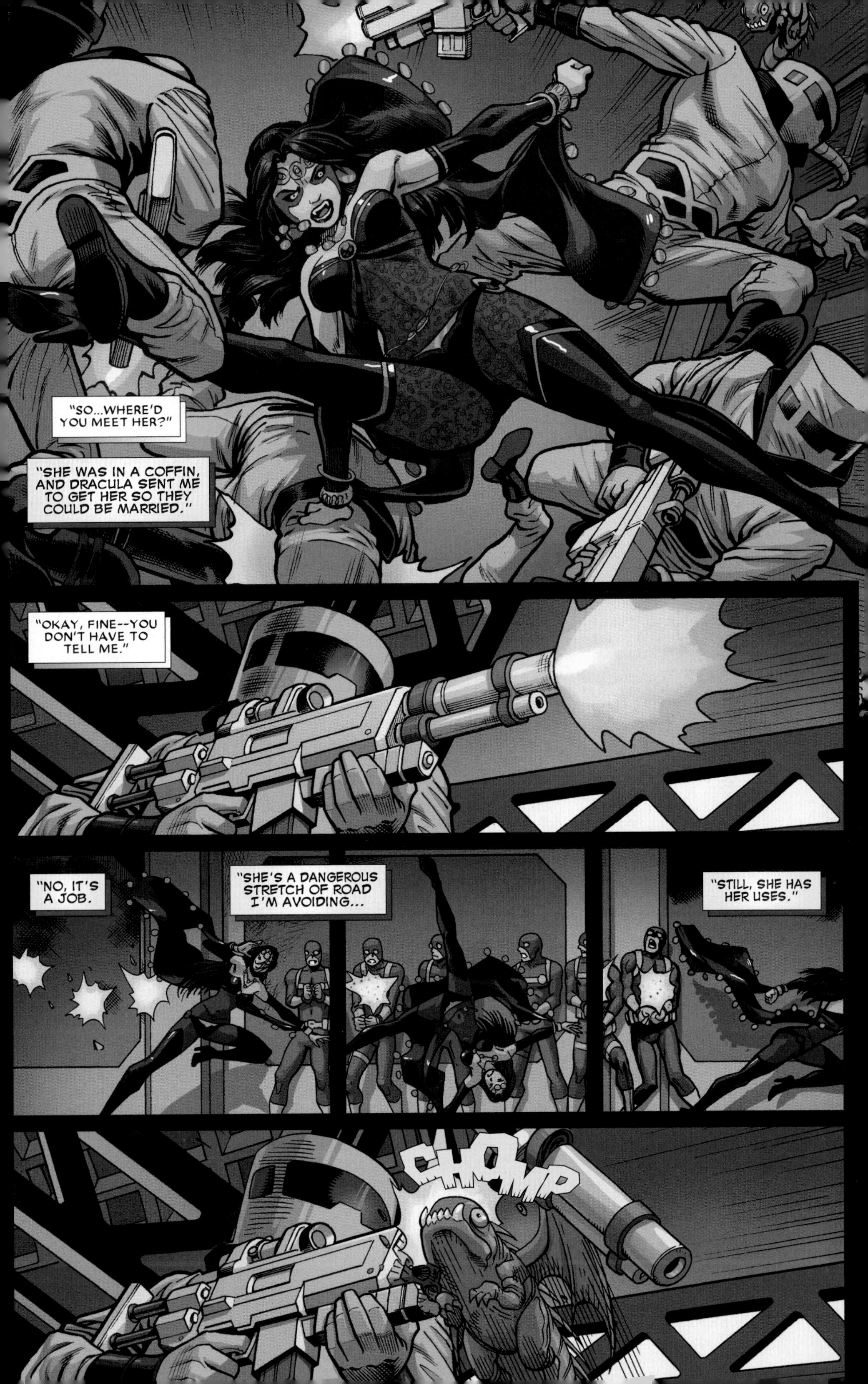
"SO...WHERE'D YOU MEET HER?"
"SHE WAS IN A COFFIN, AND DRACULA SENT ME TO GET HER SO THEY COULD BE MARRIED."
"OKAY, FINE--YOU DON'T HAVE TO TELL ME."
"NO, IT'S A JOB.
"SHE'S A DANGEROUS STRETCH OF ROAD I'M AVOIDING...
"STILL, SHE HAS HER USES."
CHOMP

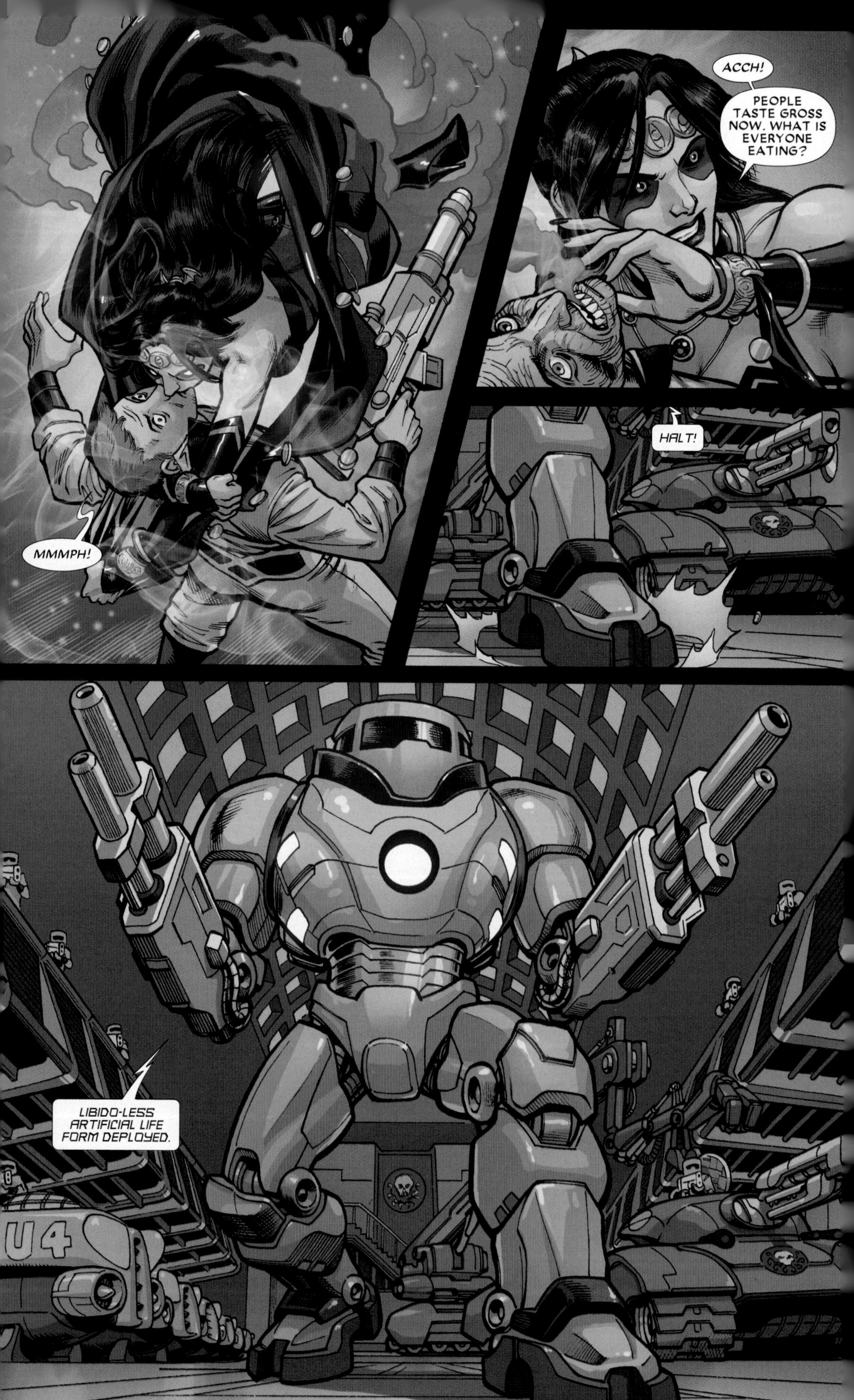
MMMPH!
ACCH!
PEOPLE TASTE GROSS NOW. WHAT IS EVERYONE EATING?
HALT!
LIBIDO-LESS ARTIFICIAL LIFE FORM DEPLOYED.
U4

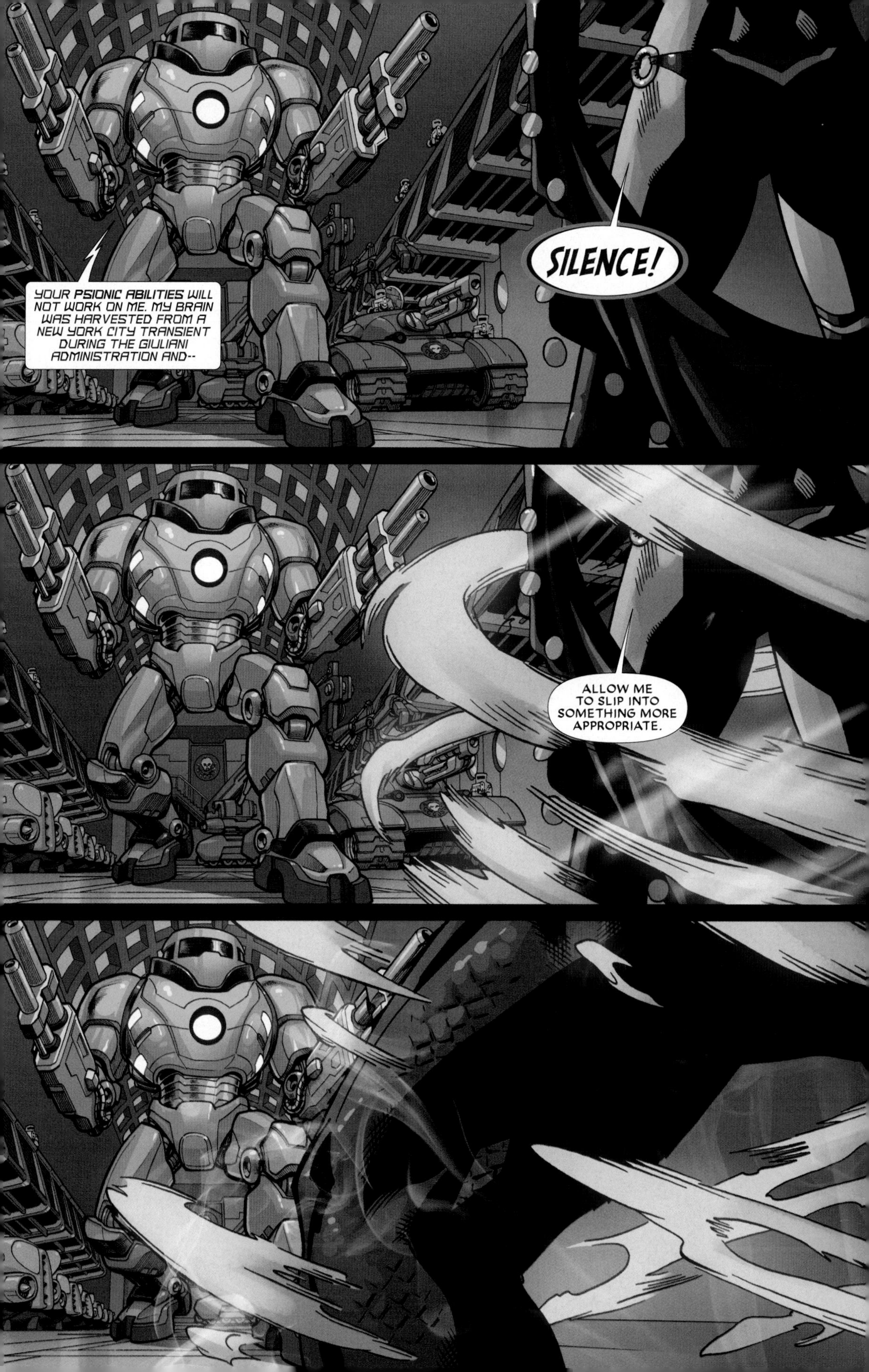
YOUR PSIONIC ABILITIES WILL NOT WORK ON ME. MY BRAIN WAS HARVESTED FROM A NEW YORK CITY TRANSIENT DURING THE GIULIANI ADMINISTRATION AND--
SILENCE!
ALLOW ME TO SLIP INTO SOMETHING MORE APPROPRIATE.

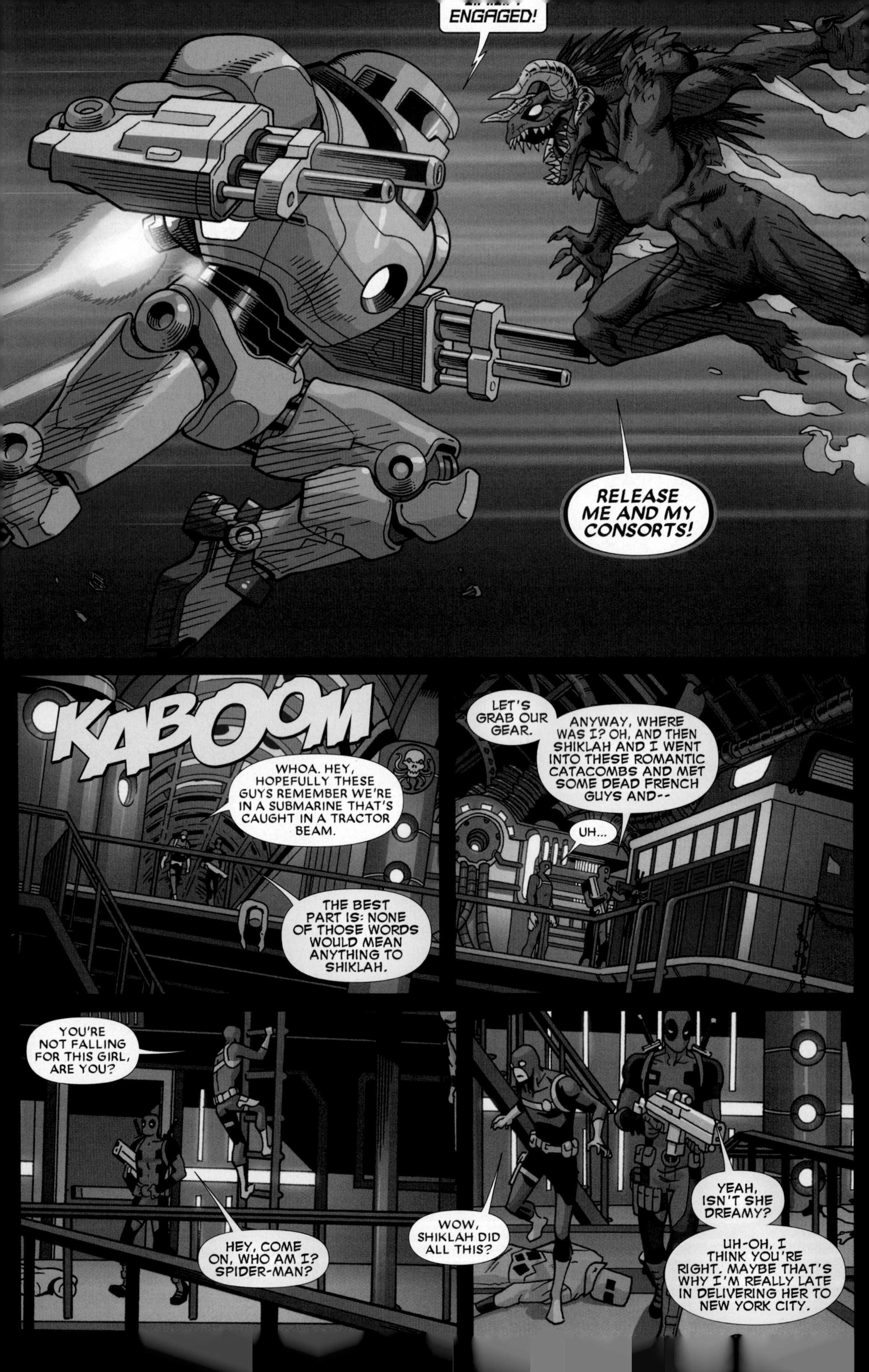
ENGAGED!
RELEASE ME AND MY CONSORTS!
KABOOM
WHOA. HEY, HOPEFULLY THESE GUYS REMEMBER WE'RE IN A SUBMARINE THAT'S CAUGHT IN A TRACTOR BEAM.
THE BEST PART IS: NONE OF THOSE WORDS WOULD MEAN ANYTHING TO SHIKLAH.
LET'S GRAB OUR GEAR.
ANYWAY, WHERE WAS I? OH, AND THEN SHIKLAH AND I WENT INTO THESE ROMANTIC CATACOMBS AND MET SOME DEAD FRENCH GUYS AND--
UH...
YOU'RE NOT FALLING FOR THIS GIRL, ARE YOU?
HEY, COME ON, WHO AM I? SPIDER-MAN?
WOW, SHIKLAH DID ALL THIS?
YEAH, ISN'T SHE DREAMY?
UH-OH, I THINK YOU'RE RIGHT. MAYBE THAT'S WHY I'M REALLY LATE IN DELIVERING HER TO NEW YORK CITY.

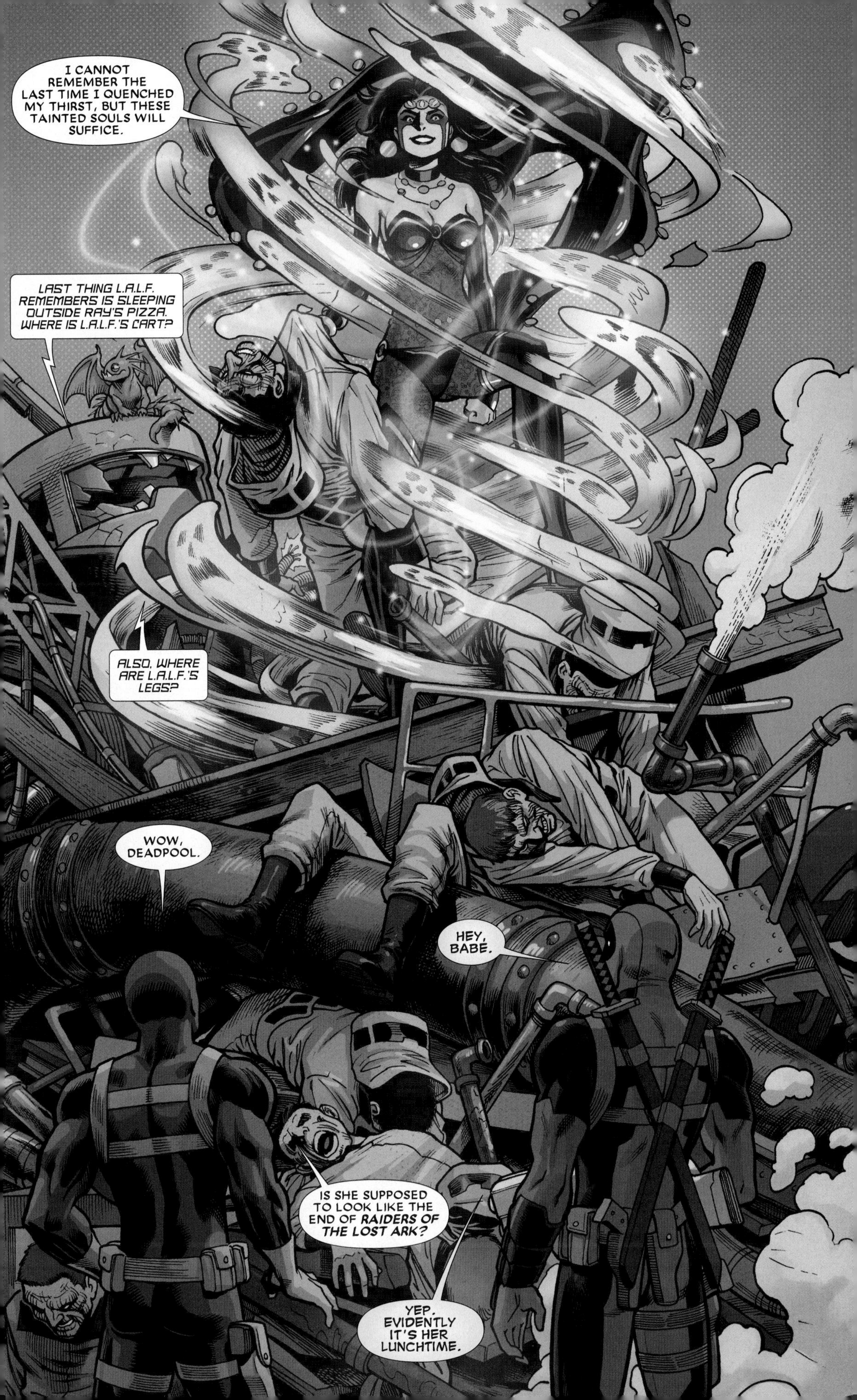
I CANNOT REMEMBER THE LAST TIME I QUENCHED MY THIRST, BUT THESE TAINTED SOULS WILL SUFFICE.
LAST THING L.A.L.F. REMEMBERS IS SLEEPING OUTSIDE RAY'S PIZZA. WHERE IS L.A.L.F.'S CART?
ALSO, WHERE ARE L.A.L.F.'S LEGS?
WOW, DEADPOOL.
HEY, BABE.
IS SHE SUPPOSED TO LOOK LIKE THE END OF RAIDERS OF THE LOST ARK?
YEP, EVIDENTLY IT'S HER LUNCHTIME.

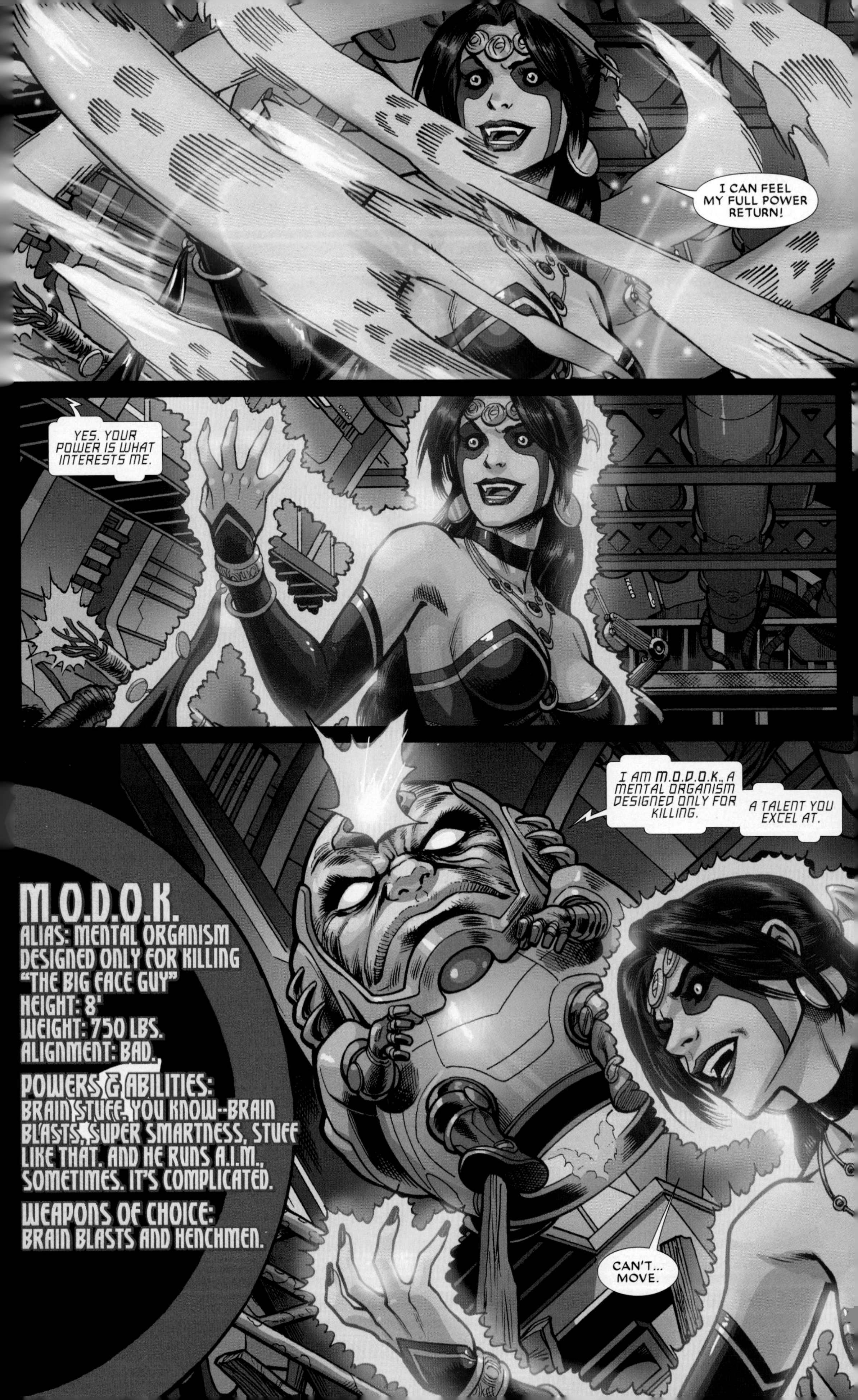
I CAN FEEL MY FULL POWER RETURN!
YES. YOUR POWER IS WHAT INTERESTS ME.
I AM M.O.D.O.K.. A MENTAL ORGANISM DESIGNED ONLY FOR KILLING.
A TALENT YOU EXCEL AT.
M.O.D.O.K.
ALIAS: MENTAL ORGANISM DESIGNED ONLY FOR KILLING "THE BIG FACE GUY"
HEIGHT: 8'
WEIGHT: 750 LBS.
ALIGNMENT: BAD.
POWERS & ABILITIES:
BRAIN STUFF. YOU KNOW--BRAIN BLASTS, SUPER SMARTNESS, STUFF LIKE THAT. AND HE RUNS A.I.M., SOMETIMES. IT'S COMPLICATED.
WEAPONS OF CHOICE:
BRAIN BLASTS AND HENCHMEN.
CAN'T... MOVE.

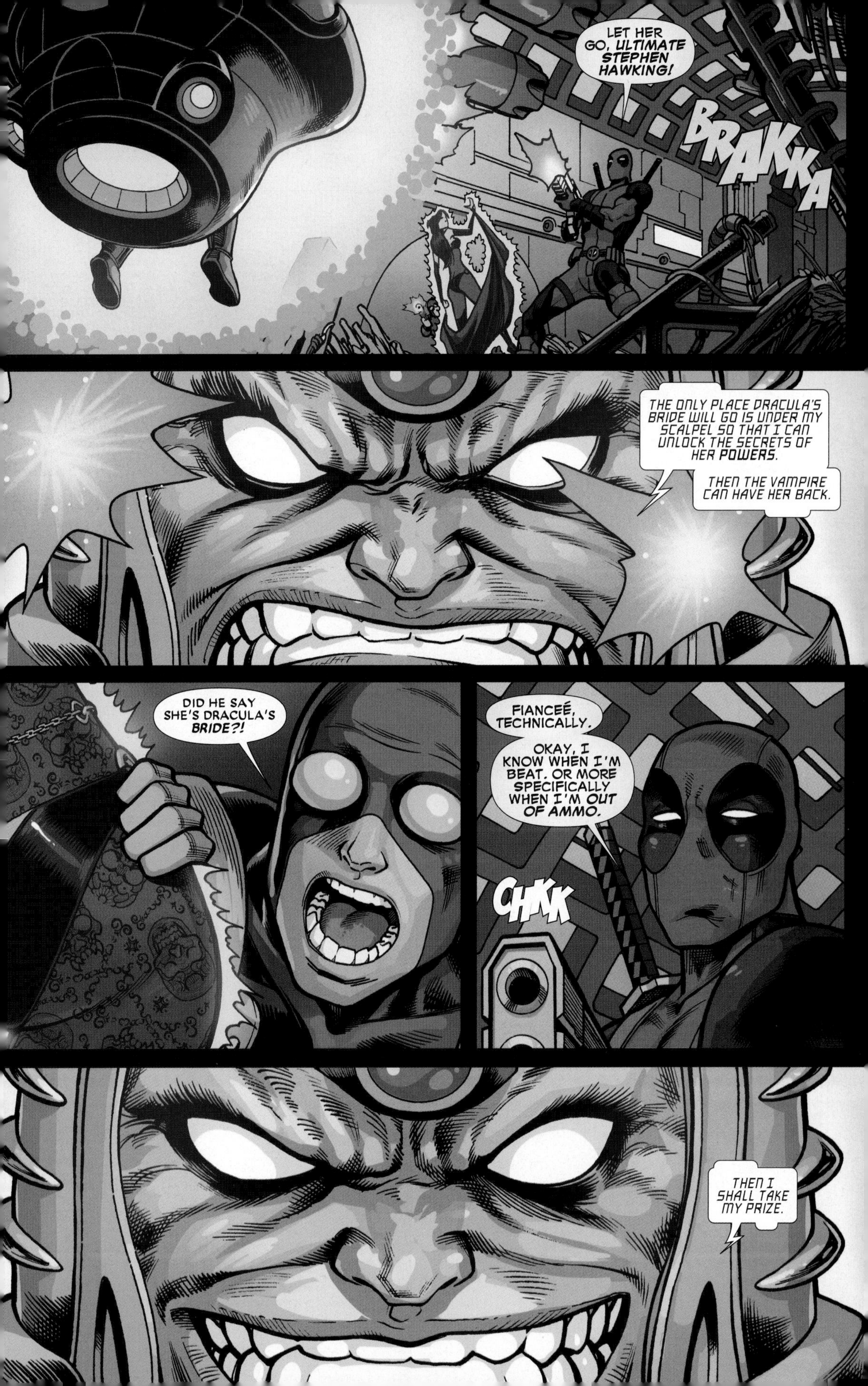
LET HER GO, ULTIMATE STEPHEN HAWKING!
BRAKKA
THE ONLY PLACE DRACULA'S BRIDE WILL GO IS UNDER MY SCALPEL SO THAT I CAN UNLOCK THE SECRETS OF HER POWERS.
THEN THE VAMPIRE CAN HAVE HER BACK.
DID HE SAY SHE'S DRACULA'S BRIDE?!
FIANCEÉ, TECHNICALLY.
OKAY, I KNOW WHEN I'M BEAT. OR MORE SPECIFICALLY WHEN I'M OUT OF AMMO.
CHKK
THEN I SHALL TAKE MY PRIZE.

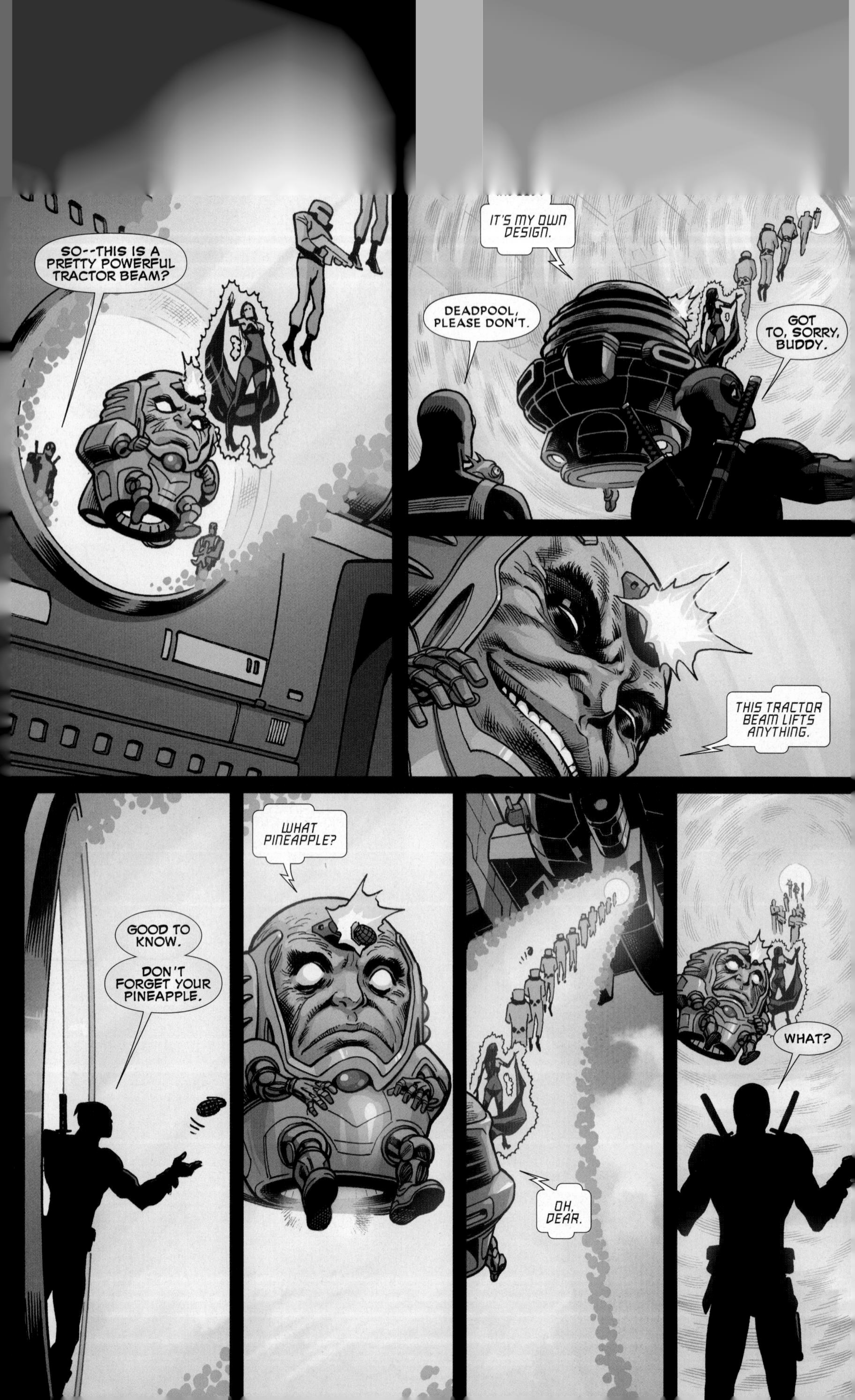

SO--THIS IS A PRETTY POWERFUL TRACTOR BEAM?
IT'S MY OWN DESIGN.
DEADPOOL, PLEASE DON'T.
GOT TO, SORRY, BUDDY.
THIS TRACTOR BEAM LIFTS ANYTHING.
GOOD TO KNOW.
DON'T FORGET YOUR PINEAPPLE.
WHAT PINEAPPLE?
OH, DEAR.
WHAT?

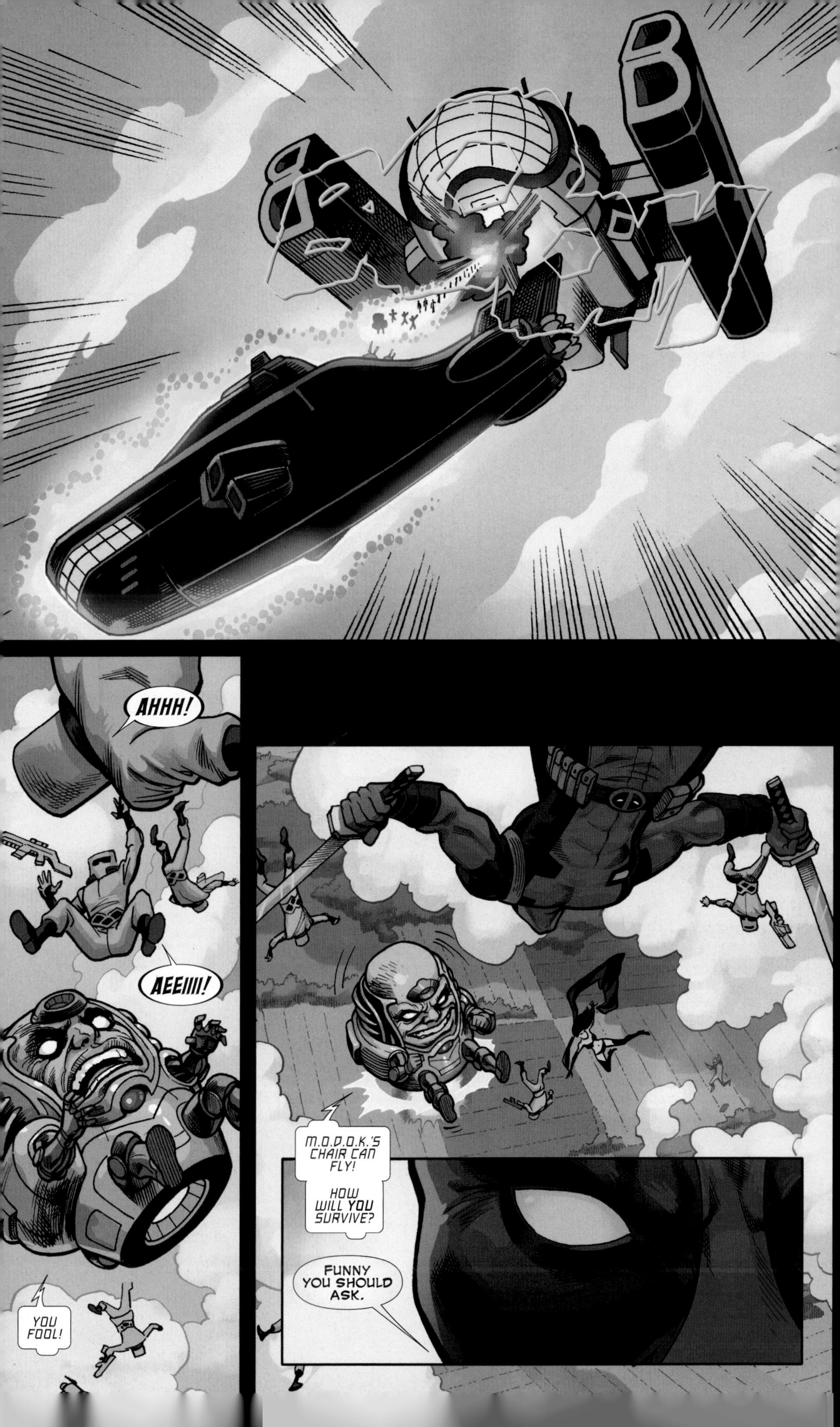
AHHH!
AEEIIII!
YOU FOOL!
M.O.D.O.K.'S CHAIR CAN FLY!
HOW WILL YOU SURVIVE?
FUNNY YOU SHOULD ASK.

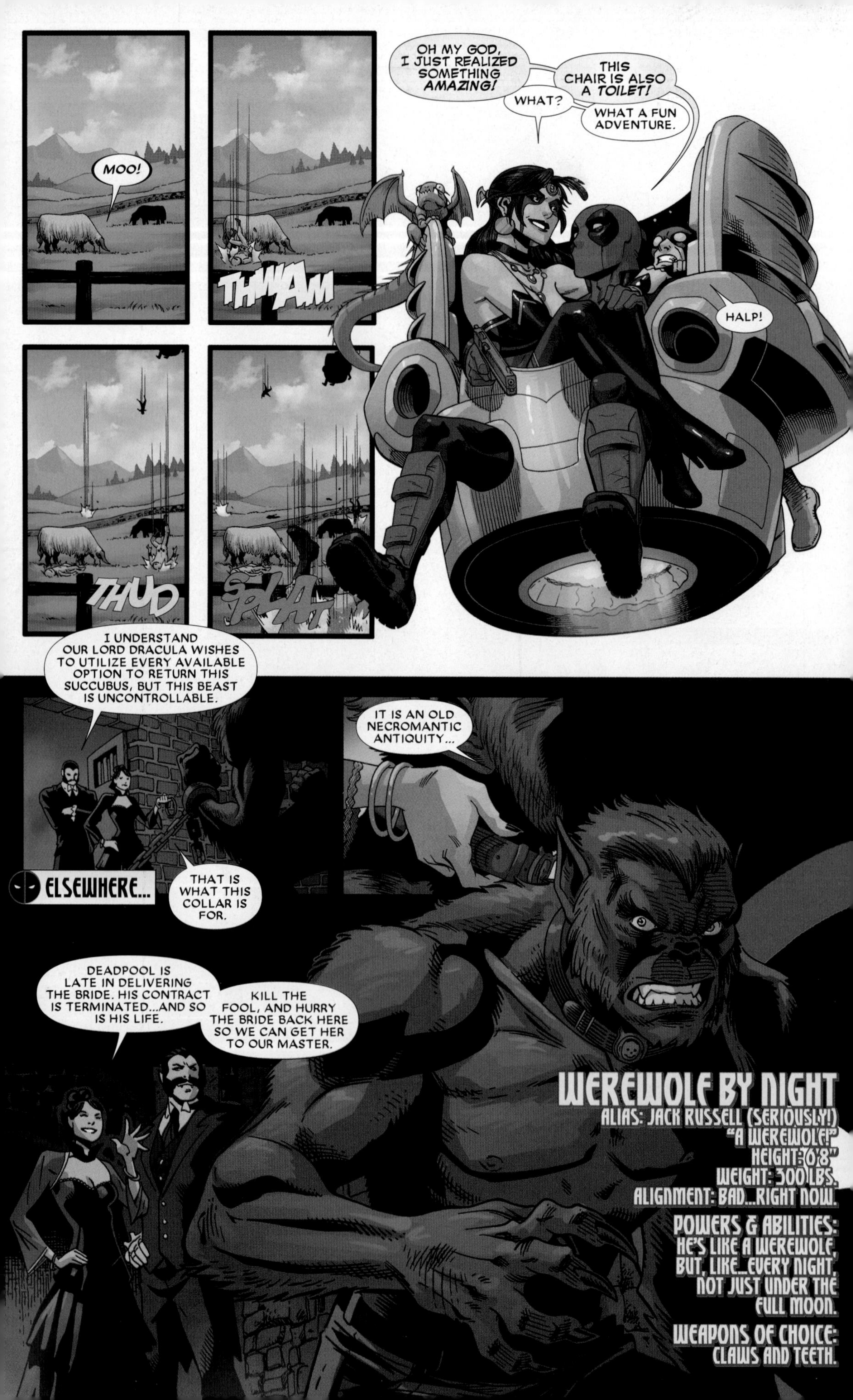
MOO!
THWAM
THUD
SPLAT
OH MY GOD, I JUST REALIZED SOMETHING AMAZING!
WHAT?
THIS CHAIR IS ALSO A TOILET!
WHAT A FUN ADVENTURE.
HALP!
I UNDERSTAND OUR LORD DRACULA WISHES TO UTILIZE EVERY AVAILABLE OPTION TO RETURN THIS SUCCUBUS, BUT THIS BEAST IS UNCONTROLLABLE.
IT IS AN OLD NECROMANTIC ANTIQUITY...
ELSEWHERE...
THAT IS WHAT THIS COLLAR IS FOR.
DEADPOOL IS LATE IN DELIVERING THE BRIDE. HIS CONTRACT IS TERMINATED...AND SO IS HIS LIFE.
KILL THE FOOL, AND HURRY THE BRIDE BACK HERE SO WE CAN GET HER TO OUR MASTER.
WEREWOLF BY NIGHT
ALIAS: JACK RUSSELL (SERIOUSLY!)
"A WEREWOLF"
HEIGHT: 6'8"
WEIGHT: 300 LBS.
ALIGNMENT: BAD...RIGHT NOW.
POWERS & ABILITIES: HE'S LIKE A WEREWOLF, BUT, LIKE...EVERY NIGHT, NOT JUST UNDER THE FULL MOON.
WEAPONS OF CHOICE: CLAWS AND TEETH.

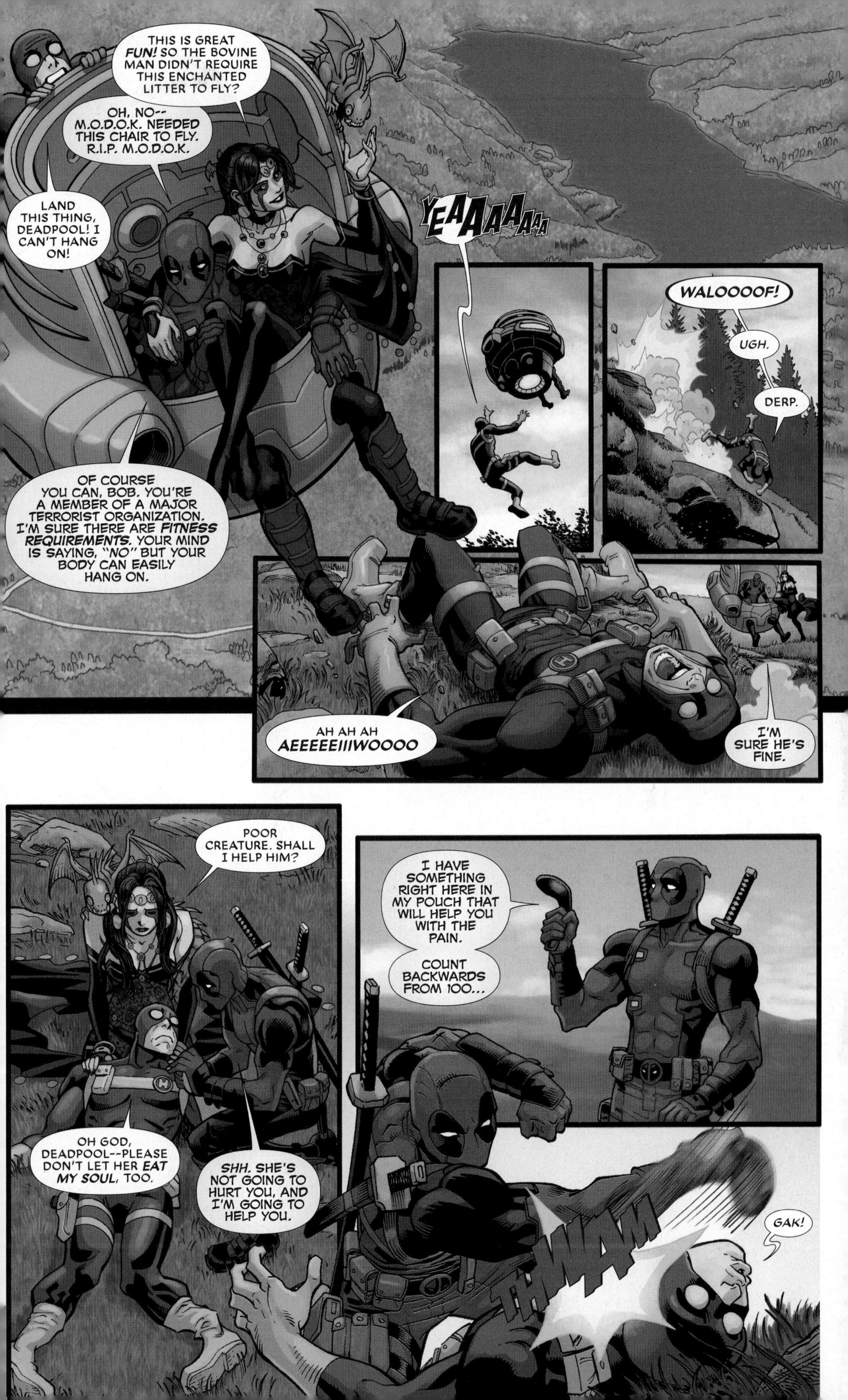
THIS IS GREAT FUN! SO THE BOVINE MAN DIDN'T REQUIRE THIS ENCHANTED LITTER TO FLY?
OH, NO-- M.O.D.O.K. NEEDED THIS CHAIR TO FLY. R.I.P. M.O.D.O.K.
LAND THIS THING, DEADPOOL! I CAN'T HANG ON!
OF COURSE YOU CAN, BOB. YOU'RE A MEMBER OF A MAJOR TERRORIST ORGANIZATION. I'M SURE THERE ARE FITNESS REQUIREMENTS. YOUR MIND IS SAYING, "NO" BUT YOUR BODY CAN EASILY HANG ON.
YEAAAAAAA
WALOOOOF!
UGH.
DERP.
AH AH AH AEEEEEIIIWOOOO
I'M SURE HE'S FINE.
POOR CREATURE. SHALL I HELP HIM?
OH GOD, DEADPOOL--PLEASE DON'T LET HER EAT MY SOUL, TOO.
SHH. SHE'S NOT GOING TO HURT YOU, AND I'M GOING TO HELP YOU.
I HAVE SOMETHING RIGHT HERE IN MY POUCH THAT WILL HELP YOU WITH THE PAIN.
COUNT BACKWARDS FROM 100...
THWAM
GAK!

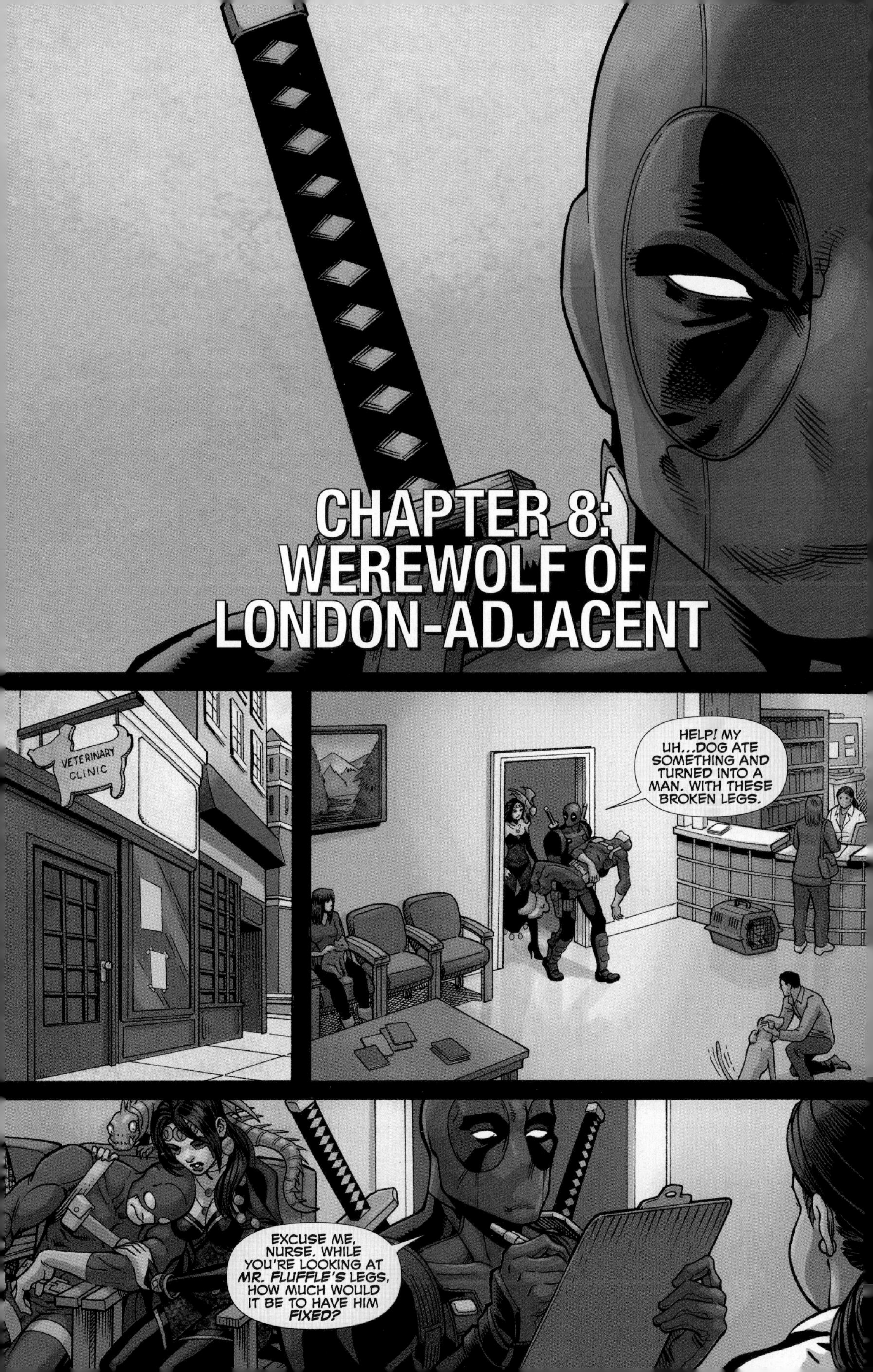
CHAPTER 8:
WEREWOLF OF
LONDON-ADJACENT
VETERINARY CLINIC
HELP! MY UH...DOG ATE SOMETHING AND TURNED INTO A MAN. WITH THESE BROKEN LEGS.
EXCUSE ME, NURSE. WHILE YOU'RE LOOKING AT MR. FLUFFLE'S LEGS, HOW MUCH WOULD IT BE TO HAVE HIM FIXED?

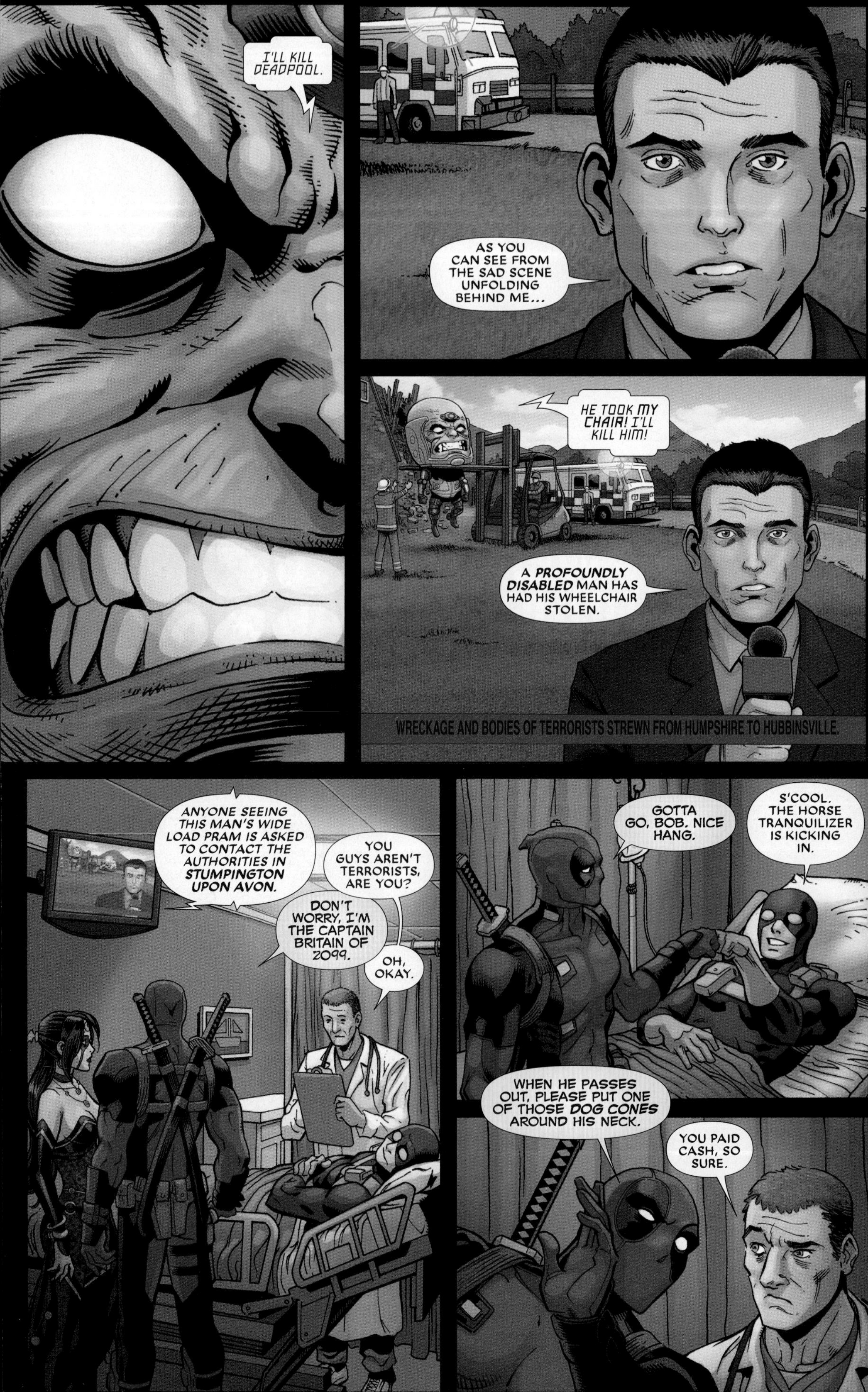
I'LL KILL DEADPOOL.
AS YOU CAN SEE FROM THE SAD SCENE UNFOLDING BEHIND ME...
HE TOOK MY CHAIR! I'LL KILL HIM!
A PROFOUNDLY DISABLED MAN HAS HAD HIS WHEELCHAIR STOLEN.
WRECKAGE AND BODIES OF TERRORISTS STREWN FROM HUMPSHIRE TO HUBBINSVILLE.
ANYONE SEEING THIS MAN'S WIDE LOAD PRAM IS ASKED TO CONTACT THE AUTHORITIES IN STUMPINGTON UPON AVON.
YOU GUYS AREN'T TERRORISTS, ARE YOU?
DON'T WORRY, I'M THE CAPTAIN BRITAIN OF 2099.
OH, OKAY.
GOTTA GO, BOB. NICE HANG.
S'COOL. THE HORSE TRANQUILIZER IS KICKING IN.
WHEN HE PASSES OUT, PLEASE PUT ONE OF THOSE DOG CONES AROUND HIS NECK.
YOU PAID CASH, SO SURE.

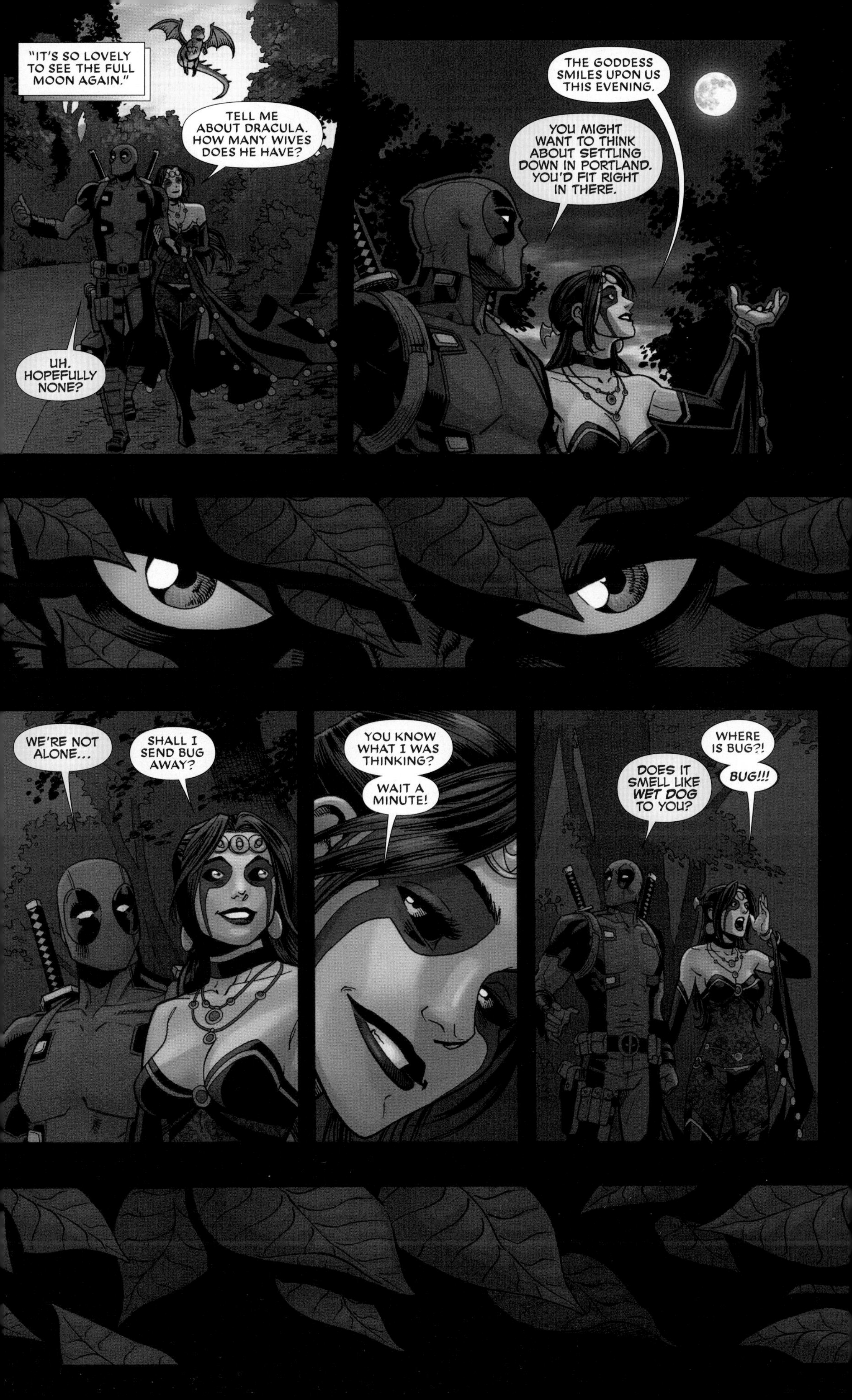
"IT'S SO LOVELY TO SEE THE FULL MOON AGAIN."
TELL ME ABOUT DRACULA. HOW MANY WIVES DOES HE HAVE?
UH. HOPEFULLY NONE?
THE GODDESS SMILES UPON US THIS EVENING.
YOU MIGHT WANT TO THINK ABOUT SETTLING DOWN IN PORTLAND. YOU'D FIT RIGHT IN THERE.
WE'RE NOT ALONE...
SHALL I SEND BUG AWAY?
YOU KNOW WHAT I WAS THINKING?
WAIT A MINUTE!
DOES IT SMELL LIKE WET DOG TO YOU?
WHERE IS BUG?!
BUG!!!

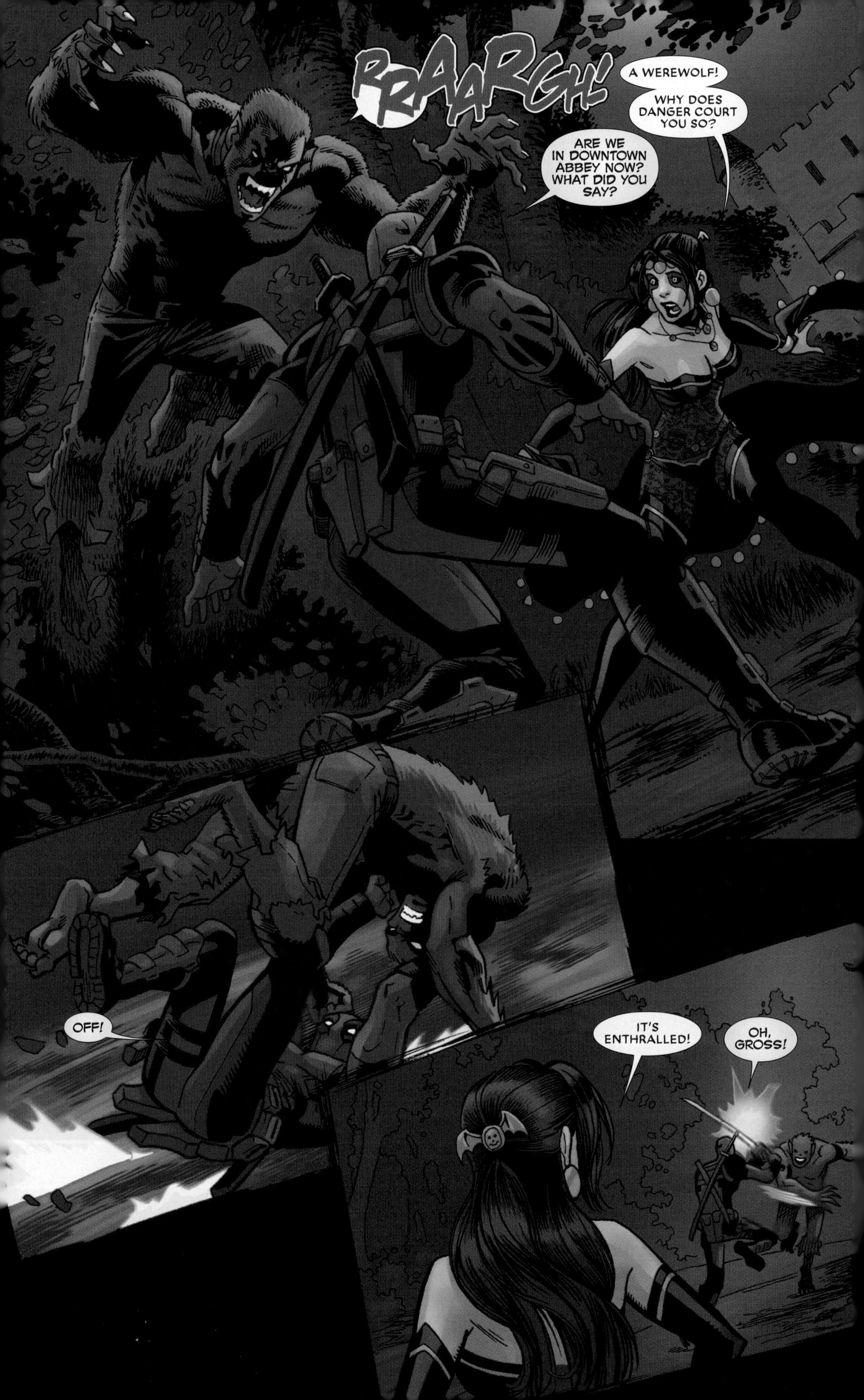
RRAARGH!
A WEREWOLF!
WHY DOES DANGER COURT YOU SO?
ARE WE IN DOWNTOWN ABBEY NOW? WHAT DID YOU SAY?
OFF!
IT'S ENTHRALLED!
OH, GROSS!

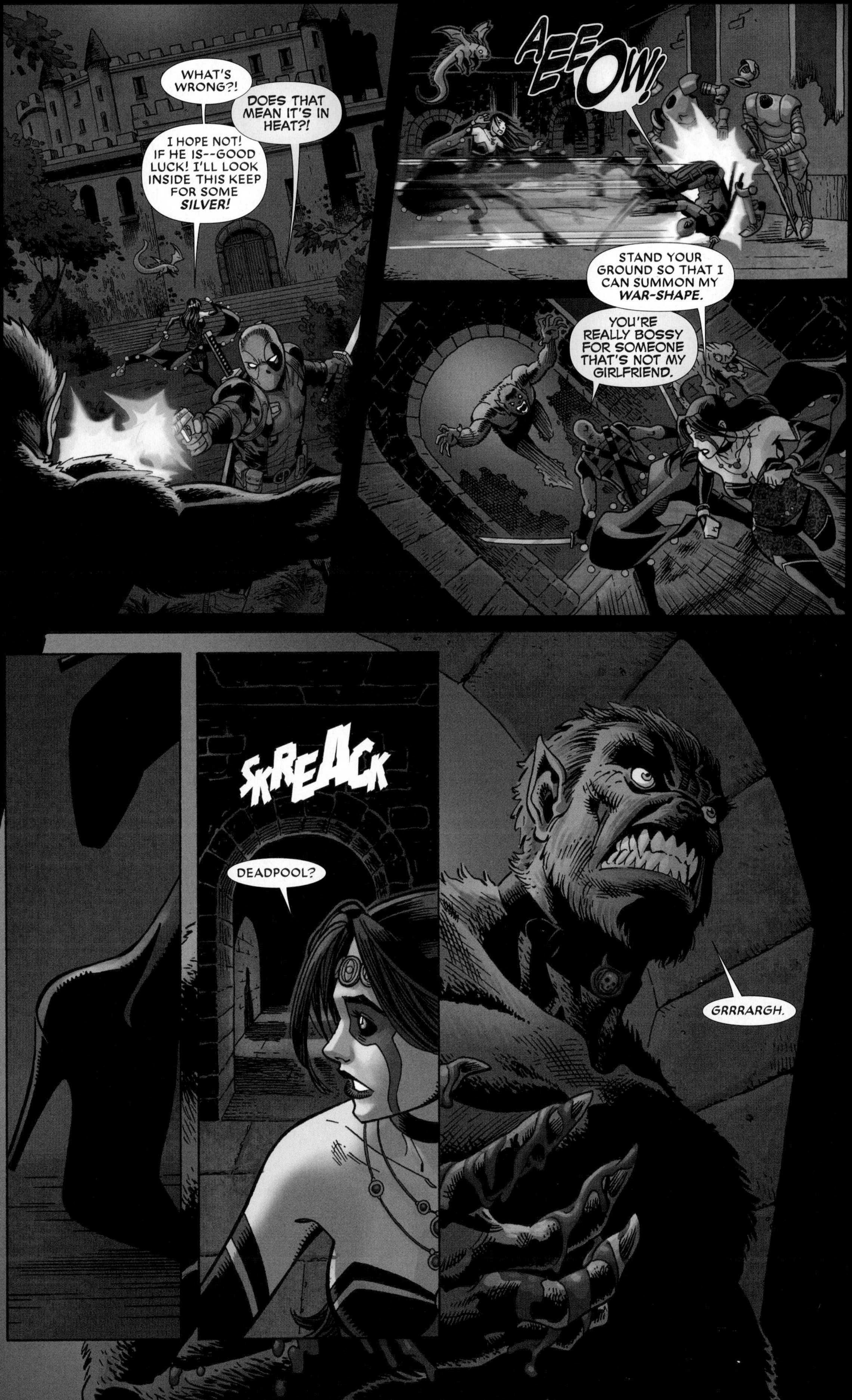

WHAT'S WRONG?!
DOES THAT MEAN IT'S IN HEAT?!
I HOPE NOT! IF HE IS--GOOD LUCK! I'LL LOOK INSIDE THIS KEEP FOR SOME SILVER!
AEEEOW!
STAND YOUR GROUND SO THAT I CAN SUMMON MY WAR-SHAPE.
YOU'RE REALLY BOSSY FOR SOMEONE THAT'S NOT MY GIRLFRIEND.
SKREACK
DEADPOOL?
GRRRARGH.

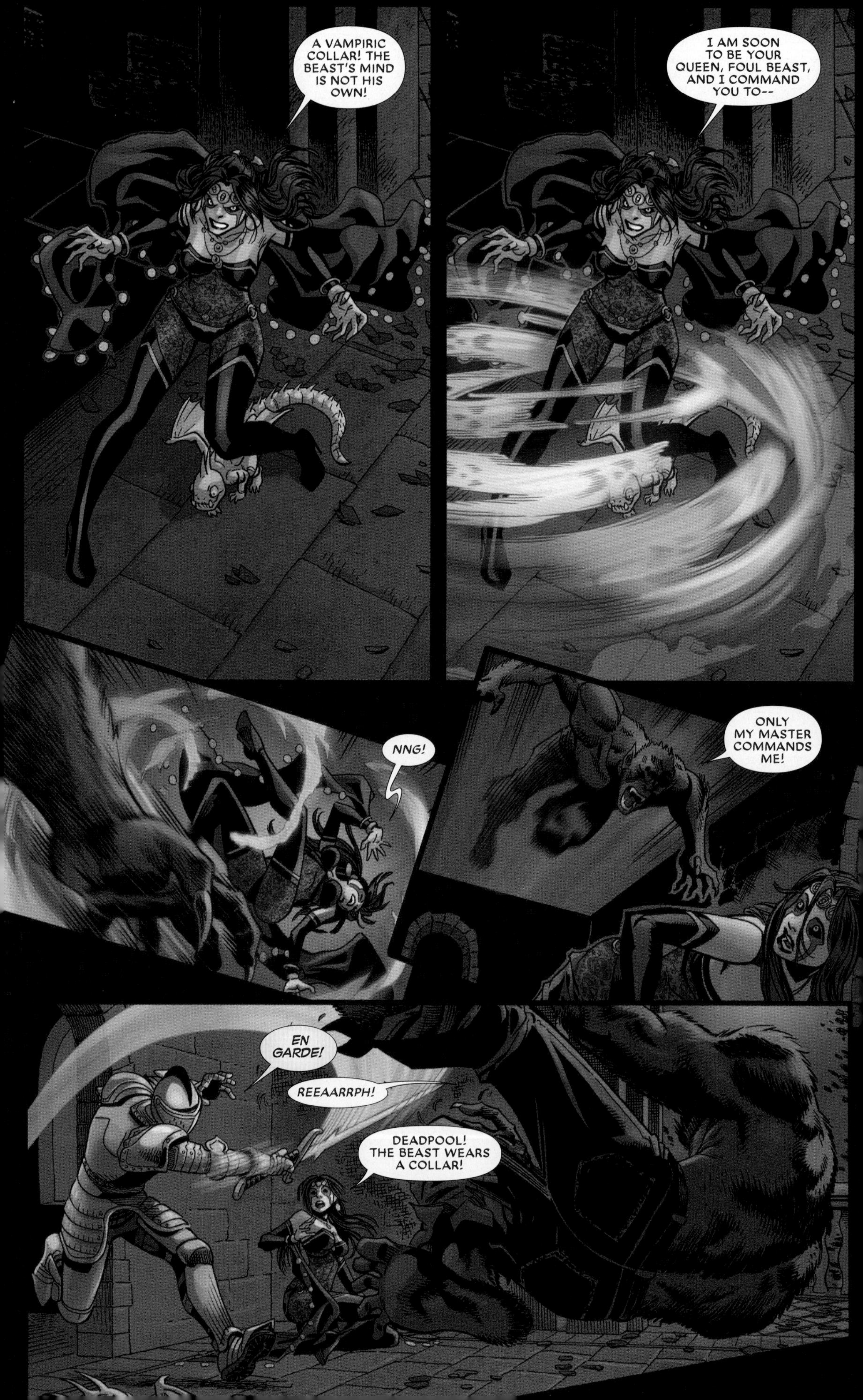
A VAMPIRIC COLLAR! THE BEAST'S MIND IS NOT HIS OWN!
I AM SOON TO BE YOUR QUEEN, FOUL BEAST, AND I COMMAND YOU TO--
NNG!
ONLY MY MASTER COMMANDS ME!
EN GARDE!
REEEAARRPH!
DEADPOOL! THE BEAST WEARS A COLLAR!

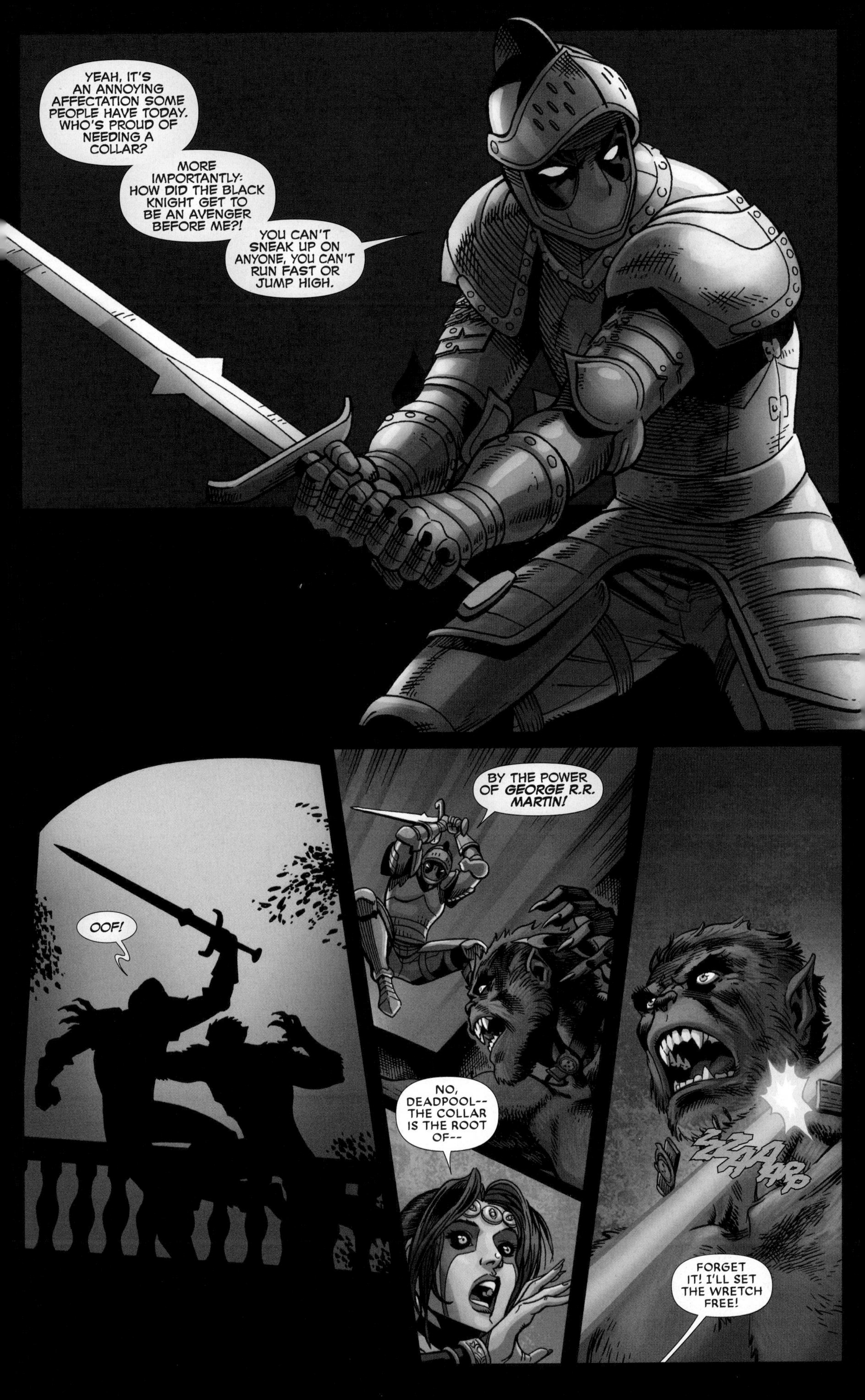
YEAH, IT'S AN ANNOYING AFFECTATION SOME PEOPLE HAVE TODAY. WHO'S PROUD OF NEEDING A COLLAR?
MORE IMPORTANTLY: HOW DID THE BLACK KNIGHT GET TO BE AN AVENGER BEFORE ME?!
YOU CAN'T SNEAK UP ON ANYONE, YOU CAN'T RUN FAST OR JUMP HIGH.
OOF!
BY THE POWER OF GEORGE R.R. MARTIN!
NO, DEADPOOL-- THE COLLAR IS THE ROOT OF--
ZZAARP
FORGET IT! I'LL SET THE WRETCH FREE!

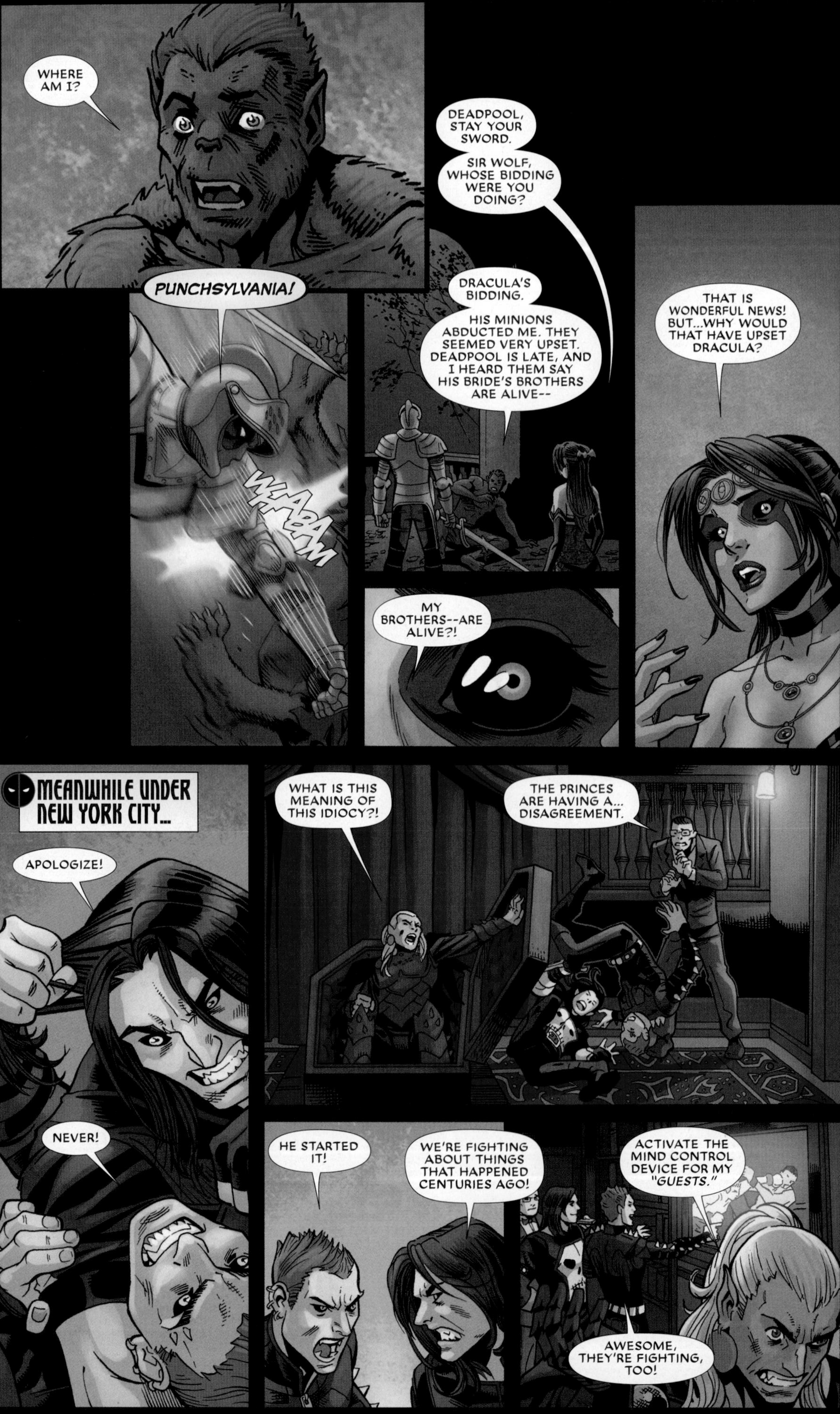
WHERE AM I?
DEADPOOL, STAY YOUR SWORD.
SIR WOLF, WHOSE BIDDING WERE YOU DOING?
PUNCHSYLVANIA!
WHABAM
DRACULA'S BIDDING.
HIS MINIONS ABDUCTED ME. THEY SEEMED VERY UPSET. DEADPOOL IS LATE, AND I HEARD THEM SAY HIS BRIDE'S BROTHERS ARE ALIVE--
THAT IS WONDERFUL NEWS! BUT...WHY WOULD THAT HAVE UPSET DRACULA?
MY BROTHERS--ARE ALIVE?!
MEANWHILE UNDER NEW YORK CITY...
APOLOGIZE!
NEVER!
WHAT IS THIS MEANING OF THIS IDIOCY?!
THE PRINCES ARE HAVING A... DISAGREEMENT.
HE STARTED IT!
WE'RE FIGHTING ABOUT THINGS THAT HAPPENED CENTURIES AGO!
ACTIVATE THE MIND CONTROL DEVICE FOR MY "GUESTS."
AWESOME, THEY'RE FIGHTING, TOO!

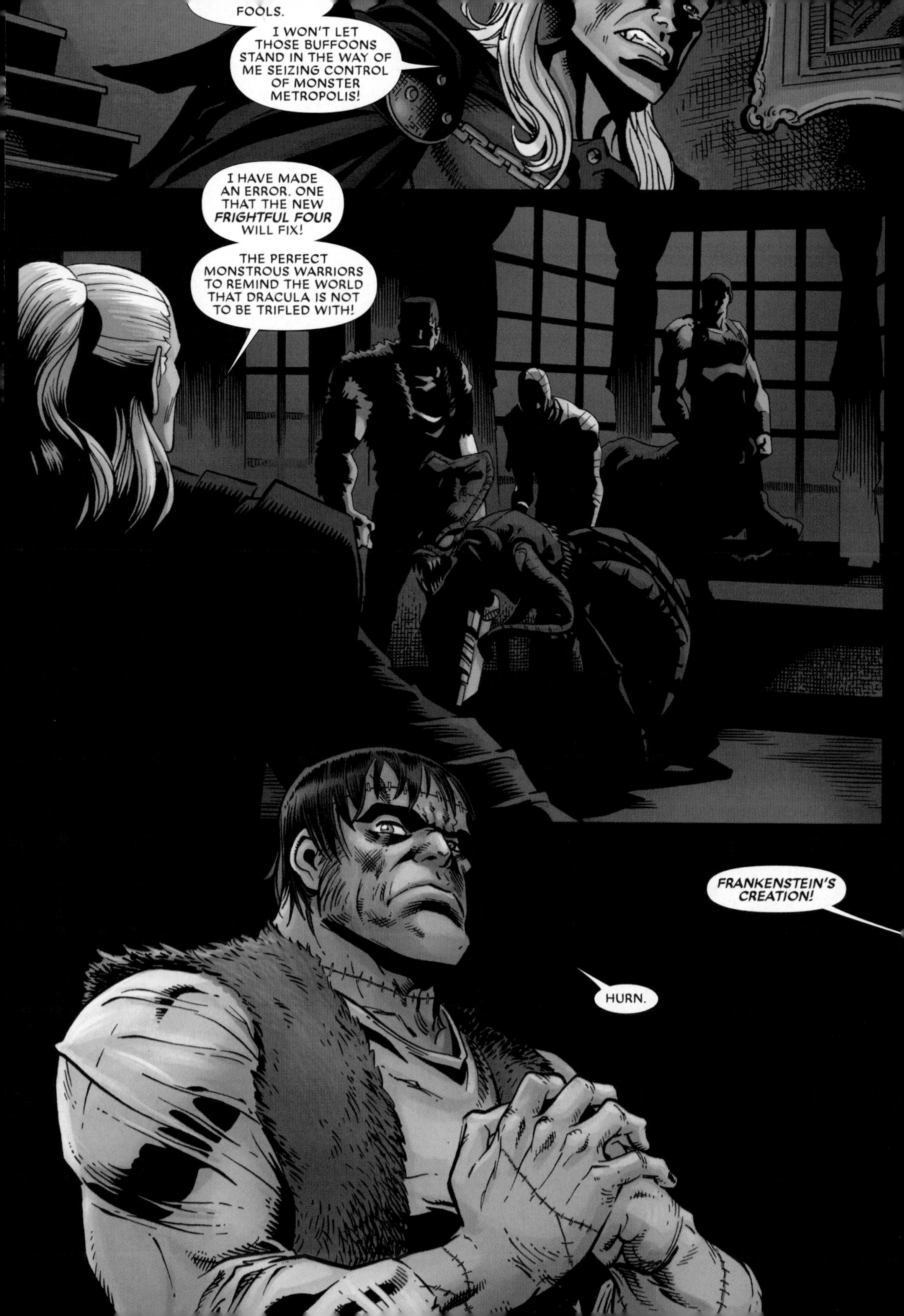
FOOLS.
I WON'T LET THOSE BUFFOONS STAND IN THE WAY OF ME SEIZING CONTROL OF MONSTER METROPOLIS!
I HAVE MADE AN ERROR. ONE THAT THE NEW *FRIGHTFUL FOUR* WILL FIX!
THE PERFECT MONSTROUS WARRIORS TO REMIND THE WORLD THAT DRACULA IS NOT TO BE TRIFLED WITH!
FRANKENSTEIN'S CREATION!
HURN.

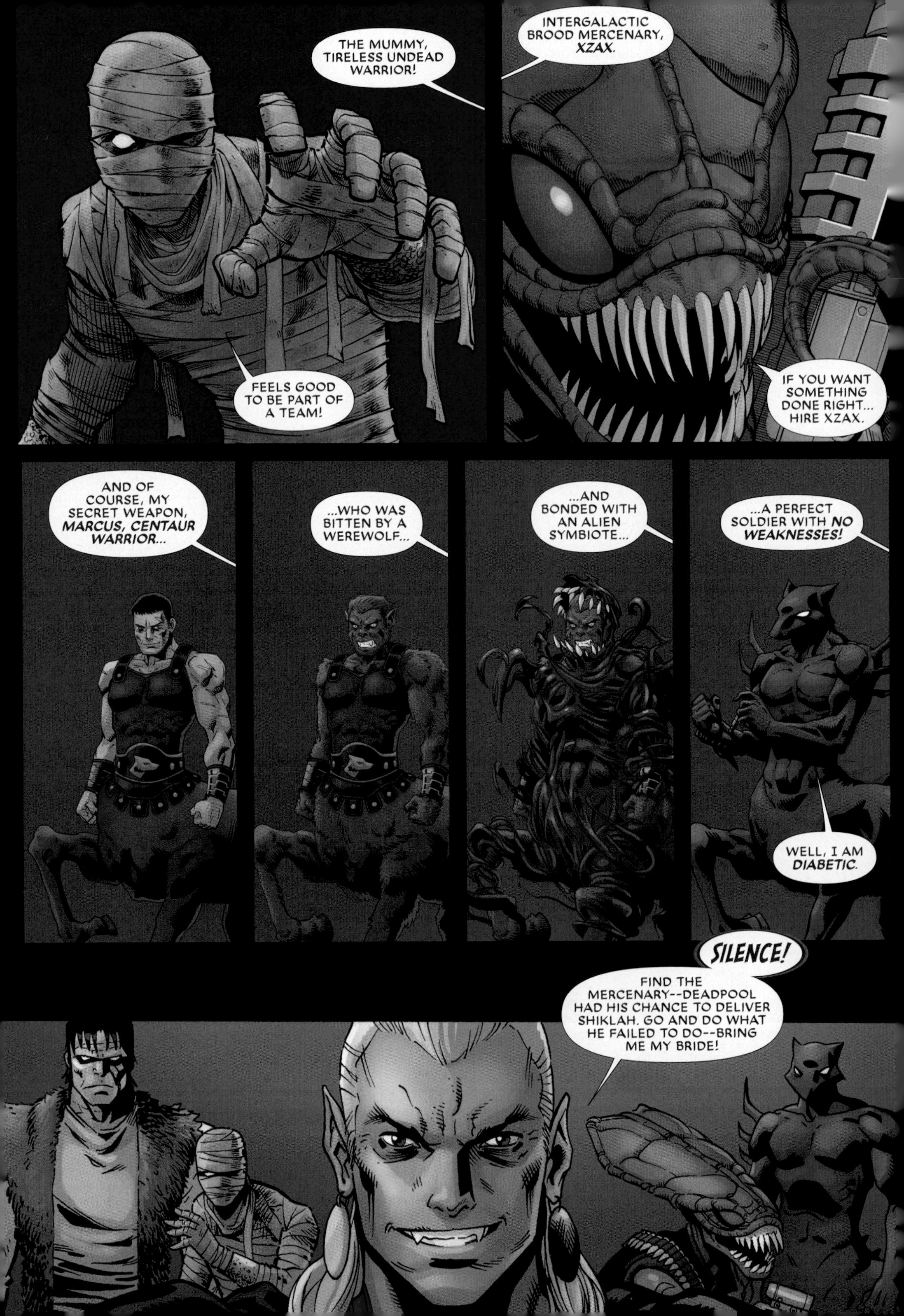
THE MUMMY, TIRELESS UNDEAD WARRIOR!
FEELS GOOD TO BE PART OF A TEAM!
INTERGALACTIC BROOD MERCENARY, XZAX.
IF YOU WANT SOMETHING DONE RIGHT... HIRE XZAX.
AND OF COURSE, MY SECRET WEAPON, MARCUS, CENTAUR WARRIOR...
...WHO WAS BITTEN BY A WEREWOLF...
...AND BONDED WITH AN ALIEN SYMBIOTE...
...A PERFECT SOLDIER WITH NO WEAKNESSES!
WELL, I AM DIABETIC.
SILENCE!
FIND THE MERCENARY--DEADPOOL HAD HIS CHANCE TO DELIVER SHIKLAH. GO AND DO WHAT HE FAILED TO DO--BRING ME MY BRIDE!

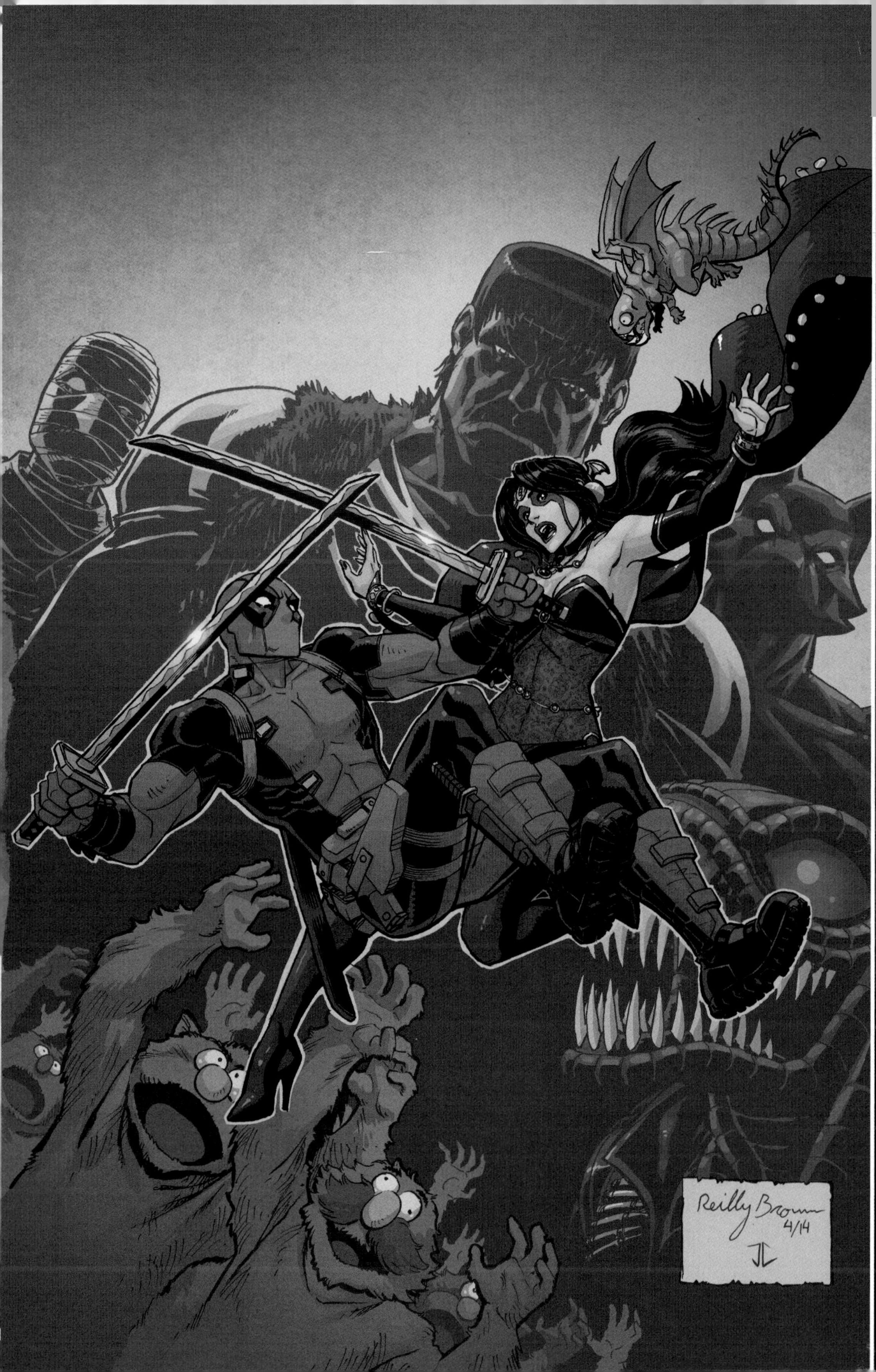
Reilly Brown
4/14
JL

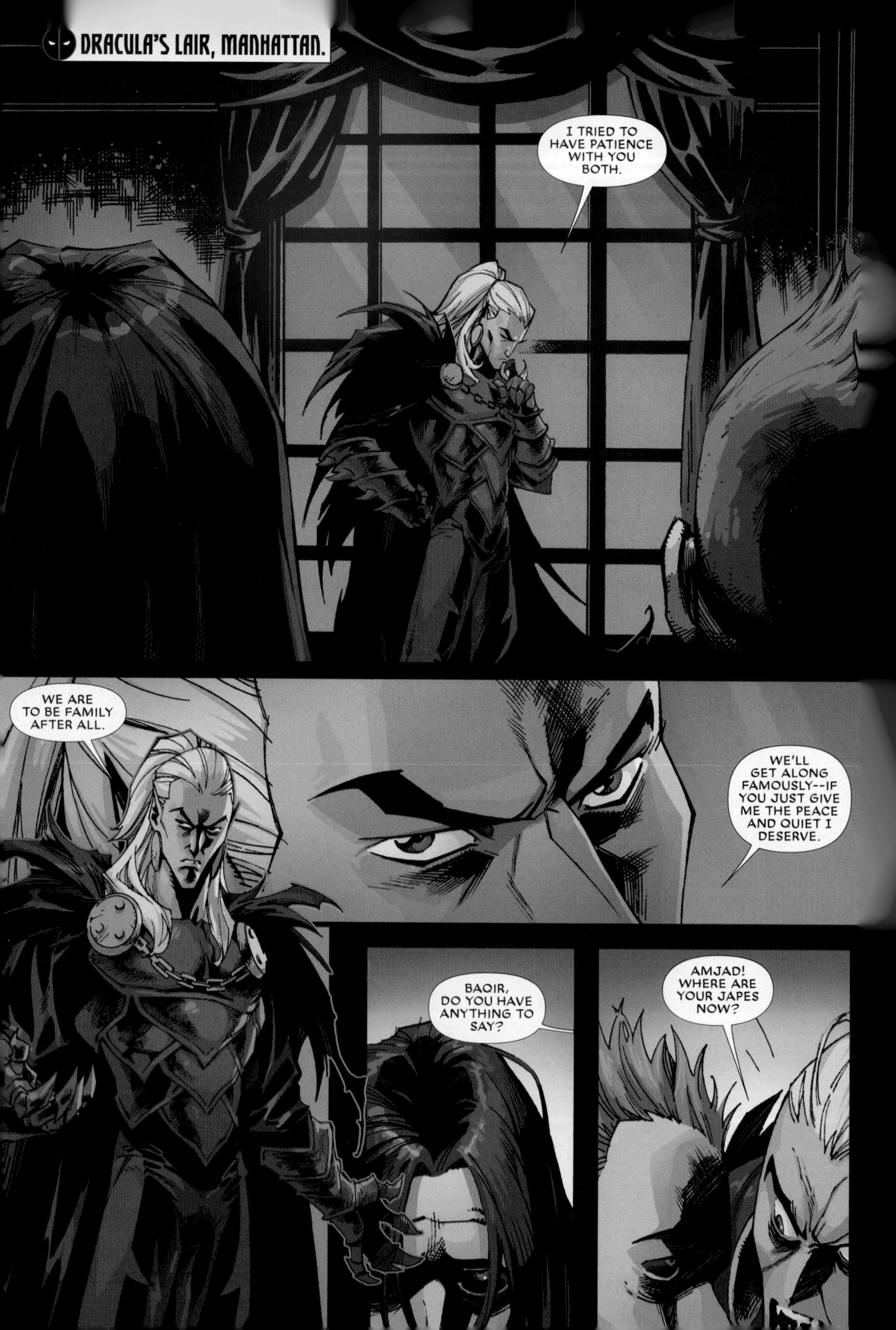
DRACULA'S LAIR, MANHATTAN.
I TRIED TO HAVE PATIENCE WITH YOU BOTH.
WE ARE TO BE FAMILY AFTER ALL.
WE'LL GET ALONG FAMOUSLY--IF YOU JUST GIVE ME THE PEACE AND QUIET I DESERVE.
BAQIR, DO YOU HAVE ANYTHING TO SAY?
AMJAD! WHERE ARE YOUR JAPES NOW?

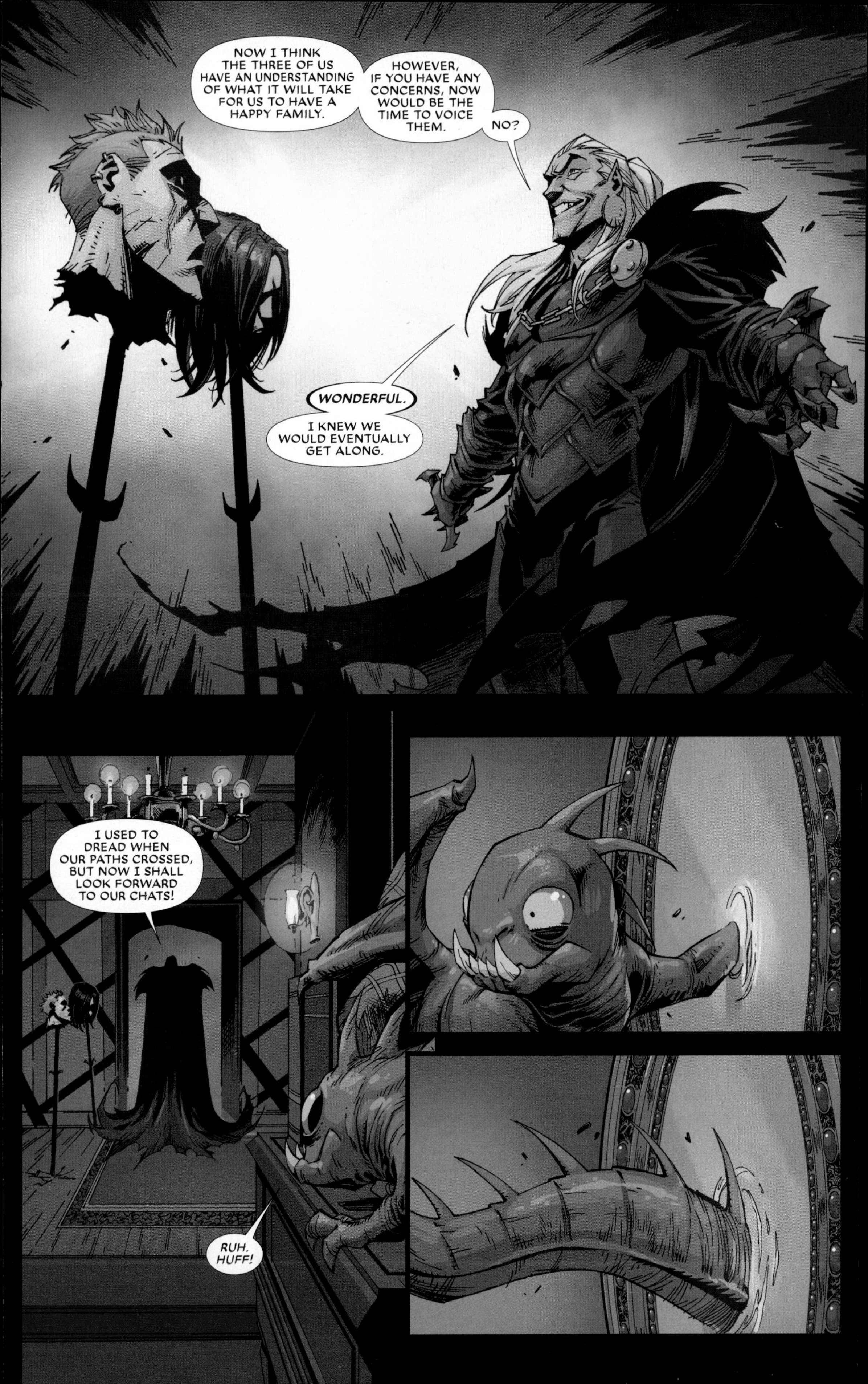
NOW I THINK THE THREE OF US HAVE AN UNDERSTANDING OF WHAT IT WILL TAKE FOR US TO HAVE A HAPPY FAMILY.
HOWEVER, IF YOU HAVE ANY CONCERNS, NOW WOULD BE THE TIME TO VOICE THEM.
NO?
WONDERFUL.
I KNEW WE WOULD EVENTUALLY GET ALONG.
I USED TO DREAD WHEN OUR PATHS CROSSED, BUT NOW I SHALL LOOK FORWARD TO OUR CHATS!
RUH. HUFF!

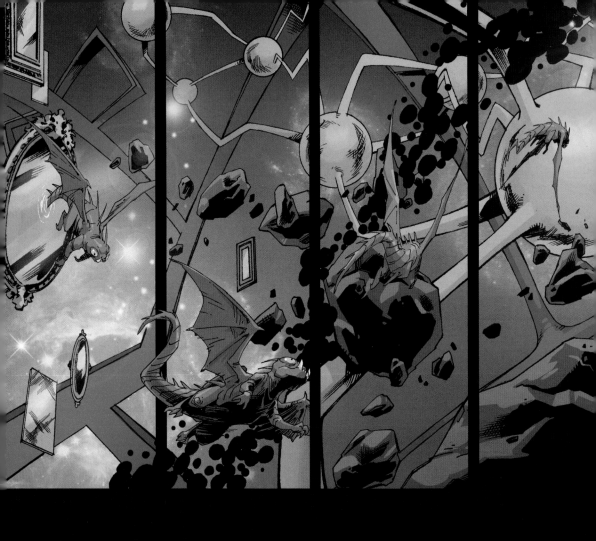

DEADPOOL
The Gauntlet
CHAPTER 9: GANGS OF NEW YORK

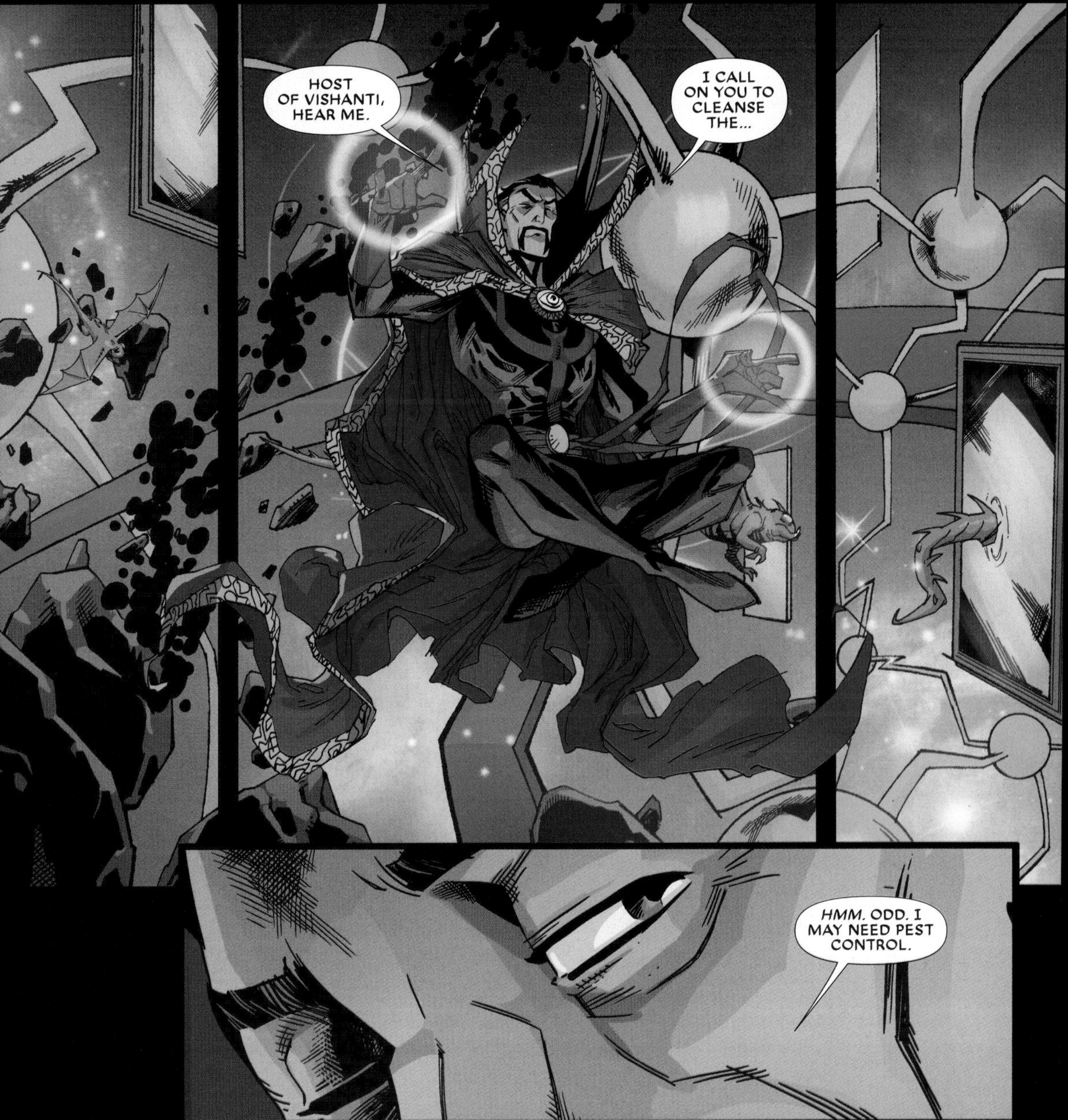
HOST OF VISHANTI, HEAR ME.
I CALL ON YOU TO CLEANSE THE...
HMM. ODD. I MAY NEED PEST CONTROL.

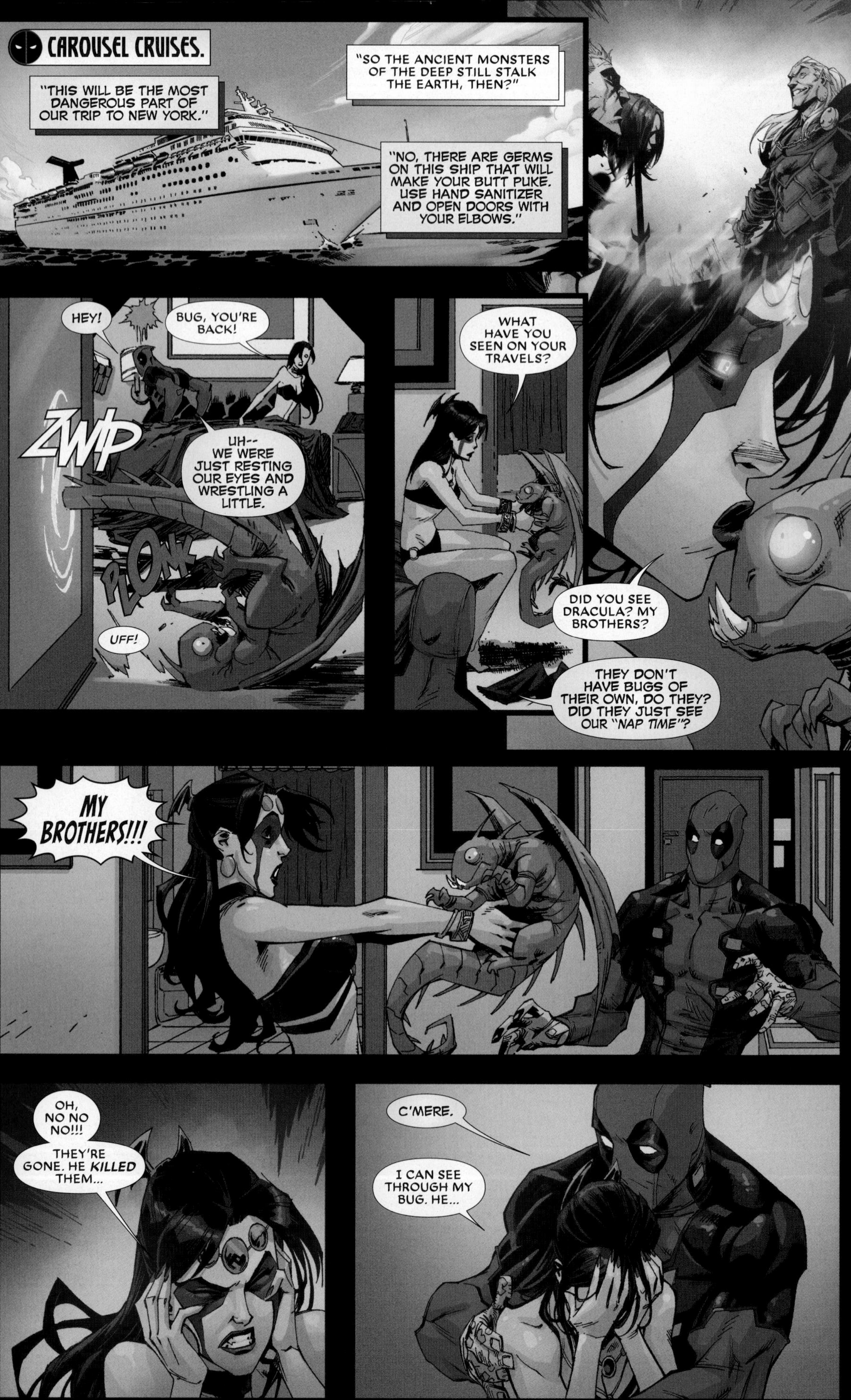
CAROUSEL CRUISES.
"THIS WILL BE THE MOST DANGEROUS PART OF OUR TRIP TO NEW YORK."
"SO THE ANCIENT MONSTERS OF THE DEEP STILL STALK THE EARTH, THEN?"
"NO, THERE ARE GERMS ON THIS SHIP THAT WILL MAKE YOUR BUTT PUKE. USE HAND SANITIZER AND OPEN DOORS WITH YOUR ELBOWS."
HEY!
BUG, YOU'RE BACK!
ZWIP
UH-- WE WERE JUST RESTING OUR EYES AND WRESTLING A LITTLE.
PLONK
UFF!
WHAT HAVE YOU SEEN ON YOUR TRAVELS?
DID YOU SEE DRACULA? MY BROTHERS?
THEY DON'T HAVE BUGS OF THEIR OWN, DO THEY? DID THEY JUST SEE OUR "NAP TIME"?
MY BROTHERS!!!
OH, NO NO NO!!! THEY'RE GONE. HE KILLED THEM...
C'MERE.
I CAN SEE THROUGH MY BUG. HE...

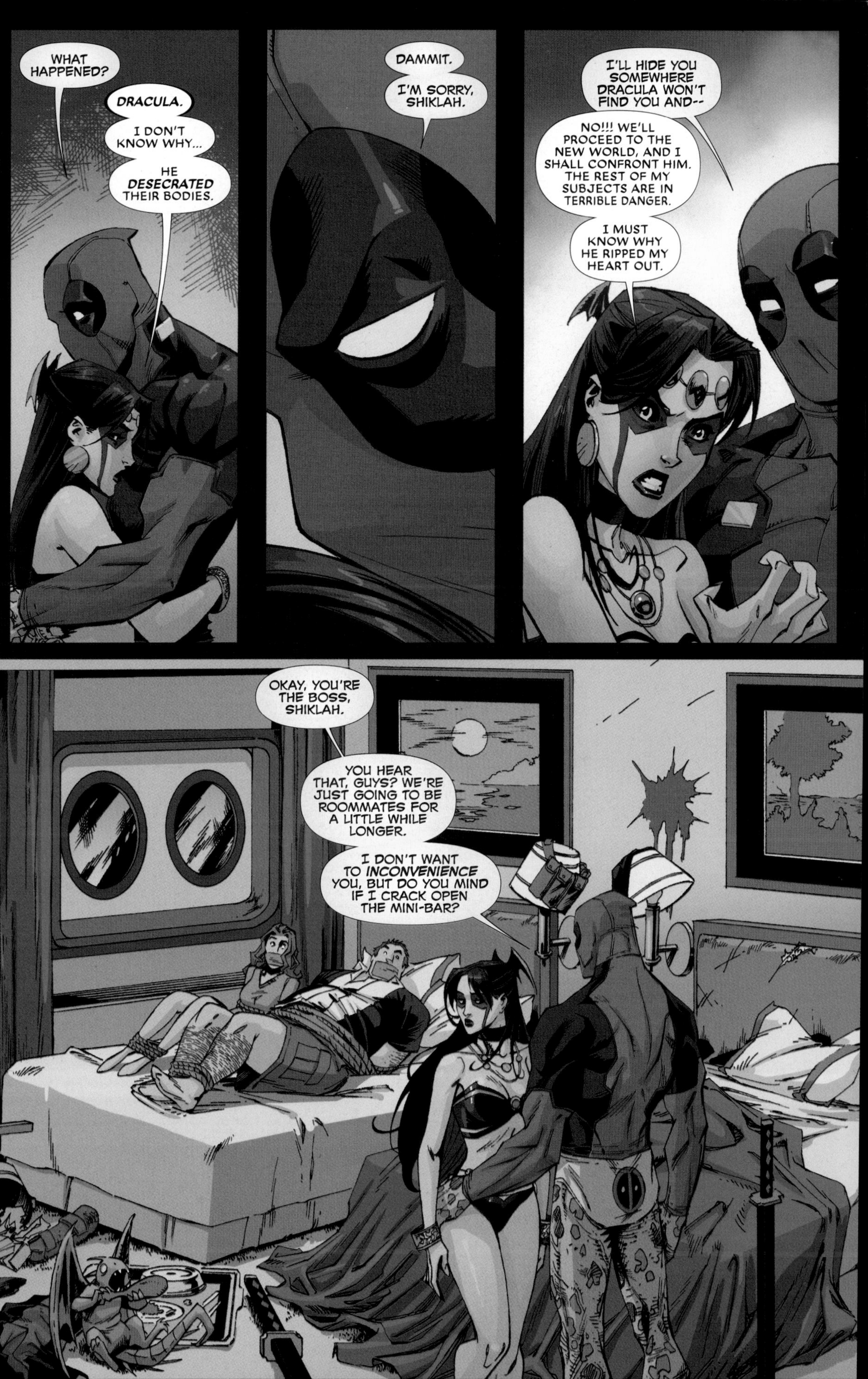

WHAT HAPPENED?
DRACULA.
I DON'T KNOW WHY...
HE DESECRATED THEIR BODIES.
DAMMIT.
I'M SORRY, SHIKLAH.
I'LL HIDE YOU SOMEWHERE DRACULA WON'T FIND YOU AND--
NO!!! WE'LL PROCEED TO THE NEW WORLD, AND I SHALL CONFRONT HIM. THE REST OF MY SUBJECTS ARE IN TERRIBLE DANGER.
I MUST KNOW WHY HE RIPPED MY HEART OUT.
OKAY, YOU'RE THE BOSS, SHIKLAH.
YOU HEAR THAT, GUYS? WE'RE JUST GOING TO BE ROOMMATES FOR A LITTLE WHILE LONGER.
I DON'T WANT TO INCONVENIENCE YOU, BUT DO YOU MIND IF I CRACK OPEN THE MINI-BAR?

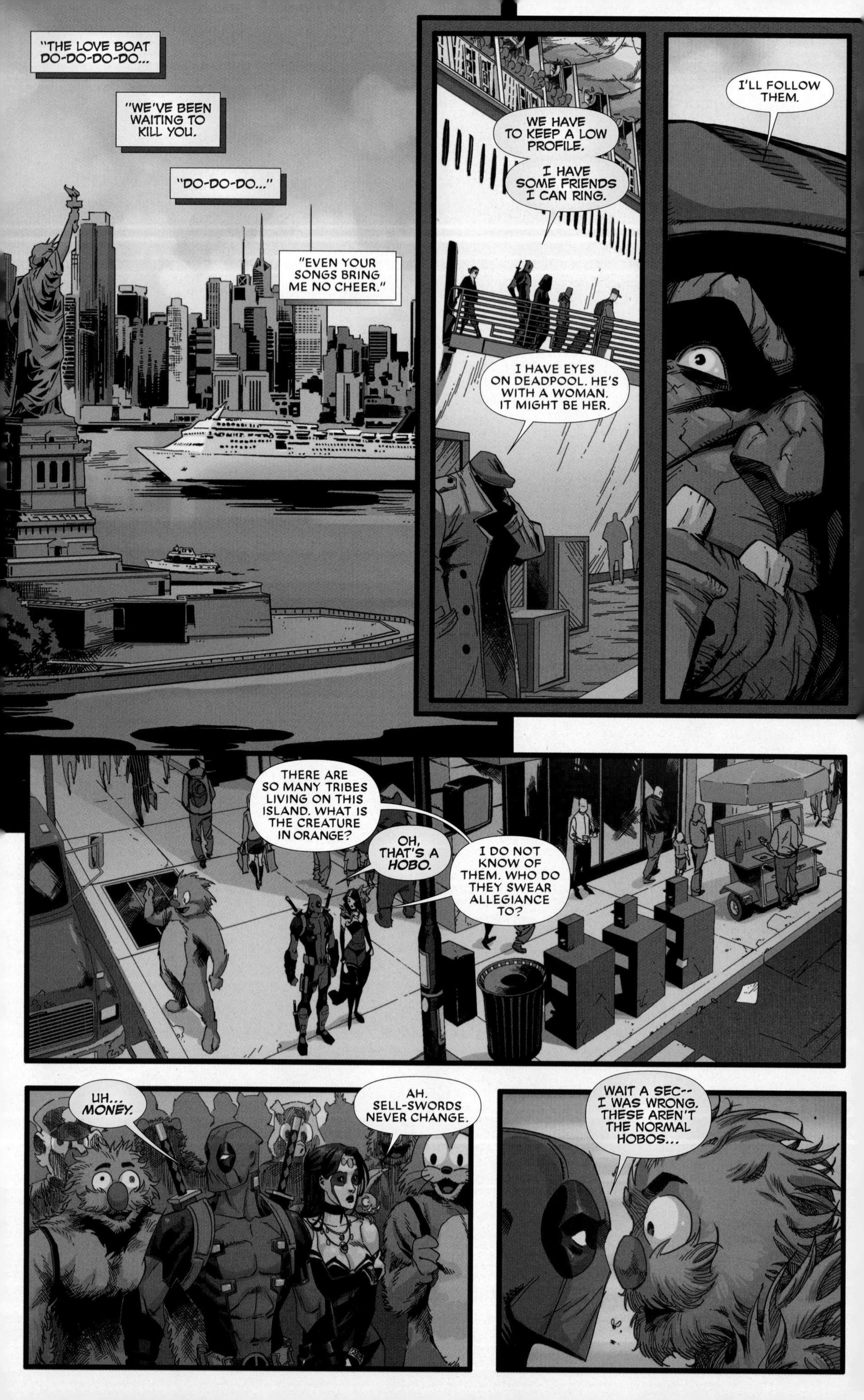
"THE LOVE BOAT DO-DO-DO-DO...
"WE'VE BEEN WAITING TO KILL YOU.
"DO-DO-DO..."
"EVEN YOUR SONGS BRING ME NO CHEER."
WE HAVE TO KEEP A LOW PROFILE.
I HAVE SOME FRIENDS I CAN RING.
I HAVE EYES ON DEADPOOL. HE'S WITH A WOMAN. IT MIGHT BE HER.
I'LL FOLLOW THEM.
THERE ARE SO MANY TRIBES LIVING ON THIS ISLAND. WHAT IS THE CREATURE IN ORANGE?
OH, THAT'S A *HOBO.*
I DO NOT KNOW OF THEM. WHO DO THEY SWEAR ALLEGIANCE TO?
UH... *MONEY.*
AH. SELL-SWORDS NEVER CHANGE.
WAIT A SEC-- I WAS WRONG. THESE AREN'T THE NORMAL HOBOS...

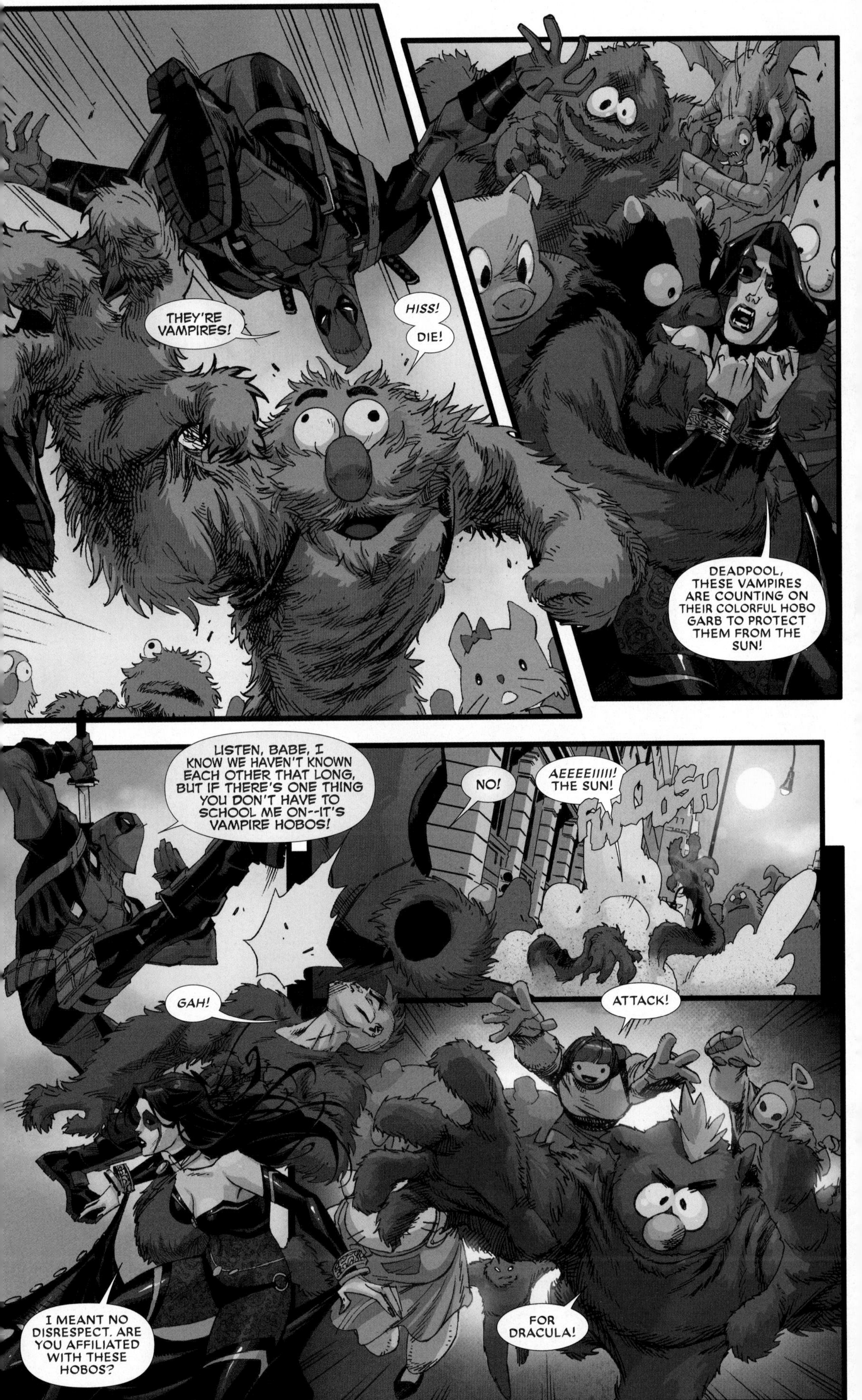
THEY'RE VAMPIRES!
HISS!
DIE!
DEADPOOL, THESE VAMPIRES ARE COUNTING ON THEIR COLORFUL HOBO GARB TO PROTECT THEM FROM THE SUN!
LISTEN, BABE, I KNOW WE HAVEN'T KNOWN EACH OTHER THAT LONG, BUT IF THERE'S ONE THING YOU DON'T HAVE TO SCHOOL ME ON--IT'S VAMPIRE HOBOS!
NO!
AEEEIIIIII! THE SUN!
FWOOSH
GAH!
ATTACK!
I MEANT NO DISRESPECT. ARE YOU AFFILIATED WITH THESE HOBOS?
FOR DRACULA!

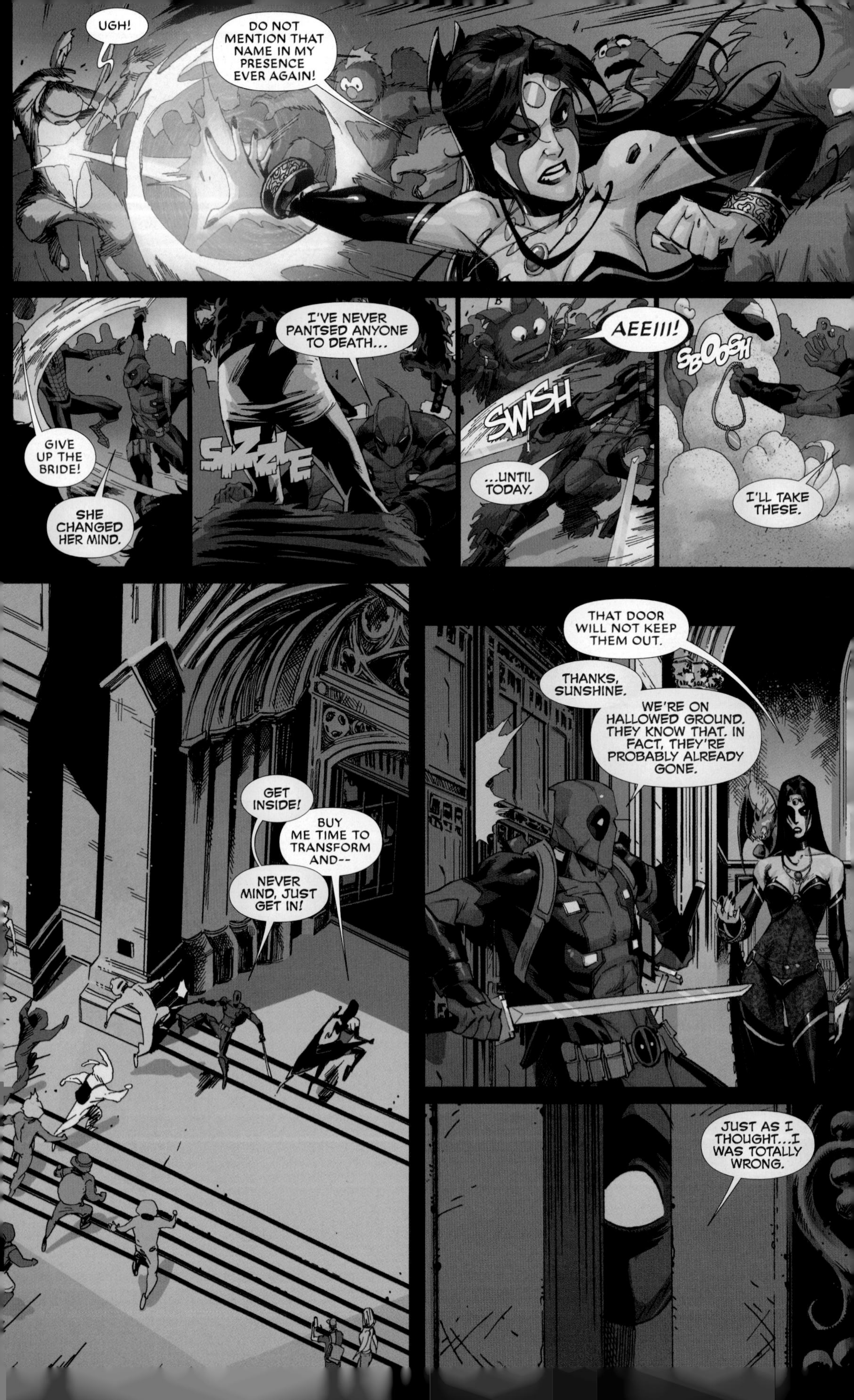

UGH!
DO NOT MENTION THAT NAME IN MY PRESENCE EVER AGAIN!
GIVE UP THE BRIDE!
SHE CHANGED HER MIND.
I'VE NEVER PANTSED ANYONE TO DEATH...
SIZZLE
AEEIII!
SWISH
...UNTIL TODAY.
SBOOSH
I'LL TAKE THESE.
GET INSIDE!
BUY ME TIME TO TRANSFORM AND--
NEVER MIND, JUST GET IN!
THAT DOOR WILL NOT KEEP THEM OUT.
THANKS, SUNSHINE.
WE'RE ON HALLOWED GROUND. THEY KNOW THAT. IN FACT, THEY'RE PROBABLY ALREADY GONE.
JUST AS I THOUGHT...I WAS TOTALLY WRONG.

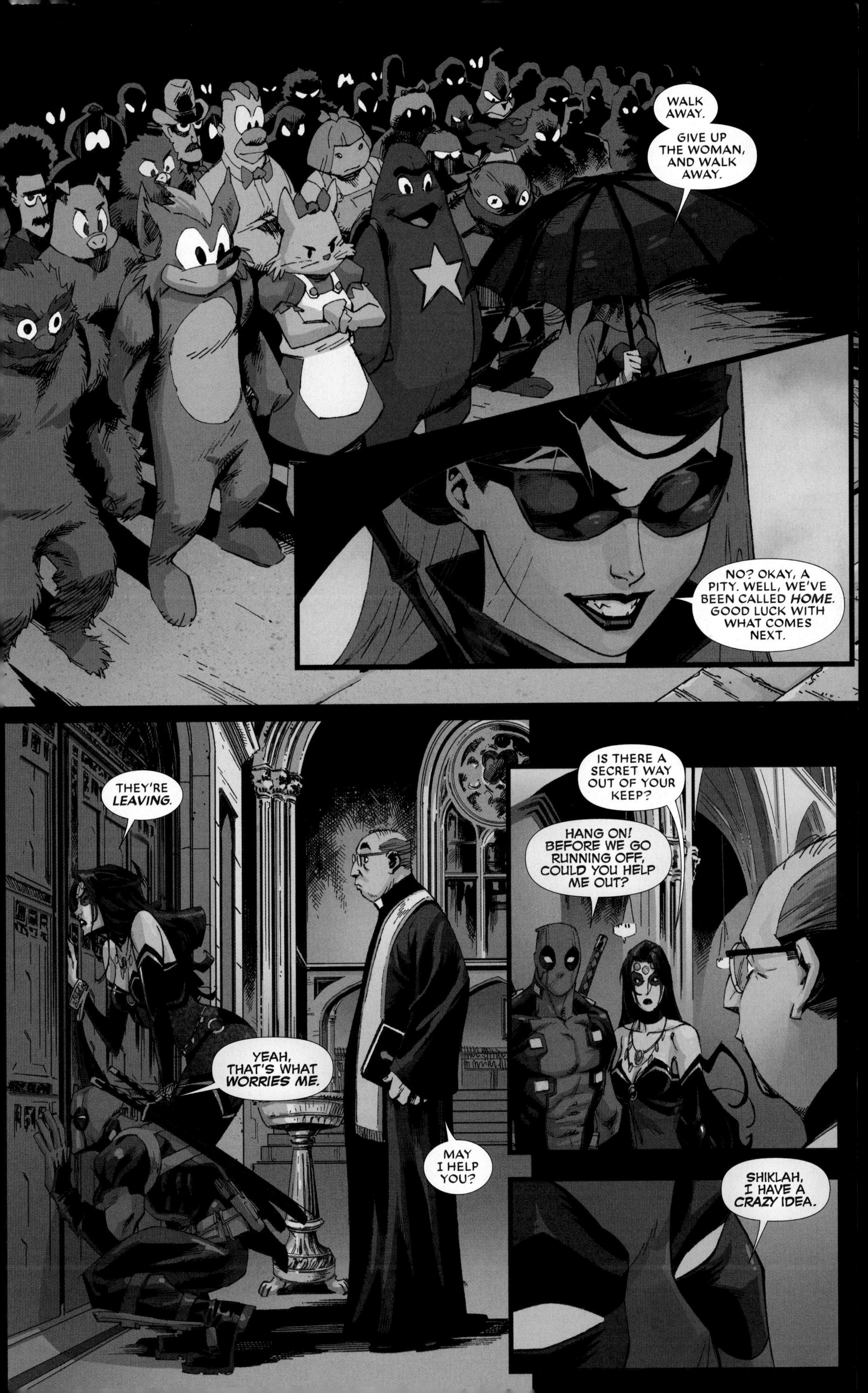
WALK AWAY.
GIVE UP THE WOMAN, AND WALK AWAY.
NO? OKAY, A PITY. WELL, WE'VE BEEN CALLED HOME. GOOD LUCK WITH WHAT COMES NEXT.
THEY'RE LEAVING.
YEAH, THAT'S WHAT WORRIES ME.
MAY I HELP YOU?
IS THERE A SECRET WAY OUT OF YOUR KEEP?
HANG ON! BEFORE WE GO RUNNING OFF, COULD YOU HELP ME OUT?
SHIKLAH, I HAVE A CRAZY IDEA.

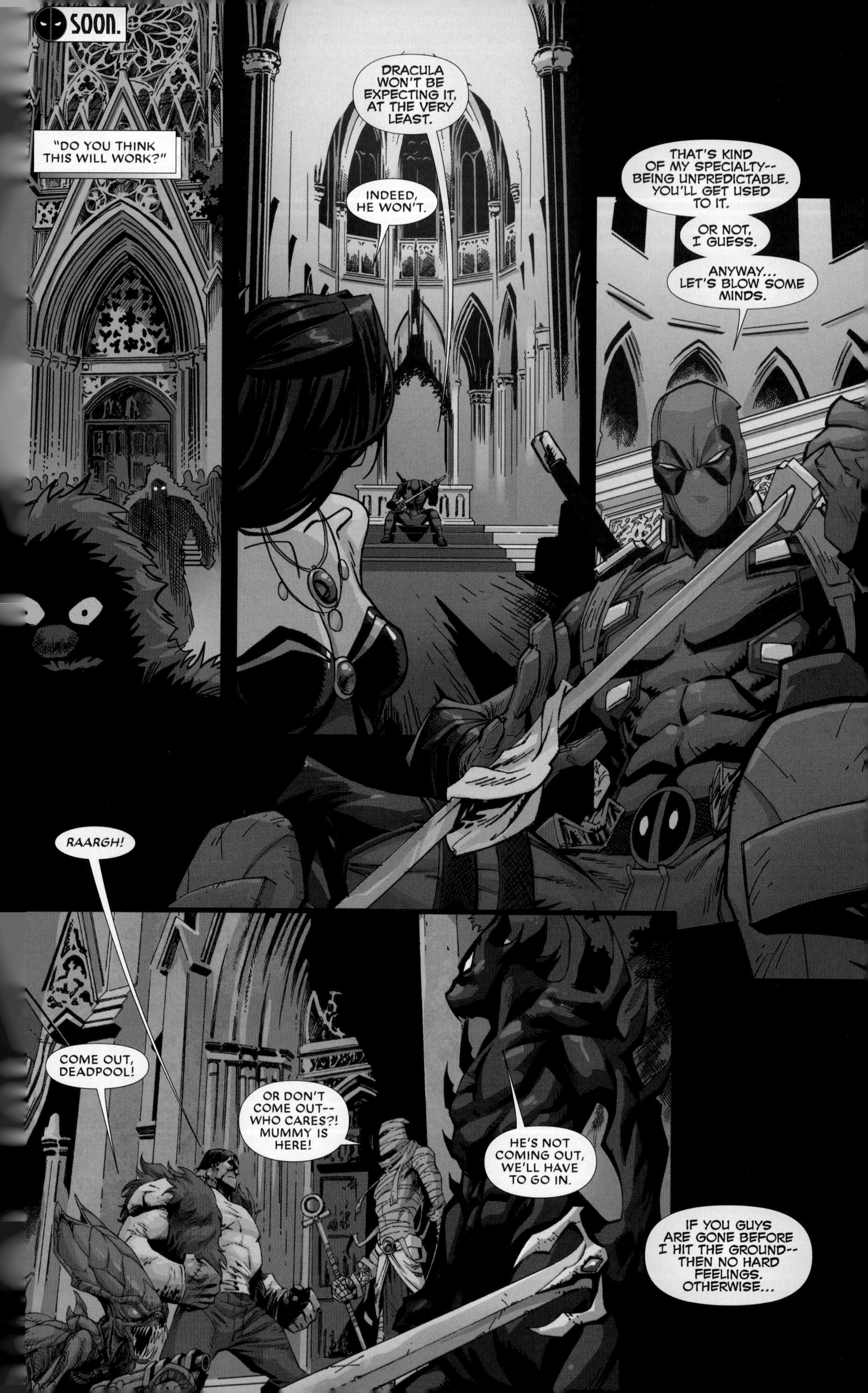

SOON.
"DO YOU THINK THIS WILL WORK?"
DRACULA WON'T BE EXPECTING IT, AT THE VERY LEAST.
INDEED, HE WON'T.
THAT'S KIND OF MY SPECIALTY-- BEING UNPREDICTABLE. YOU'LL GET USED TO IT.
OR NOT, I GUESS.
ANYWAY... LET'S BLOW SOME MINDS.
RAARGH!
COME OUT, DEADPOOL!
OR DON'T COME OUT-- WHO CARES?! MUMMY IS HERE!
HE'S NOT COMING OUT, WE'LL HAVE TO GO IN.
IF YOU GUYS ARE GONE BEFORE I HIT THE GROUND-- THEN NO HARD FEELINGS. OTHERWISE...

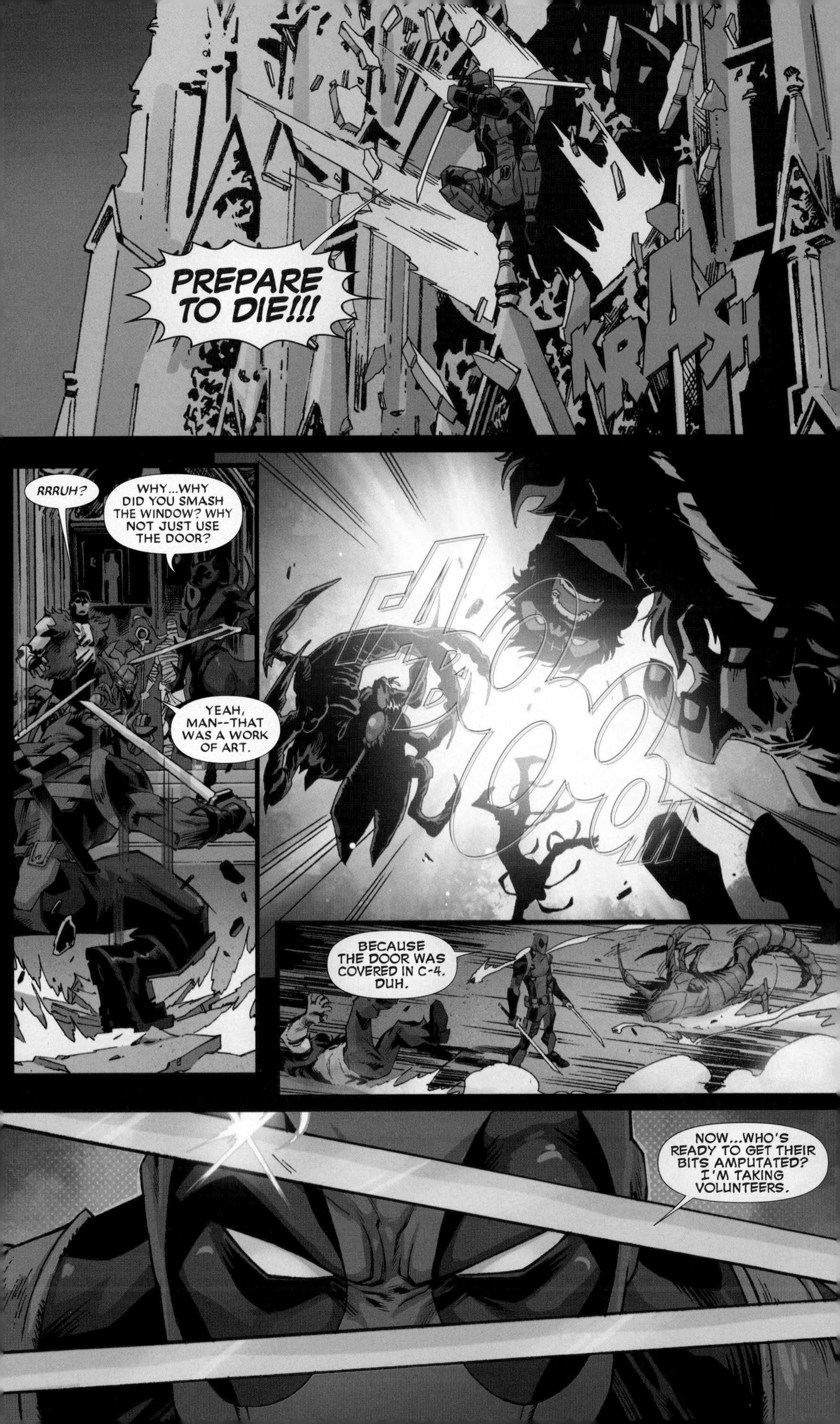
PREPARE TO DIE!!!
KRASH
RRRUH?
WHY...WHY DID YOU SMASH THE WINDOW? WHY NOT JUST USE THE DOOR?
YEAH, MAN--THAT WAS A WORK OF ART.
BECAUSE THE DOOR WAS COVERED IN C-4. DUH.
NOW...WHO'S READY TO GET THEIR BITS AMPUTATED? I'M TAKING VOLUNTEERS.

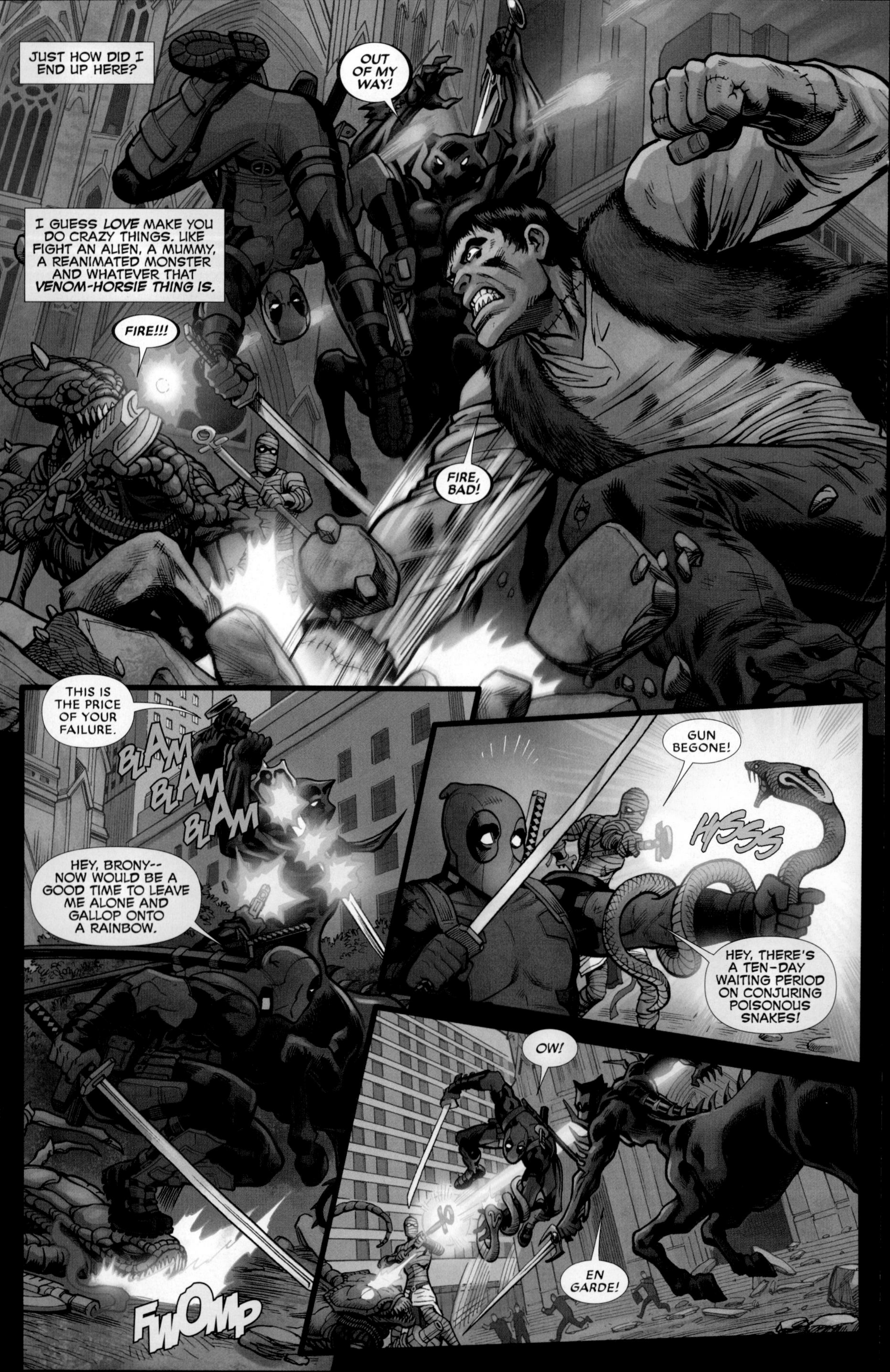
JUST HOW DID I END UP HERE?
OUT OF MY WAY!
I GUESS LOVE MAKE YOU DO CRAZY THINGS. LIKE FIGHT AN ALIEN, A MUMMY, A REANIMATED MONSTER AND WHATEVER THAT VENOM-HORSIE THING IS.
FIRE!!!
FIRE, BAD!
THIS IS THE PRICE OF YOUR FAILURE.
BLAM BLAM BLAM
HEY, BRONY-- NOW WOULD BE A GOOD TIME TO LEAVE ME ALONE AND GALLOP ONTO A RAINBOW.
GUN BEGONE!
HSSS
HEY, THERE'S A TEN-DAY WAITING PERIOD ON CONJURING POISONOUS SNAKES!
OW!
EN GARDE!
FWOMP

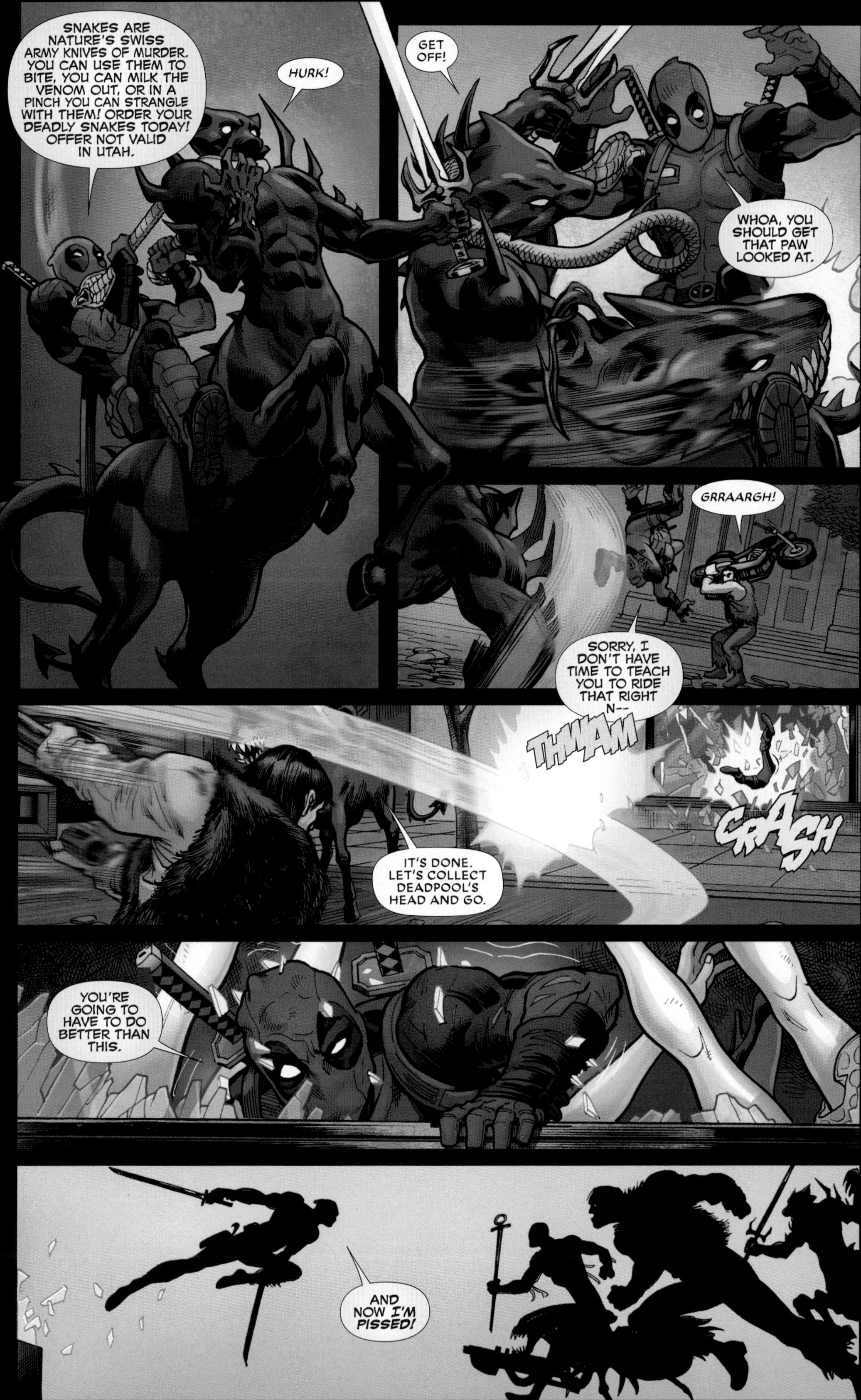
SNAKES ARE NATURE'S SWISS ARMY KNIVES OF MURDER. YOU CAN USE THEM TO BITE, YOU CAN MILK THE VENOM OUT, OR IN A PINCH YOU CAN STRANGLE WITH THEM! ORDER YOUR DEADLY SNAKES TODAY! OFFER NOT VALID IN UTAH.
HURK!
GET OFF!
WHOA, YOU SHOULD GET THAT PAW LOOKED AT.
GRRAARGH!
SORRY, I DON'T HAVE TIME TO TEACH YOU TO RIDE THAT RIGHT N--
THWAM
CRASH
IT'S DONE. LET'S COLLECT DEADPOOL'S HEAD AND GO.
YOU'RE GOING TO HAVE TO DO BETTER THAN THIS.
AND NOW I'M PISSED!

DEADPOOL
The Gauntlet

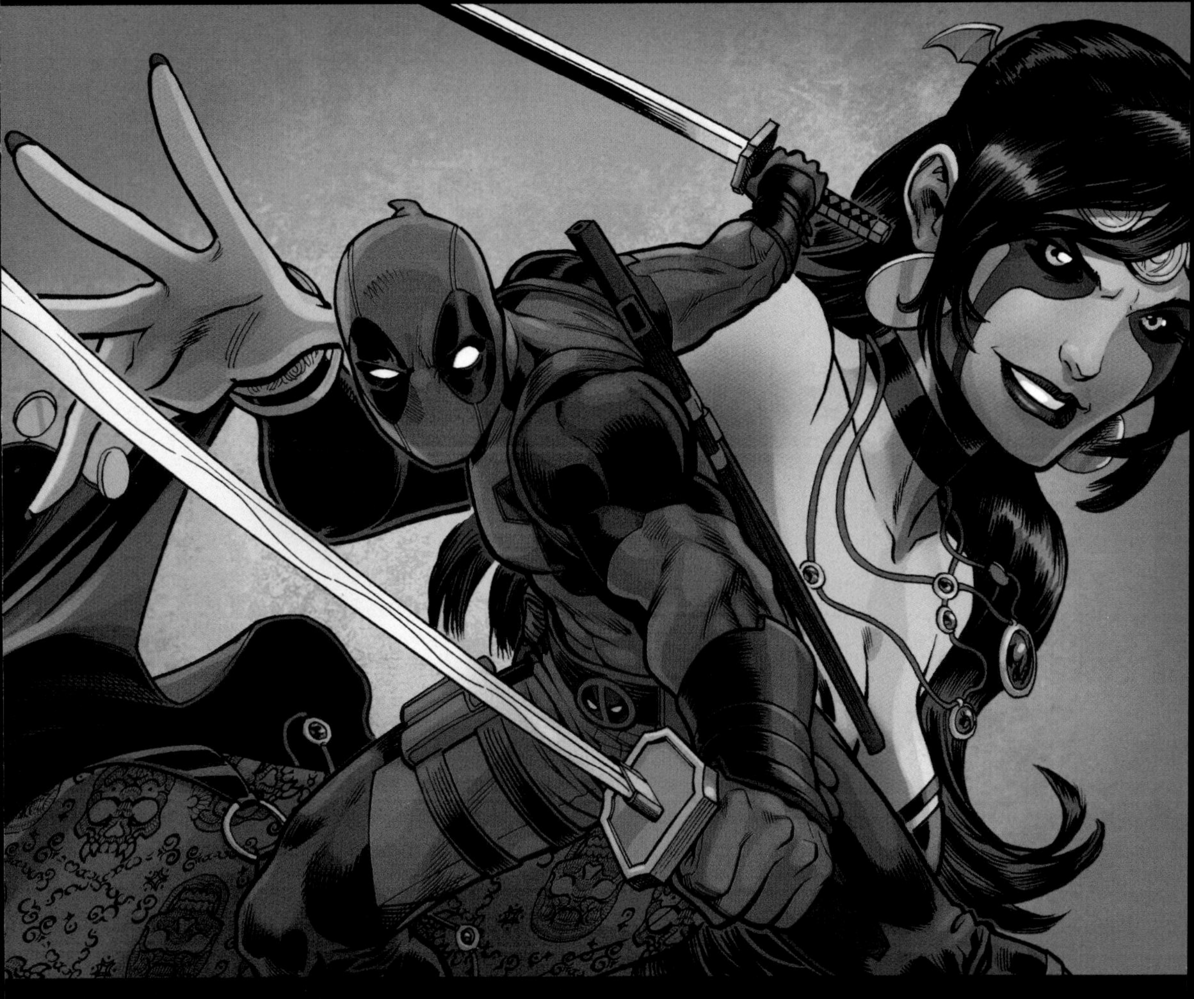

CHAPTER 10: WHEN COMETH THE FRIGHTFUL FOUR

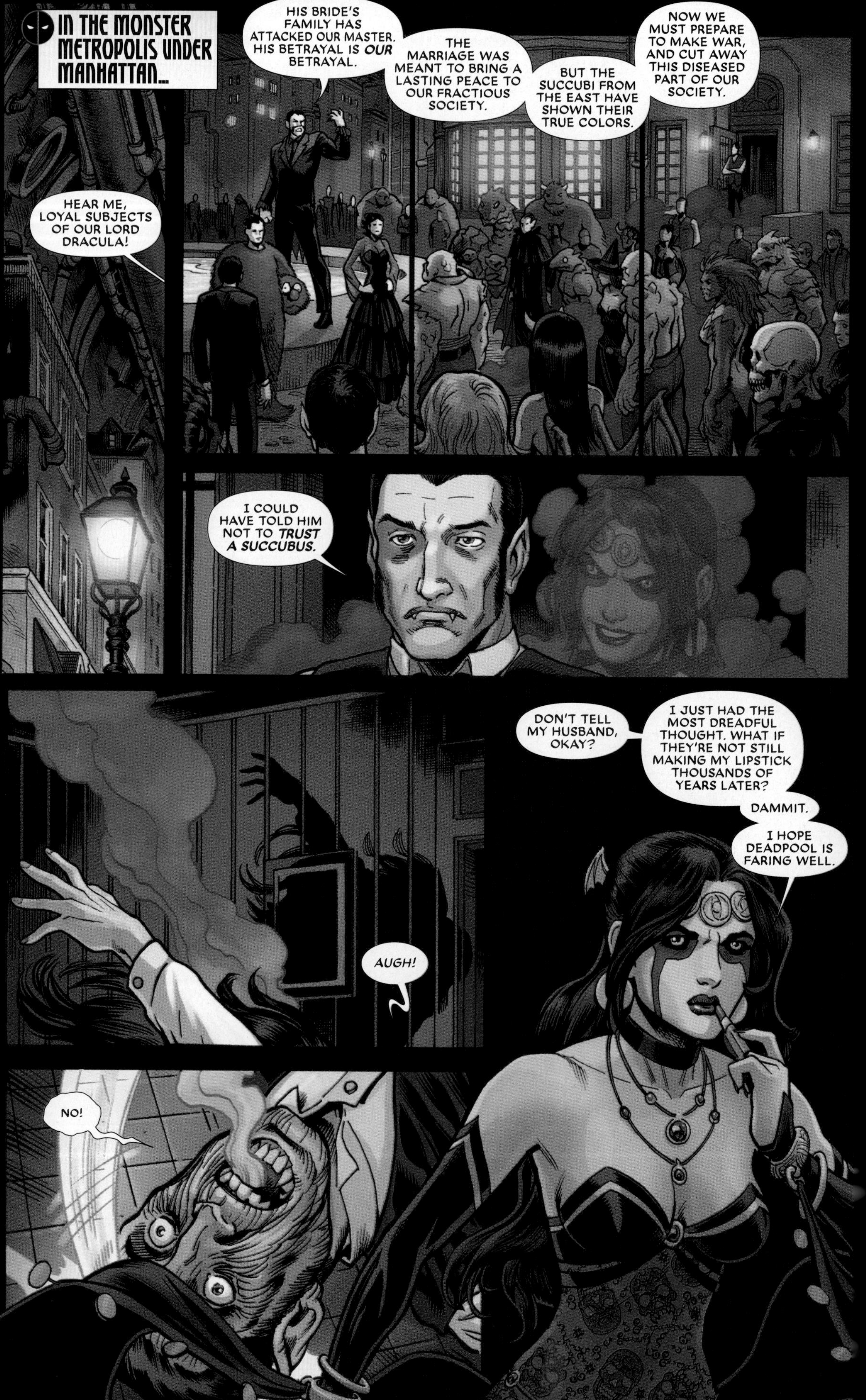
IN THE MONSTER METROPOLIS UNDER MANHATTAN...
HEAR ME, LOYAL SUBJECTS OF OUR LORD DRACULA!
HIS BRIDE'S FAMILY HAS ATTACKED OUR MASTER. HIS BETRAYAL IS OUR BETRAYAL.
THE MARRIAGE WAS MEANT TO BRING A LASTING PEACE TO OUR FRACTIOUS SOCIETY.
BUT THE SUCCUBI FROM THE EAST HAVE SHOWN THEIR TRUE COLORS.
NOW WE MUST PREPARE TO MAKE WAR, AND CUT AWAY THIS DISEASED PART OF OUR SOCIETY.
I COULD HAVE TOLD HIM NOT TO TRUST A SUCCUBUS.
DON'T TELL MY HUSBAND, OKAY?
I JUST HAD THE MOST DREADFUL THOUGHT. WHAT IF THEY'RE NOT STILL MAKING MY LIPSTICK THOUSANDS OF YEARS LATER?
DAMMIT.
I HOPE DEADPOOL IS FARING WELL.
AUGH!
NO!

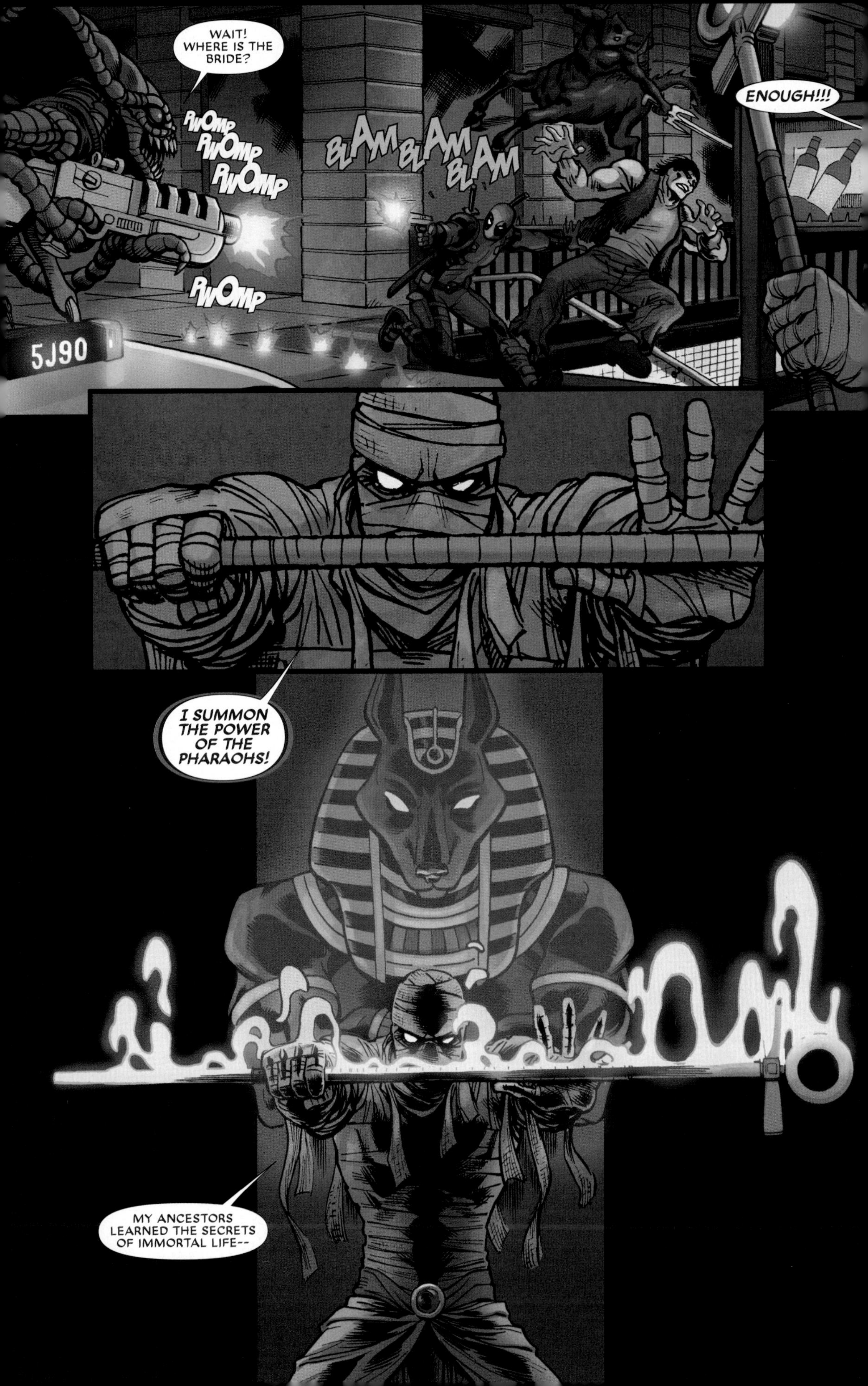
WAIT! WHERE IS THE BRIDE?
RWOMP RWOMP RWOMP
BLAM BLAM BLAM
ENOUGH!!!
RWOMP
5J90
I SUMMON THE POWER OF THE PHARAOHS!
MY ANCESTORS LEARNED THE SECRETS OF IMMORTAL LIFE--

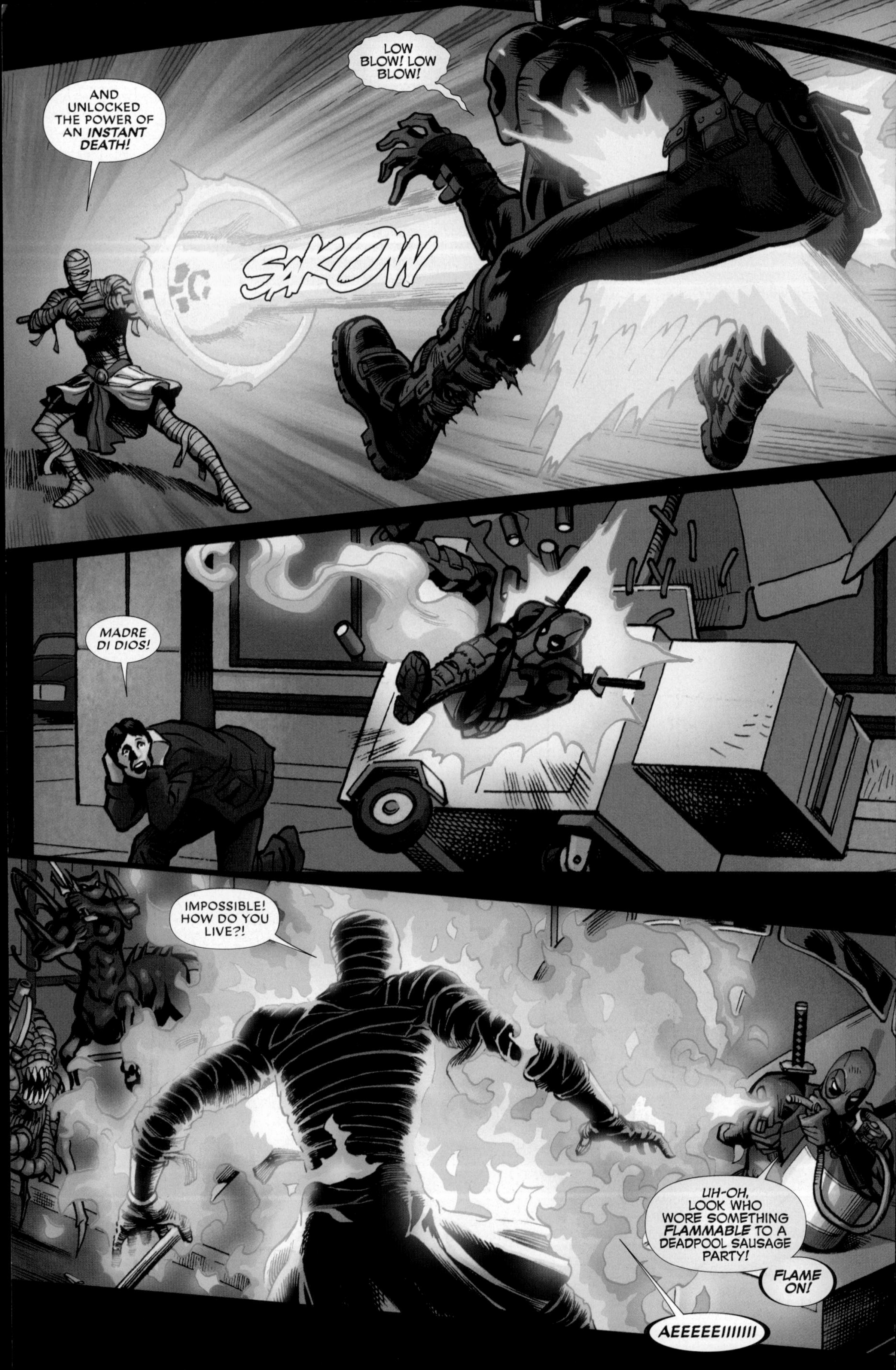
AND UNLOCKED THE POWER OF AN *INSTANT DEATH!*
LOW BLOW! LOW BLOW!
SAKOW
MADRE DI DIOS!
IMPOSSIBLE! HOW DO YOU LIVE?!
UH-OH, LOOK WHO WORE SOMETHING *FLAMMABLE* TO A DEADPOOL SAUSAGE PARTY!
FLAME ON!
AEEEEEIIIIIII

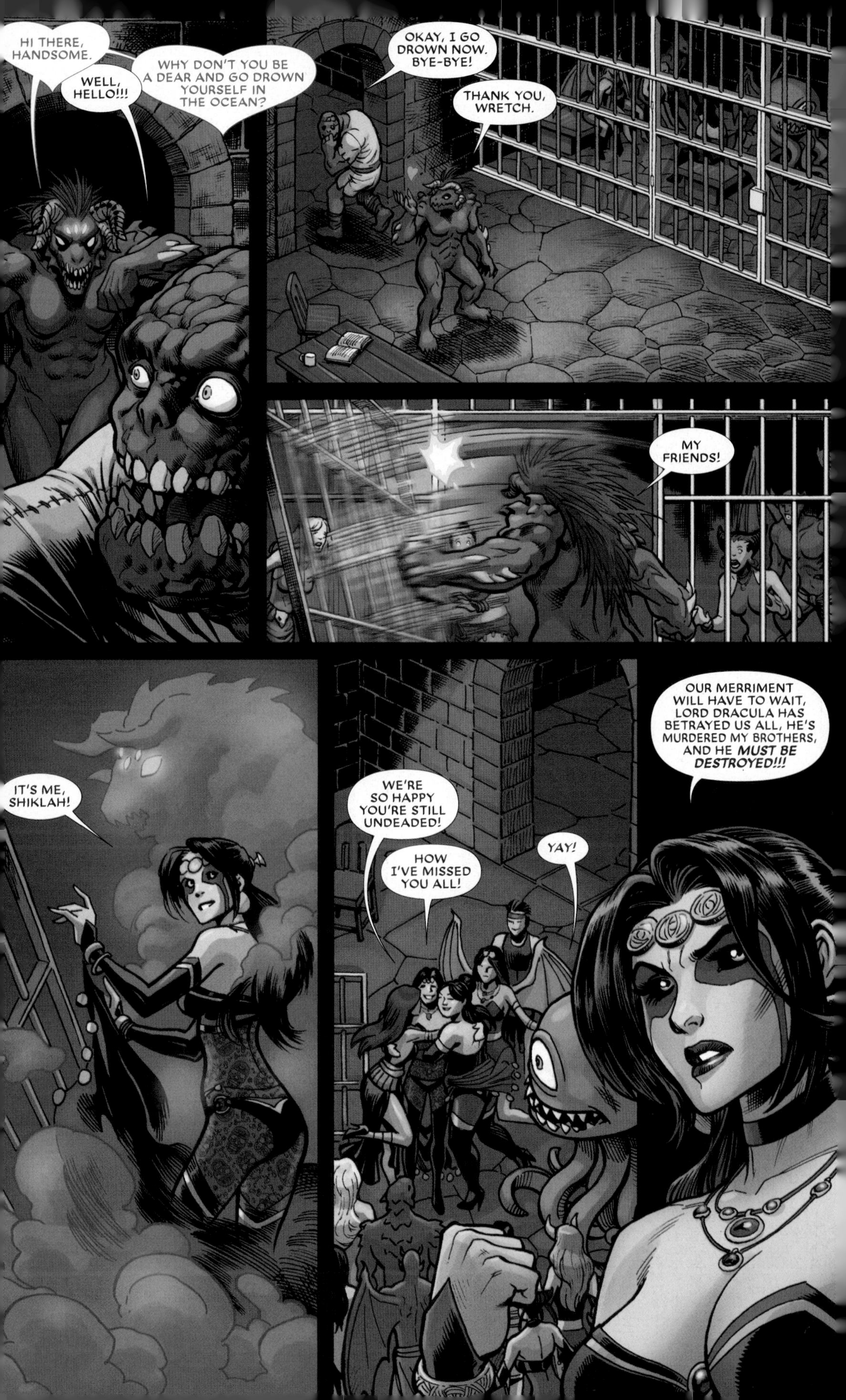
HI THERE, HANDSOME.
WELL, HELLO!!!
WHY DON'T YOU BE A DEAR AND GO DROWN YOURSELF IN THE OCEAN?
OKAY, I GO DROWN NOW. BYE-BYE!
THANK YOU, WRETCH.
MY FRIENDS!
IT'S ME, SHIKLAH!
WE'RE SO HAPPY YOU'RE STILL UNDEADED!
HOW I'VE MISSED YOU ALL!
YAY!
OUR MERRIMENT WILL HAVE TO WAIT, LORD DRACULA HAS BETRAYED US ALL, HE'S MURDERED MY BROTHERS, AND HE *MUST BE DESTROYED!!!*

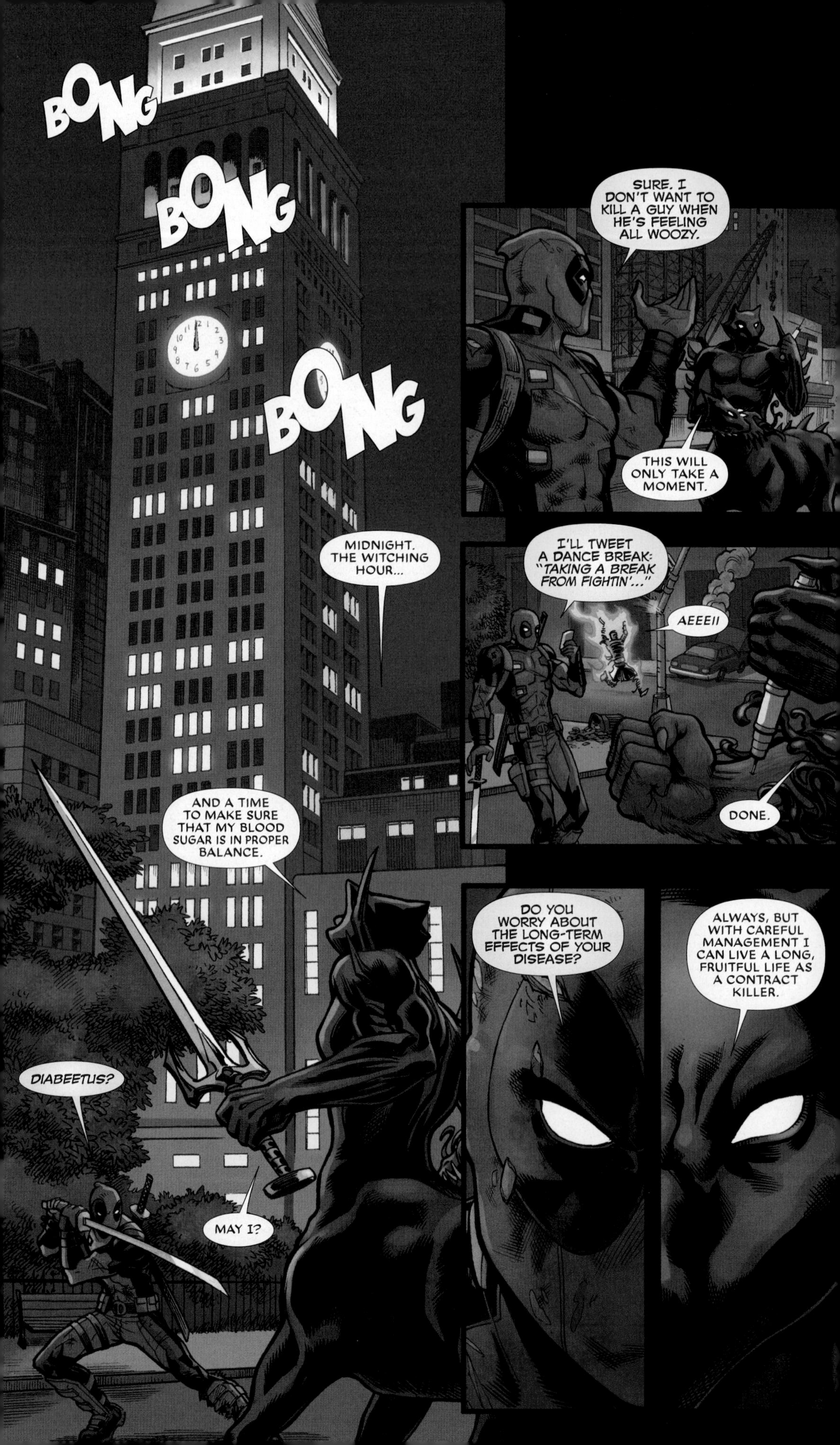
BONG
BONG
BONG
MIDNIGHT. THE WITCHING HOUR...
AND A TIME TO MAKE SURE THAT MY BLOOD SUGAR IS IN PROPER BALANCE.
DIABEETUS?
MAY I?
SURE. I DON'T WANT TO KILL A GUY WHEN HE'S FEELING ALL WOOZY.
THIS WILL ONLY TAKE A MOMENT.
I'LL TWEET A DANCE BREAK: *"TAKING A BREAK FROM FIGHTIN'..."*
AEEEII
DONE.
DO YOU WORRY ABOUT THE LONG-TERM EFFECTS OF YOUR DISEASE?
ALWAYS, BUT WITH CAREFUL MANAGEMENT I CAN LIVE A LONG, FRUITFUL LIFE AS A CONTRACT KILLER.

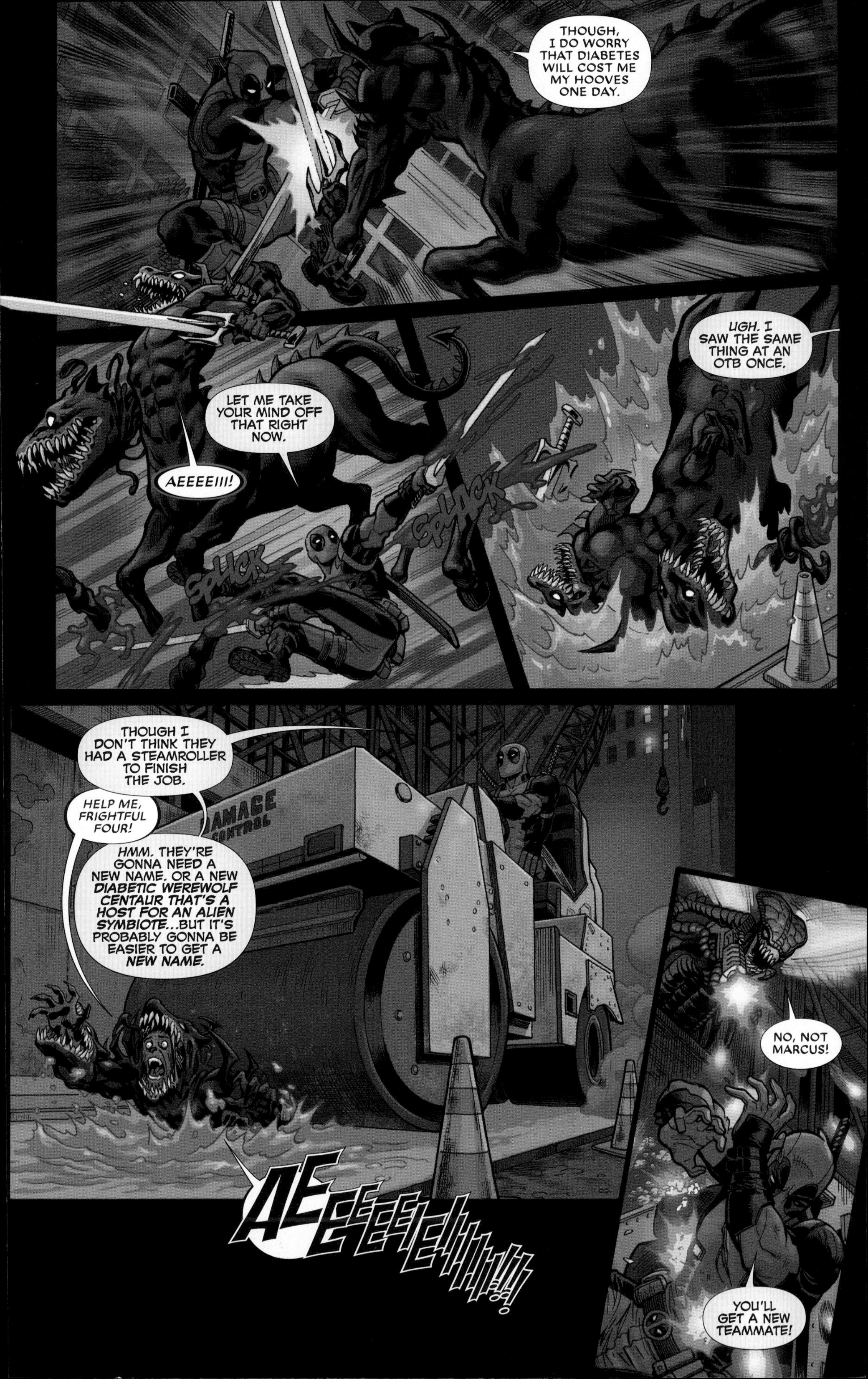
THOUGH, I DO WORRY THAT DIABETES WILL COST ME MY HOOVES ONE DAY.
LET ME TAKE YOUR MIND OFF THAT RIGHT NOW.
AEEEEIII!
SPLACK
SPLACK
UGH. I SAW THE SAME THING AT AN OTB ONCE.
THOUGH I DON'T THINK THEY HAD A STEAMROLLER TO FINISH THE JOB.
HELP ME, FRIGHTFUL FOUR!
HMM. THEY'RE GONNA NEED A NEW NAME. OR A NEW DIABETIC WEREWOLF CENTAUR THAT'S A HOST FOR AN ALIEN SYMBIOTE...BUT IT'S PROBABLY GONNA BE EASIER TO GET A NEW NAME.
DAMAGE CONTROL
NO, NOT MARCUS!
YOU'LL GET A NEW TEAMMATE!

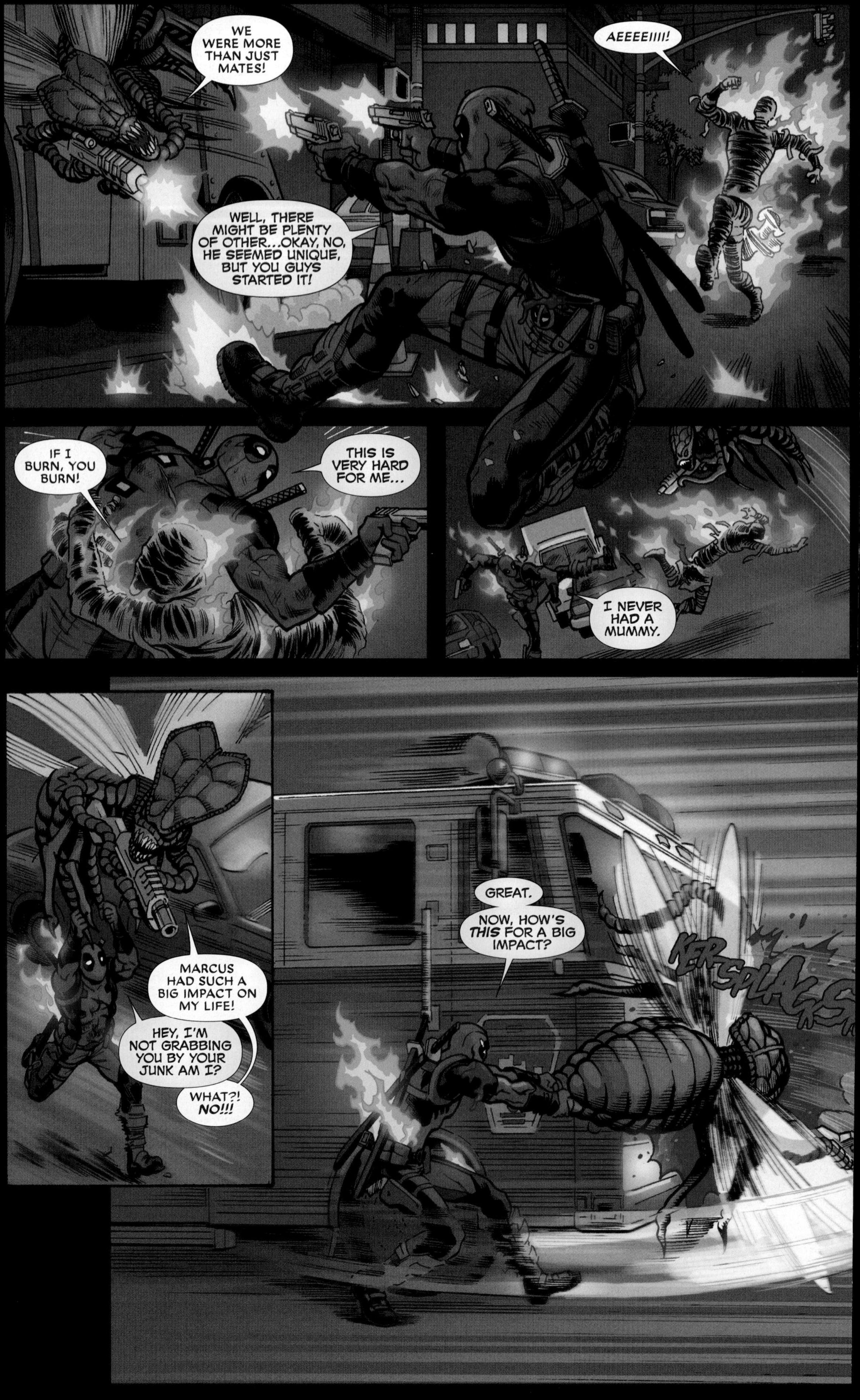
WE WERE MORE THAN JUST MATES!
AEEEIIII!
WELL, THERE MIGHT BE PLENTY OF OTHER...OKAY, NO, HE SEEMED UNIQUE, BUT YOU GUYS STARTED IT!
IF I BURN, YOU BURN!
THIS IS VERY HARD FOR ME...
I NEVER HAD A MUMMY.
MARCUS HAD SUCH A BIG IMPACT ON MY LIFE!
HEY, I'M NOT GRABBING YOU BY YOUR JUNK AM I?
WHAT?! NO!!!
GREAT.
NOW, HOW'S THIS FOR A BIG IMPACT?

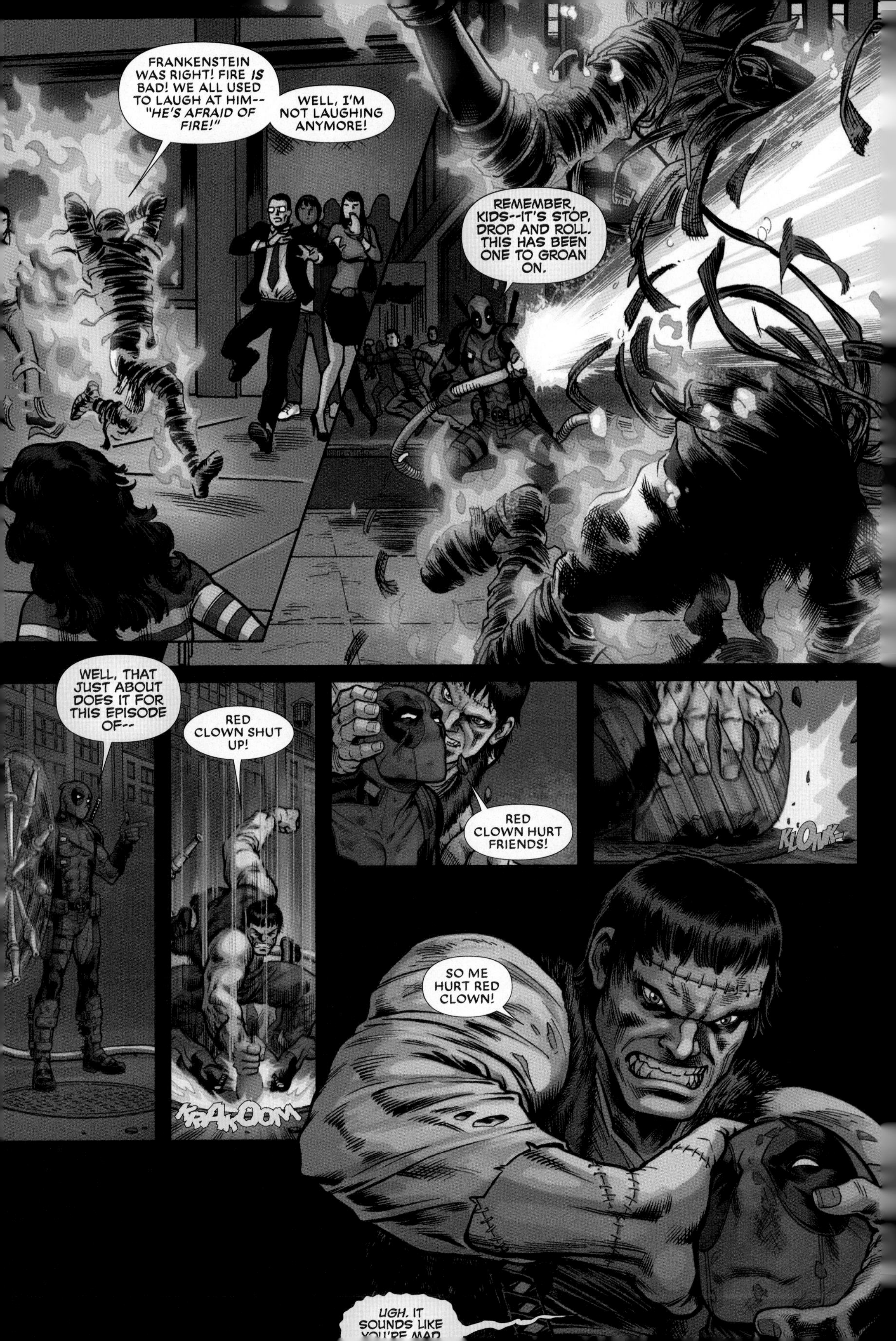
FRANKENSTEIN WAS RIGHT! FIRE *IS* BAD! WE ALL USED TO LAUGH AT HIM-- *"HE'S AFRAID OF FIRE!"*
WELL, I'M NOT LAUGHING ANYMORE!
REMEMBER, KIDS--IT'S STOP, DROP AND ROLL. THIS HAS BEEN ONE TO GROAN ON.
WELL, THAT JUST ABOUT DOES IT FOR THIS EPISODE OF--
RED CLOWN SHUT UP!
KRAKOOM
RED CLOWN HURT FRIENDS!
KLONK
SO ME HURT RED CLOWN!
UGH. IT SOUNDS LIKE

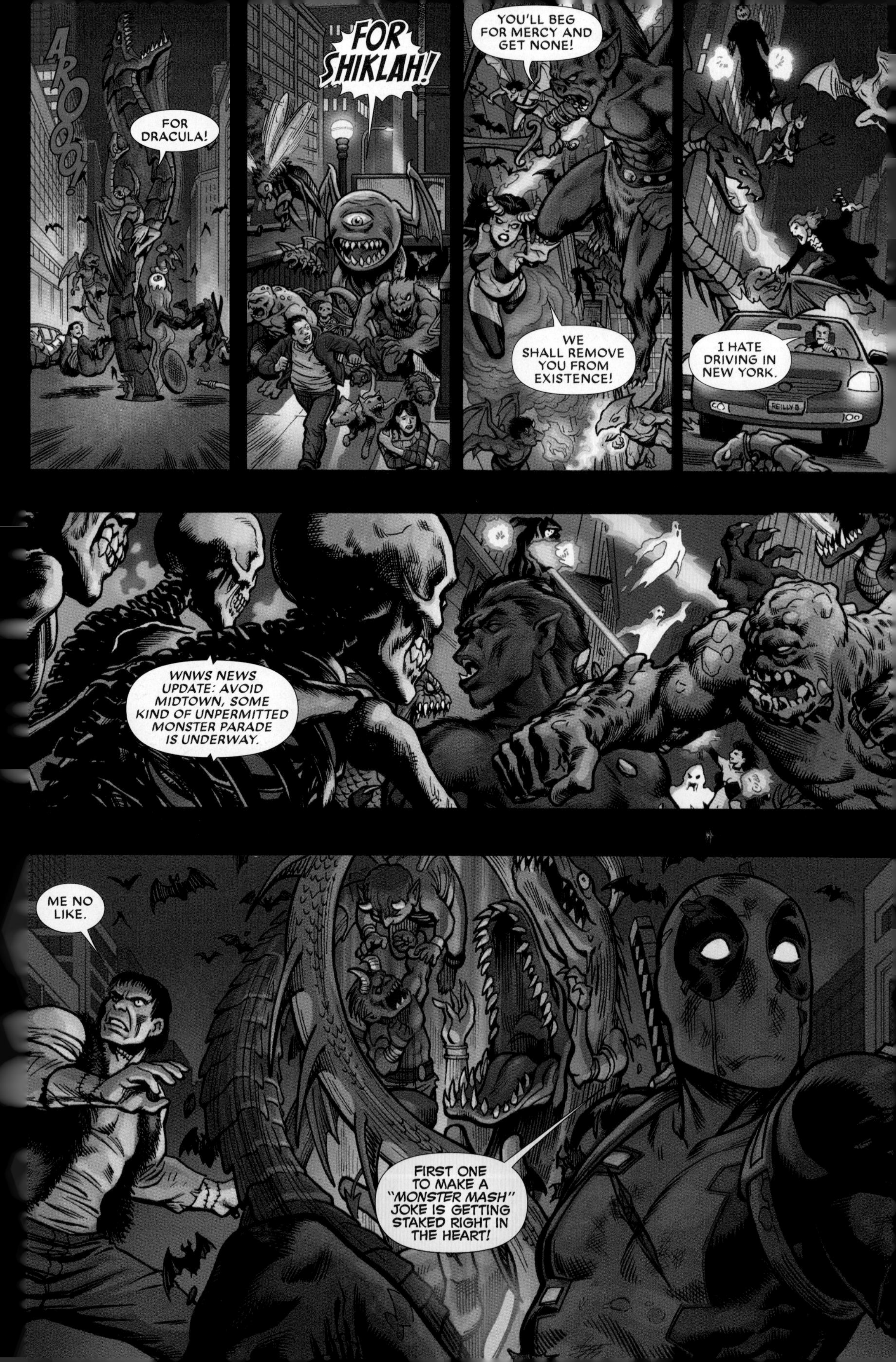
AROOOO
FOR DRACULA!
FOR SHIKLAH!
YOU'LL BEG FOR MERCY AND GET NONE!
WE SHALL REMOVE YOU FROM EXISTENCE!
I HATE DRIVING IN NEW YORK.
REILLY B
WNWS NEWS UPDATE: AVOID MIDTOWN, SOME KIND OF UNPERMITTED MONSTER PARADE IS UNDERWAY.
ME NO LIKE.
FIRST ONE TO MAKE A "MONSTER MASH" JOKE IS GETTING STAKED RIGHT IN THE HEART!

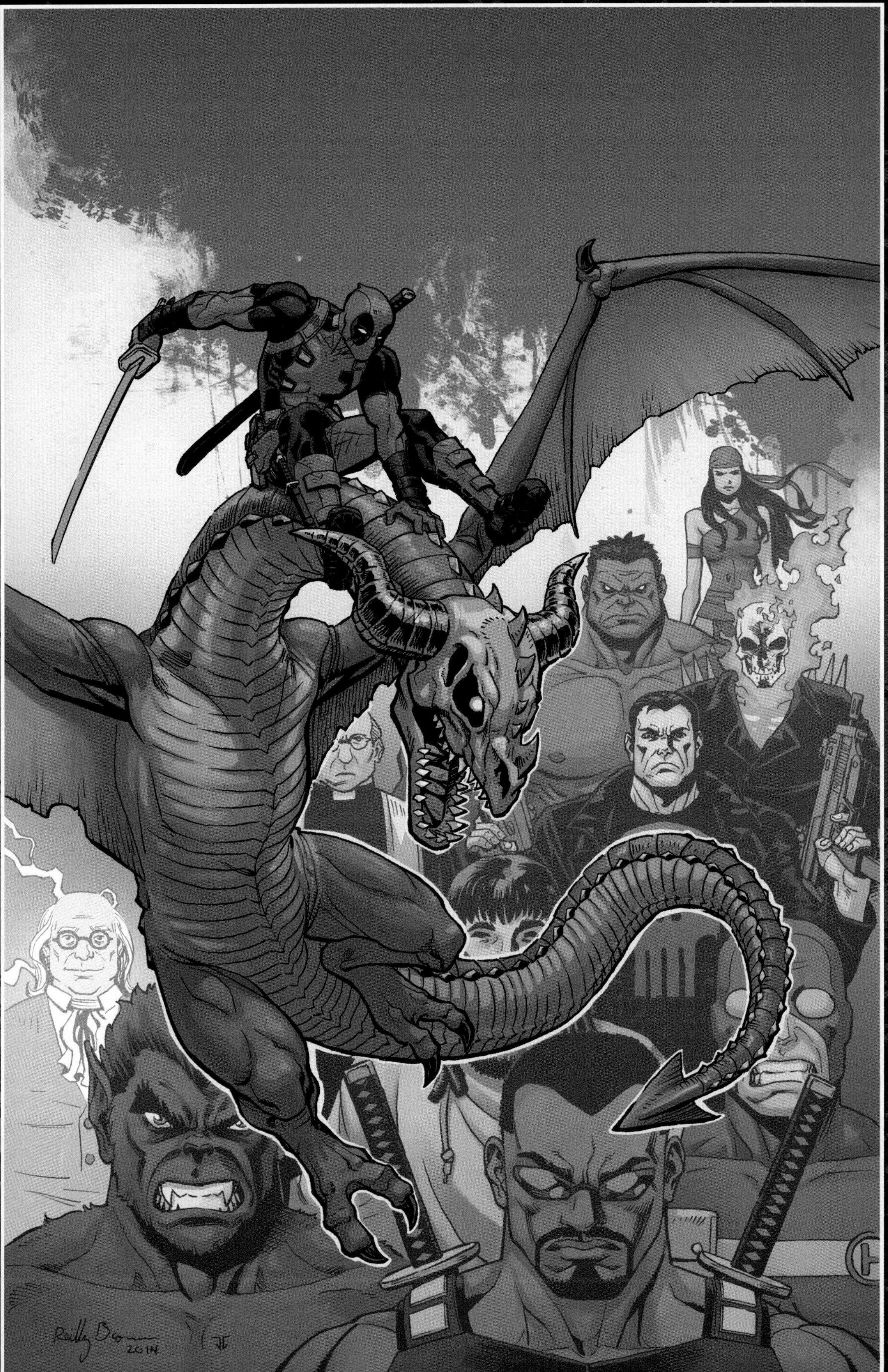
Reilly Brown
2014
JC

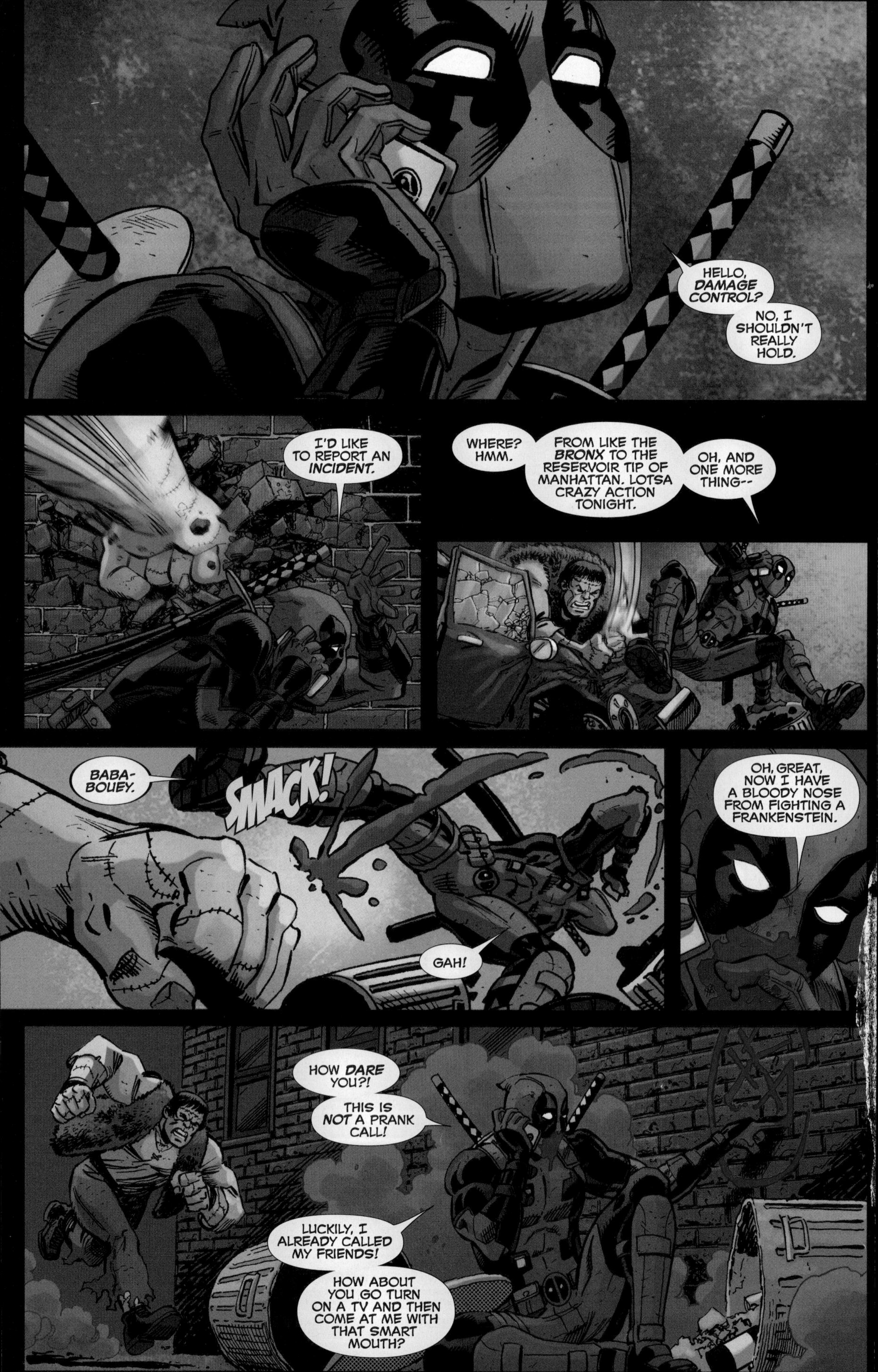
HELLO, DAMAGE CONTROL?
NO, I SHOULDN'T REALLY HOLD.
I'D LIKE TO REPORT AN INCIDENT.
WHERE? HMM.
FROM LIKE THE BRONX TO THE RESERVOIR TIP OF MANHATTAN. LOTSA CRAZY ACTION TONIGHT.
OH, AND ONE MORE THING--
BABA-BOUEY.
SMACK!
GAH!
OH, GREAT, NOW I HAVE A BLOODY NOSE FROM FIGHTING A FRANKENSTEIN.
HOW DARE YOU?!
THIS IS NOT A PRANK CALL!
LUCKILY, I ALREADY CALLED MY FRIENDS!
HOW ABOUT YOU GO TURN ON A TV AND THEN COME AT ME WITH THAT SMART MOUTH?

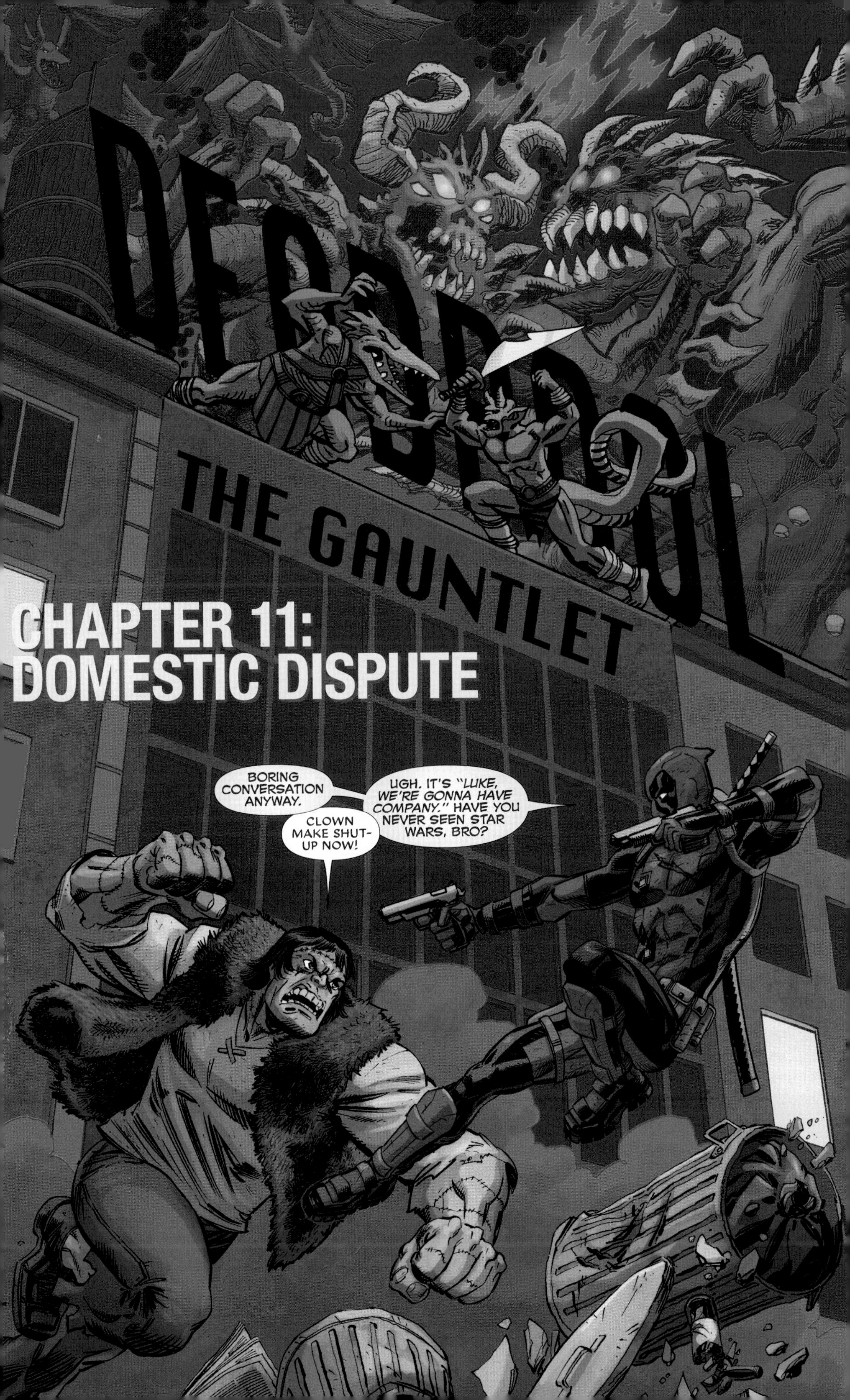
DEADPOOL
THE GAUNTLET
CHAPTER 11:
DOMESTIC DISPUTE
BORING CONVERSATION ANYWAY.
UGH. IT'S "LUKE, WE'RE GONNA HAVE COMPANY." HAVE YOU NEVER SEEN STAR WARS, BRO?
CLOWN MAKE SHUT-UP NOW!

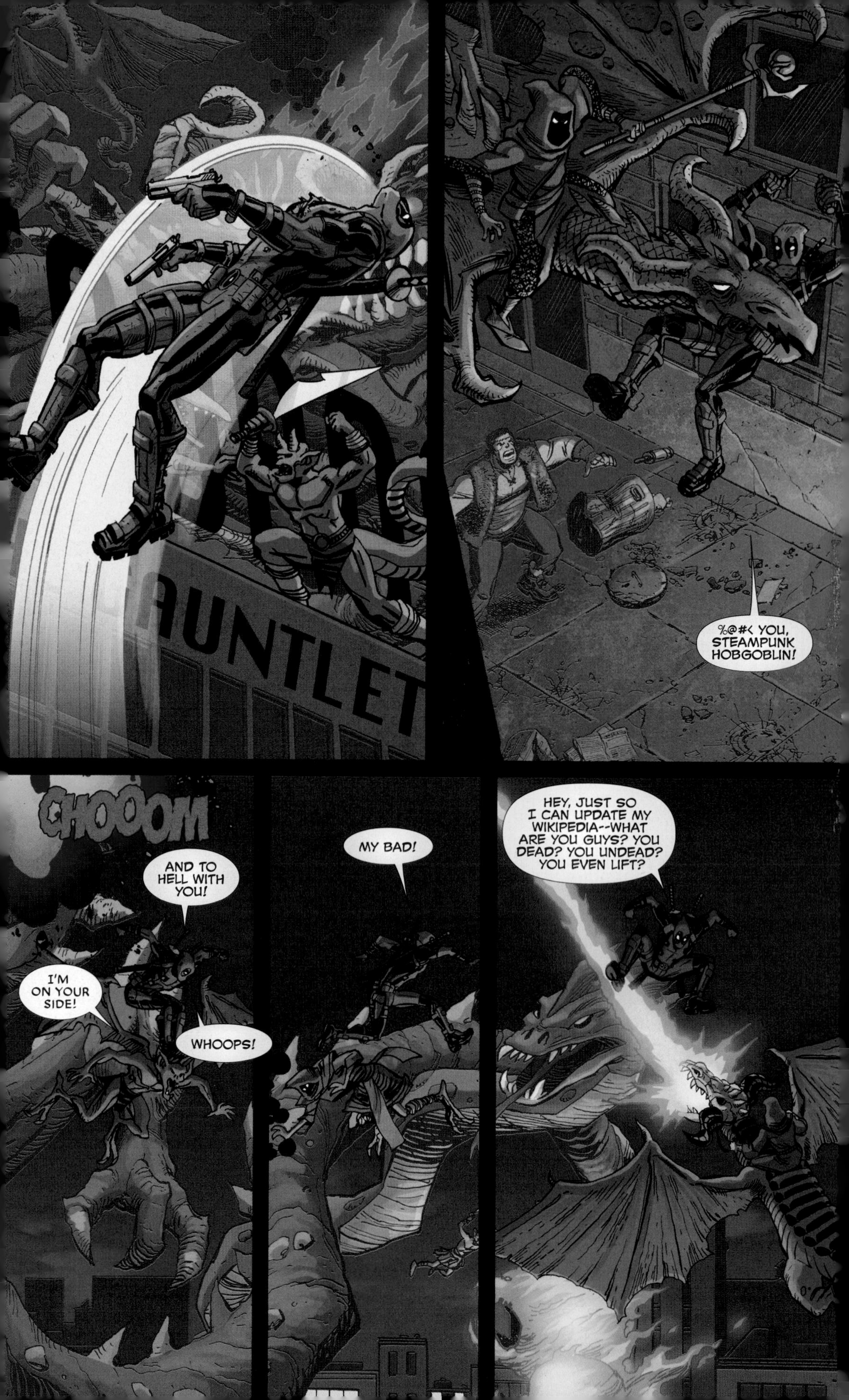
AUNTLET
%@#< YOU, STEAMPUNK HOBGOBLIN!
CHOOOM
AND TO HELL WITH YOU!
I'M ON YOUR SIDE!
WHOOPS!
MY BAD!
HEY, JUST SO I CAN UPDATE MY WIKIPEDIA--WHAT ARE YOU GUYS? YOU DEAD? YOU UNDEAD? YOU EVEN LIFT?

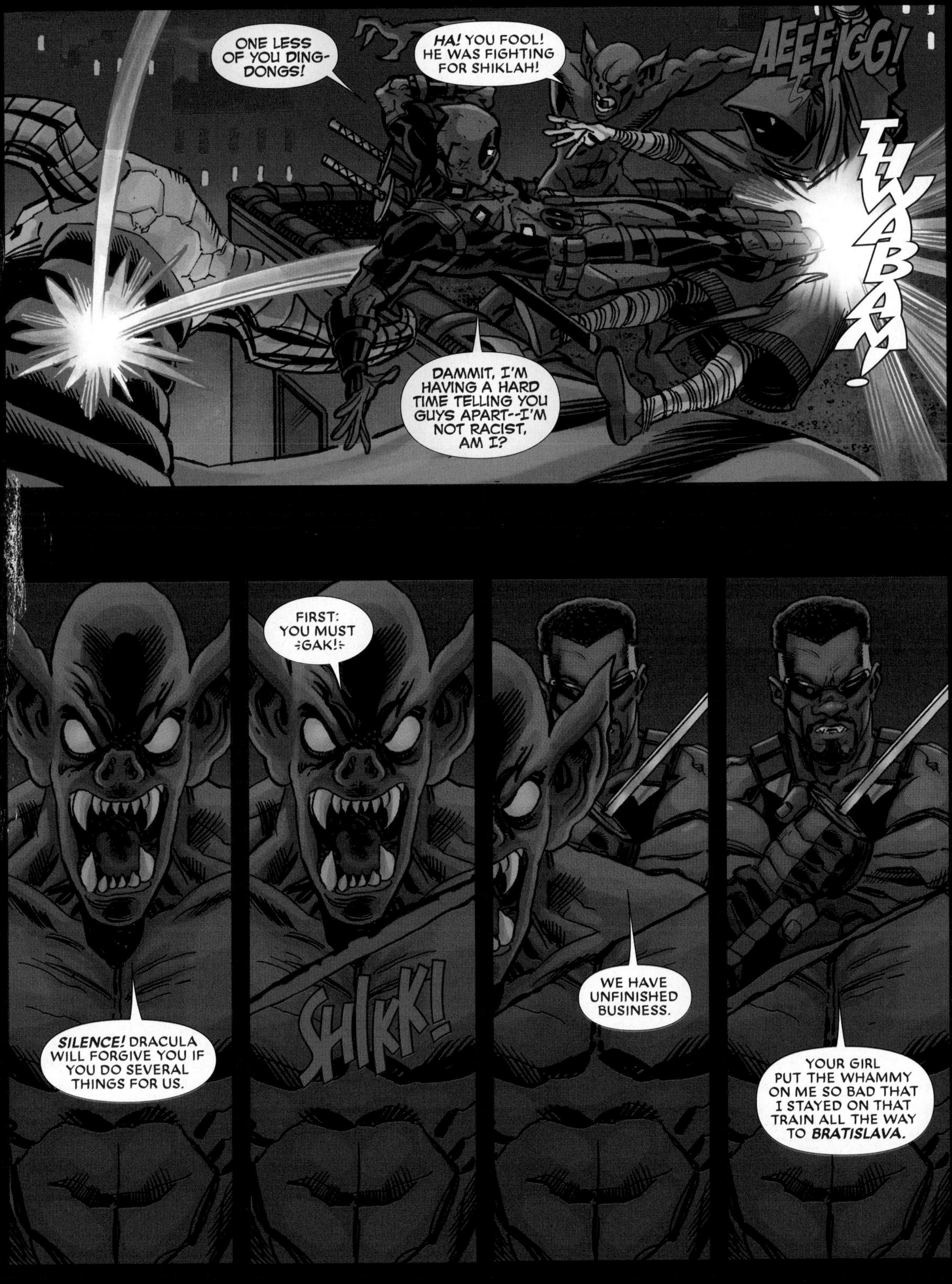
ONE LESS OF YOU DING-DONGS!
HA! YOU FOOL! HE WAS FIGHTING FOR SHIKLAH!
AEEEIGG!
THWABAM!
DAMMIT, I'M HAVING A HARD TIME TELLING YOU GUYS APART--I'M NOT RACIST, AM I?
SILENCE! DRACULA WILL FORGIVE YOU IF YOU DO SEVERAL THINGS FOR US.
FIRST: YOU MUST -GAK!-
SHIKK!
WE HAVE UNFINISHED BUSINESS.
YOUR GIRL PUT THE WHAMMY ON ME SO BAD THAT I STAYED ON THAT TRAIN ALL THE WAY TO BRATISLAVA.

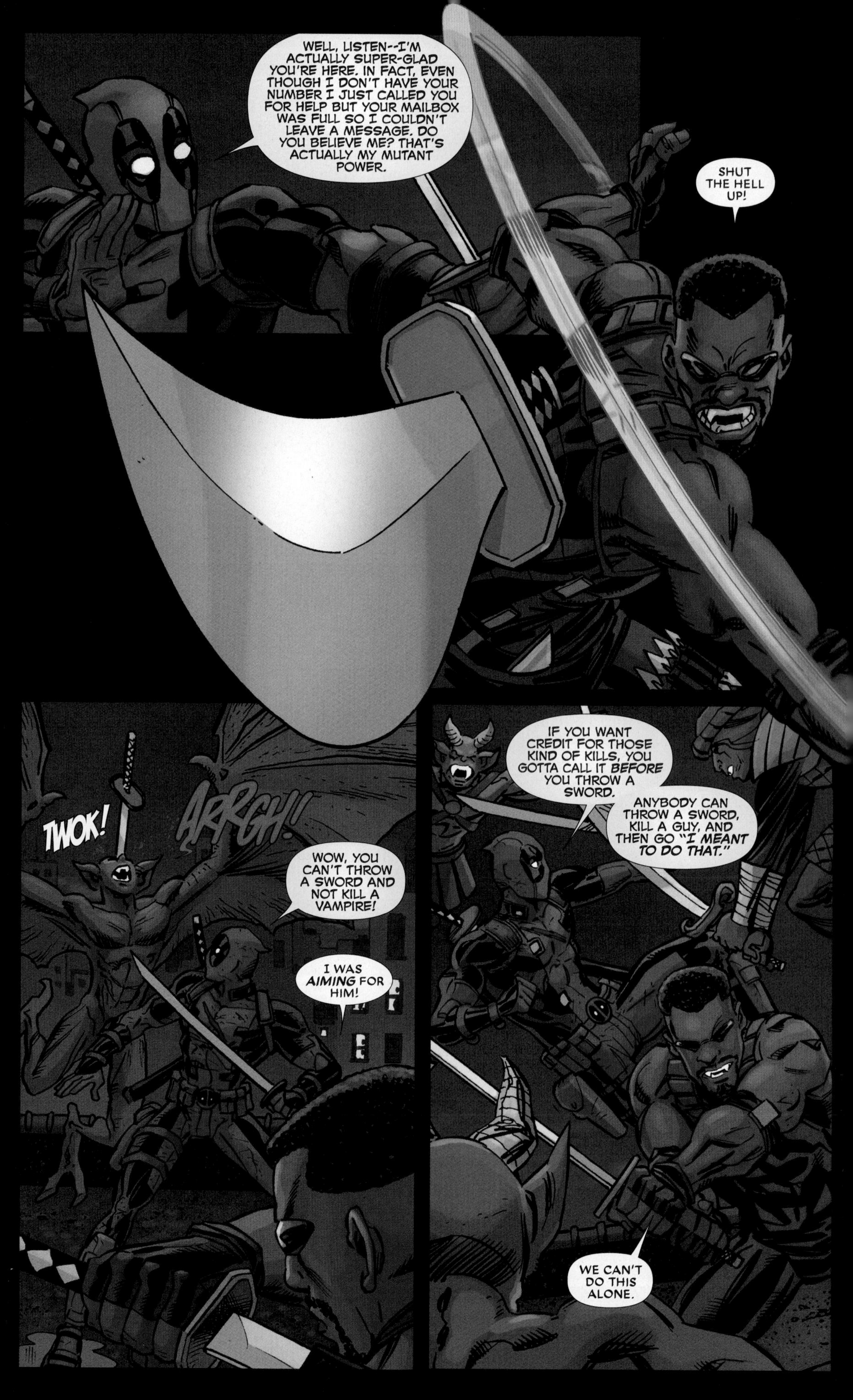
WELL, LISTEN--I'M ACTUALLY SUPER-GLAD YOU'RE HERE. IN FACT, EVEN THOUGH I DON'T HAVE YOUR NUMBER I JUST CALLED YOU FOR HELP BUT YOUR MAILBOX WAS FULL SO I COULDN'T LEAVE A MESSAGE. DO YOU BELIEVE ME? THAT'S ACTUALLY MY MUTANT POWER.
SHUT THE HELL UP!
TWOK!
ARRGH!
WOW, YOU CAN'T THROW A SWORD AND NOT KILL A VAMPIRE!
I WAS AIMING FOR HIM!
IF YOU WANT CREDIT FOR THOSE KIND OF KILLS, YOU GOTTA CALL IT BEFORE YOU THROW A SWORD.
ANYBODY CAN THROW A SWORD, KILL A GUY, AND THEN GO "I MEANT TO DO THAT."
WE CAN'T DO THIS ALONE.

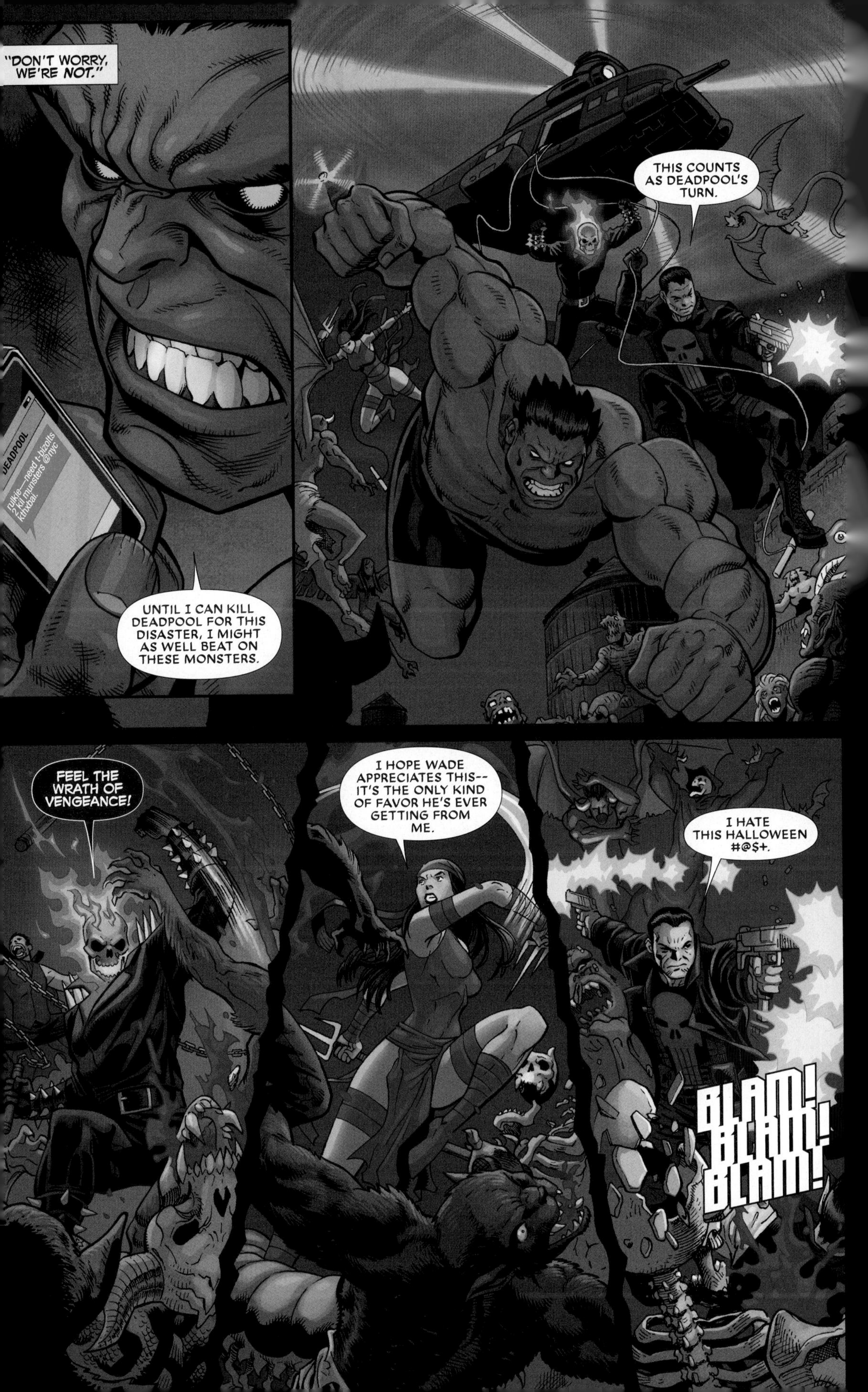

"DON'T WORRY, WE'RE NOT."
DEADPOOL
rulkie—need t-bizolts 2 kil munsters @nyc kthxbai.
UNTIL I CAN KILL DEADPOOL FOR THIS DISASTER, I MIGHT AS WELL BEAT ON THESE MONSTERS.
THIS COUNTS AS DEADPOOL'S TURN.
FEEL THE WRATH OF VENGEANCE!
I HOPE WADE APPRECIATES THIS-- IT'S THE ONLY KIND OF FAVOR HE'S EVER GETTING FROM ME.
I HATE THIS HALLOWEEN #@$+.
BLAM! BLAM! BLAM!

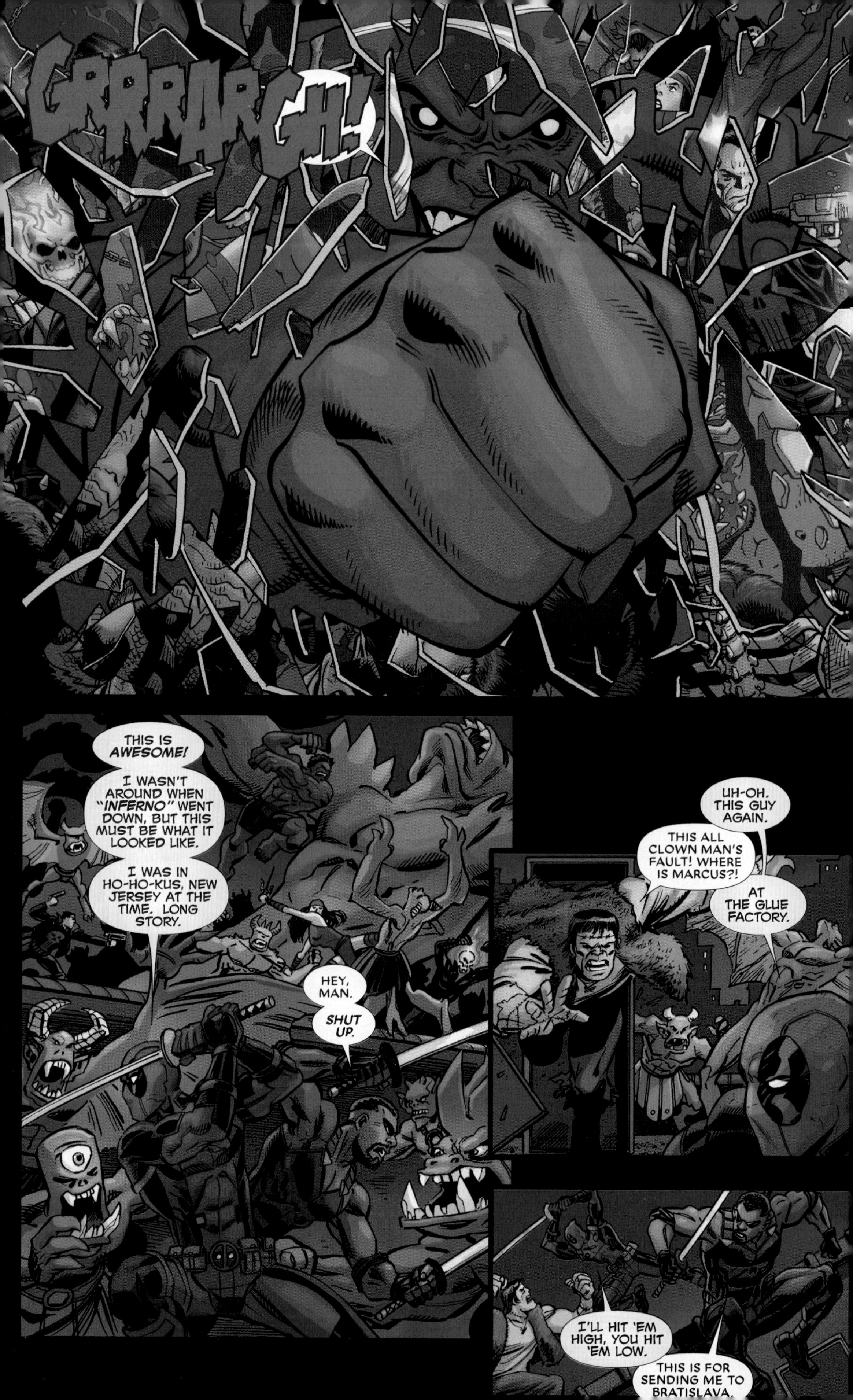

GRRRARGH!
THIS IS AWESOME!
I WASN'T AROUND WHEN "INFERNO" WENT DOWN, BUT THIS MUST BE WHAT IT LOOKED LIKE.
I WAS IN HO-HO-KUS, NEW JERSEY AT THE TIME. LONG STORY.
HEY, MAN. SHUT UP.
UH-OH. THIS GUY AGAIN.
THIS ALL CLOWN MAN'S FAULT! WHERE IS MARCUS?!
AT THE GLUE FACTORY.
I'LL HIT 'EM HIGH, YOU HIT 'EM LOW.
THIS IS FOR SENDING ME TO BRATISLAVA.

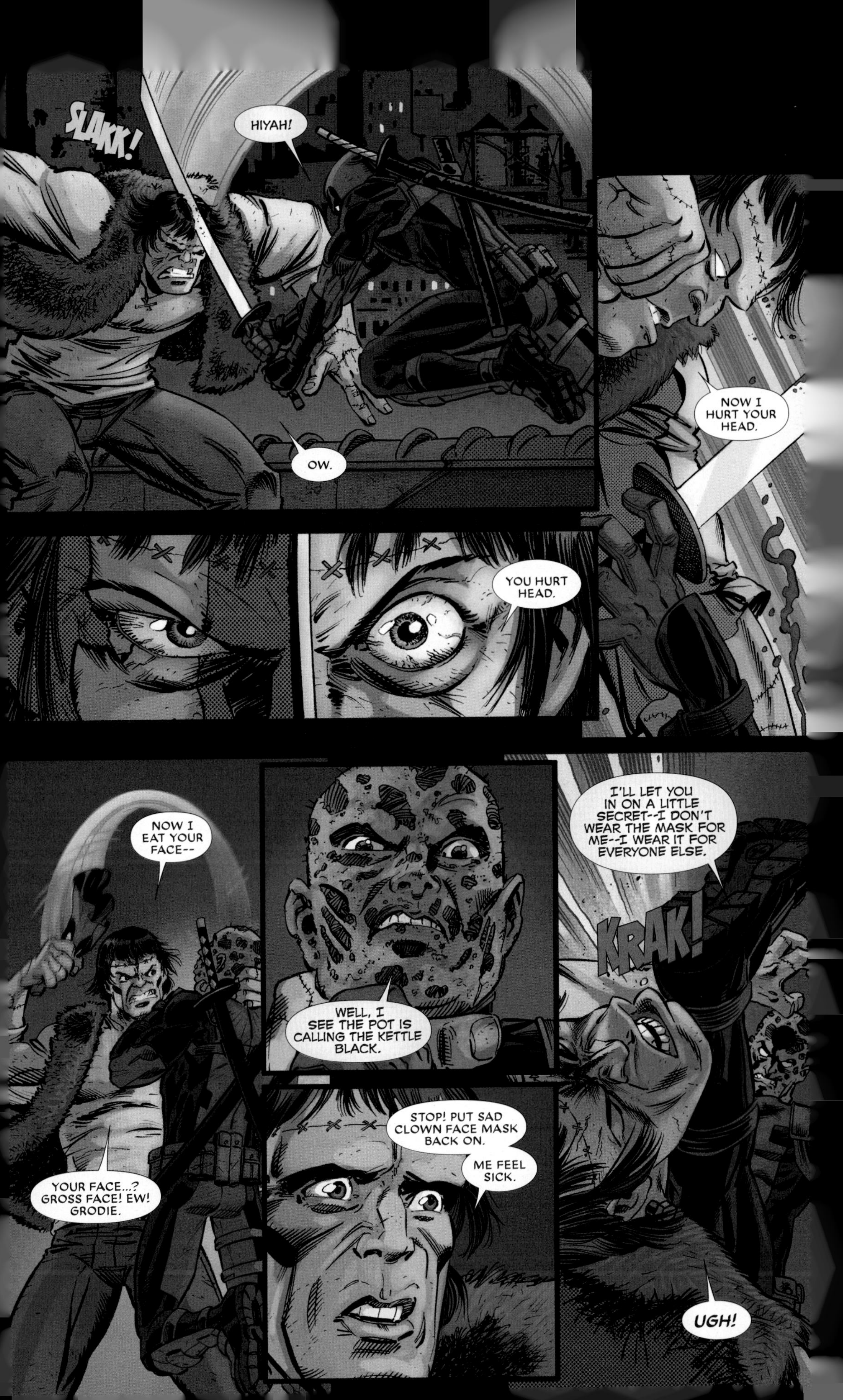
SLAKK!
HIYAH!
OW.
NOW I HURT YOUR HEAD.
YOU HURT HEAD.
NOW I EAT YOUR FACE--
YOUR FACE...? GROSS FACE! EW! GRODIE.
WELL, I SEE THE POT IS CALLING THE KETTLE BLACK.
STOP! PUT SAD CLOWN FACE MASK BACK ON.
ME FEEL SICK.
I'LL LET YOU IN ON A LITTLE SECRET--I DON'T WEAR THE MASK FOR ME--I WEAR IT FOR EVERYONE ELSE.
KRAK!
UGH!

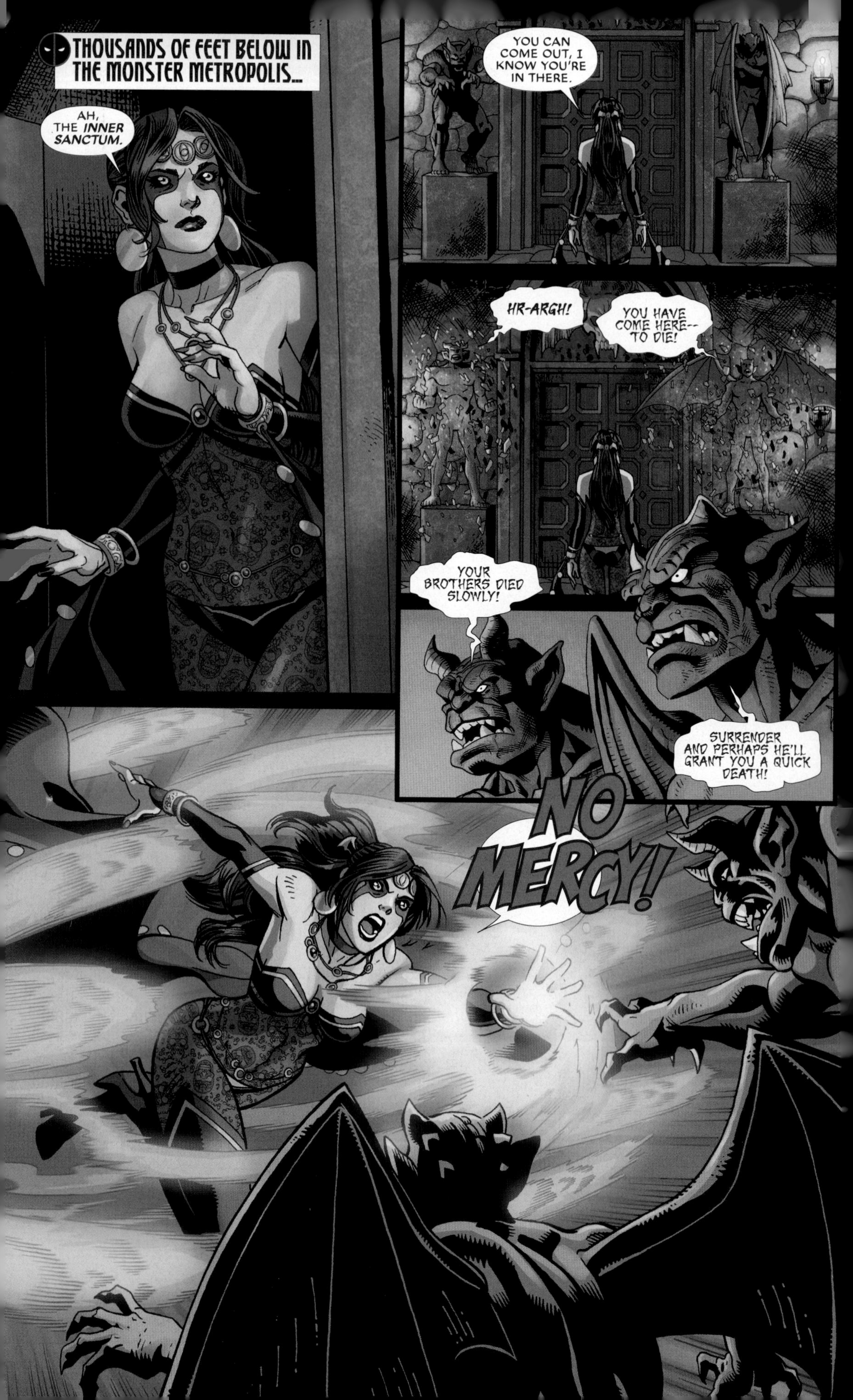
THOUSANDS OF FEET BELOW IN THE MONSTER METROPOLIS...
AH, THE INNER SANCTUM.
YOU CAN COME OUT, I KNOW YOU'RE IN THERE.
HR-ARGH!
YOU HAVE COME HERE-- TO DIE!
YOUR BROTHERS DIED SLOWLY!
SURRENDER AND PERHAPS HE'LL GRANT YOU A QUICK DEATH!
NO MERCY!

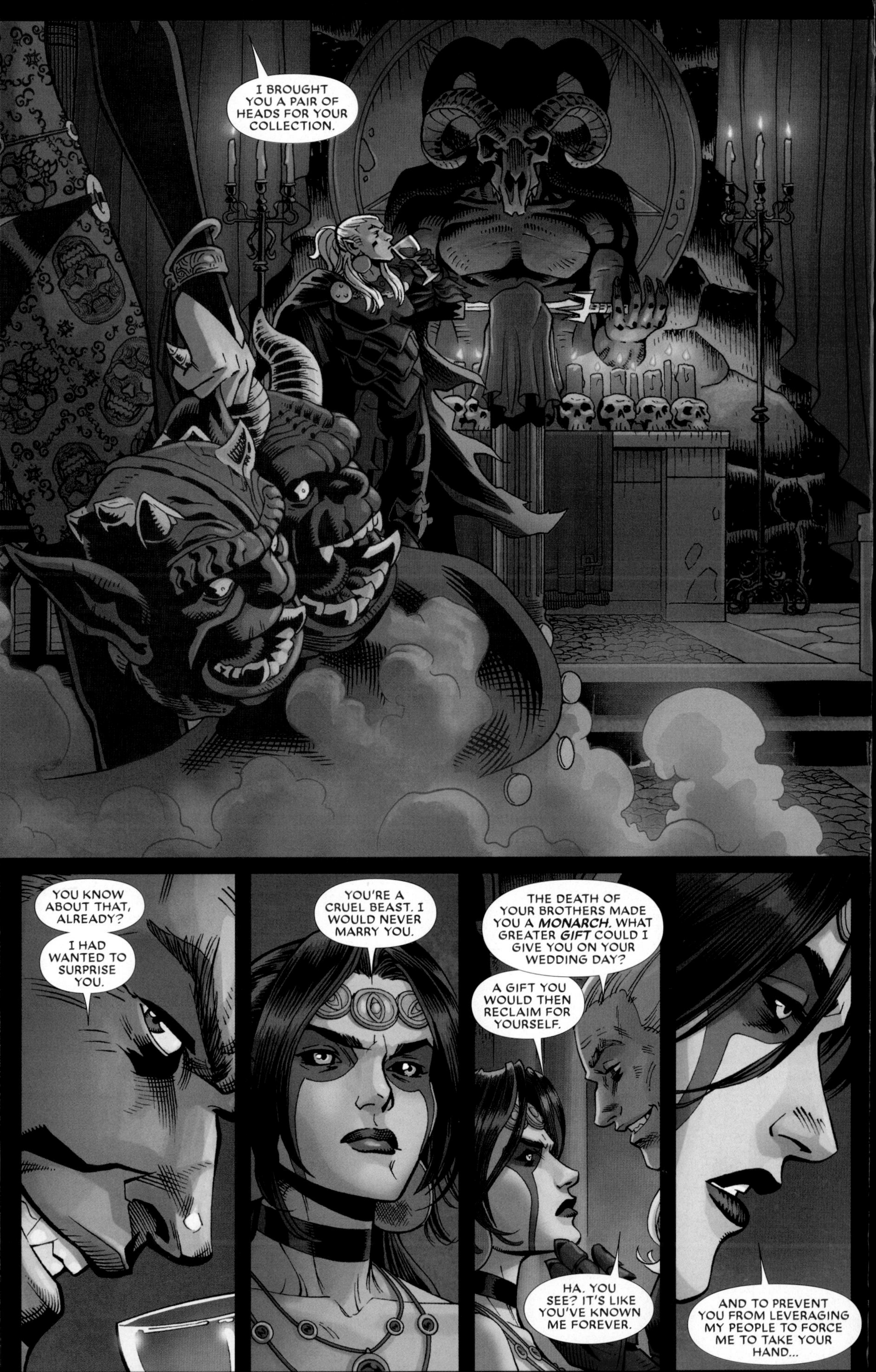
I BROUGHT YOU A PAIR OF HEADS FOR YOUR COLLECTION.
YOU KNOW ABOUT THAT, ALREADY?
I HAD WANTED TO SURPRISE YOU.
YOU'RE A CRUEL BEAST. I WOULD NEVER MARRY YOU.
THE DEATH OF YOUR BROTHERS MADE YOU A *MONARCH.* WHAT GREATER *GIFT* COULD I GIVE YOU ON YOUR WEDDING DAY?
A GIFT YOU WOULD THEN RECLAIM FOR YOURSELF.
HA. YOU SEE? IT'S LIKE YOU'VE KNOWN ME FOREVER.
AND TO PREVENT YOU FROM LEVERAGING MY PEOPLE TO FORCE ME TO TAKE YOUR HAND...

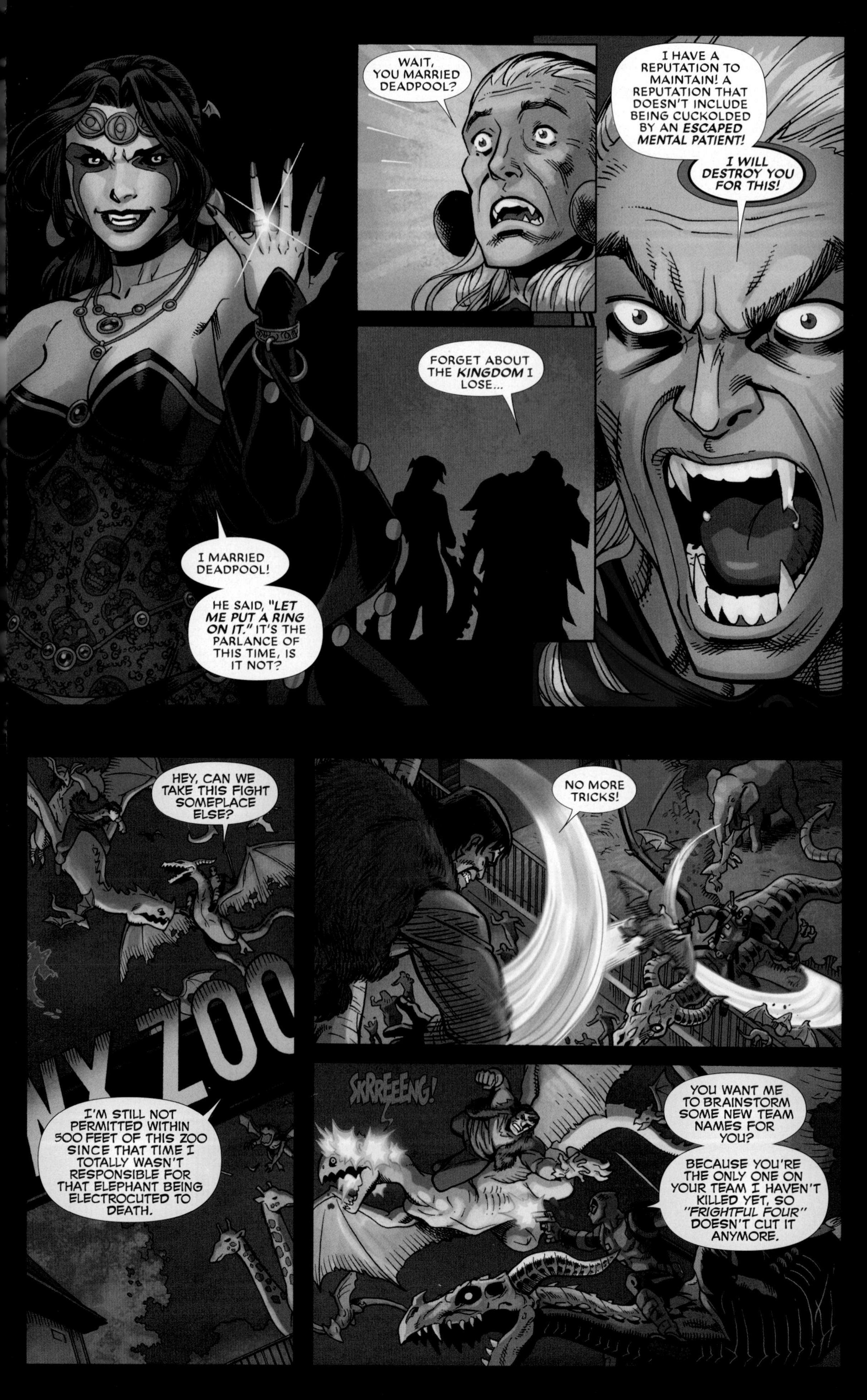
WAIT, YOU MARRIED DEADPOOL?
I MARRIED DEADPOOL!
HE SAID, "LET ME PUT A RING ON IT." IT'S THE PARLANCE OF THIS TIME, IS IT NOT?
FORGET ABOUT THE KINGDOM I LOSE...
I HAVE A REPUTATION TO MAINTAIN! A REPUTATION THAT DOESN'T INCLUDE BEING CUCKOLDED BY AN ESCAPED MENTAL PATIENT!
I WILL DESTROY YOU FOR THIS!
HEY, CAN WE TAKE THIS FIGHT SOMEPLACE ELSE?
NY ZOO
I'M STILL NOT PERMITTED WITHIN 500 FEET OF THIS ZOO SINCE THAT TIME I TOTALLY WASN'T RESPONSIBLE FOR THAT ELEPHANT BEING ELECTROCUTED TO DEATH.
NO MORE TRICKS!
SKRREEEENG!
YOU WANT ME TO BRAINSTORM SOME NEW TEAM NAMES FOR YOU?
BECAUSE YOU'RE THE ONLY ONE ON YOUR TEAM I HAVEN'T KILLED YET, SO "FRIGHTFUL FOUR" DOESN'T CUT IT ANYMORE.

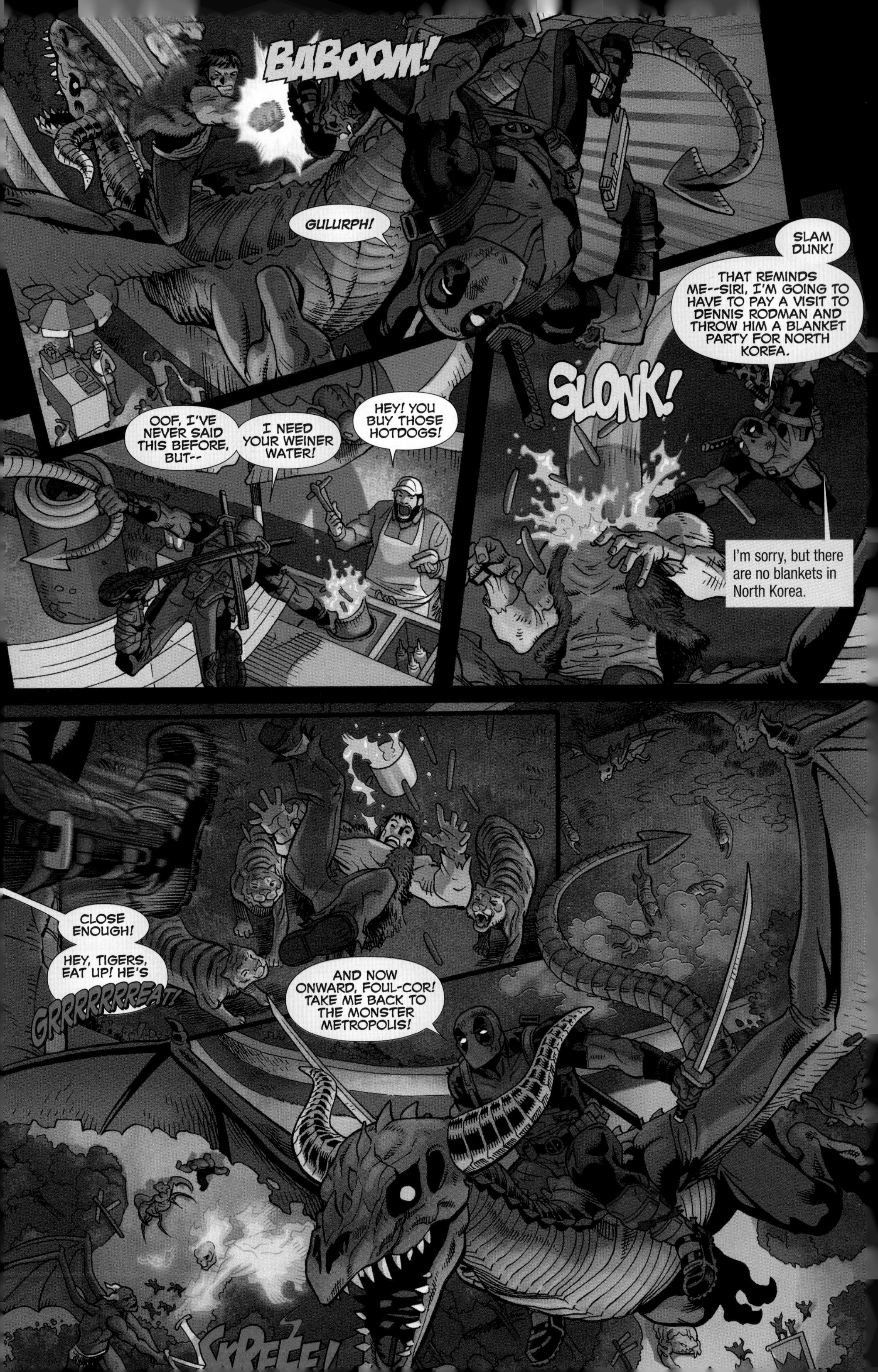
BABOOM!
GULURPH!
SLAM DUNK!
THAT REMINDS ME--SIRI, I'M GOING TO HAVE TO PAY A VISIT TO DENNIS RODMAN AND THROW HIM A BLANKET PARTY FOR NORTH KOREA.
OOF, I'VE NEVER SAID THIS BEFORE, BUT--
I NEED YOUR WEINER WATER!
HEY! YOU BUY THOSE HOTDOGS!
SLONK!
I'm sorry, but there are no blankets in North Korea.
CLOSE ENOUGH!
HEY, TIGERS, EAT UP! HE'S
GRRRRRRREAT!
AND NOW ONWARD, FOUL-COR! TAKE ME BACK TO THE MONSTER METROPOLIS!

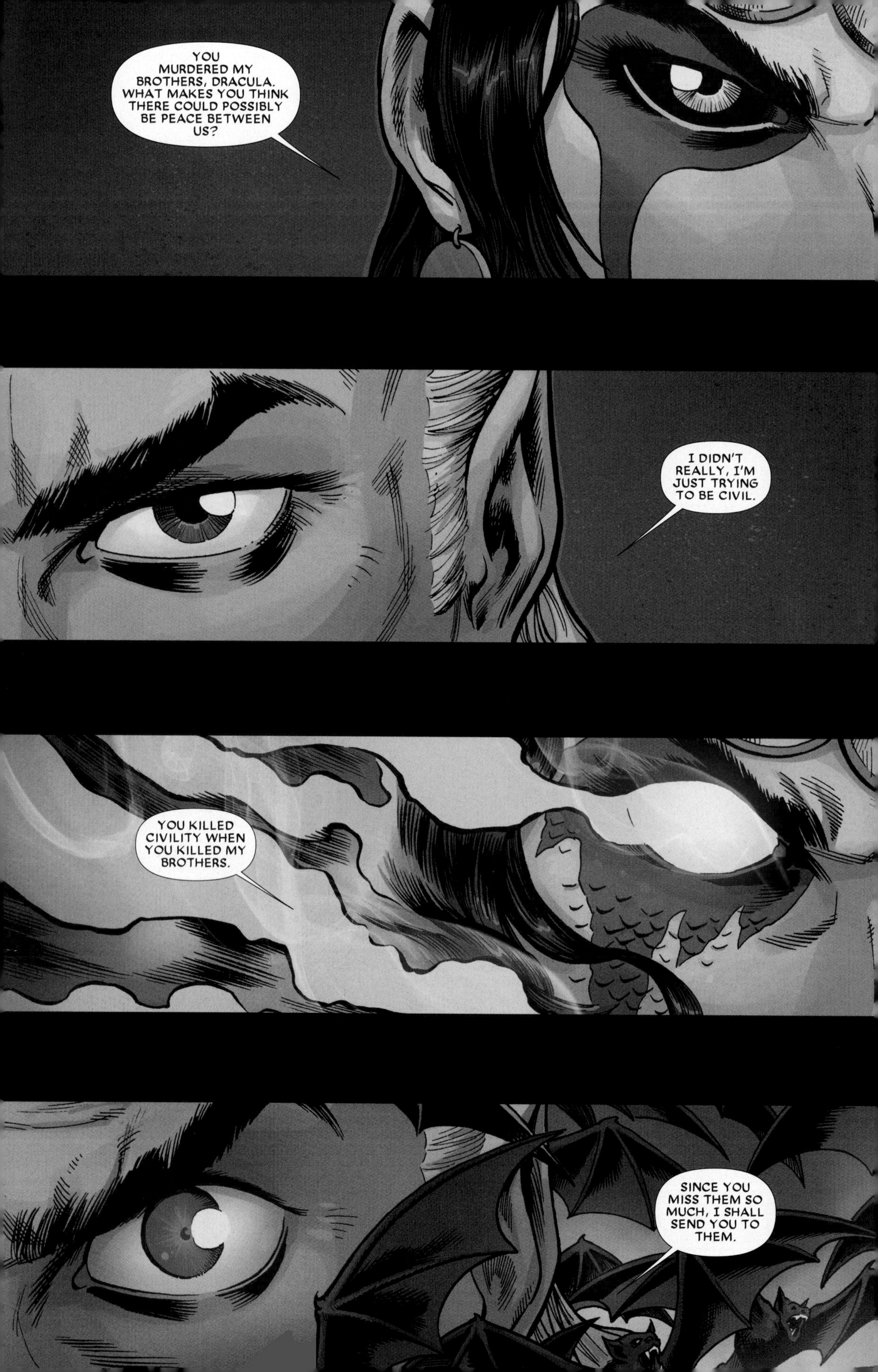
YOU MURDERED MY BROTHERS, DRACULA. WHAT MAKES YOU THINK THERE COULD POSSIBLY BE PEACE BETWEEN US?
I DIDN'T REALLY, I'M JUST TRYING TO BE CIVIL.
YOU KILLED CIVILITY WHEN YOU KILLED MY BROTHERS.
SINCE YOU MISS THEM SO MUCH, I SHALL SEND YOU TO THEM.

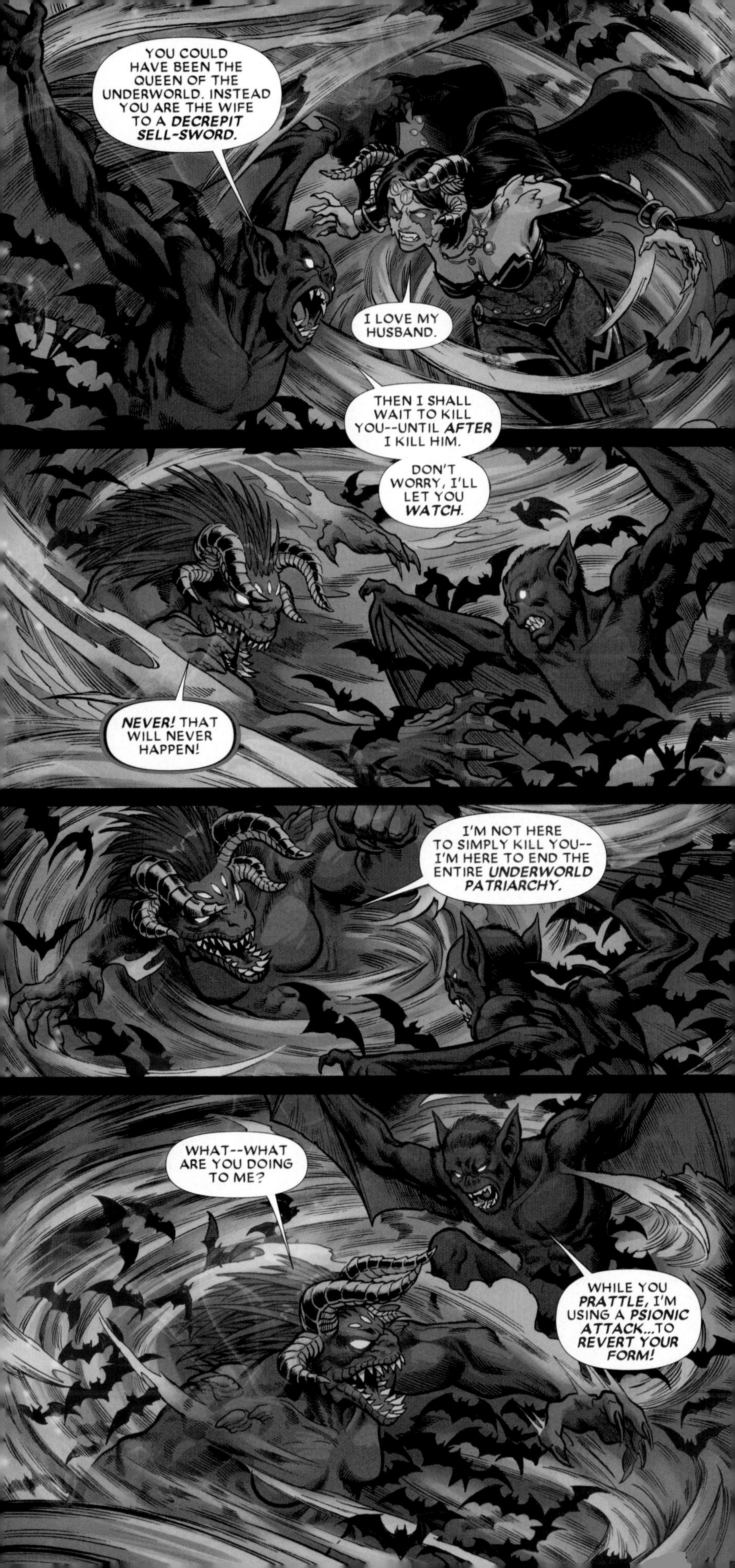
YOU COULD HAVE BEEN THE QUEEN OF THE UNDERWORLD. INSTEAD YOU ARE THE WIFE TO A DECREPIT SELL-SWORD.
I LOVE MY HUSBAND.
THEN I SHALL WAIT TO KILL YOU--UNTIL AFTER I KILL HIM.
DON'T WORRY, I'LL LET YOU WATCH.
NEVER! THAT WILL NEVER HAPPEN!
I'M NOT HERE TO SIMPLY KILL YOU-- I'M HERE TO END THE ENTIRE UNDERWORLD PATRIARCHY.
WHAT--WHAT ARE YOU DOING TO ME?
WHILE YOU PRATTLE, I'M USING A PSIONIC ATTACK...TO REVERT YOUR FORM!

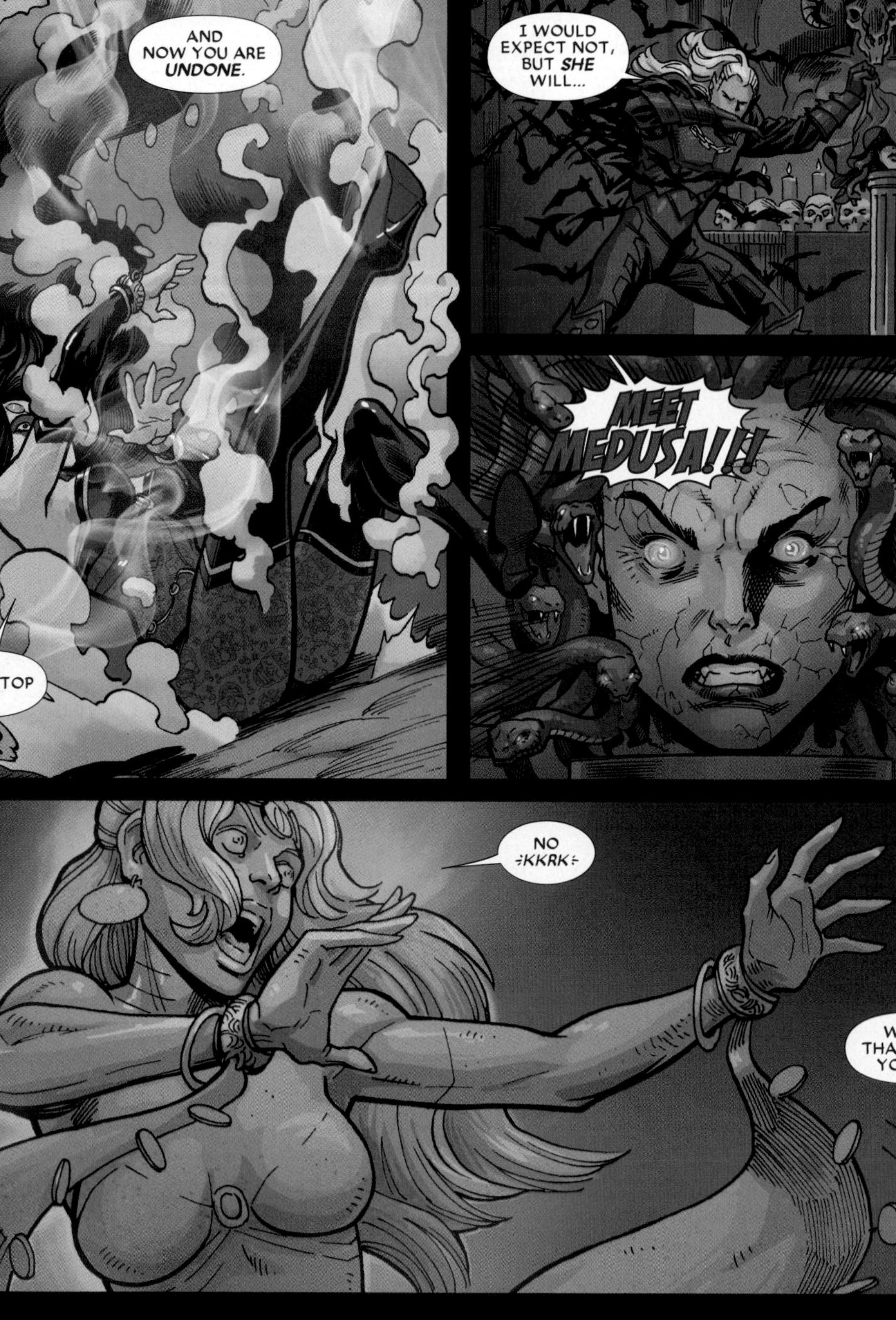
AND NOW YOU ARE UNDONE.
I WOULD EXPECT NOT, BUT SHE WILL...
MEET MEDUSA!!!
NO -KKRK-

DEADPOOL
The Gauntlet

CHAPTER 12: DEADPOOL, DISARMED

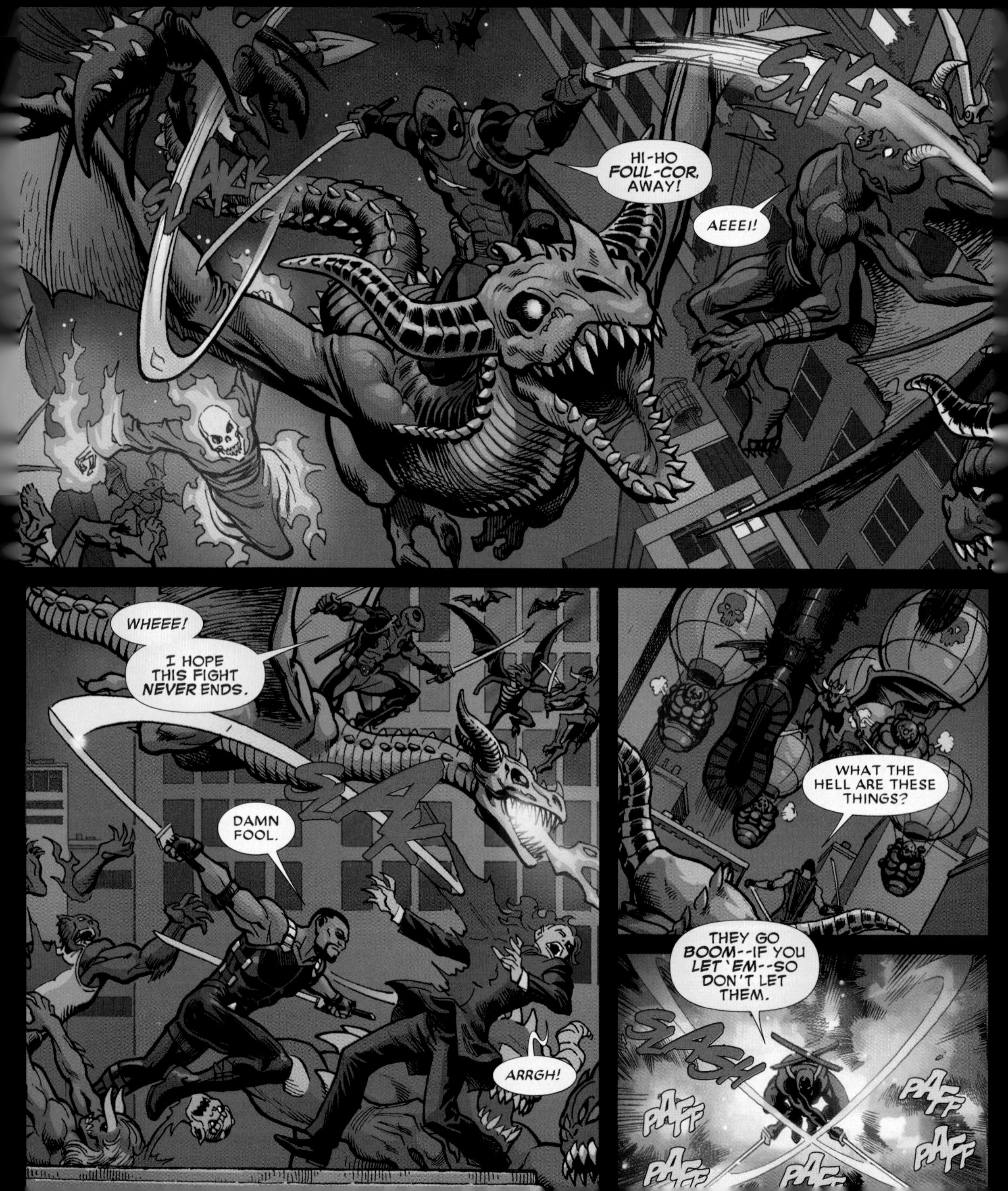
HI-HO FOUL-COR, AWAY!
AEEEI!
WHEEE!
I HOPE THIS FIGHT NEVER ENDS.
DAMN FOOL.
ARRGH!
WHAT THE HELL ARE THESE THINGS?
THEY GO BOOM--IF YOU LET 'EM--SO DON'T LET THEM.
SLASH
PAFF
PAFF
PAFF
PAFF

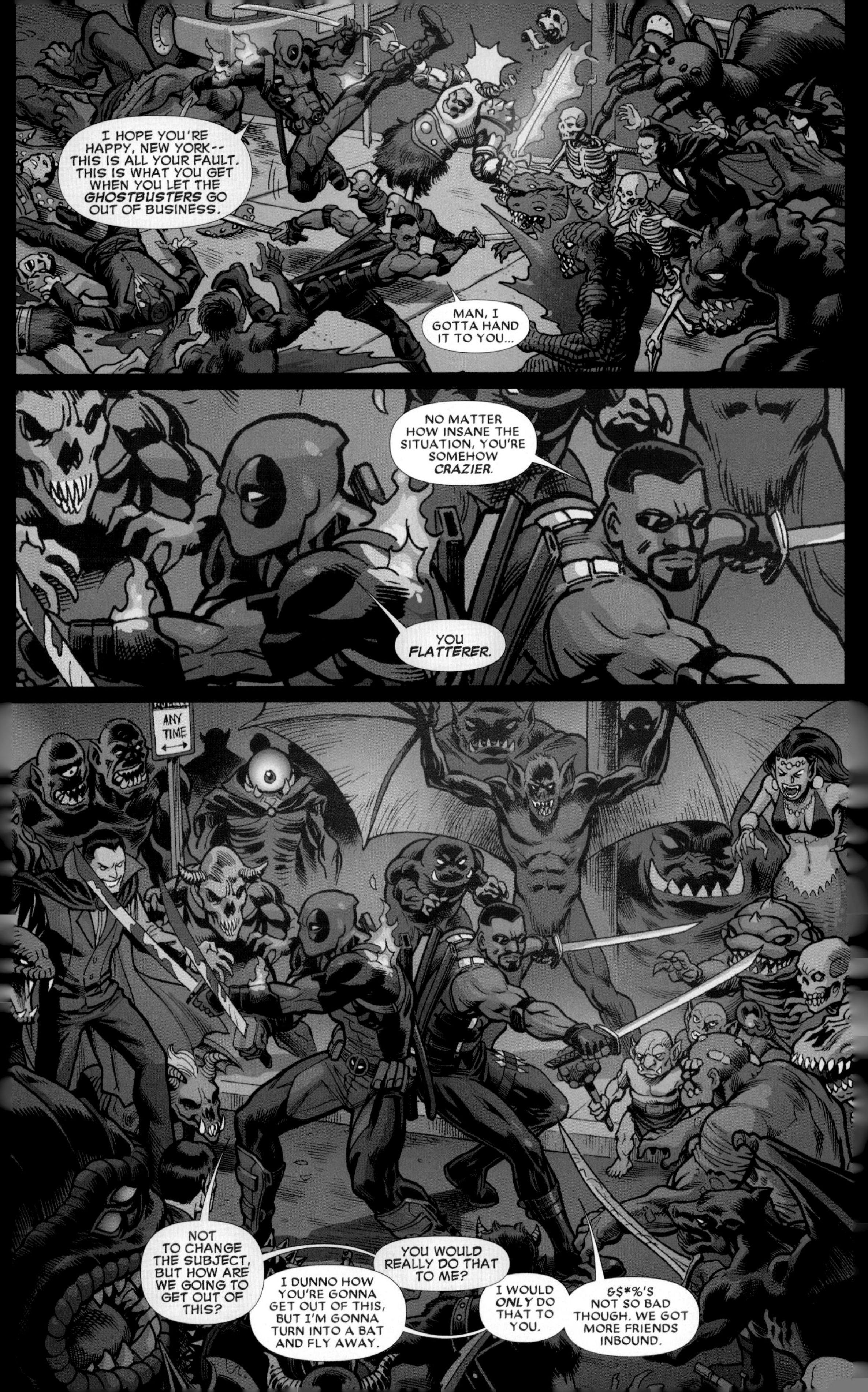
I HOPE YOU'RE HAPPY, NEW YORK-- THIS IS ALL YOUR FAULT. THIS IS WHAT YOU GET WHEN YOU LET THE GHOSTBUSTERS GO OUT OF BUSINESS.
MAN, I GOTTA HAND IT TO YOU...
NO MATTER HOW INSANE THE SITUATION, YOU'RE SOMEHOW CRAZIER.
YOU FLATTERER.
ANY TIME
NOT TO CHANGE THE SUBJECT, BUT HOW ARE WE GOING TO GET OUT OF THIS?
I DUNNO HOW YOU'RE GONNA GET OUT OF THIS, BUT I'M GONNA TURN INTO A BAT AND FLY AWAY.
YOU WOULD REALLY DO THAT TO ME?
I WOULD ONLY DO THAT TO YOU.
&$*%'S NOT SO BAD THOUGH. WE GOT MORE FRIENDS INBOUND.

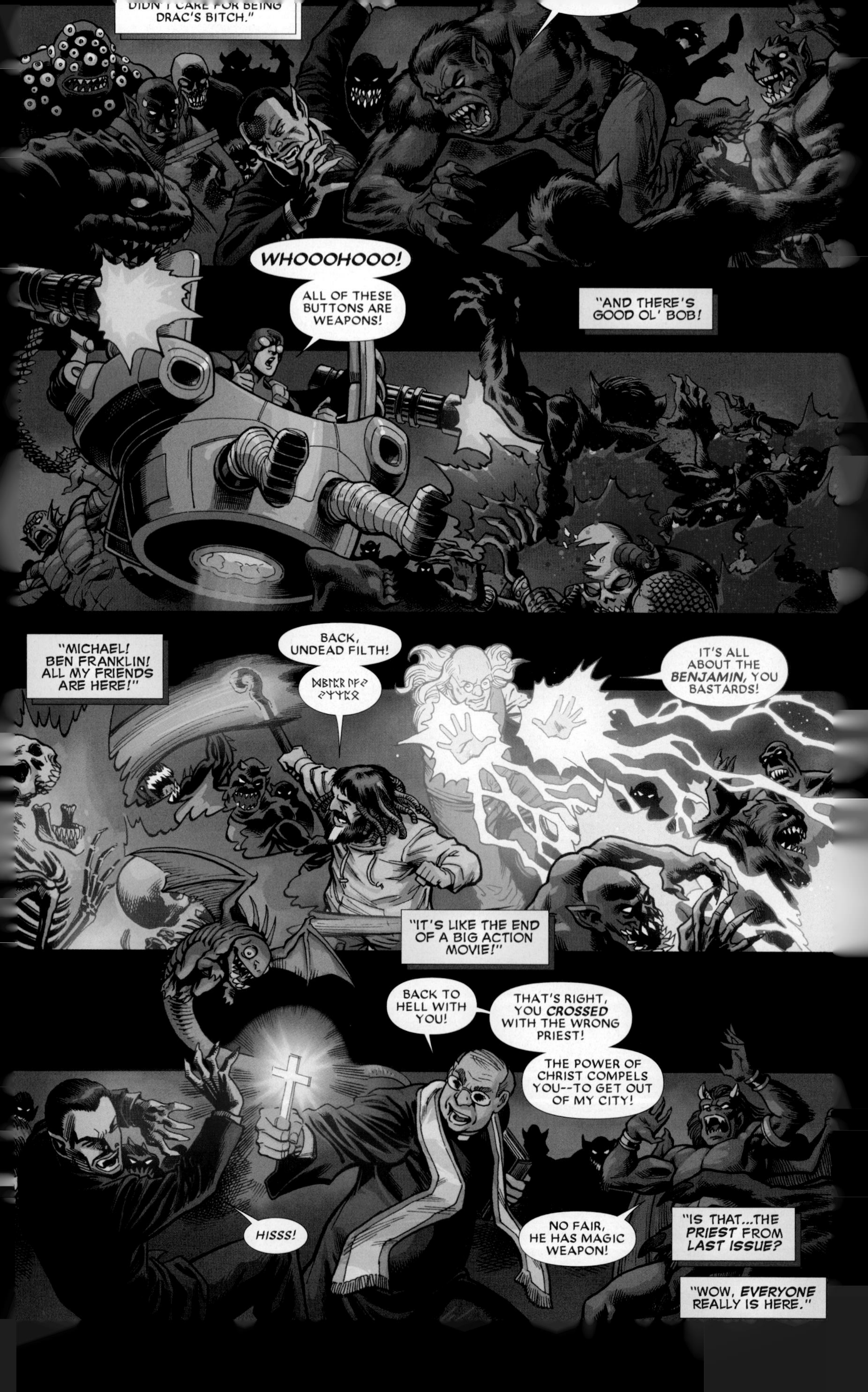
DIDN'T CARE FOR BEING DRAC'S BITCH."
WHOOOHOOO!
ALL OF THESE BUTTONS ARE WEAPONS!
"AND THERE'S GOOD OL' BOB!
"MICHAEL! BEN FRANKLIN! ALL MY FRIENDS ARE HERE!"
BACK, UNDEAD FILTH!
IT'S ALL ABOUT THE BENJAMIN, YOU BASTARDS!
"IT'S LIKE THE END OF A BIG ACTION MOVIE!"
BACK TO HELL WITH YOU!
THAT'S RIGHT, YOU CROSSED WITH THE WRONG PRIEST!
THE POWER OF CHRIST COMPELS YOU--TO GET OUT OF MY CITY!
HISSS!
NO FAIR, HE HAS MAGIC WEAPON!
"IS THAT...THE PRIEST FROM LAST ISSUE?
"WOW, EVERYONE REALLY IS HERE."

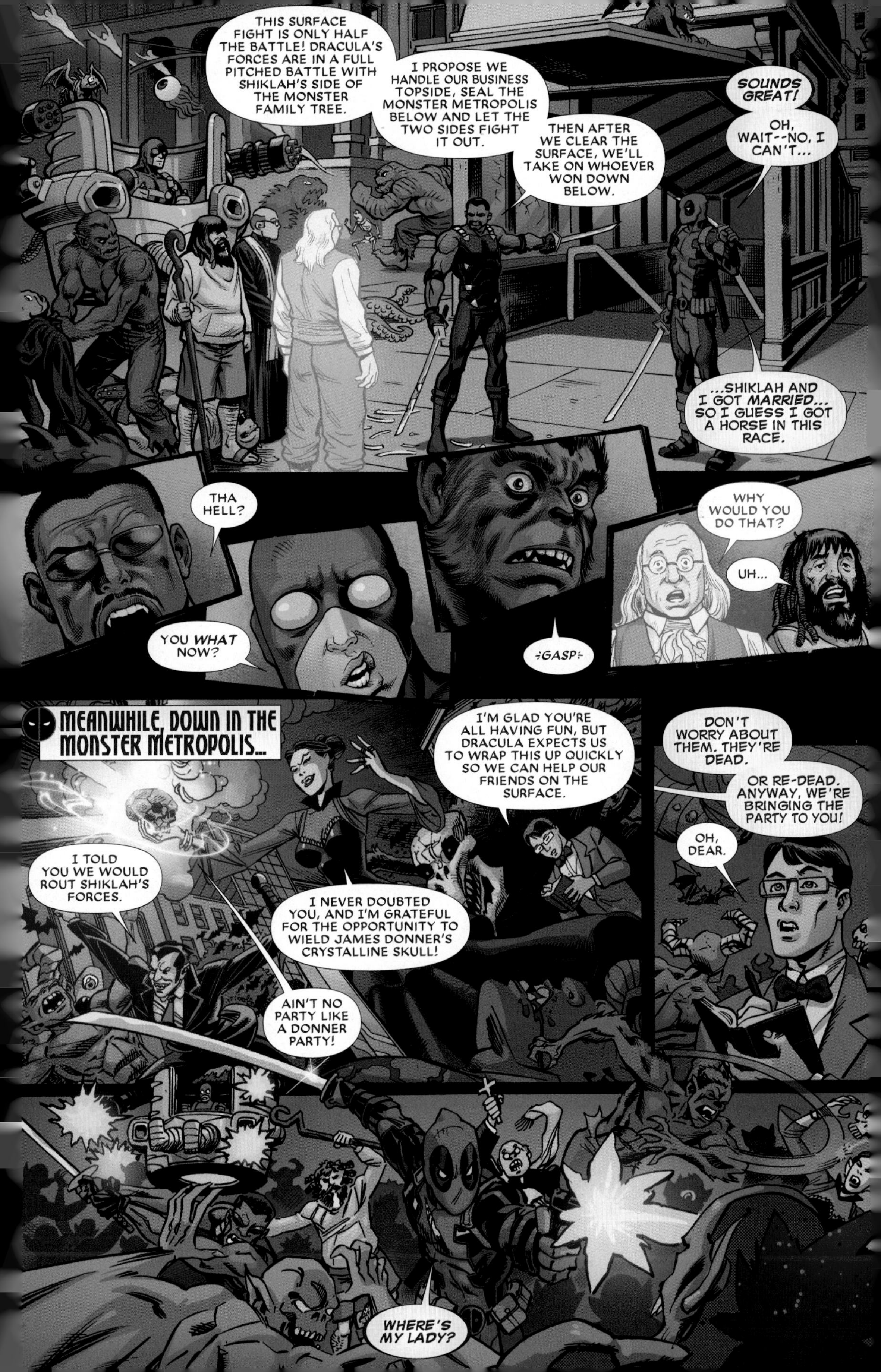
THIS SURFACE FIGHT IS ONLY HALF THE BATTLE! DRACULA'S FORCES ARE IN A FULL PITCHED BATTLE WITH SHIKLAH'S SIDE OF THE MONSTER FAMILY TREE.
I PROPOSE WE HANDLE OUR BUSINESS TOPSIDE, SEAL THE MONSTER METROPOLIS BELOW AND LET THE TWO SIDES FIGHT IT OUT.
THEN AFTER WE CLEAR THE SURFACE, WE'LL TAKE ON WHOEVER WON DOWN BELOW.
SOUNDS GREAT!
OH, WAIT--NO, I CAN'T...
...SHIKLAH AND I GOT MARRIED... SO I GUESS I GOT A HORSE IN THIS RACE.
THA HELL?
YOU WHAT NOW?
GASP
WHY WOULD YOU DO THAT?
UH...
MEANWHILE, DOWN IN THE MONSTER METROPOLIS...
I'M GLAD YOU'RE ALL HAVING FUN, BUT DRACULA EXPECTS US TO WRAP THIS UP QUICKLY SO WE CAN HELP OUR FRIENDS ON THE SURFACE.
DON'T WORRY ABOUT THEM. THEY'RE DEAD.
OR RE-DEAD. ANYWAY, WE'RE BRINGING THE PARTY TO YOU!
OH, DEAR.
I TOLD YOU WE WOULD ROUT SHIKLAH'S FORCES.
I NEVER DOUBTED YOU, AND I'M GRATEFUL FOR THE OPPORTUNITY TO WIELD JAMES DONNER'S CRYSTALLINE SKULL!
AIN'T NO PARTY LIKE A DONNER PARTY!
WHERE'S MY LADY?

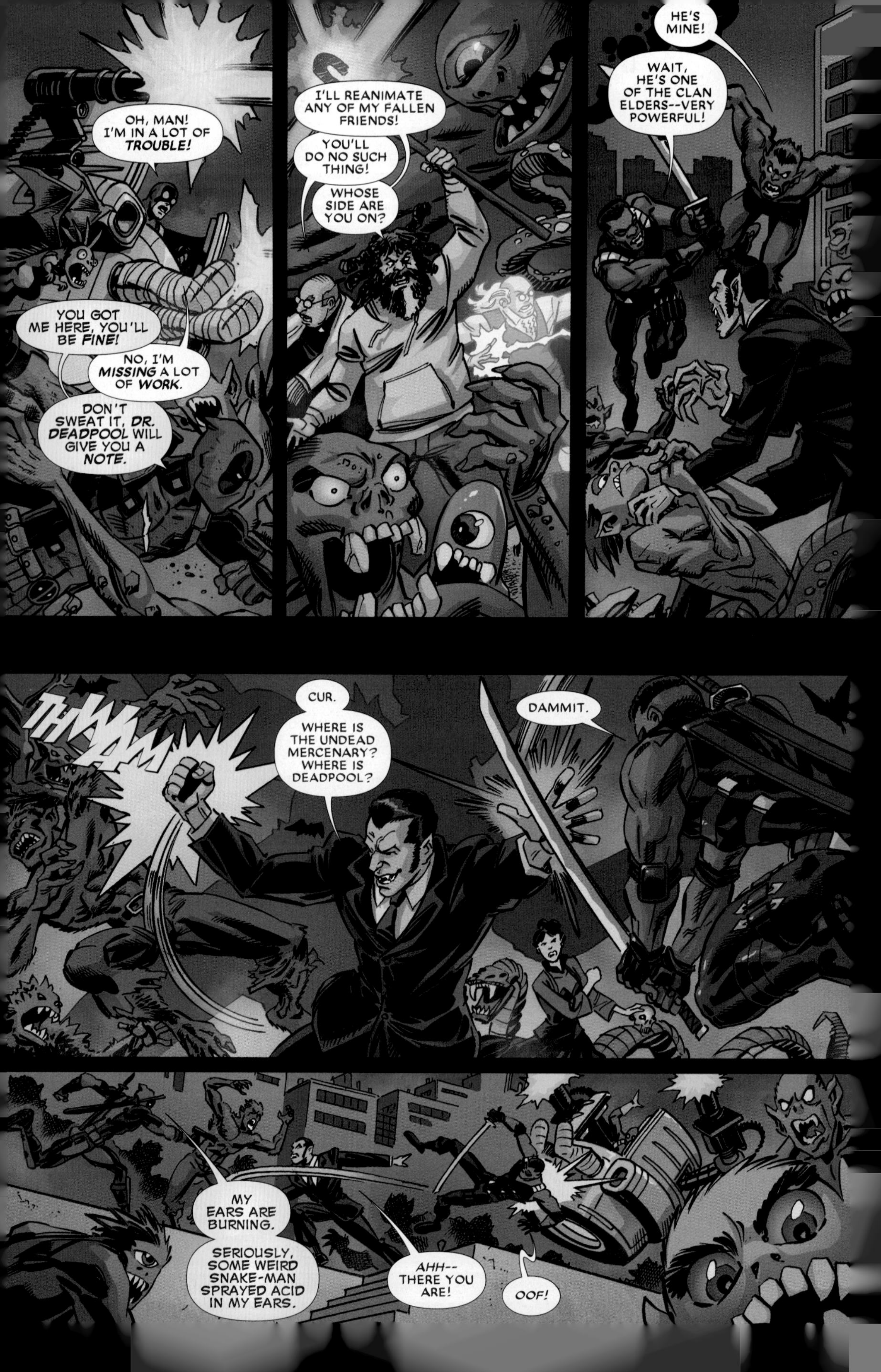

OH, MAN! I'M IN A LOT OF TROUBLE!
YOU GOT ME HERE, YOU'LL BE FINE!
NO, I'M MISSING A LOT OF WORK.
DON'T SWEAT IT, DR. DEADPOOL WILL GIVE YOU A NOTE.
I'LL REANIMATE ANY OF MY FALLEN FRIENDS!
YOU'LL DO NO SUCH THING!
WHOSE SIDE ARE YOU ON?
HE'S MINE!
WAIT, HE'S ONE OF THE CLAN ELDERS--VERY POWERFUL!
THWAM
CUR.
WHERE IS THE UNDEAD MERCENARY? WHERE IS DEADPOOL?
DAMMIT.
MY EARS ARE BURNING.
SERIOUSLY, SOME WEIRD SNAKE-MAN SPRAYED ACID IN MY EARS.
AHH-- THERE YOU ARE!
OOF!

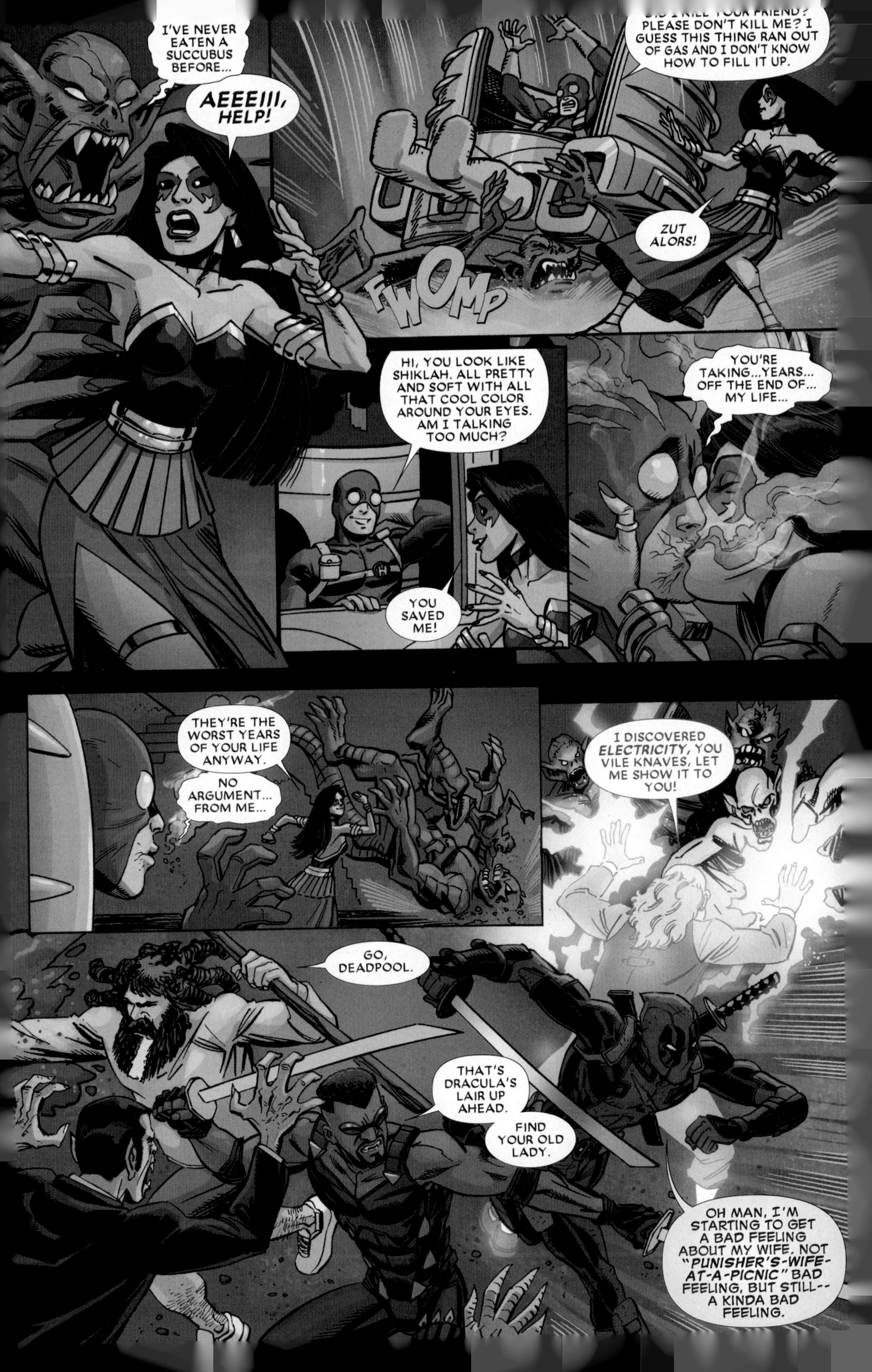
I'VE NEVER EATEN A SUCCUBUS BEFORE...
AEEEIII, HELP!
PLEASE DON'T KILL ME? I GUESS THIS THING RAN OUT OF GAS AND I DON'T KNOW HOW TO FILL IT UP.
ZUT ALORS!
FWOMP
HI, YOU LOOK LIKE SHIKLAH. ALL PRETTY AND SOFT WITH ALL THAT COOL COLOR AROUND YOUR EYES. AM I TALKING TOO MUCH?
YOU SAVED ME!
YOU'RE TAKING...YEARS... OFF THE END OF... MY LIFE...
THEY'RE THE WORST YEARS OF YOUR LIFE ANYWAY.
NO ARGUMENT... FROM ME...
I DISCOVERED ELECTRICITY, YOU VILE KNAVES, LET ME SHOW IT TO YOU!
GO, DEADPOOL.
THAT'S DRACULA'S LAIR UP AHEAD.
FIND YOUR OLD LADY.
OH MAN, I'M STARTING TO GET A BAD FEELING ABOUT MY WIFE. NOT "PUNISHER'S-WIFE-AT-A-PICNIC" BAD FEELING, BUT STILL-- A KINDA BAD FEELING.

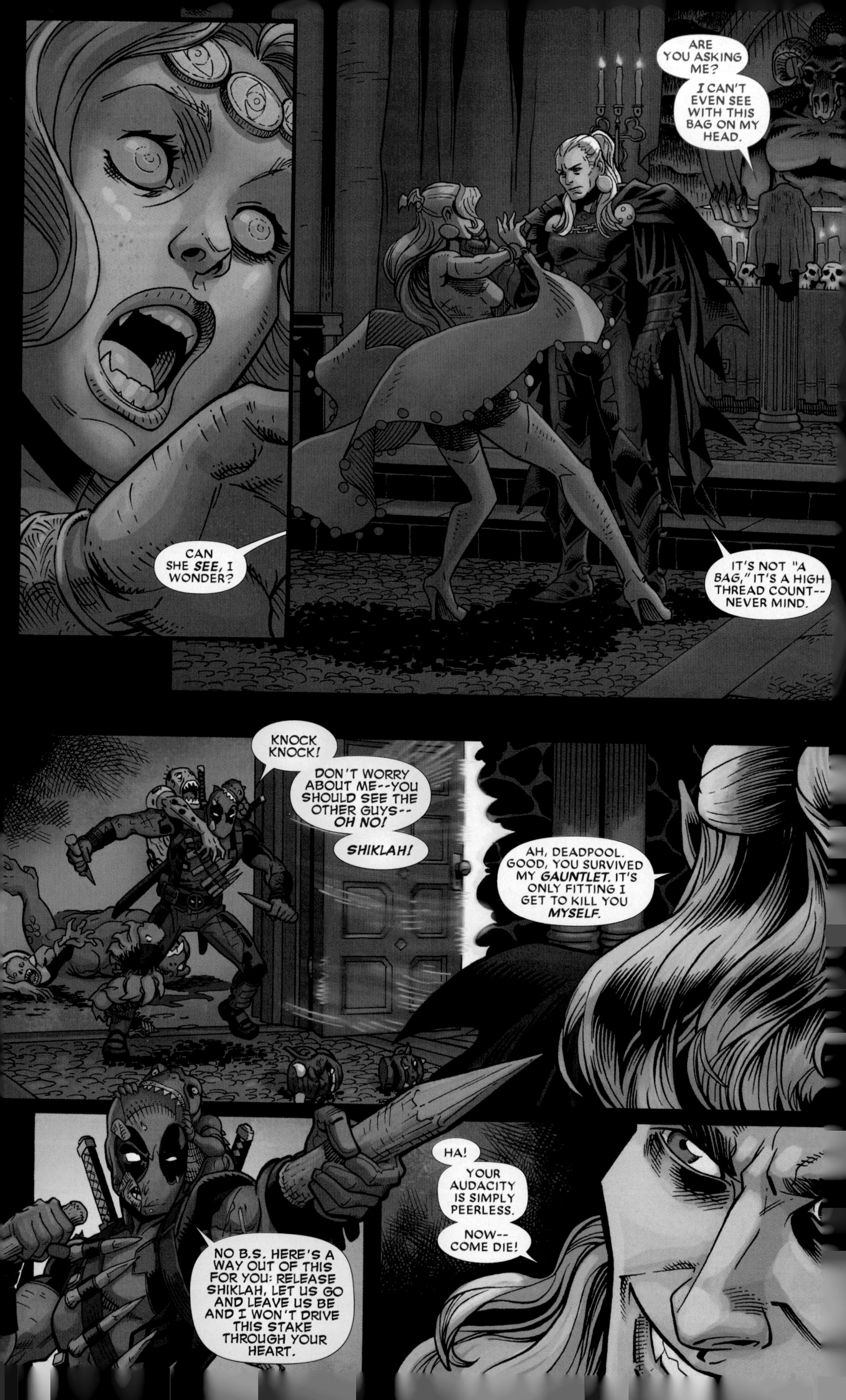

ARE YOU ASKING ME?
I CAN'T EVEN SEE WITH THIS BAG ON MY HEAD.
CAN SHE SEE, I WONDER?
IT'S NOT "A BAG," IT'S A HIGH THREAD COUNT--NEVER MIND.
KNOCK KNOCK!
DON'T WORRY ABOUT ME--YOU SHOULD SEE THE OTHER GUYS--OH NO!
SHIKLAH!
AH, DEADPOOL. GOOD, YOU SURVIVED MY GAUNTLET. IT'S ONLY FITTING I GET TO KILL YOU MYSELF.
NO B.S. HERE'S A WAY OUT OF THIS FOR YOU: RELEASE SHIKLAH, LET US GO AND LEAVE US BE AND I WON'T DRIVE THIS STAKE THROUGH YOUR HEART.
HA!
YOUR AUDACITY IS SIMPLY PEERLESS.
NOW--COME DIE!

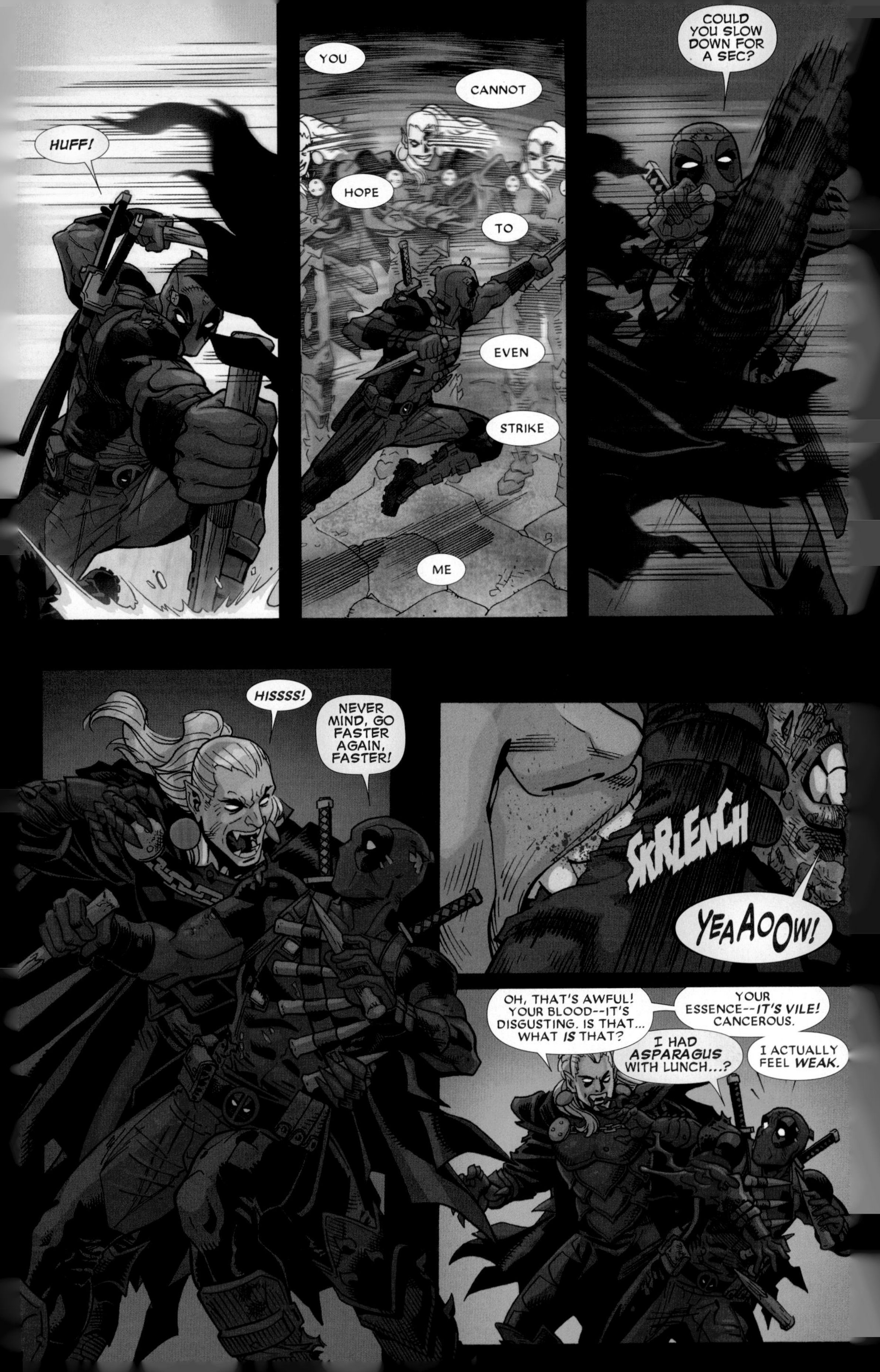
HUFF!
YOU
CANNOT
HOPE
TO
EVEN
STRIKE
ME
COULD YOU SLOW DOWN FOR A SEC?
HISSSS!
NEVER MIND, GO FASTER AGAIN, FASTER!
SKRLENCH
YEAAOOW!
OH, THAT'S AWFUL! YOUR BLOOD--IT'S DISGUSTING. IS THAT... WHAT IS THAT?
YOUR ESSENCE--IT'S VILE! CANCEROUS.
I HAD ASPARAGUS WITH LUNCH...?
I ACTUALLY FEEL WEAK.

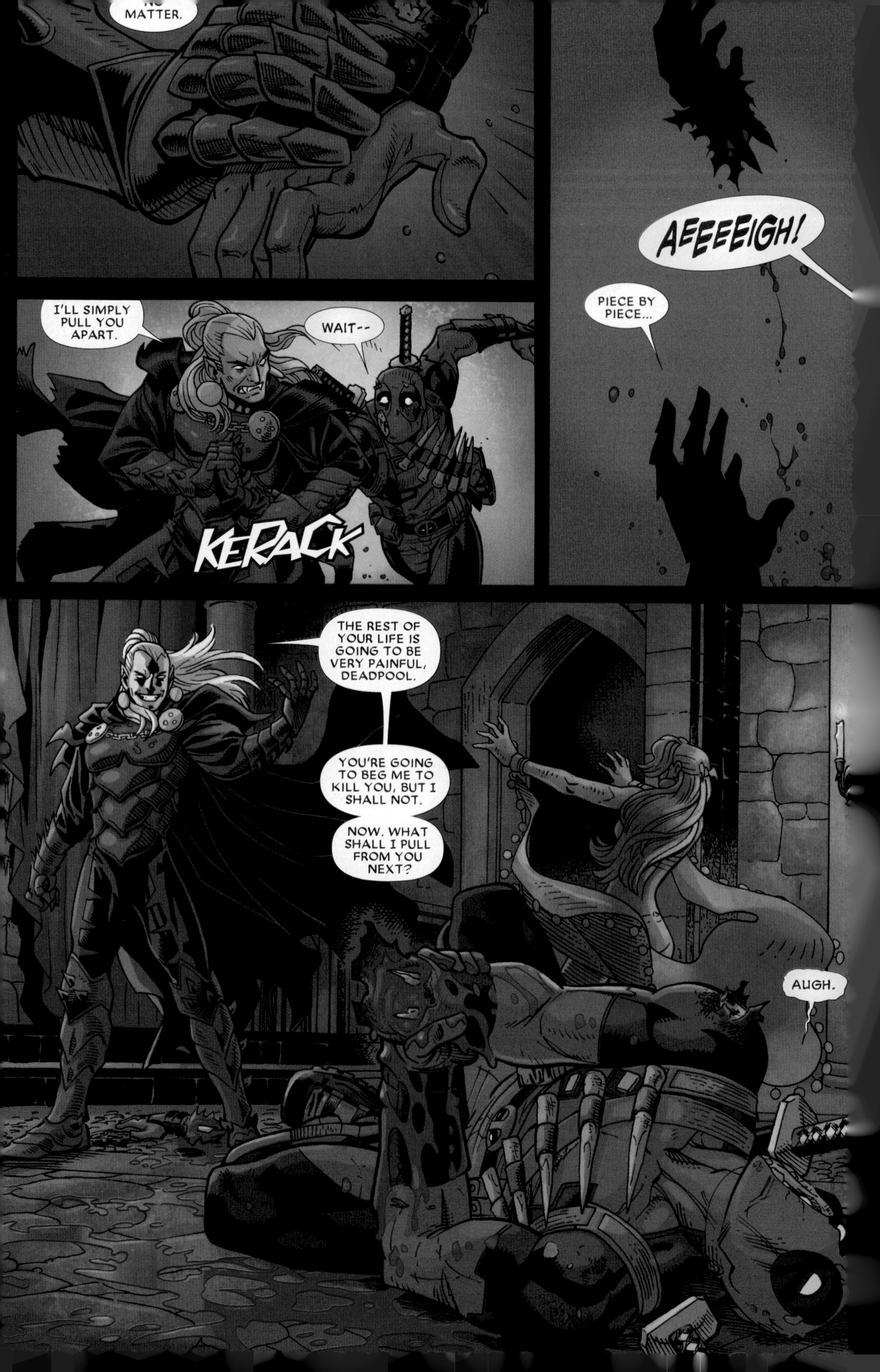
MATTER.
I'LL SIMPLY PULL YOU APART.
WAIT--
KERACK
AEEEEIGH!
PIECE BY PIECE...
THE REST OF YOUR LIFE IS GOING TO BE VERY PAINFUL, DEADPOOL.
YOU'RE GOING TO BEG ME TO KILL YOU, BUT I SHALL NOT.
NOW. WHAT SHALL I PULL FROM YOU NEXT?
AUGH.

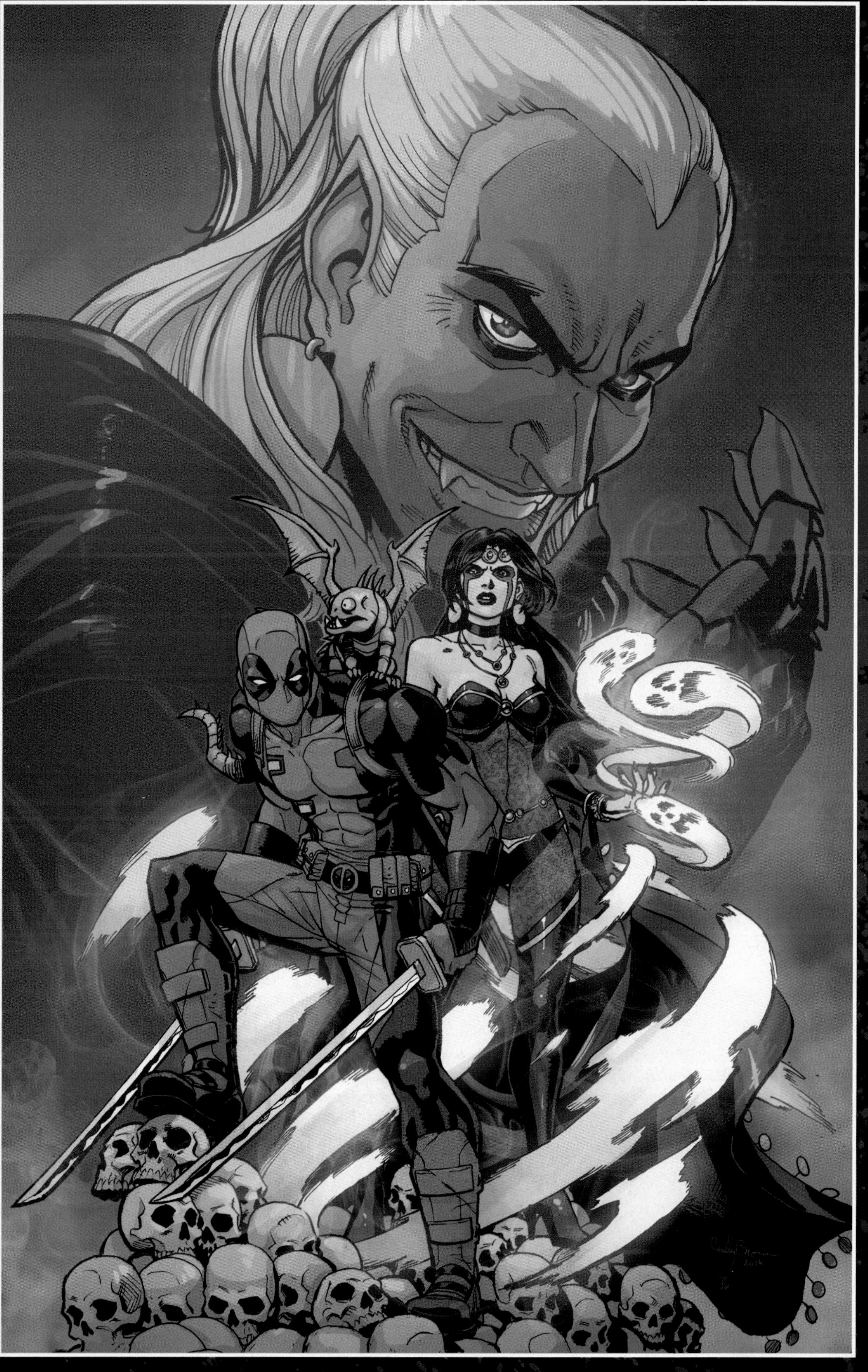

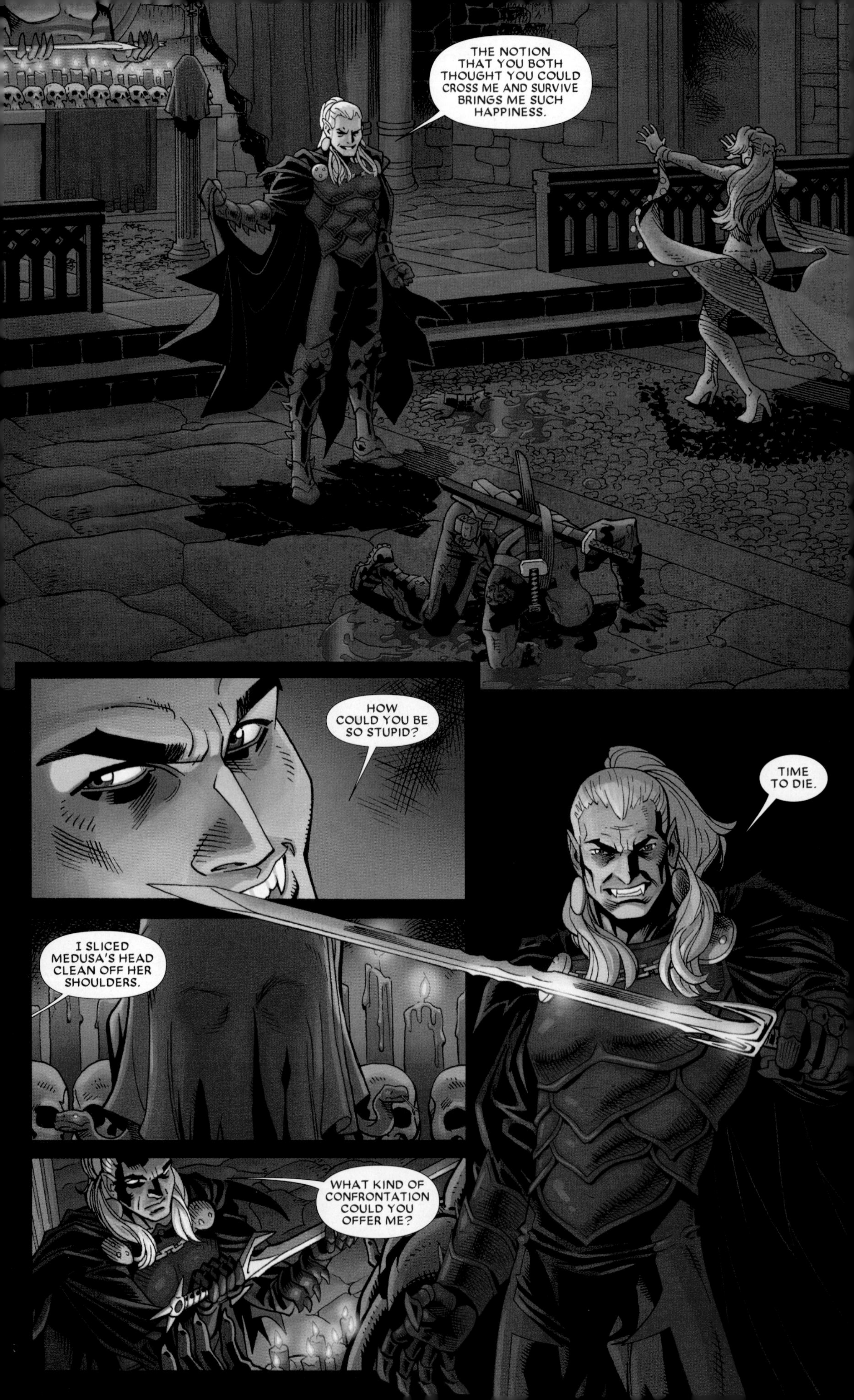
THE NOTION THAT YOU BOTH THOUGHT YOU COULD CROSS ME AND SURVIVE BRINGS ME SUCH HAPPINESS.
HOW COULD YOU BE SO STUPID?
I SLICED MEDUSA'S HEAD CLEAN OFF HER SHOULDERS.
WHAT KIND OF CONFRONTATION COULD YOU OFFER ME?
TIME TO DIE.

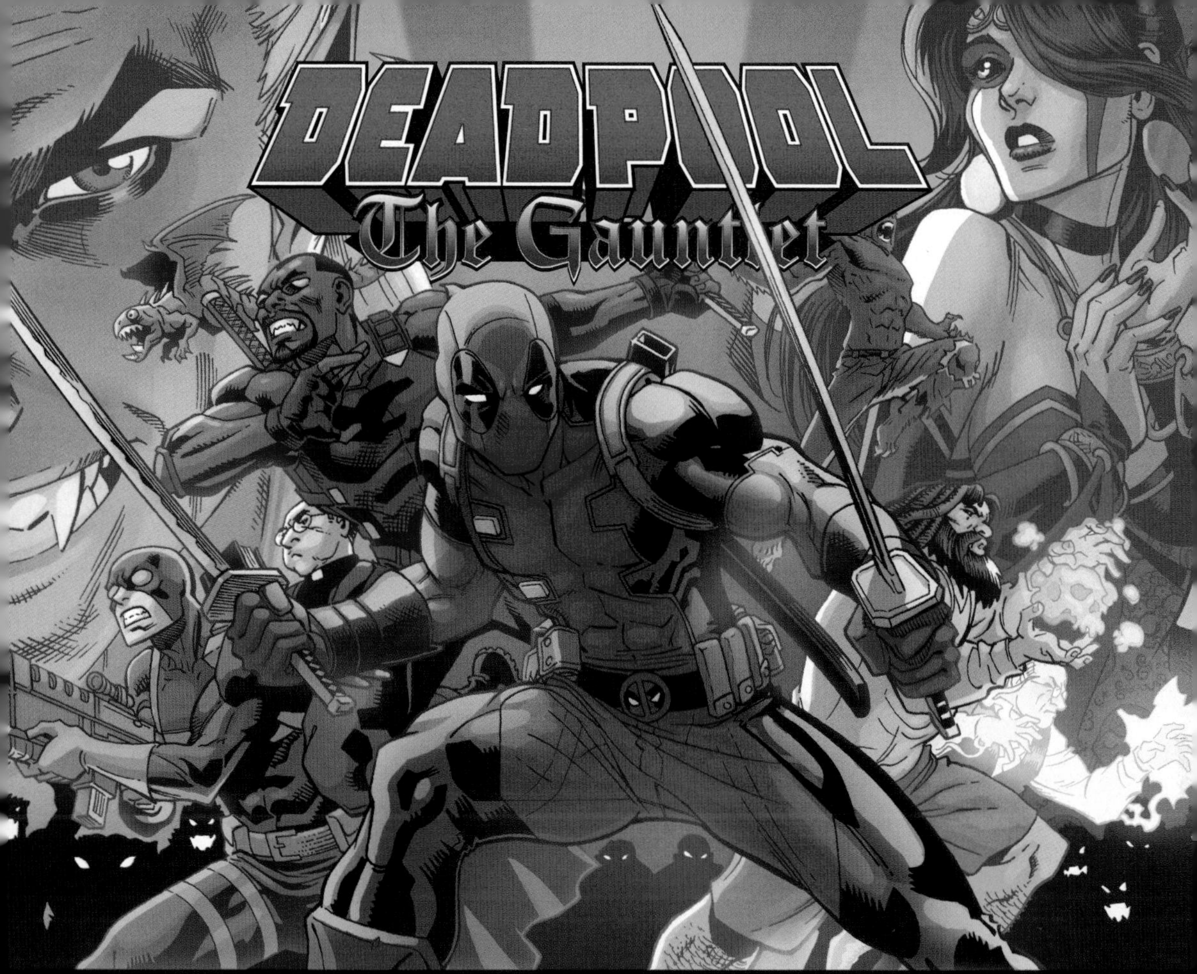
DEADPOOL
The Gauntlet

CHAPTER 13: GIVE LOVE A HAND

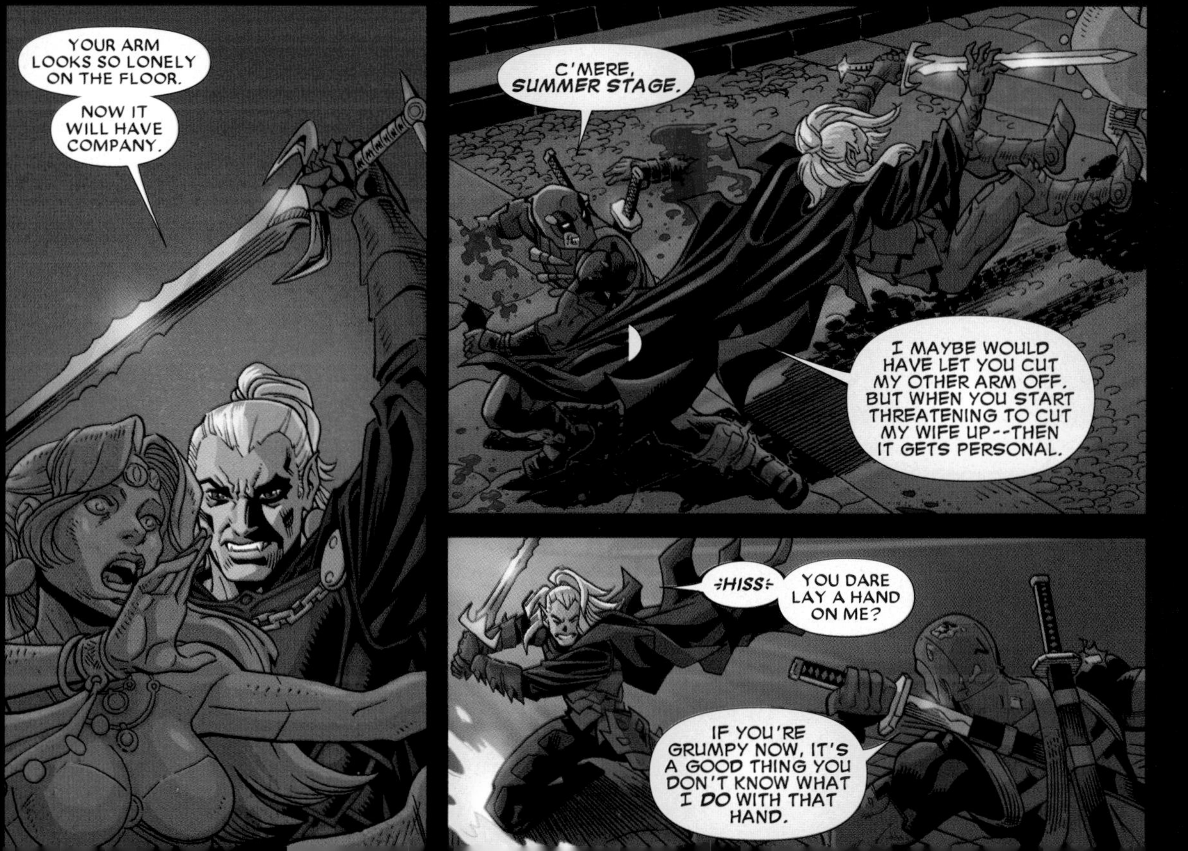
YOUR ARM LOOKS SO LONELY ON THE FLOOR.
NOW IT WILL HAVE COMPANY.
C'MERE, SUMMER STAGE.
I MAYBE WOULD HAVE LET YOU CUT MY OTHER ARM OFF. BUT WHEN YOU START THREATENING TO CUT MY WIFE UP--THEN IT GETS PERSONAL.
HISS
YOU DARE LAY A HAND ON ME?
IF YOU'RE GRUMPY NOW, IT'S A GOOD THING YOU DON'T KNOW WHAT I DO WITH THAT HAND.

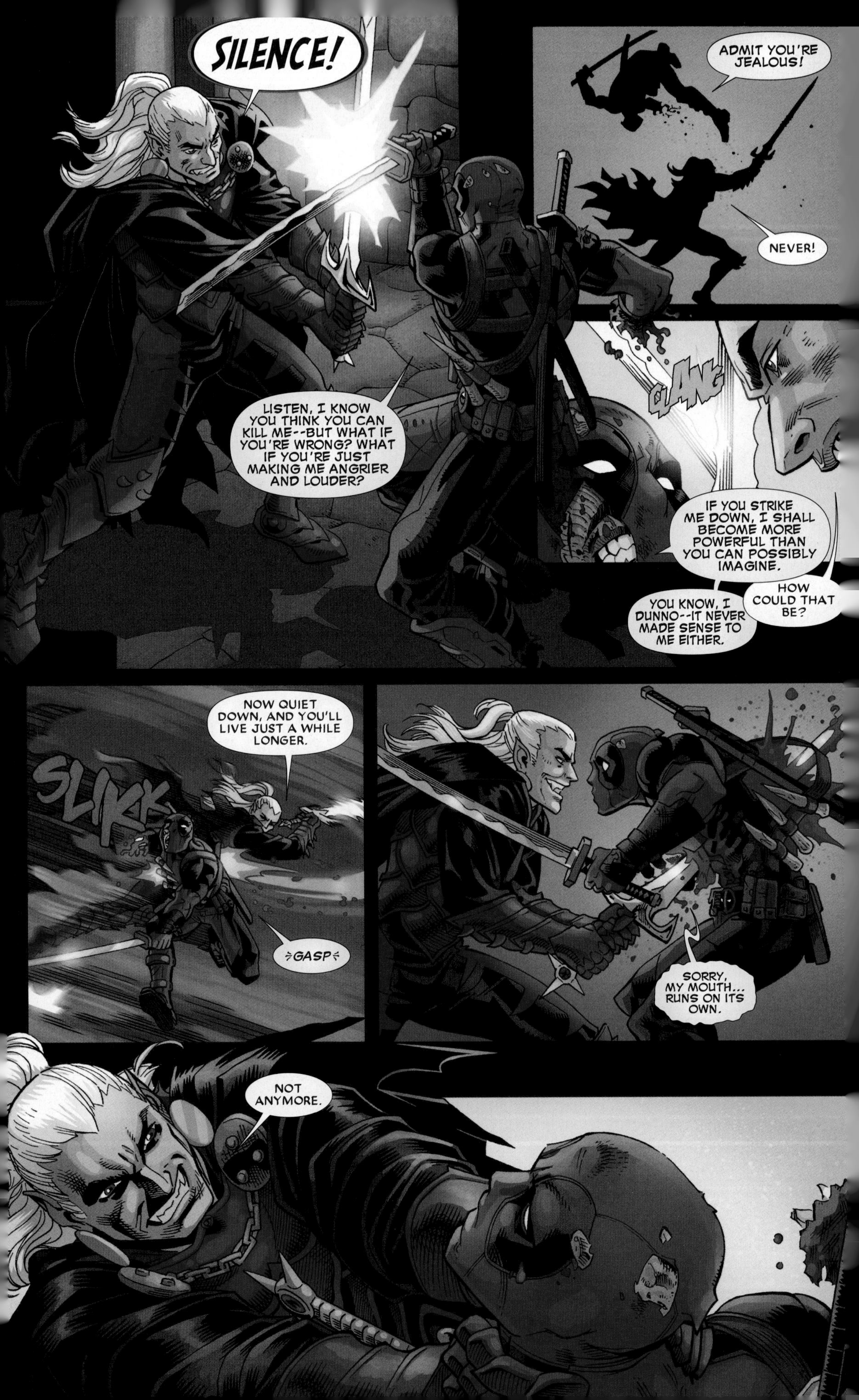
SILENCE!
LISTEN, I KNOW YOU THINK YOU CAN KILL ME--BUT WHAT IF YOU'RE WRONG? WHAT IF YOU'RE JUST MAKING ME ANGRIER AND LOUDER?
ADMIT YOU'RE JEALOUS!
NEVER!
CLANG
IF YOU STRIKE ME DOWN, I SHALL BECOME MORE POWERFUL THAN YOU CAN POSSIBLY IMAGINE.
HOW COULD THAT BE?
YOU KNOW, I DUNNO--IT NEVER MADE SENSE TO ME EITHER.
NOW QUIET DOWN, AND YOU'LL LIVE JUST A WHILE LONGER.
SLIKK
GASP
SORRY, MY MOUTH... RUNS ON ITS OWN.
NOT ANYMORE.

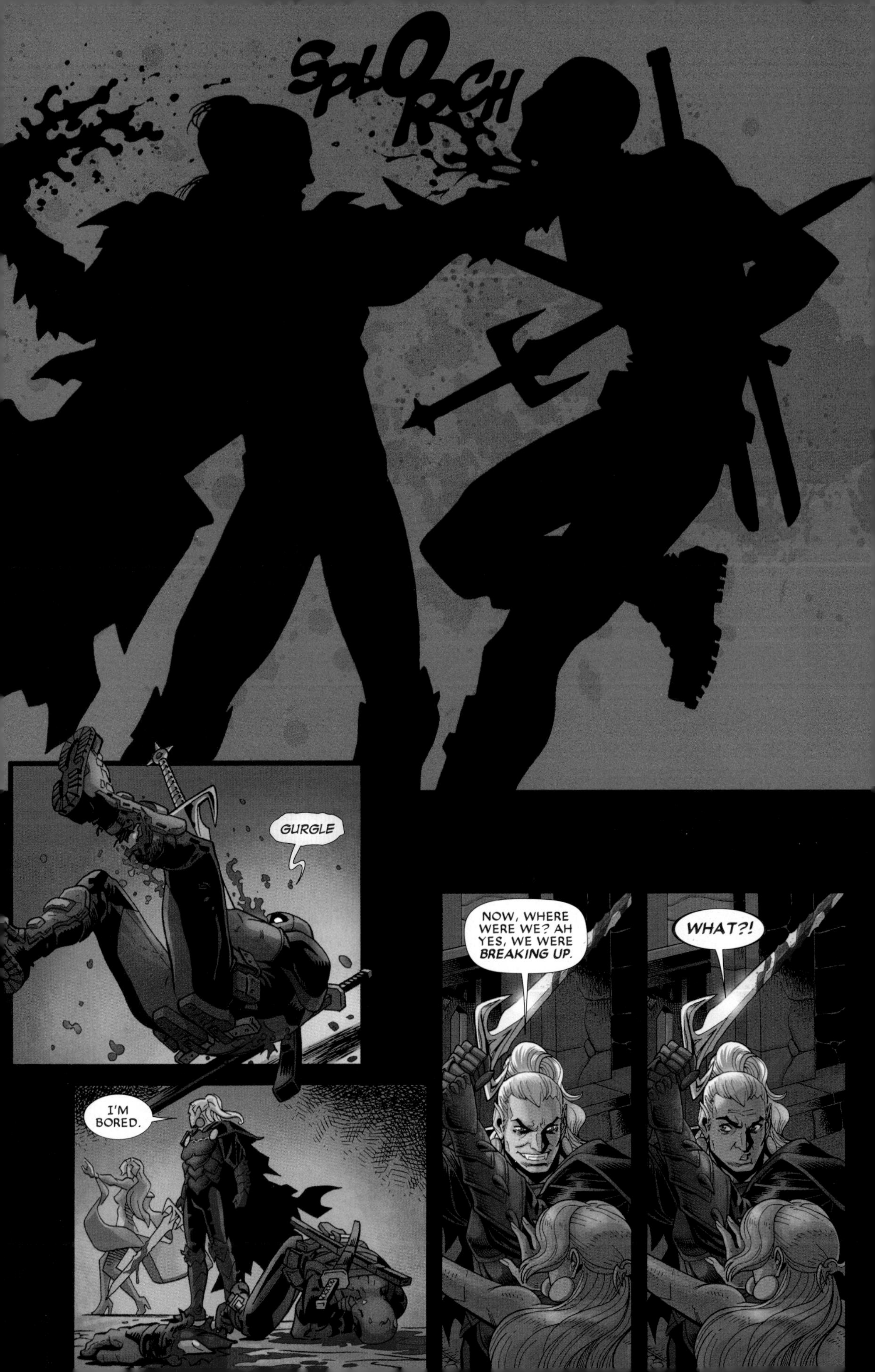
SPLORCH
GURGLE
I'M BORED.
NOW, WHERE WERE WE? AH YES, WE WERE BREAKING UP.
WHAT?!

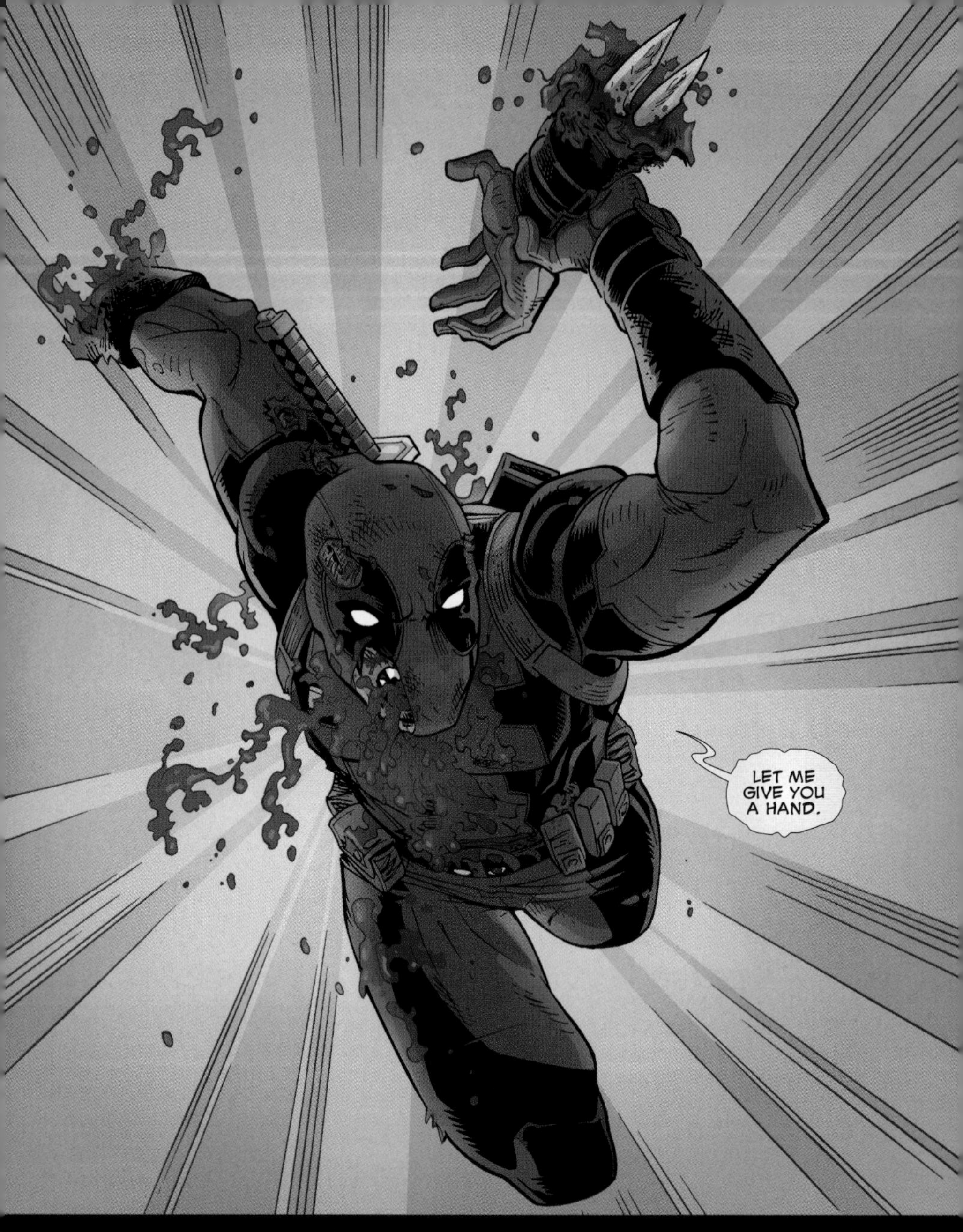
LET ME GIVE YOU A HAND.

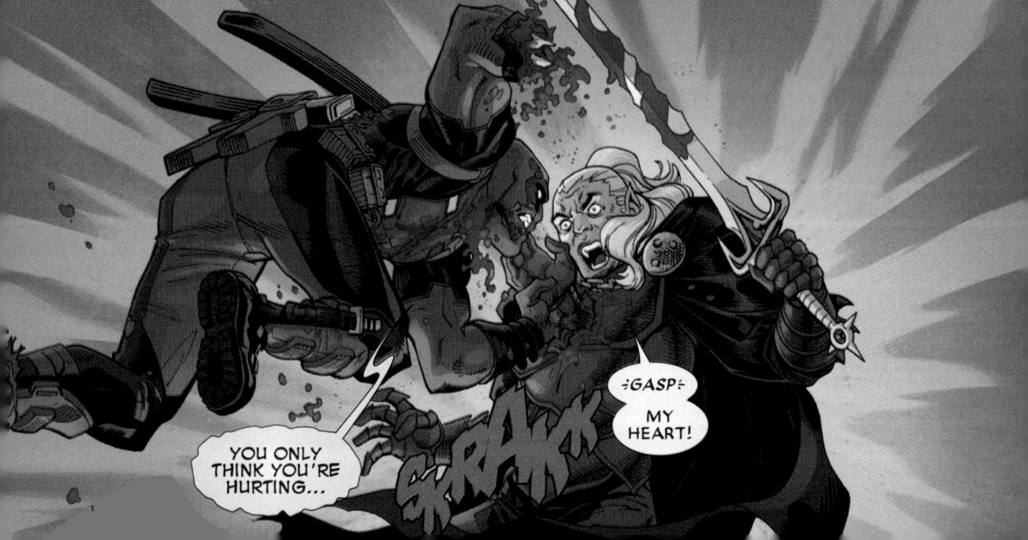
GASP
MY HEART!
YOU ONLY THINK YOU'RE HURTING...
SKRAKK

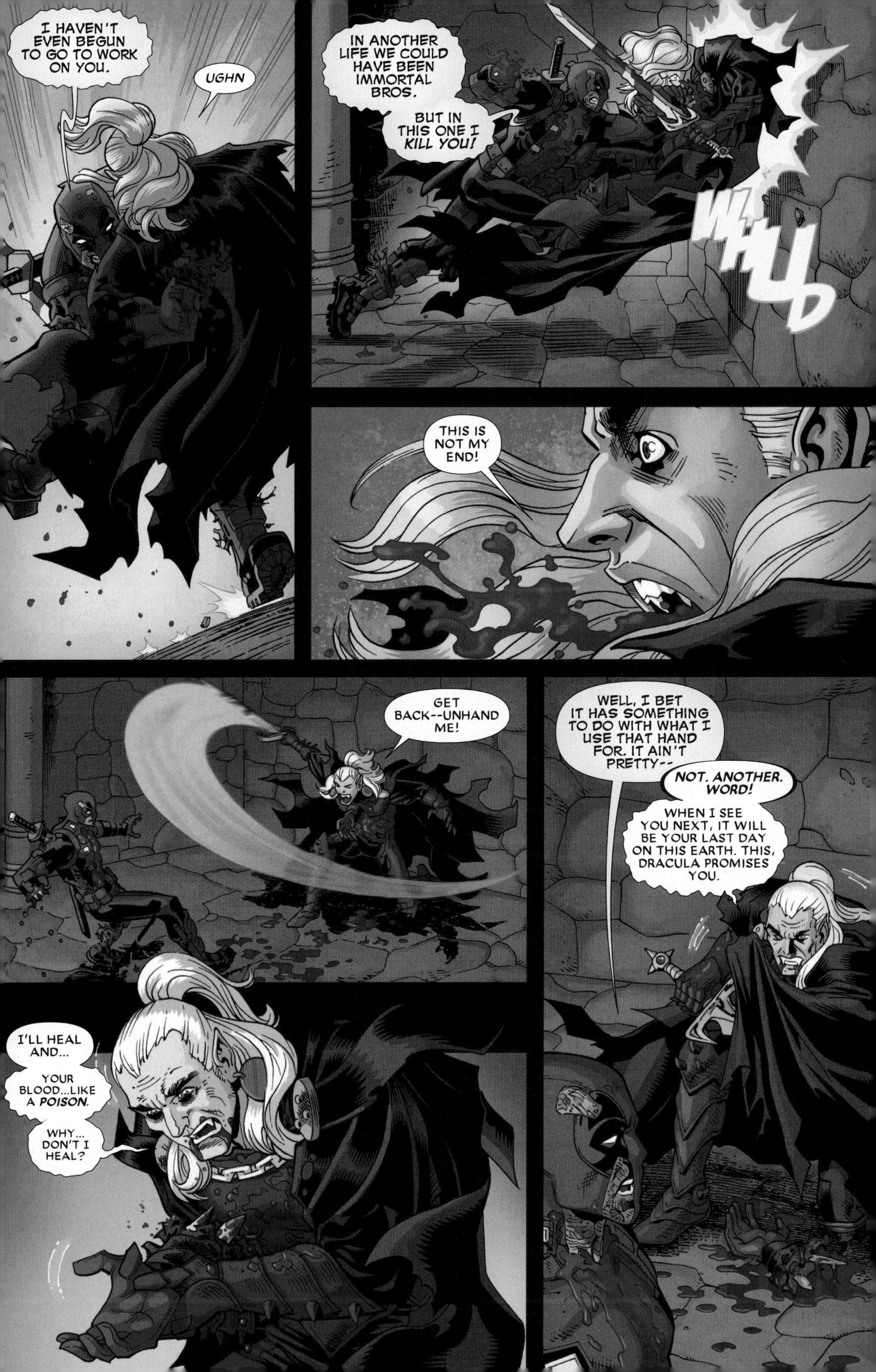

I HAVEN'T EVEN BEGUN TO GO TO WORK ON YOU.
UGHN
IN ANOTHER LIFE WE COULD HAVE BEEN IMMORTAL BROS.
BUT IN THIS ONE I *KILL YOU!*
WHUD
THIS IS NOT MY END!
GET BACK--UNHAND ME!
WELL, I BET IT HAS SOMETHING TO DO WITH WHAT I USE THAT HAND FOR. IT AIN'T PRETTY--
NOT. ANOTHER. WORD!
WHEN I SEE YOU NEXT, IT WILL BE YOUR LAST DAY ON THIS EARTH. THIS, DRACULA PROMISES YOU.
I'LL HEAL AND...
YOUR BLOOD...LIKE A *POISON*.
WHY... DON'T I HEAL?

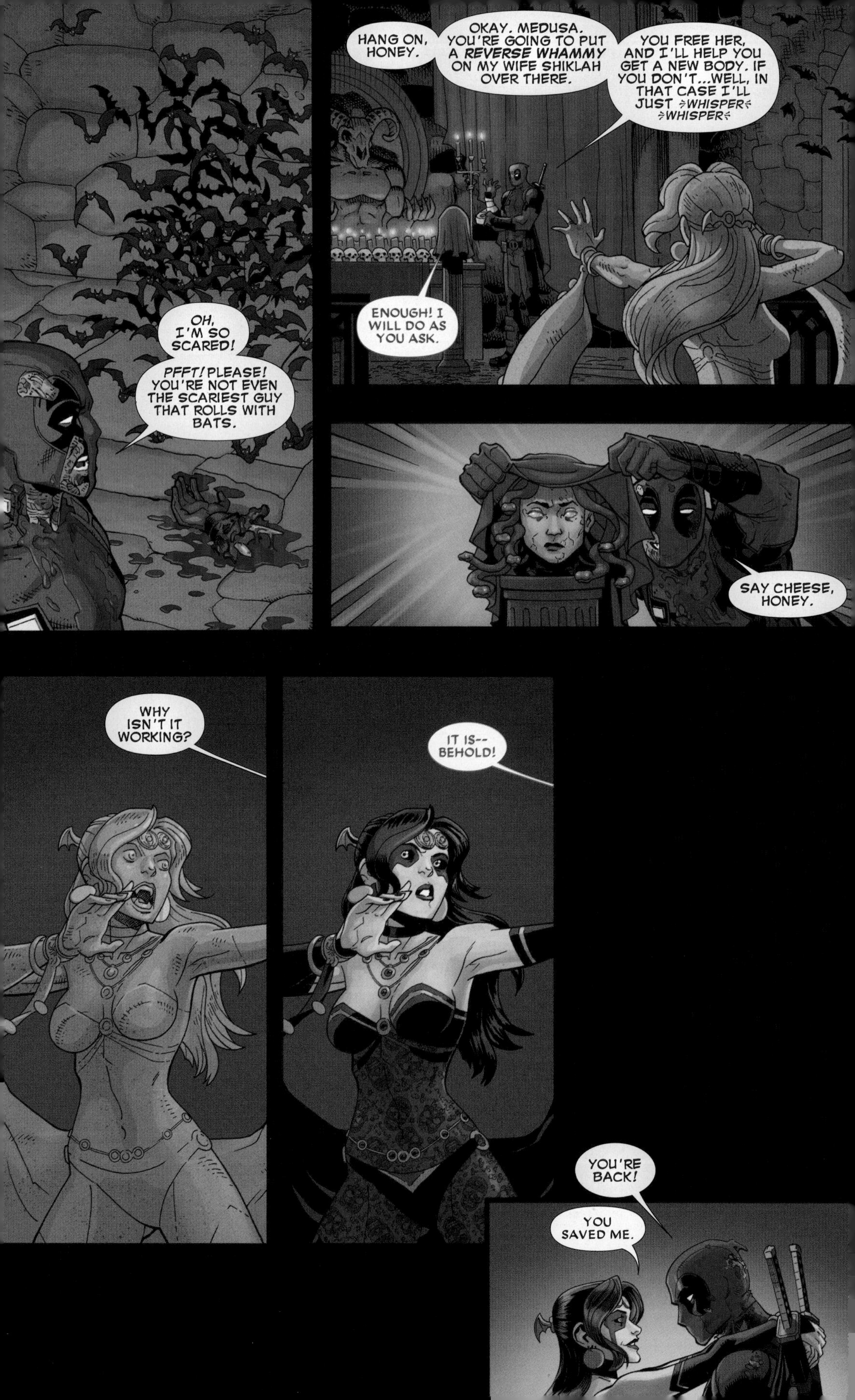
OH, I'M SO SCARED!
PFFT! PLEASE! YOU'RE NOT EVEN THE SCARIEST GUY THAT ROLLS WITH BATS.
HANG ON, HONEY.
OKAY. MEDUSA. YOU'RE GOING TO PUT A REVERSE WHAMMY ON MY WIFE SHIKLAH OVER THERE.
YOU FREE HER, AND I'LL HELP YOU GET A NEW BODY. IF YOU DON'T...WELL, IN THAT CASE I'LL JUST WHISPER WHISPER
ENOUGH! I WILL DO AS YOU ASK.
SAY CHEESE, HONEY.
WHY ISN'T IT WORKING?
IT IS-- BEHOLD!
YOU'RE BACK!
YOU SAVED ME.

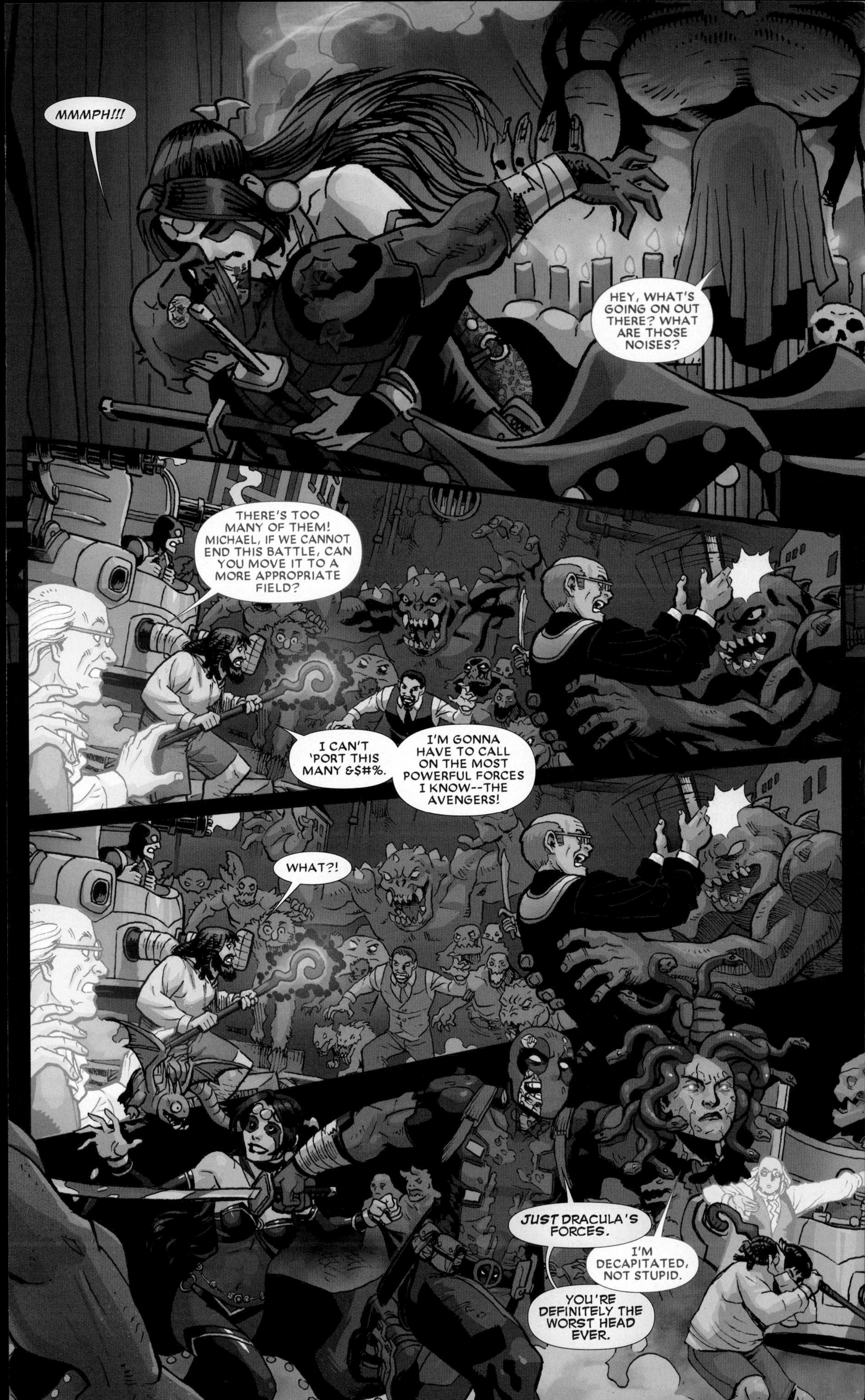
MMMPH!!!
HEY, WHAT'S GOING ON OUT THERE? WHAT ARE THOSE NOISES?
THERE'S TOO MANY OF THEM! MICHAEL, IF WE CANNOT END THIS BATTLE, CAN YOU MOVE IT TO A MORE APPROPRIATE FIELD?
I CAN'T 'PORT THIS MANY &$#%.
I'M GONNA HAVE TO CALL ON THE MOST POWERFUL FORCES I KNOW--THE AVENGERS!
WHAT?!
JUST DRACULA'S FORCES.
I'M DECAPITATED, NOT STUPID.
YOU'RE DEFINITELY THE WORST HEAD EVER.

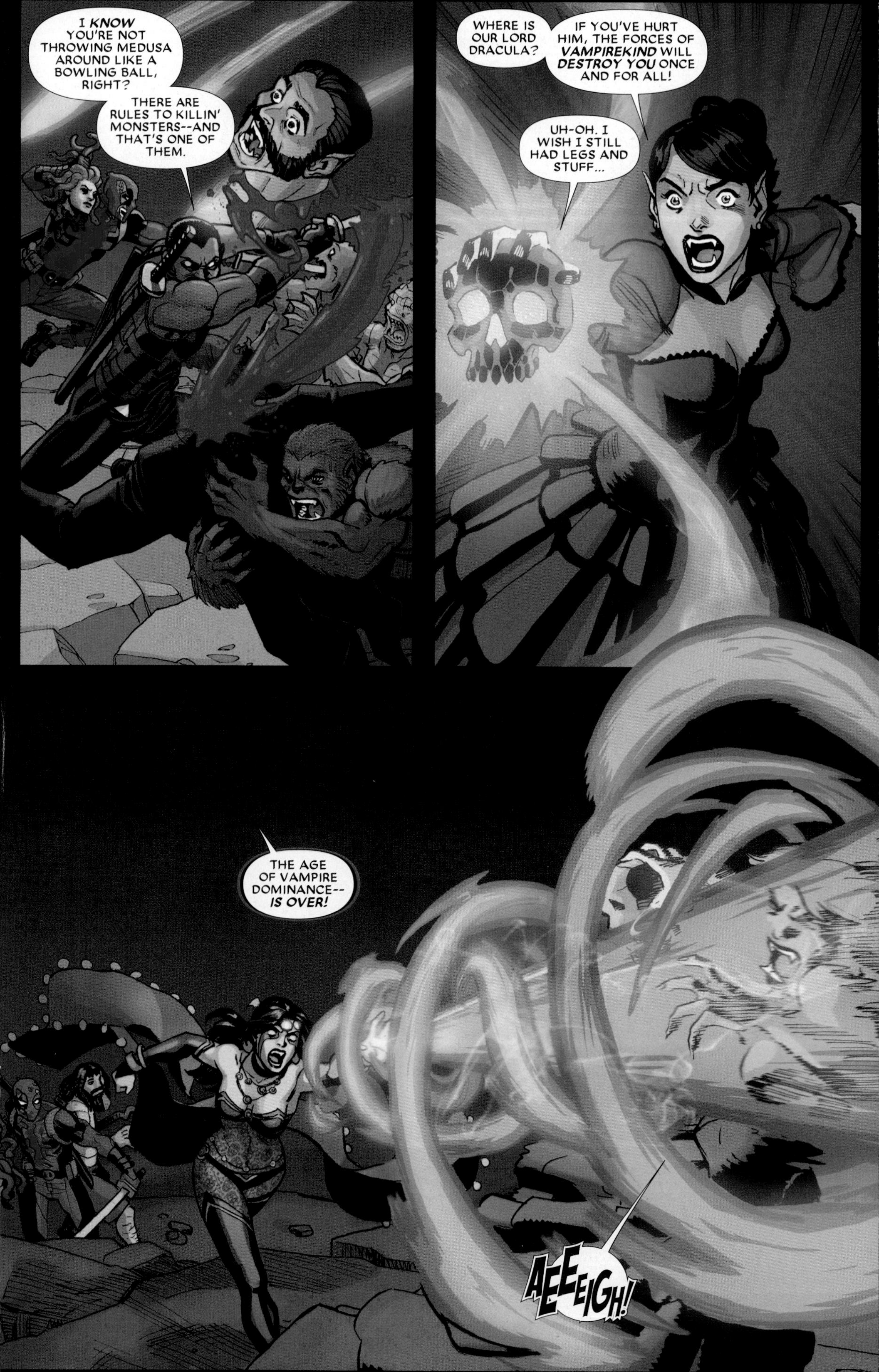
I KNOW YOU'RE NOT THROWING MEDUSA AROUND LIKE A BOWLING BALL, RIGHT?
THERE ARE RULES TO KILLIN' MONSTERS--AND THAT'S ONE OF THEM.
WHERE IS OUR LORD DRACULA?
IF YOU'VE HURT HIM, THE FORCES OF VAMPIREKIND WILL DESTROY YOU ONCE AND FOR ALL!
UH-OH. I WISH I STILL HAD LEGS AND STUFF...
THE AGE OF VAMPIRE DOMINANCE-- IS OVER!
AEEEIGH!

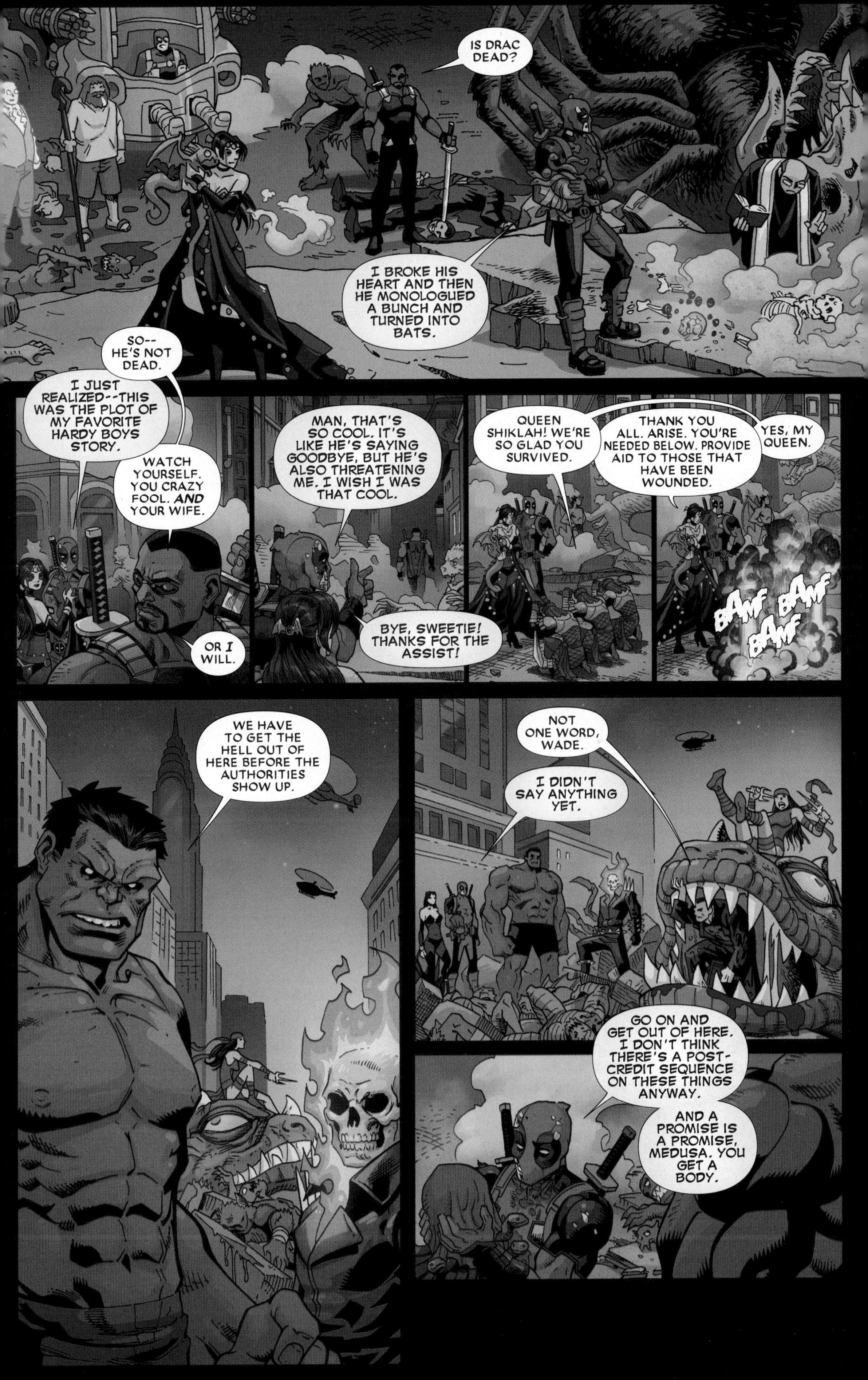
IS DRAC DEAD?
I BROKE HIS HEART AND THEN HE MONOLOGUED A BUNCH AND TURNED INTO BATS.
SO-- HE'S NOT DEAD.
I JUST REALIZED--THIS WAS THE PLOT OF MY FAVORITE HARDY BOYS STORY.
WATCH YOURSELF. YOU CRAZY FOOL. AND YOUR WIFE.
OR I WILL.
MAN, THAT'S SO COOL. IT'S LIKE HE'S SAYING GOODBYE, BUT HE'S ALSO THREATENING ME. I WISH I WAS THAT COOL.
BYE, SWEETIE! THANKS FOR THE ASSIST!
QUEEN SHIKLAH! WE'RE SO GLAD YOU SURVIVED.
THANK YOU ALL. ARISE. YOU'RE NEEDED BELOW. PROVIDE AID TO THOSE THAT HAVE BEEN WOUNDED.
YES, MY QUEEN.
BAMF BAMF BAMF
WE HAVE TO GET THE HELL OUT OF HERE BEFORE THE AUTHORITIES SHOW UP.
NOT ONE WORD, WADE.
I DIDN'T SAY ANYTHING YET.
GO ON AND GET OUT OF HERE. I DON'T THINK THERE'S A POST-CREDIT SEQUENCE ON THESE THINGS ANYWAY.
AND A PROMISE IS A PROMISE, MEDUSA. YOU GET A BODY.

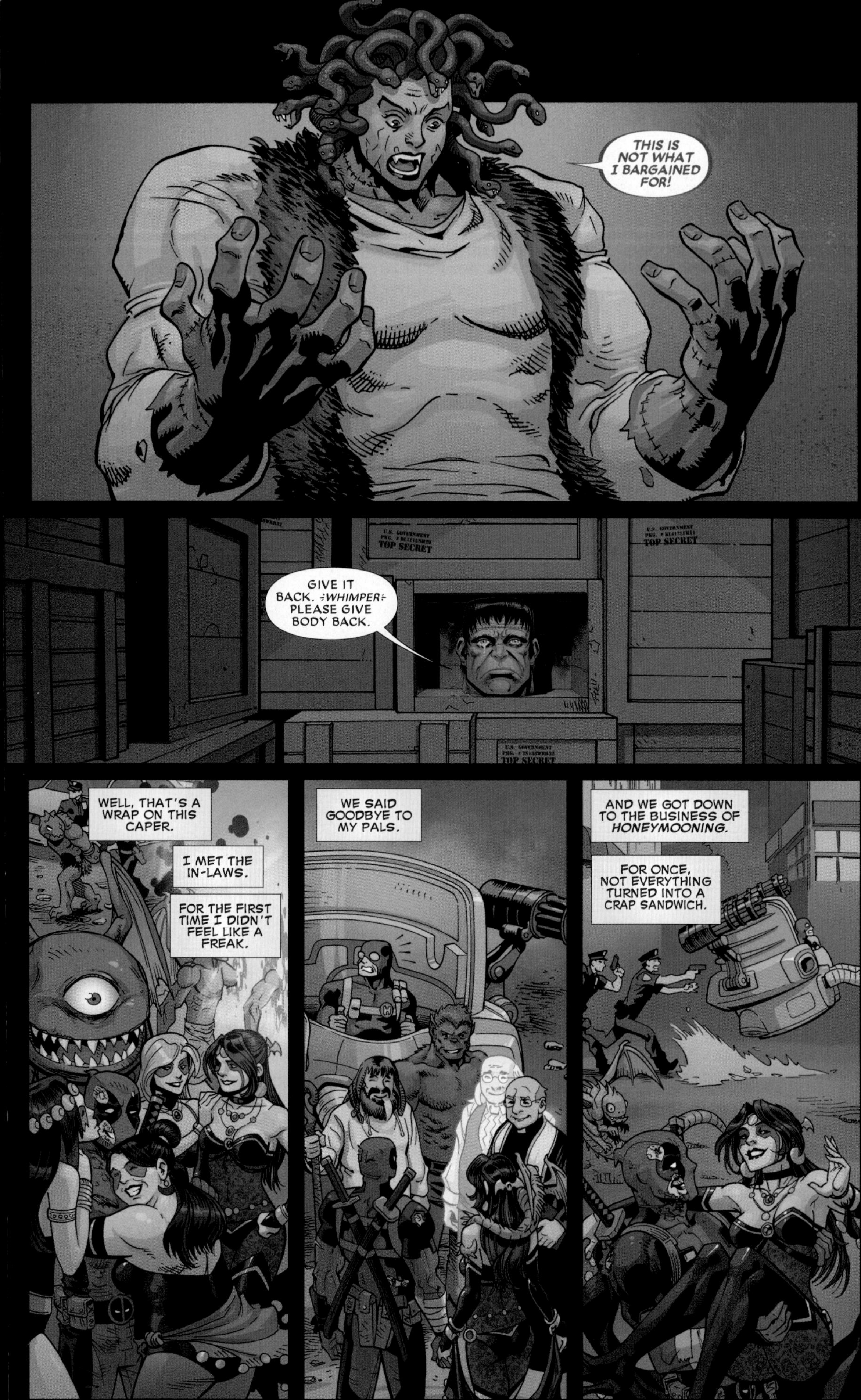
THIS IS NOT WHAT I BARGAINED FOR!
U.S. GOVERNMENT PKG. TOP SECRET
GIVE IT BACK. ~WHIMPER~ PLEASE GIVE BODY BACK.
U.S. GOVERNMENT TOP SECRET
WELL, THAT'S A WRAP ON THIS CAPER.
I MET THE IN-LAWS.
FOR THE FIRST TIME I DIDN'T FEEL LIKE A FREAK.
WE SAID GOODBYE TO MY PALS.
AND WE GOT DOWN TO THE BUSINESS OF HONEYMOONING.
FOR ONCE, NOT EVERYTHING TURNED INTO A CRAP SANDWICH.

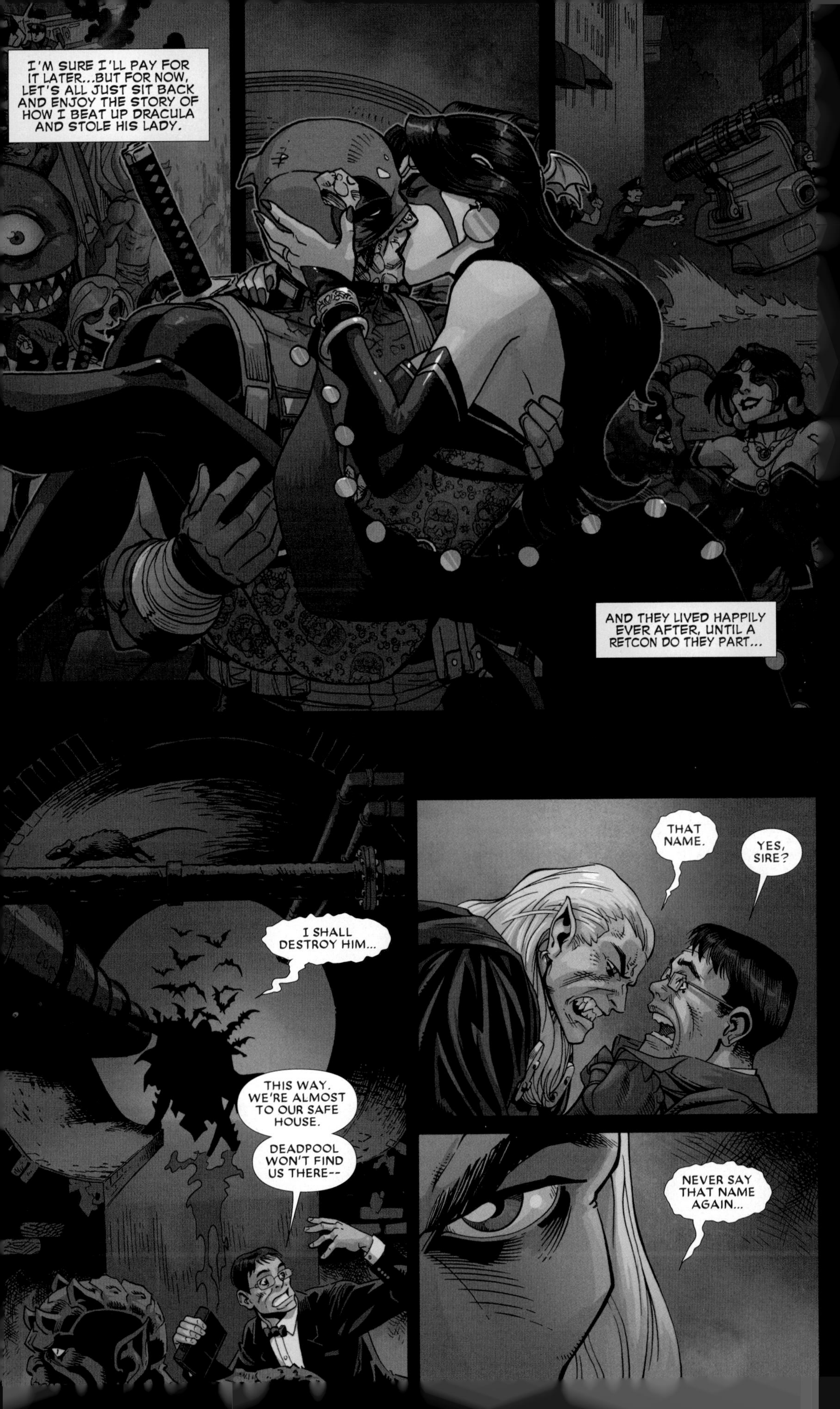
I'M SURE I'LL PAY FOR IT LATER...BUT FOR NOW, LET'S ALL JUST SIT BACK AND ENJOY THE STORY OF HOW I BEAT UP DRACULA AND STOLE HIS LADY.
AND THEY LIVED HAPPILY EVER AFTER, UNTIL A RETCON DO THEY PART...
I SHALL DESTROY HIM...
THIS WAY. WE'RE ALMOST TO OUR SAFE HOUSE.
DEADPOOL WON'T FIND US THERE--
THAT NAME.
YES, SIRE?
NEVER SAY THAT NAME AGAIN...

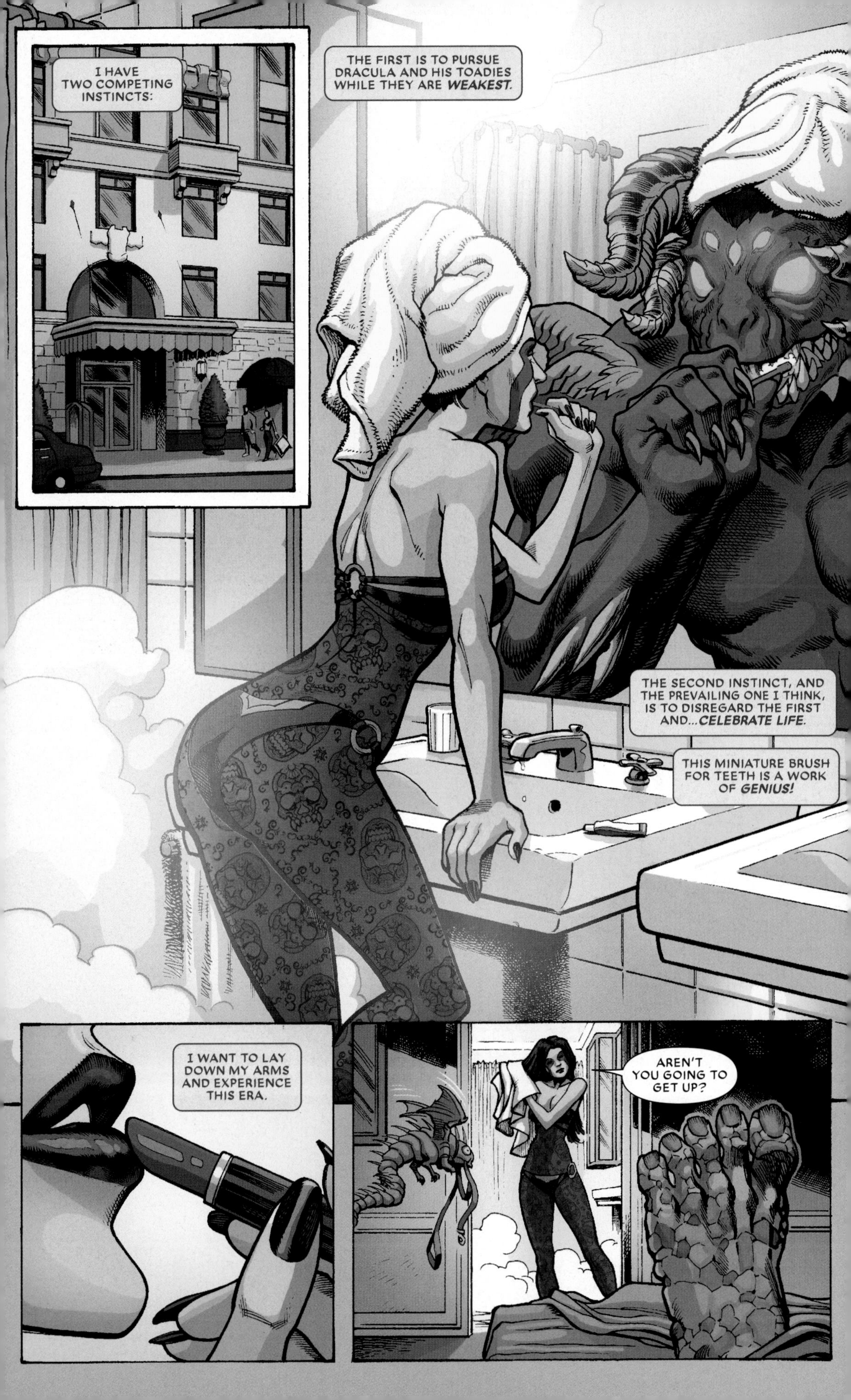
I HAVE TWO COMPETING INSTINCTS:
THE FIRST IS TO PURSUE DRACULA AND HIS TOADIES WHILE THEY ARE WEAKEST.
THE SECOND INSTINCT, AND THE PREVAILING ONE I THINK, IS TO DISREGARD THE FIRST AND...CELEBRATE LIFE.
THIS MINIATURE BRUSH FOR TEETH IS A WORK OF GENIUS!
I WANT TO LAY DOWN MY ARMS AND EXPERIENCE THIS ERA.
AREN'T YOU GOING TO GET UP?

THE PRIZE OF "ALL-TOO-PRECIOUS" YOU

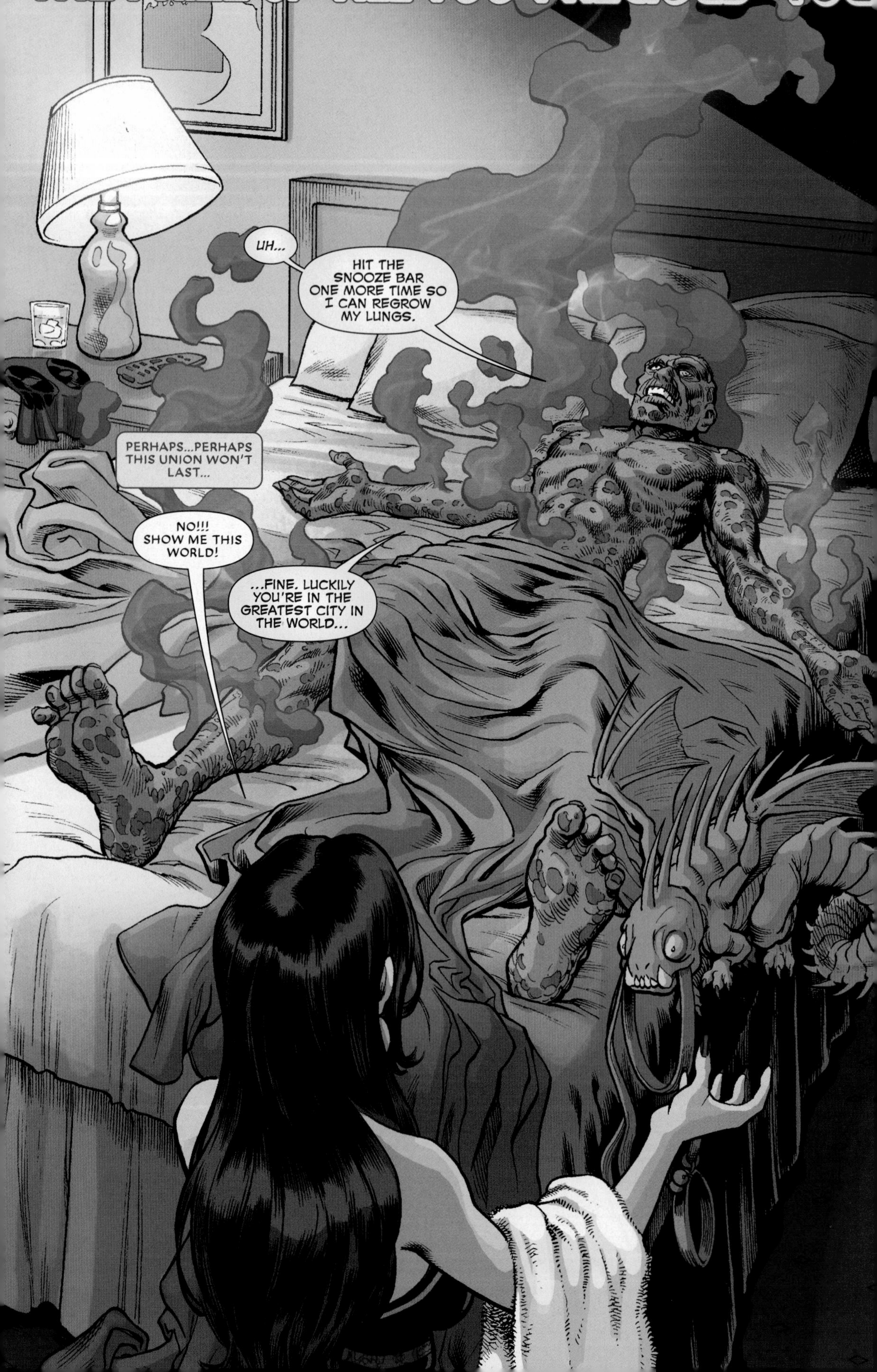
UH...
HIT THE SNOOZE BAR ONE MORE TIME SO I CAN REGROW MY LUNGS.
PERHAPS...PERHAPS THIS UNION WON'T LAST...
NO!!! SHOW ME THIS WORLD!
...FINE. LUCKILY YOU'RE IN THE GREATEST CITY IN THE WORLD...

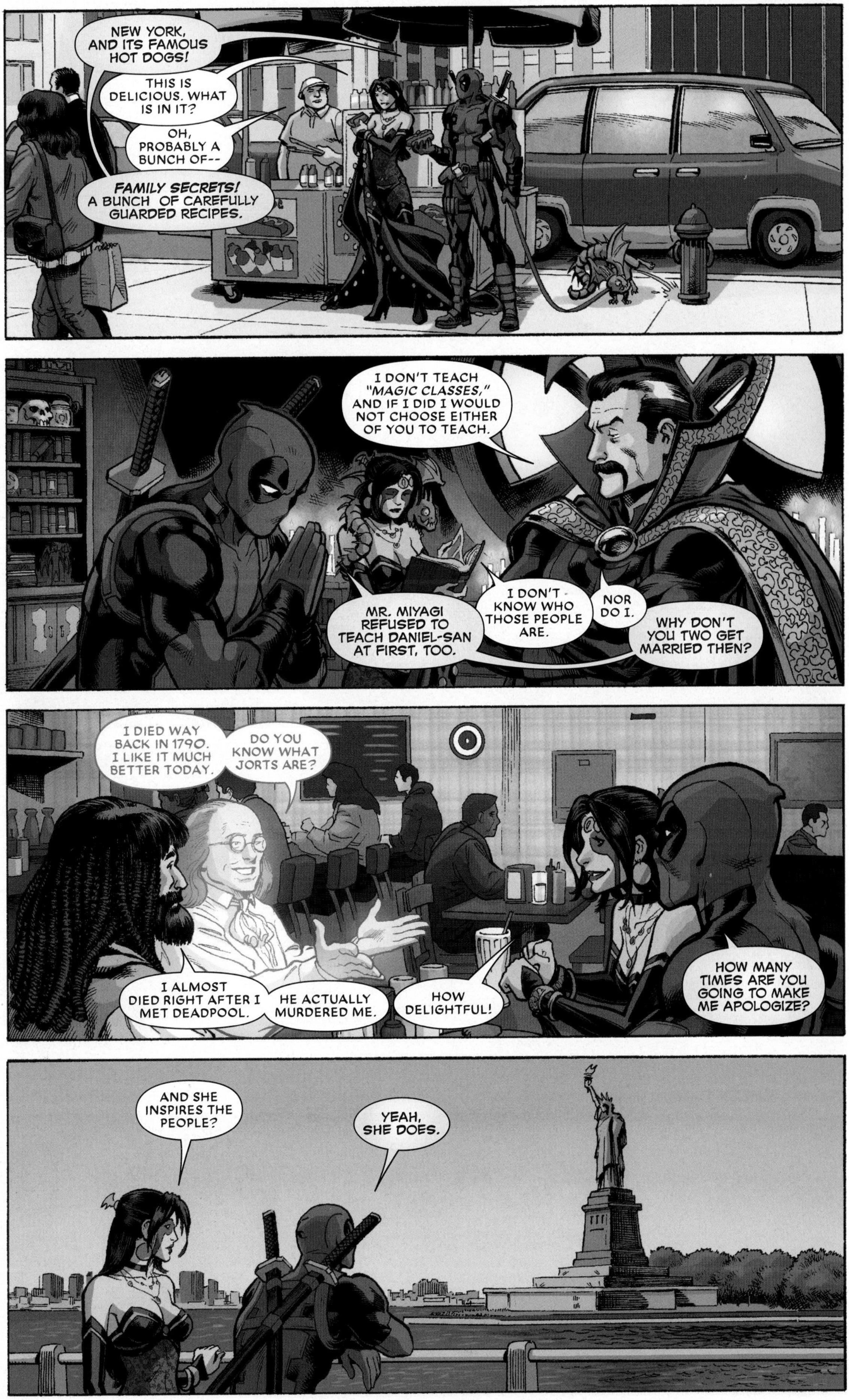

NEW YORK, AND ITS FAMOUS HOT DOGS!
THIS IS DELICIOUS. WHAT IS IN IT?
OH, PROBABLY A BUNCH OF--
FAMILY SECRETS! A BUNCH OF CAREFULLY GUARDED RECIPES.
I DON'T TEACH "MAGIC CLASSES," AND IF I DID I WOULD NOT CHOOSE EITHER OF YOU TO TEACH.
MR. MIYAGI REFUSED TO TEACH DANIEL-SAN AT FIRST, TOO.
I DON'T KNOW WHO THOSE PEOPLE ARE.
NOR DO I.
WHY DON'T YOU TWO GET MARRIED THEN?
I DIED WAY BACK IN 1790. I LIKE IT MUCH BETTER TODAY.
DO YOU KNOW WHAT JORTS ARE?
I ALMOST DIED RIGHT AFTER I MET DEADPOOL.
HE ACTUALLY MURDERED ME.
HOW DELIGHTFUL!
HOW MANY TIMES ARE YOU GOING TO MAKE ME APOLOGIZE?
AND SHE INSPIRES THE PEOPLE?
YEAH, SHE DOES.

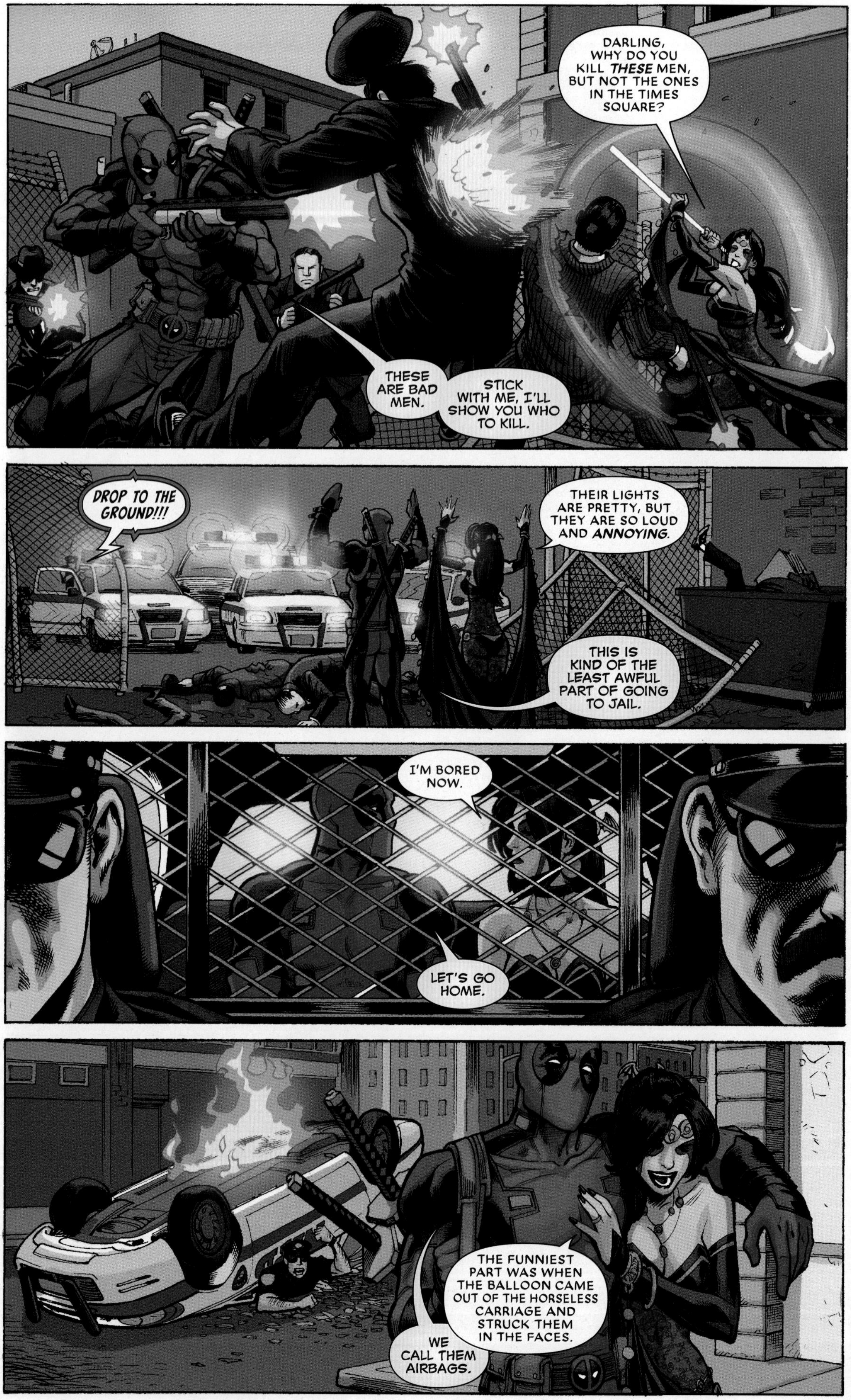
DARLING, WHY DO YOU KILL *THESE* MEN, BUT NOT THE ONES IN THE TIMES SQUARE?
THESE ARE BAD MEN.
STICK WITH ME, I'LL SHOW YOU WHO TO KILL.
DROP TO THE GROUND!!!
THEIR LIGHTS ARE PRETTY, BUT THEY ARE SO LOUD AND *ANNOYING*.
THIS IS KIND OF THE LEAST AWFUL PART OF GOING TO JAIL.
I'M BORED NOW.
LET'S GO HOME.
THE FUNNIEST PART WAS WHEN THE BALLOON CAME OUT OF THE HORSELESS CARRIAGE AND STRUCK THEM IN THE FACES.
WE CALL THEM AIRBAGS.

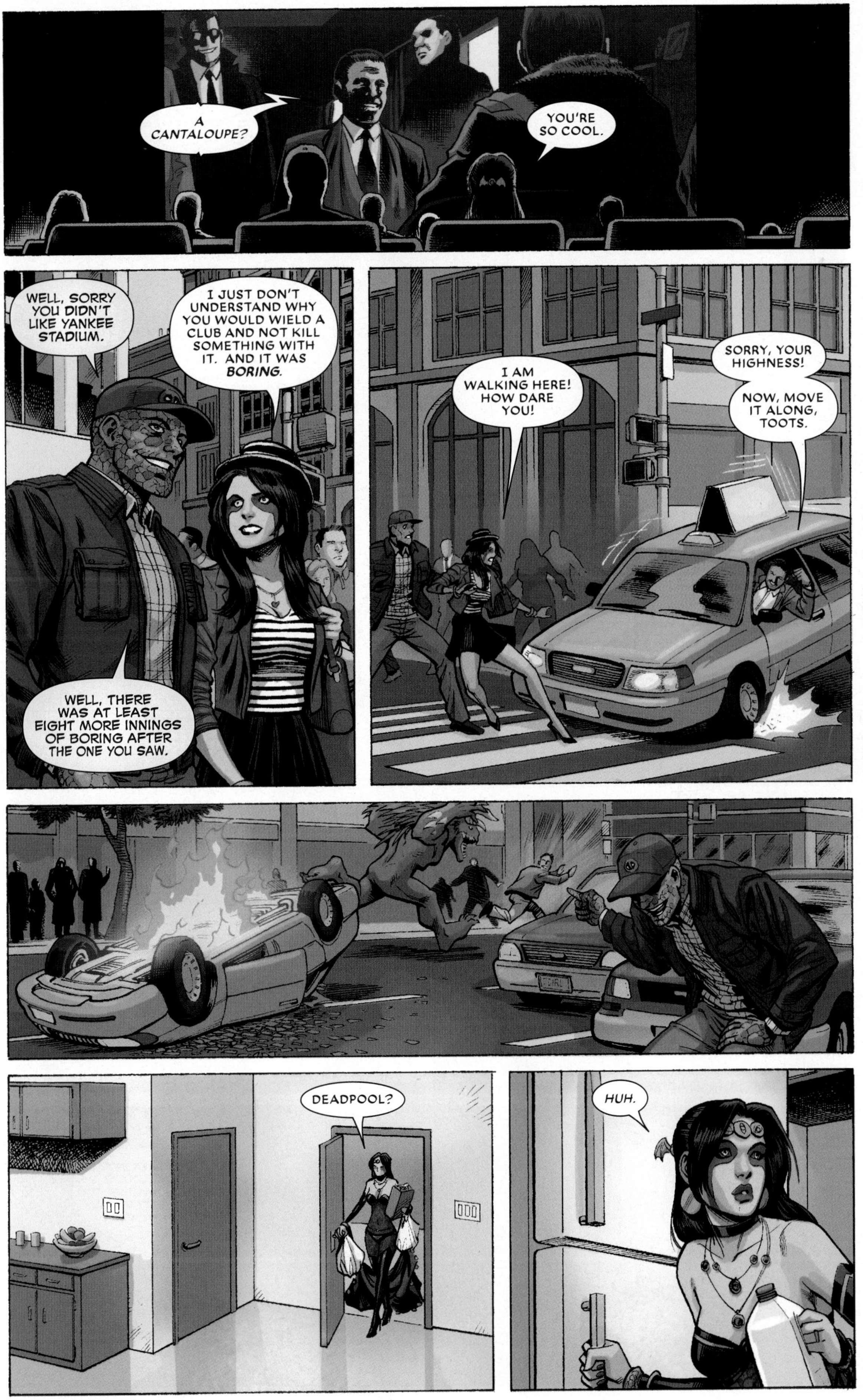
A CANTALOUPE?
YOU'RE SO COOL.
WELL, SORRY YOU DIDN'T LIKE YANKEE STADIUM.
I JUST DON'T UNDERSTAND WHY YOU WOULD WIELD A CLUB AND NOT KILL SOMETHING WITH IT. AND IT WAS BORING.
WELL, THERE WAS AT LEAST EIGHT MORE INNINGS OF BORING AFTER THE ONE YOU SAW.
I AM WALKING HERE! HOW DARE YOU!
SORRY, YOUR HIGHNESS!
NOW, MOVE IT ALONG, TOOTS.
DEADPOOL?
HUH.

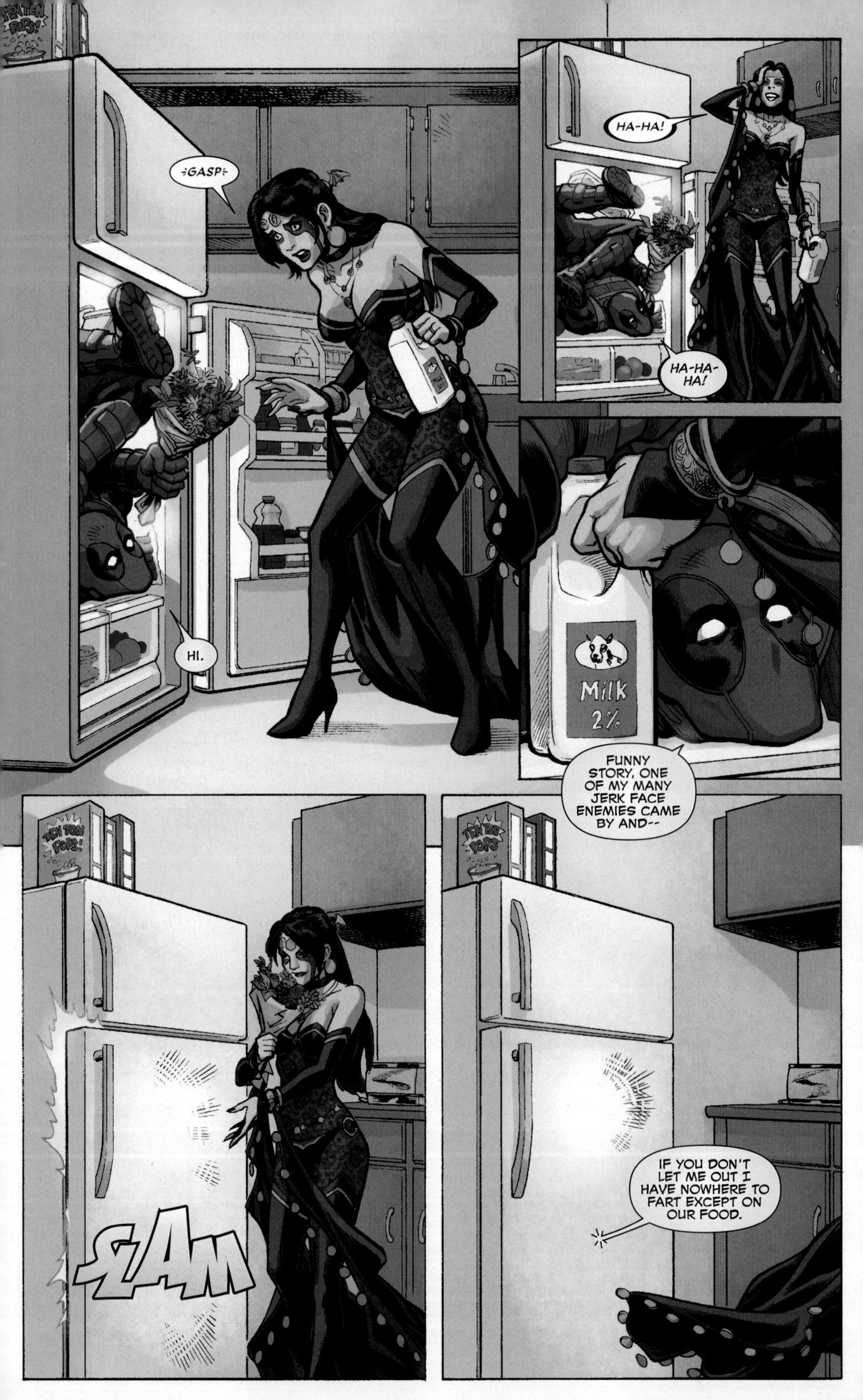
TEN TON POPS!
GASP
HI.
HA-HA!
HA-HA-HA!
Milk 2%
FUNNY STORY, ONE OF MY MANY JERK FACE ENEMIES CAME BY AND--
TEN TON POPS!
SLAM
TEN TON POPS
IF YOU DON'T LET ME OUT I HAVE NOWHERE TO FART EXCEPT ON OUR FOOD.

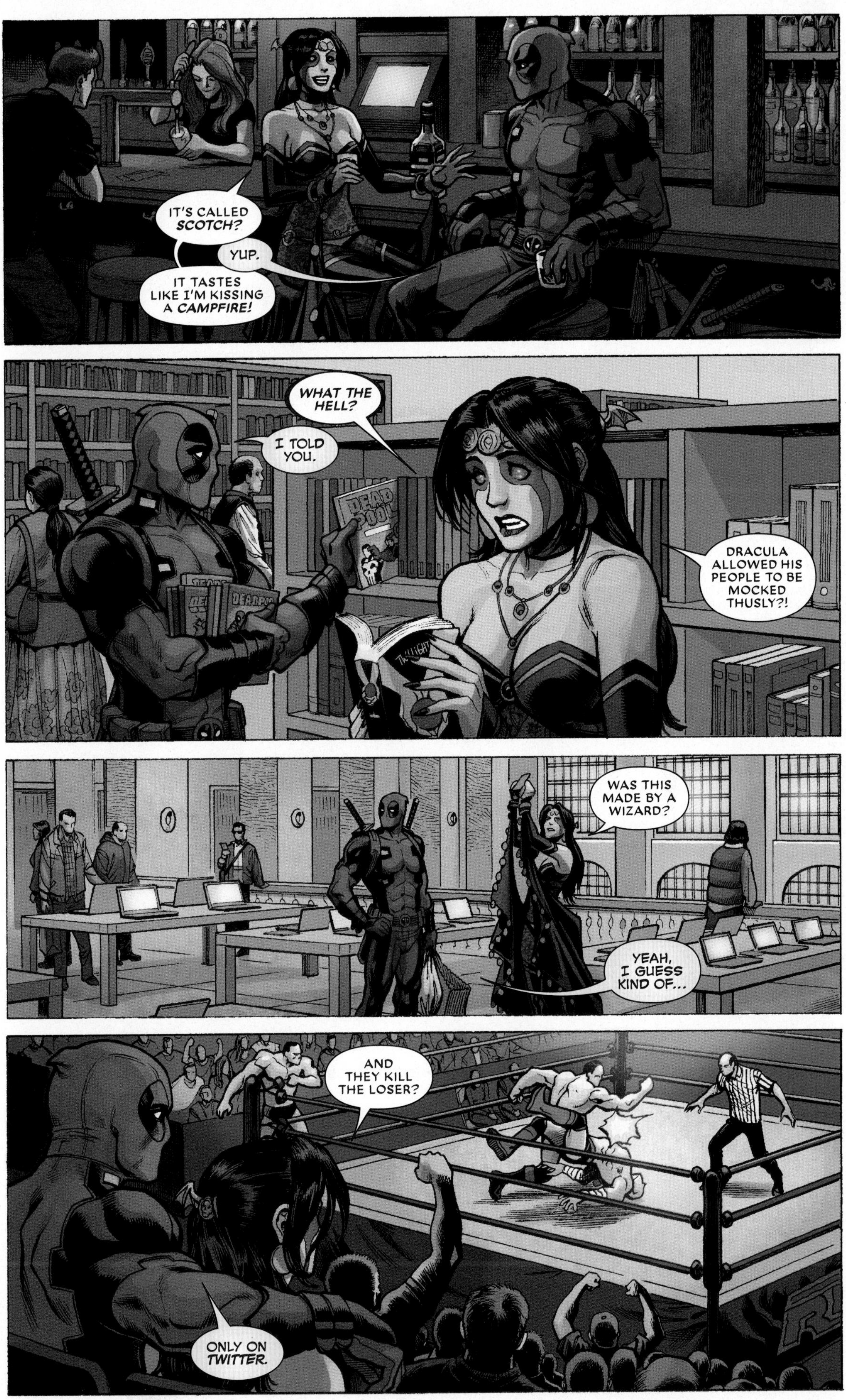
IT'S CALLED SCOTCH?
YUP.
IT TASTES LIKE I'M KISSING A CAMPFIRE!
WHAT THE HELL?
I TOLD YOU.
DRACULA ALLOWED HIS PEOPLE TO BE MOCKED THUSLY?!
WAS THIS MADE BY A WIZARD?
YEAH, I GUESS KIND OF...
AND THEY KILL THE LOSER?
ONLY ON TWITTER.

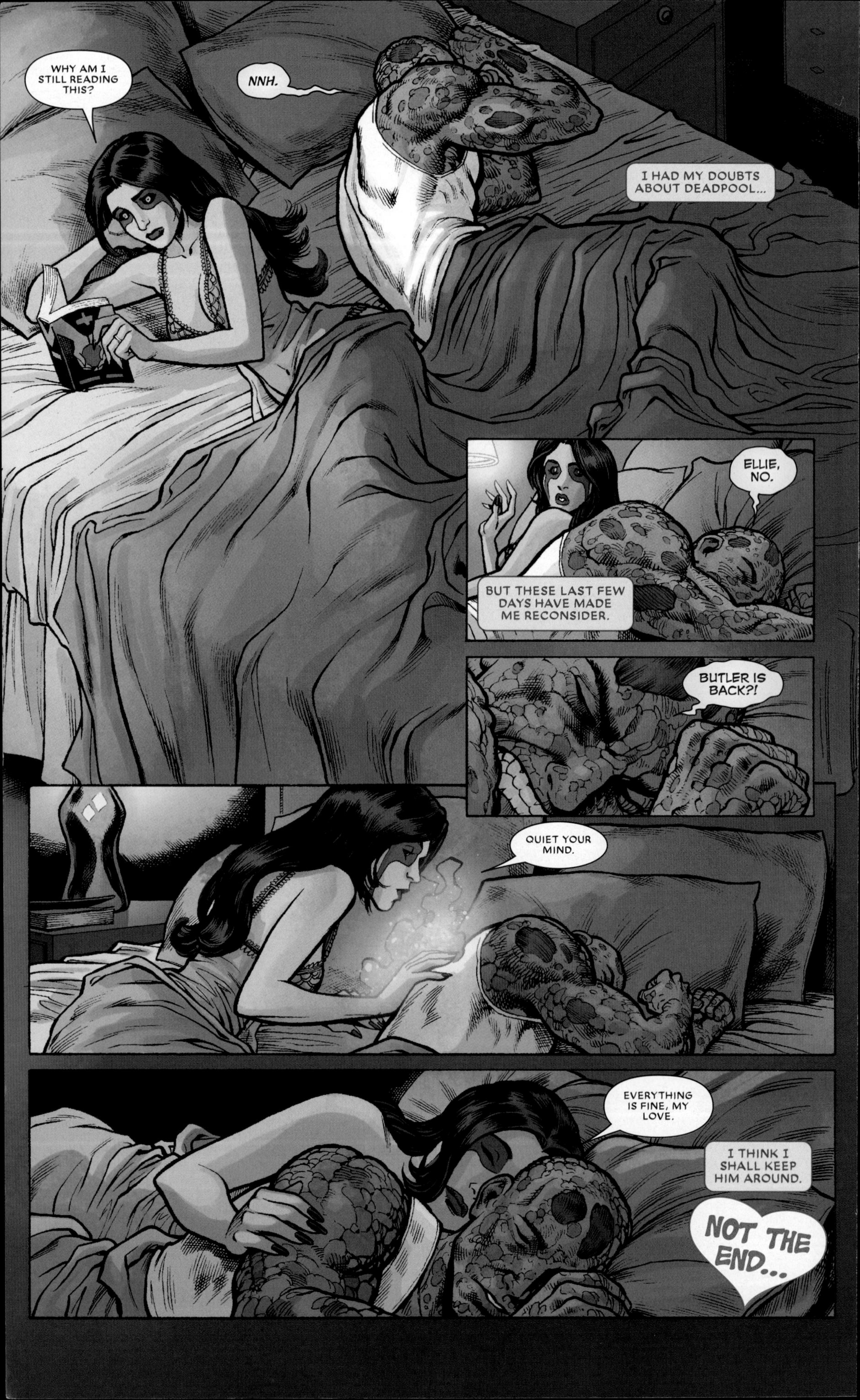
WHY AM I STILL READING THIS?
NNH.
I HAD MY DOUBTS ABOUT DEADPOOL...
ELLIE, NO.
BUT THESE LAST FEW DAYS HAVE MADE ME RECONSIDER.
BUTLER IS BACK?!
QUIET YOUR MIND.
EVERYTHING IS FINE, MY LOVE.
I THINK I SHALL KEEP HIM AROUND.
NOT THE END...

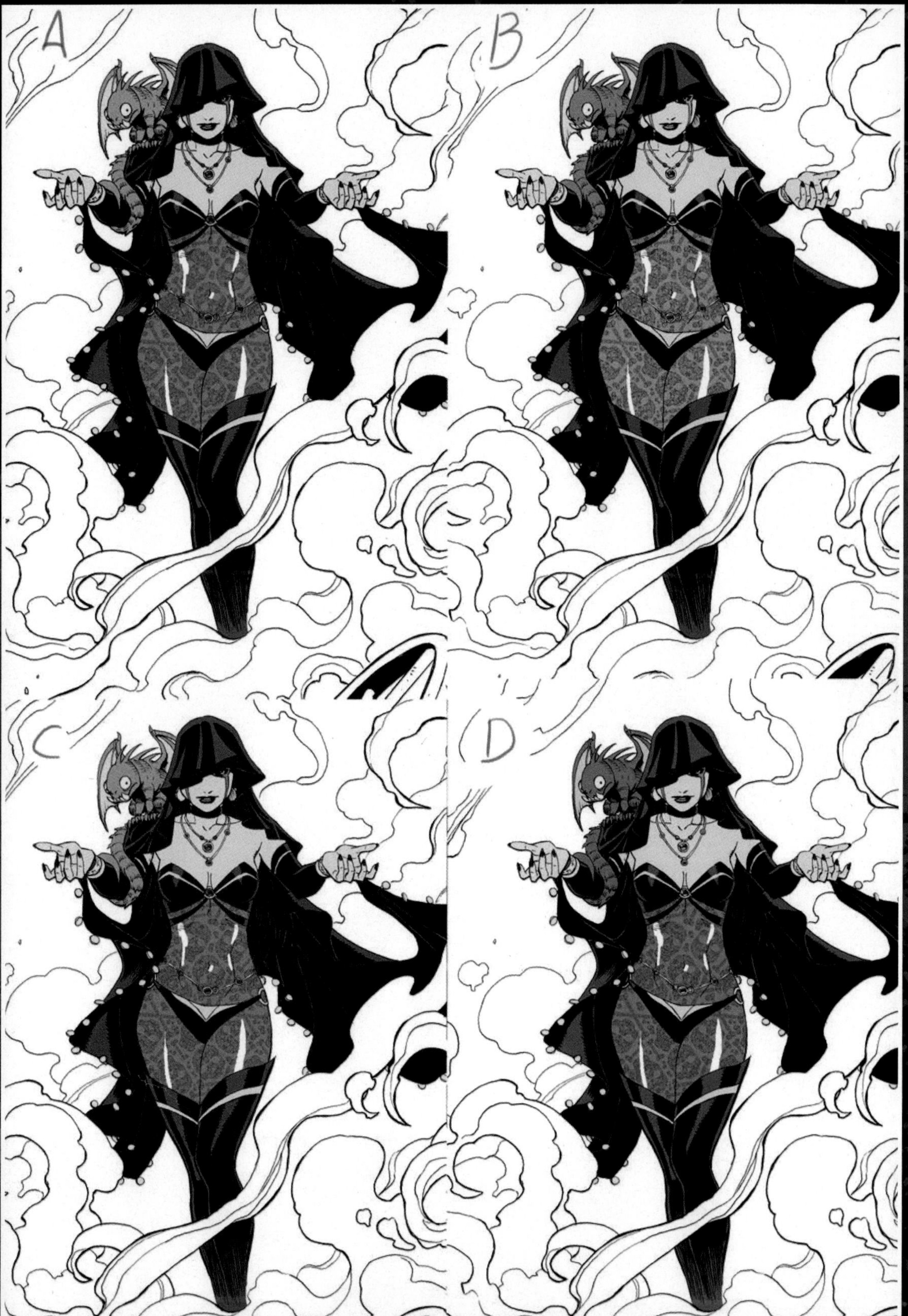
A
B
C
D

SHIKLAH COLOR STUDIES BY REILLY BROWN

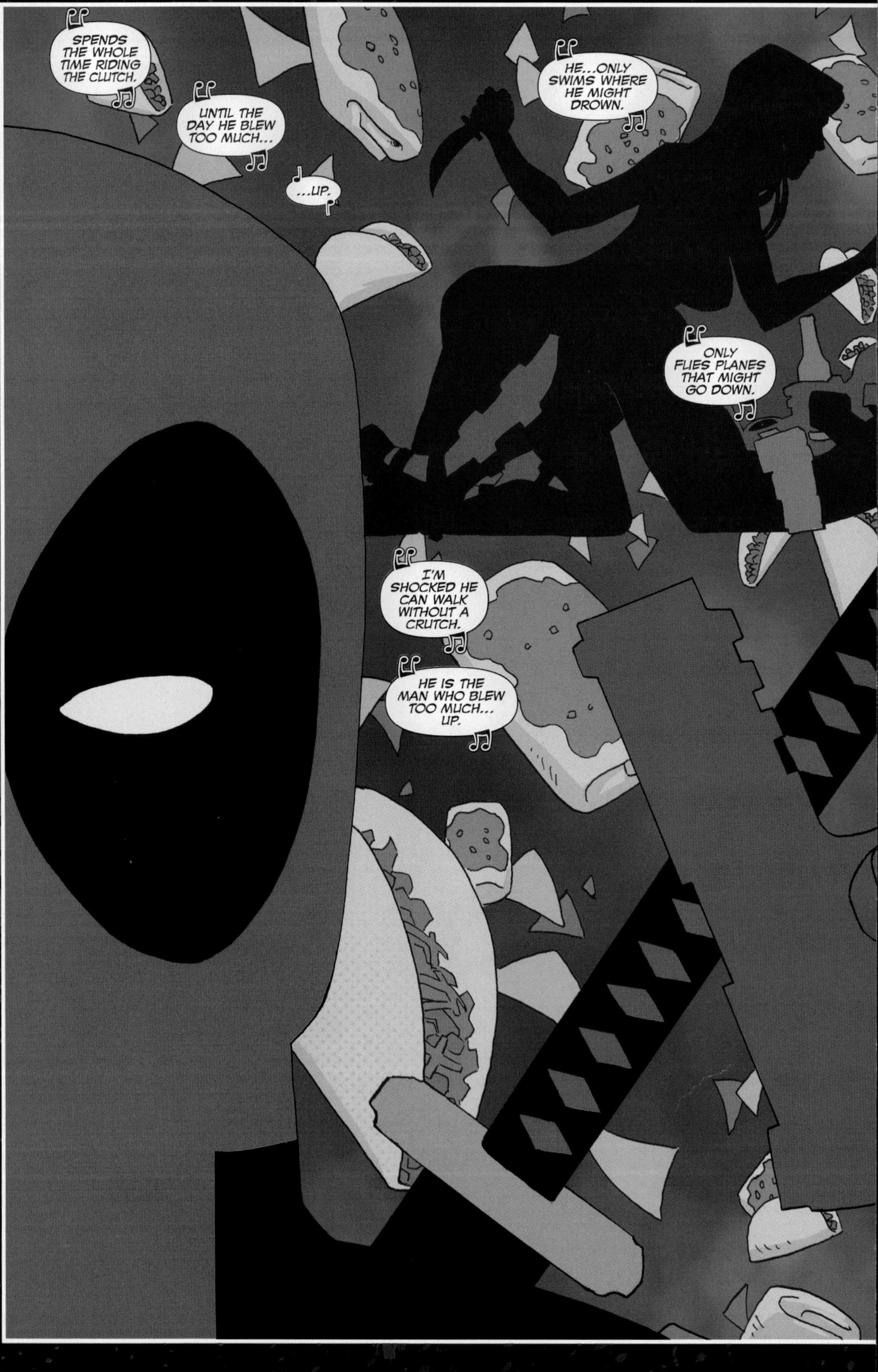
SPENDS THE WHOLE TIME RIDING THE CLUTCH.
UNTIL THE DAY HE BLEW TOO MUCH...
...UP.
HE...ONLY SWIMS WHERE HE MIGHT DROWN.
ONLY FLIES PLANES THAT MIGHT GO DOWN.
I'M SHOCKED HE CAN WALK WITHOUT A CRUTCH.
HE IS THE MAN WHO BLEW TOO MUCH... UP.

"THE MAN WHO BLEW TOO MUCH...UP"

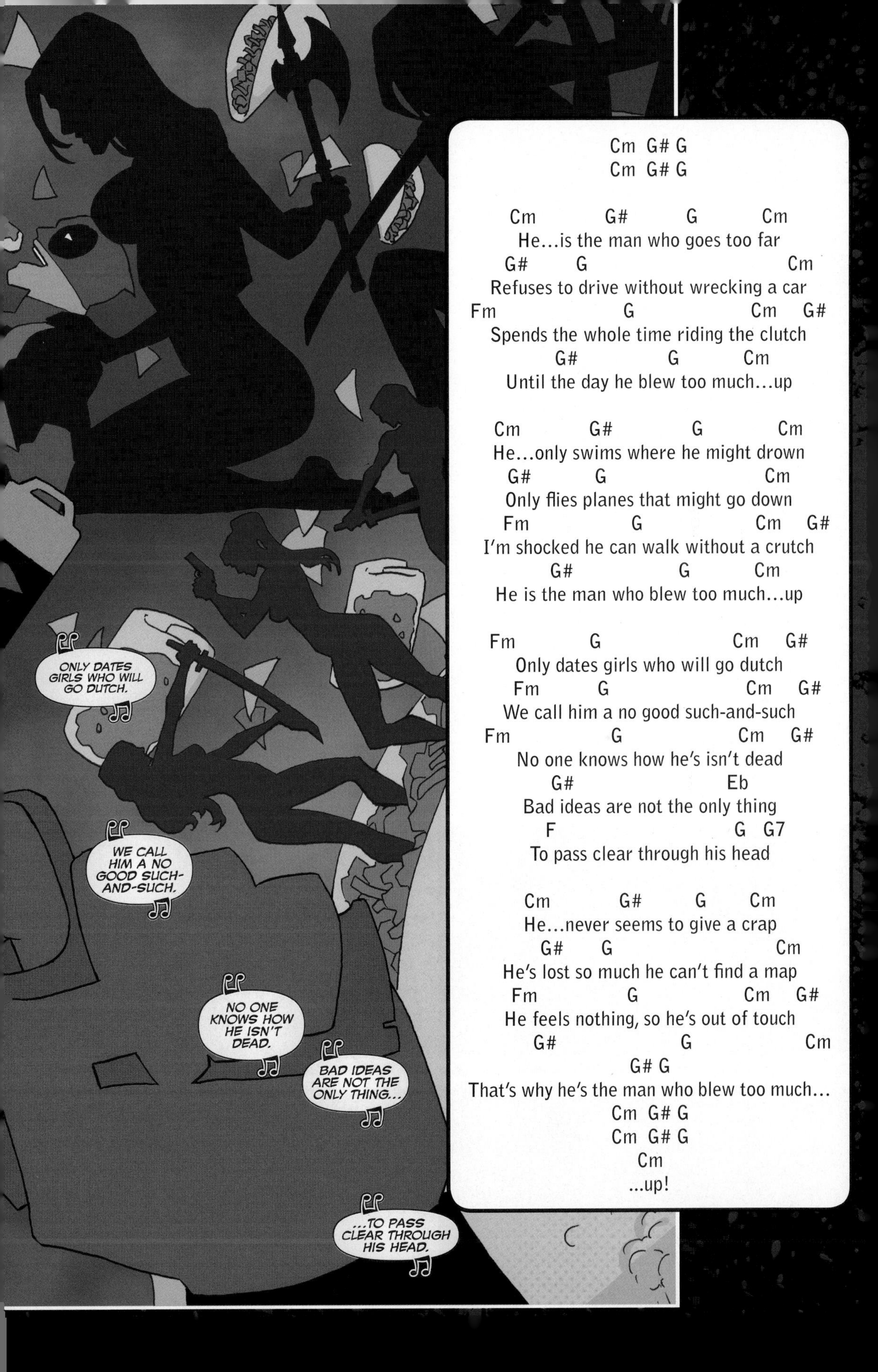
ONLY DATES GIRLS WHO WILL GO DUTCH.
WE CALL HIM A NO GOOD SUCH-AND-SUCH.
NO ONE KNOWS HOW HE ISN'T DEAD.
BAD IDEAS ARE NOT THE ONLY THING...
...TO PASS CLEAR THROUGH HIS HEAD.

Cm G# G
Cm G# G

Cm G# G Cm
He...is the man who goes too far
G# G Cm
Refuses to drive without wrecking a car
Fm G Cm G#
Spends the whole time riding the clutch
G# G Cm
Until the day he blew too much...up

Cm G# G Cm
He...only swims where he might drown
G# G Cm
Only flies planes that might go down
Fm G Cm G#
I'm shocked he can walk without a crutch
G# G Cm
He is the man who blew too much...up

Fm G Cm G#
Only dates girls who will go dutch
Fm G Cm G#
We call him a no good such-and-such
Fm G Cm G#
No one knows how he's isn't dead
G# Eb
Bad ideas are not the only thing
F G G7
To pass clear through his head

Cm G# G Cm
He...never seems to give a crap
G# G Cm
He's lost so much he can't find a map
Fm G Cm G#
He feels nothing, so he's out of touch
G# G Cm
G# G
That's why he's the man who blew too much...
Cm G# G
Cm G# G
Cm
...up!

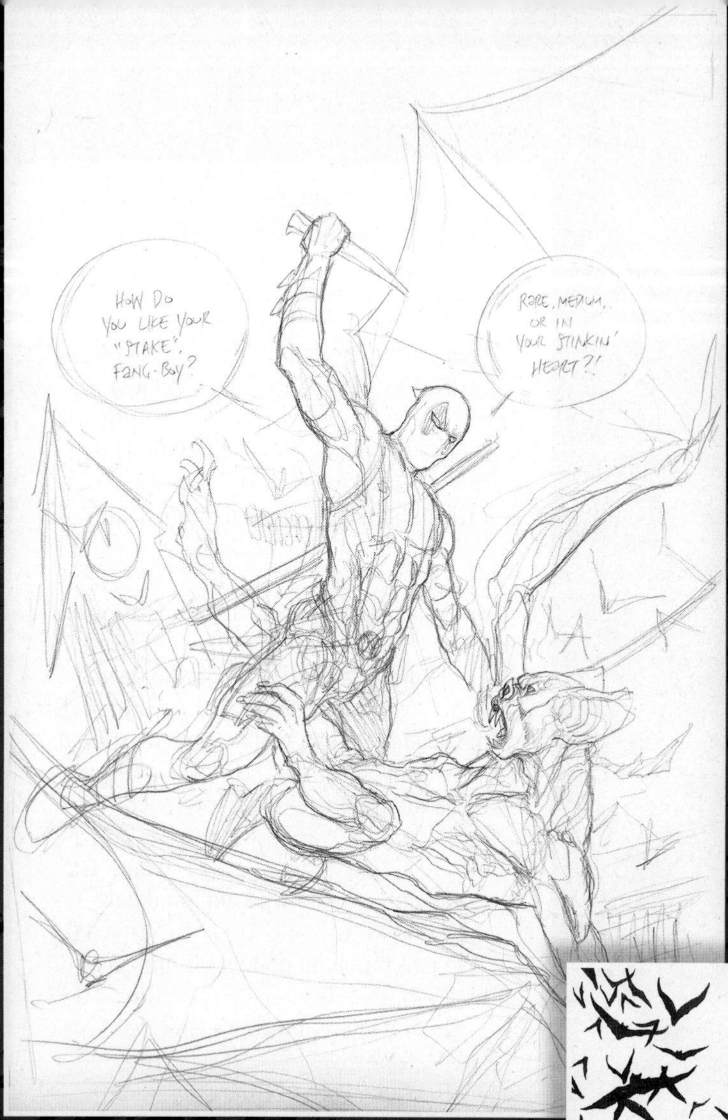
HOW DO YOU LIKE YOUR "STAKE", FANG-BOY?
RARE, MEDIUM... OR IN YOUR STINKIN' HEART?!

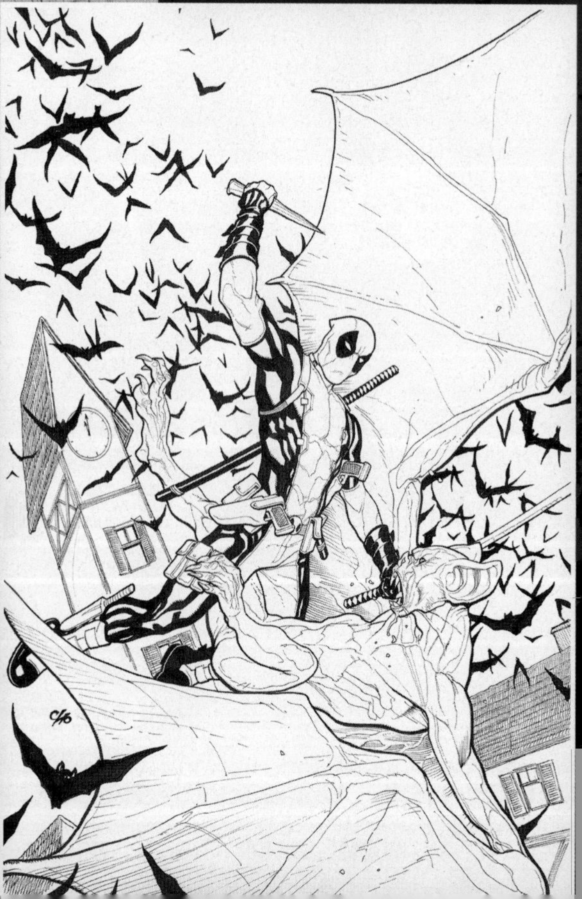

DEADPOOL: THE GAUNTLET #1
COVER PROCESS BY
FRANK CHO & JIM CAMPBELL

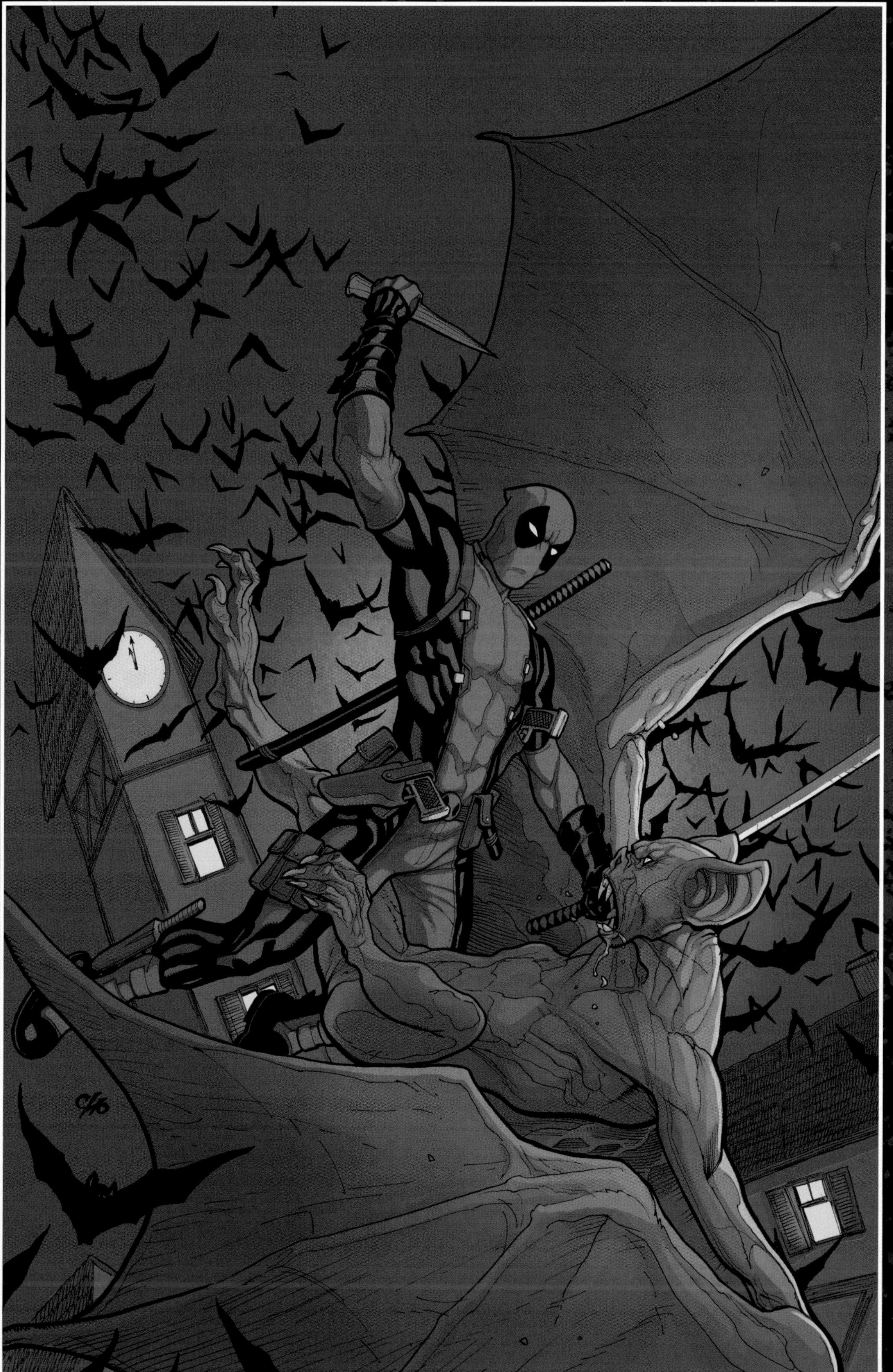

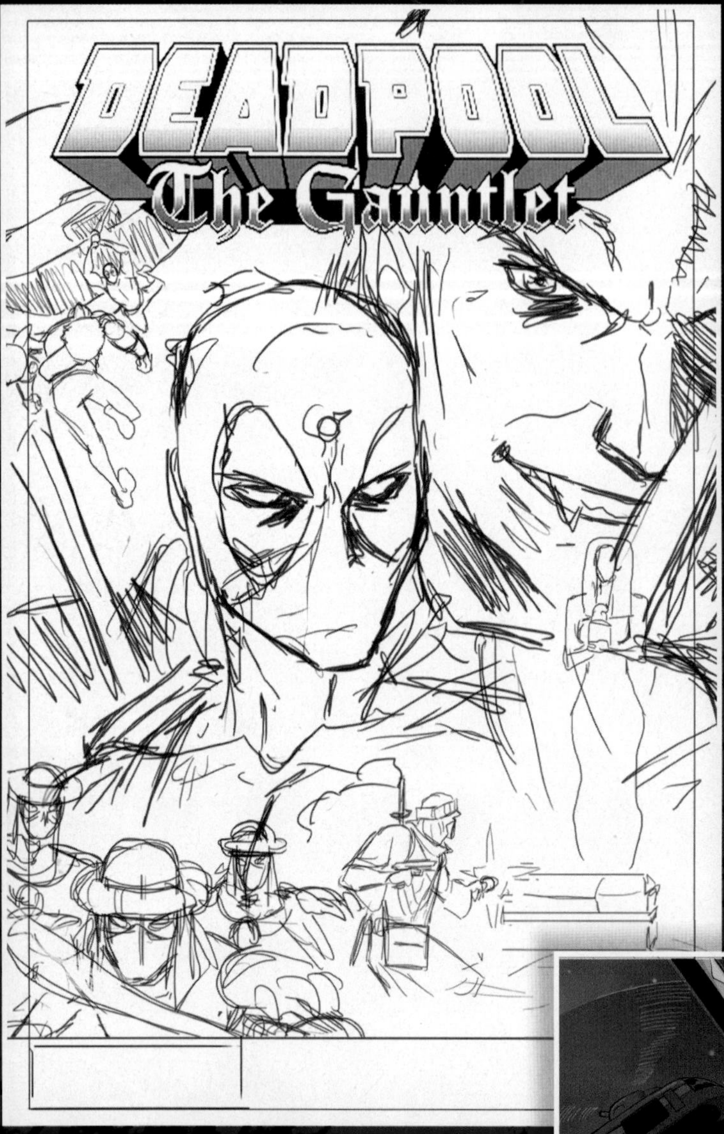
DEADPOOL
The Gauntlet

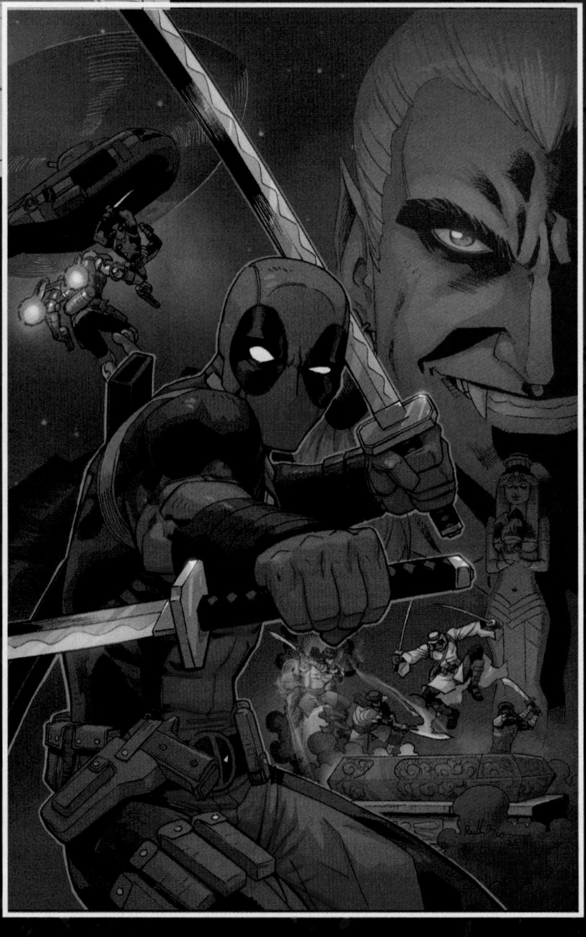

COVER PROCESS BY
REILLY BROWN

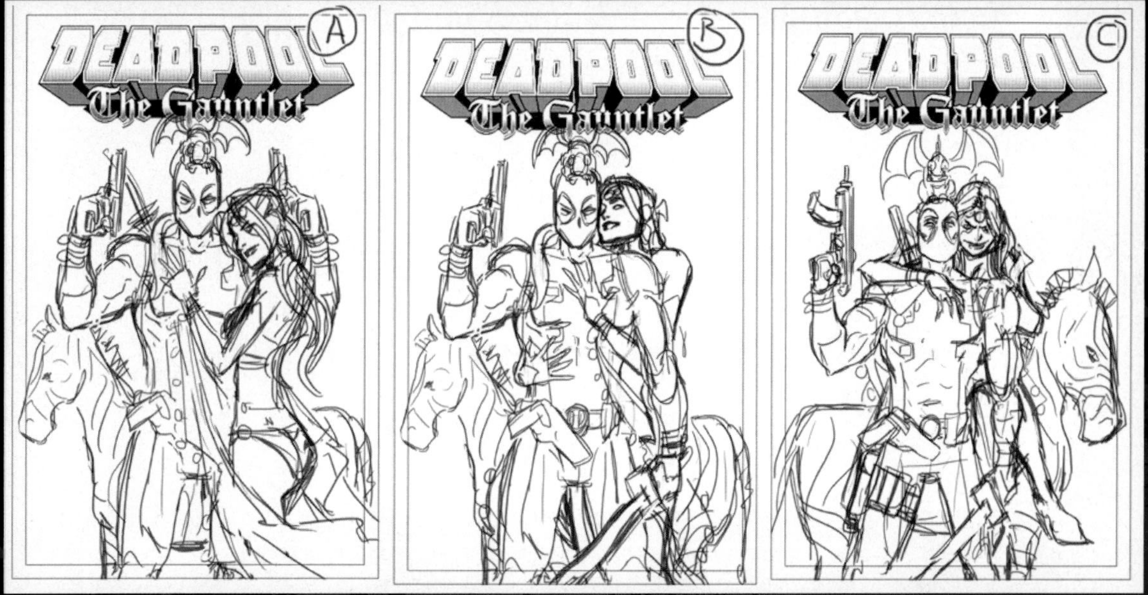
DEADPOOL
The Gauntlet
A
DEADPOOL
The Gauntlet
B
DEADPOOL
The Gauntlet
C

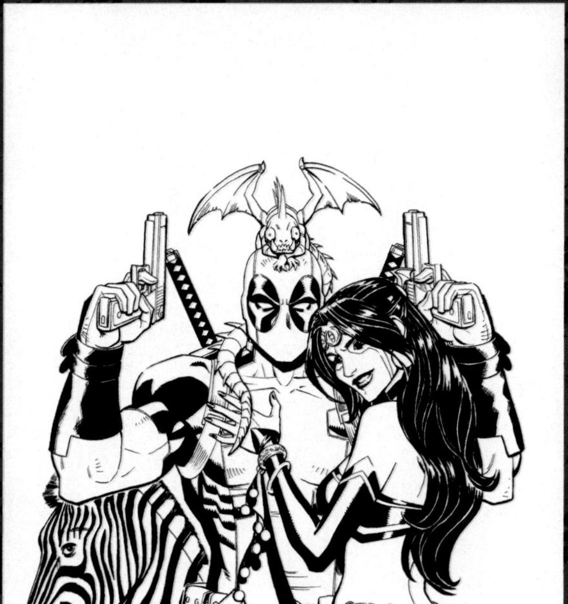
REILLY BROWN 2014

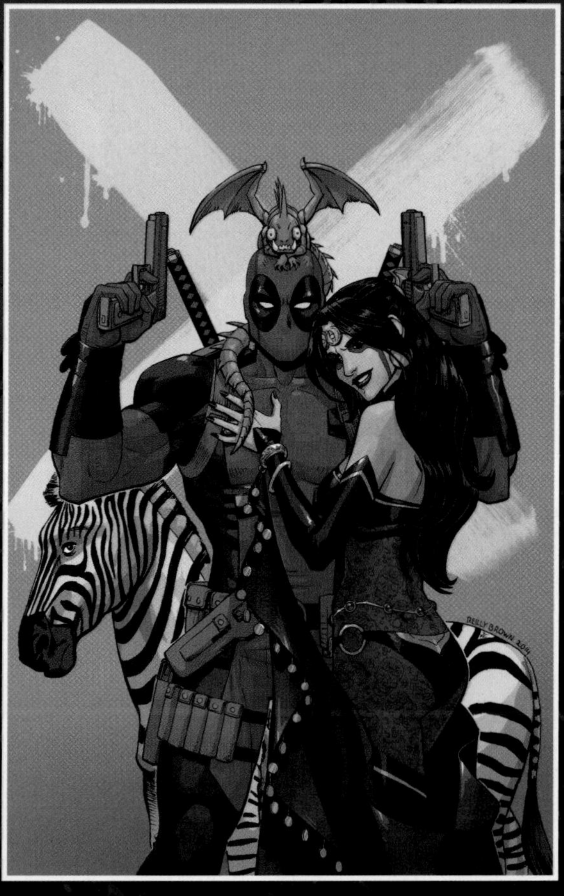
REILLY BROWN 2014

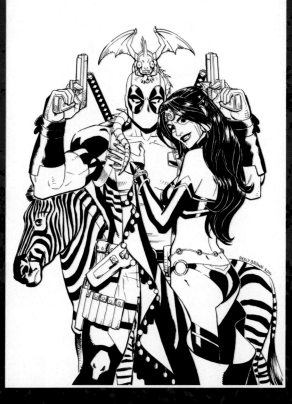

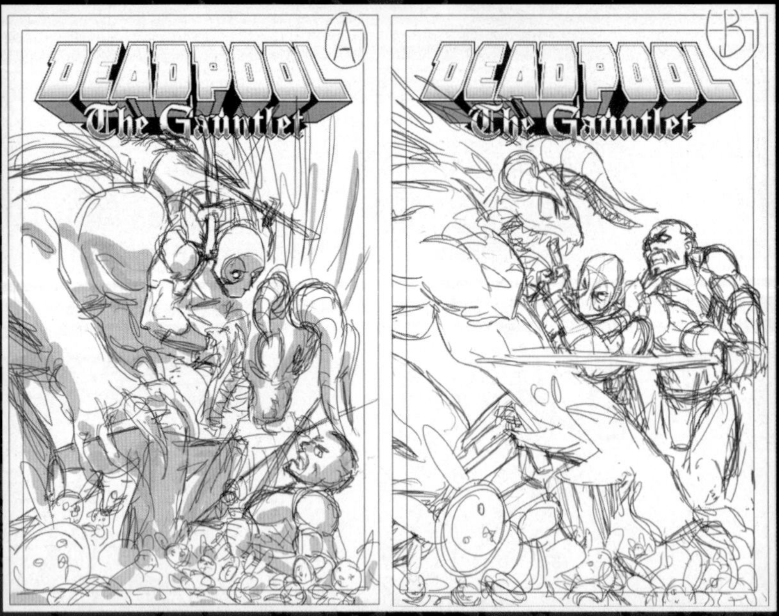
A
DEADPOOL
The Gauntlet
B
DEADPOOL
The Gauntlet

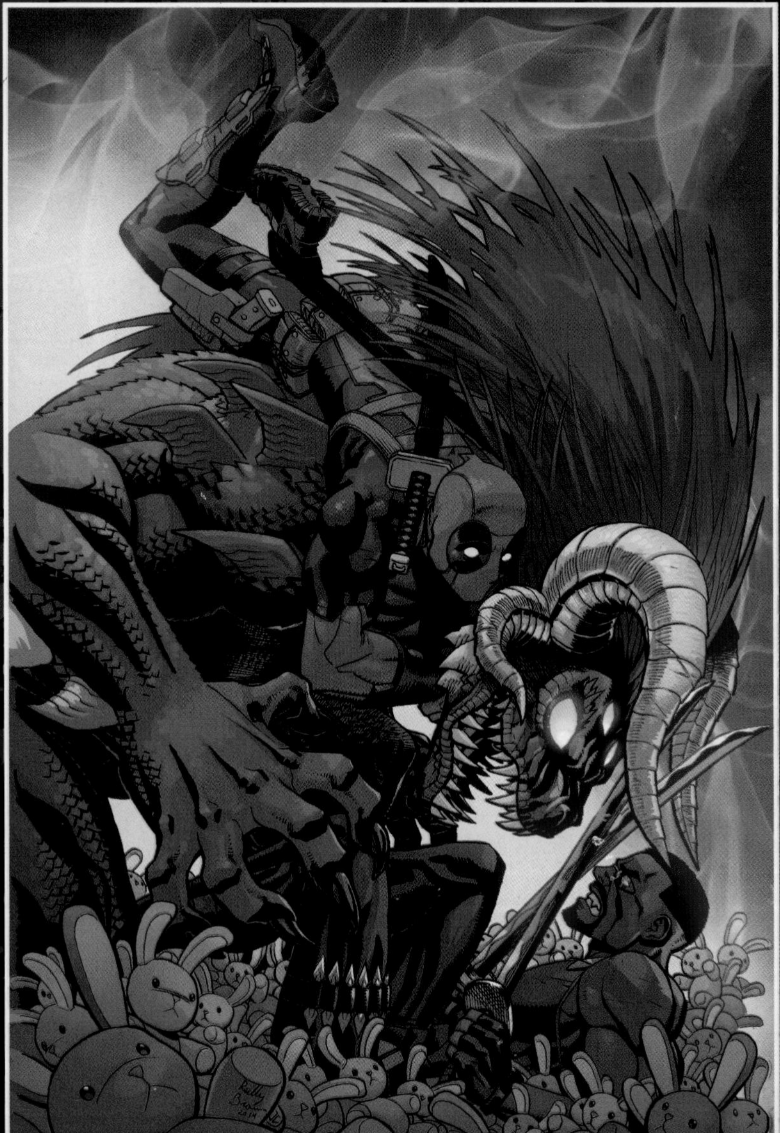

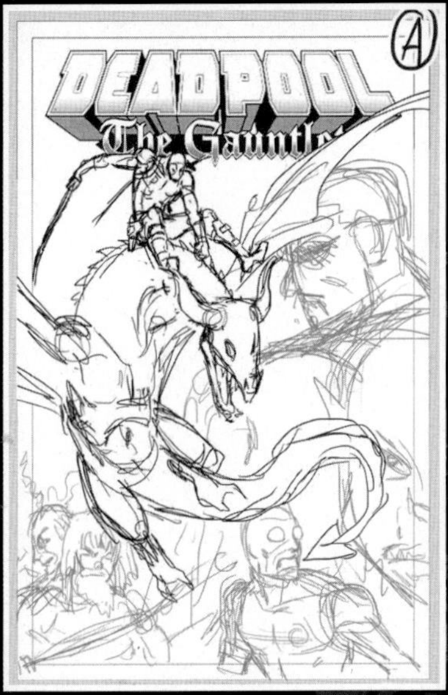
DEADPOOL
A

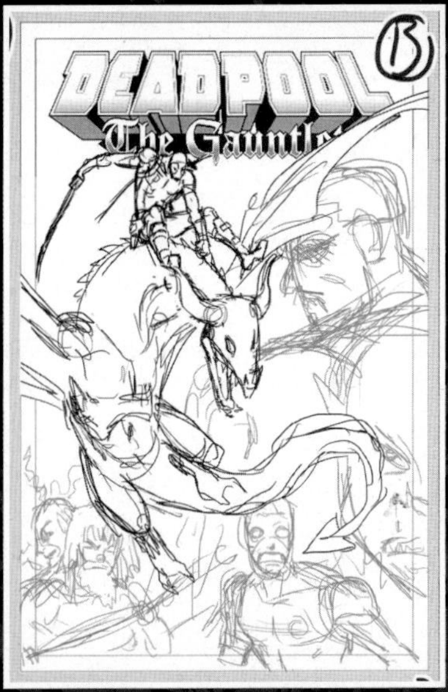
DEADPOOL
B

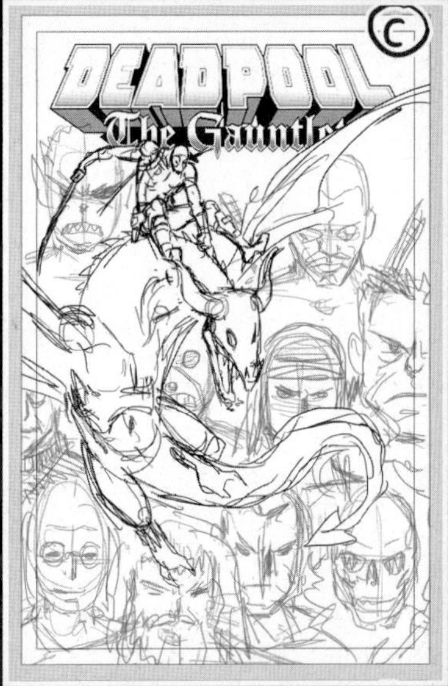
DEADPOOL
C

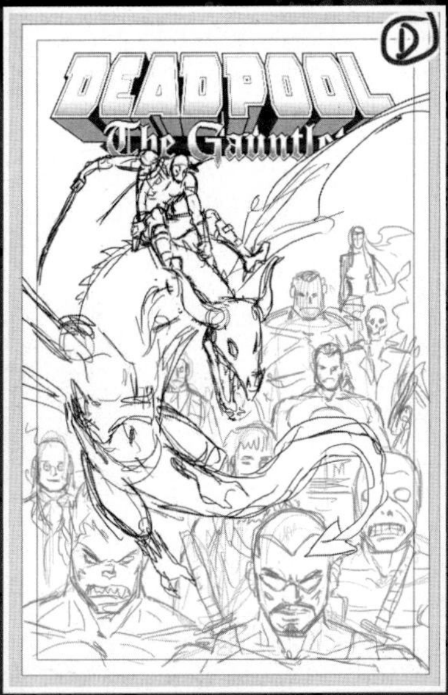
DEADPOOL
D

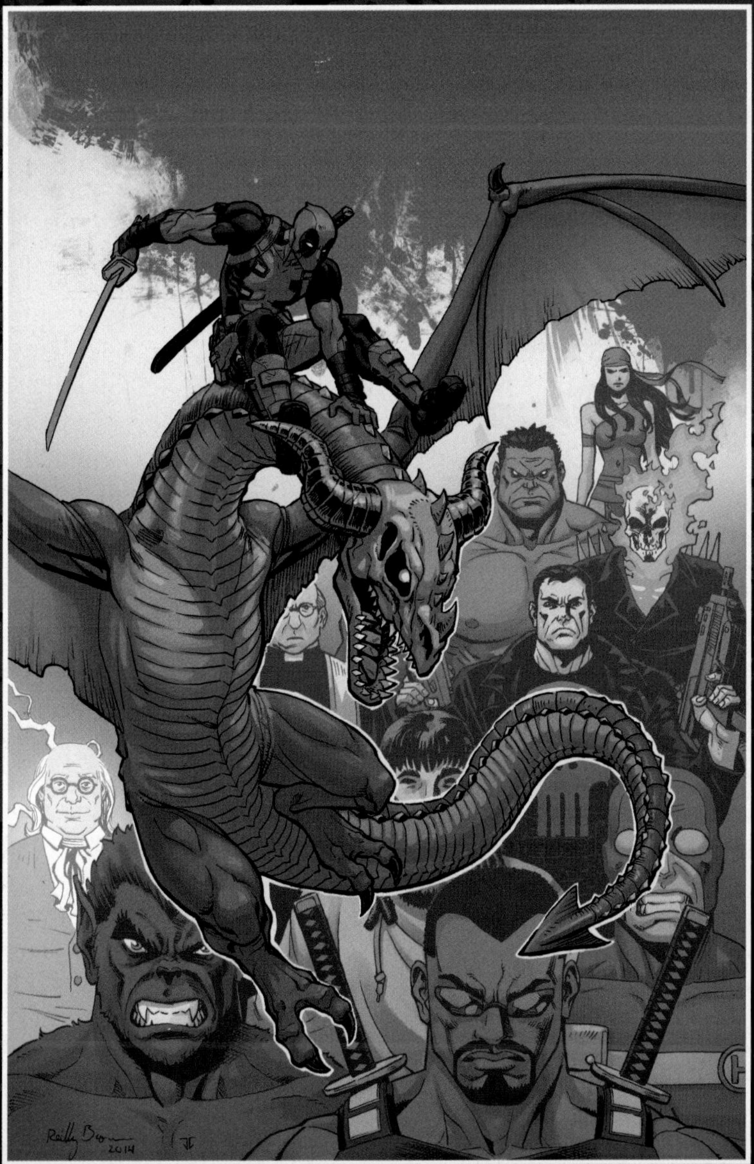
Reilly Brown
2014

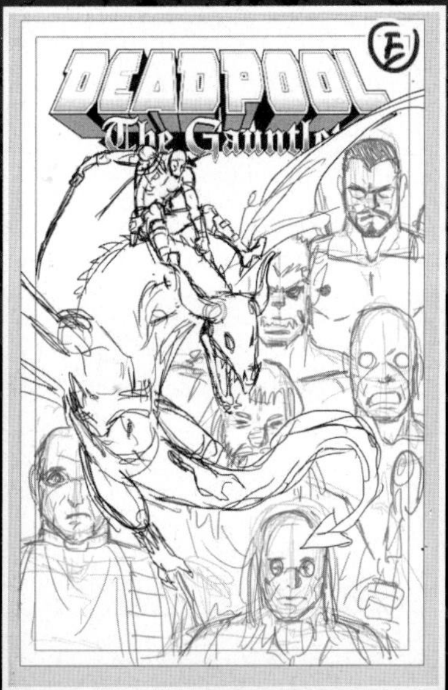
DEADPOOL
E

Infinite Comics are Marvel's newest and boldest jump into the world of digital comics. Crafted specifically to be read on the Marvel Comics App, Infinite Comics take advantage of new storytelling opportunities the digital realm makes possible. This story has been restructured into traditional print comics, but the original versions can be read on the Marvel Comics App to get the full effect.

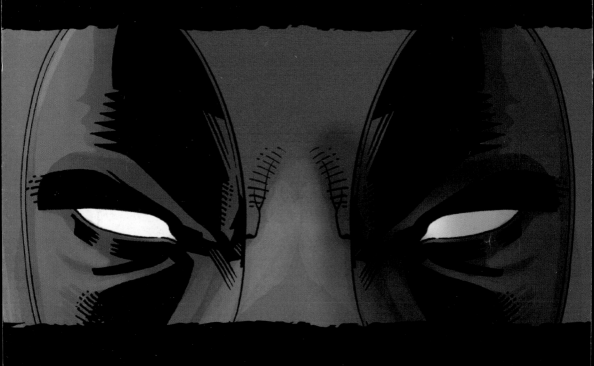